AF207886

TINA HAASE

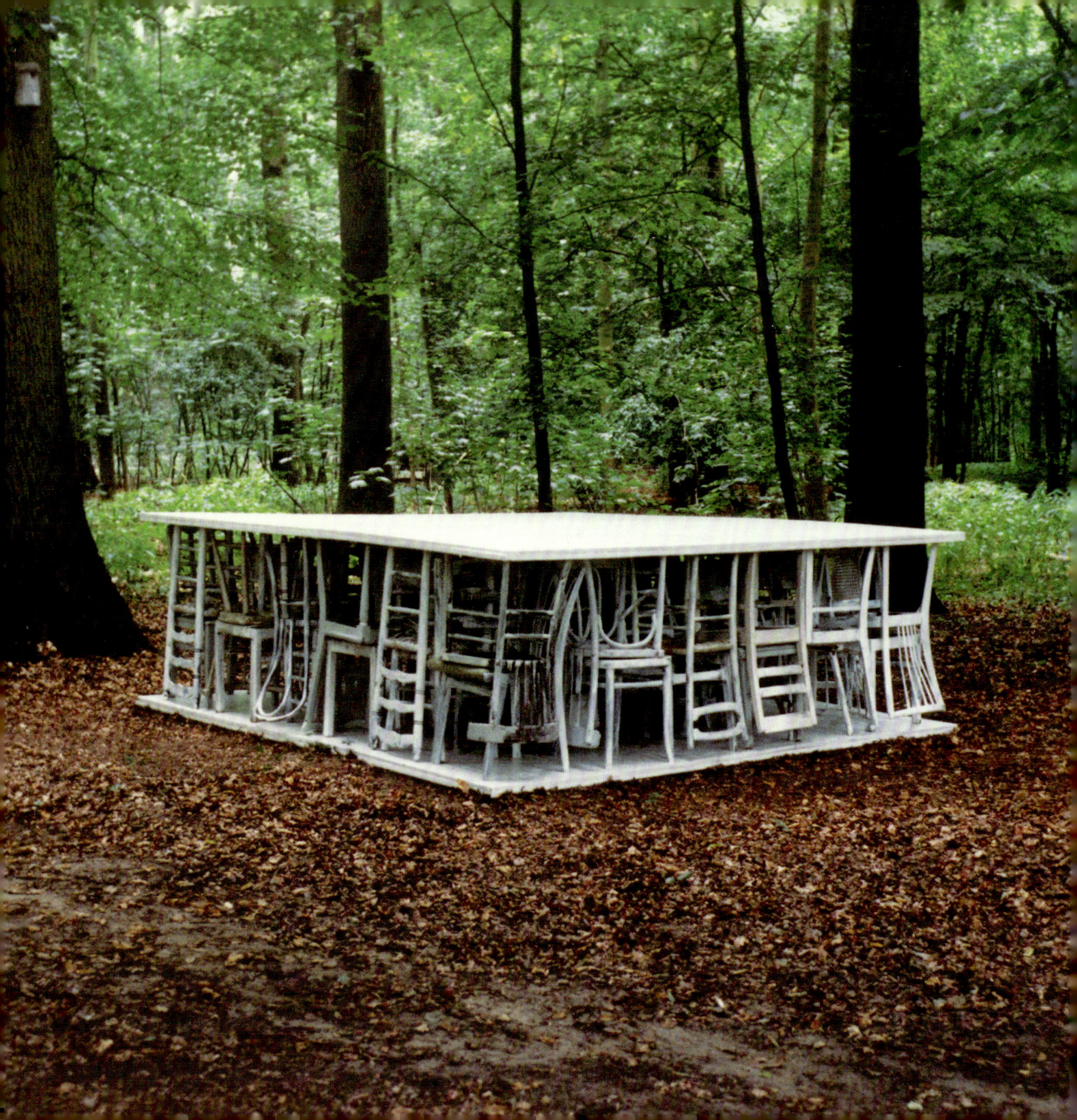

TINA HAASE

KÖNEMANN

p. 2

o.T.

1991, Wood, 85 × 250 × 250 cm, Rhijnauwen, Bunnik

KÖNEMANN

© 2018 koenemann.com GmbH
www.koenemann.com

Concept, Project Management: koenemann.com GmbH

Text: Tina Haase, Jens Peter Koerver, Sabine Elsa Müller
Translations: koenemann.com GmbH

Layout: Oliver Hessmann
Colour Separation: PREPRESS GmbH, Cologne

Picture credits:
Ron Steemers, Arnhem   p. 2
Michael Kremer, Köln   pp. 10–14, 28
Dr. Ulrich Mueller, Köln   pp. 6, 7, 20–27, 29–37, 41, 42, 44–49, 55–59, 62, 63, 66, 67, 72, 75–77, 82, 83, 96,
      97, 100–101, 103, 105, 110 b, 111, 117, 121, 126, 130, 132, 134–137, 140, 141
Enne Haehnle, Leipzig   pp. 38, 39
Eberhard Weible, Köln   pp. 60, 61, 78, 79, 106–109, 116, 122, 138, 142–144, 146, 149, 151, 156, 158, 160, 161,
      166, 177–179, 183–188, 192, 201, 206–207
Willi Ahlmer, Rheine   p. 71
Carl Victor Dahmen, Köln   p. 81
Thomas Bruns, Berlin   pp. 84–87
Astrid Eckert, TU München   pp. 94, 95
Oliver Oefelein, Berlin   p. 115
Jus Juchtmans, Antwerpen   pp. 131, 152, 153, 155
Jochen Heufelder, Köln   p. 133
Michael Wittassek, Bergisch Gladbach   pp. 145, 147
Peter Sörries, Köln   pp. 148, 150
Tina Haase, Köln   pp. 15–19, 40, 43, 50–54, 64, 65, 68, 80, 88–93, 98, 99, 102, 104, 110 t, 111 r, 112–114,
      118–120, 123–125, 127–129, 139, 157, 159, 162–165, 167, 169–176, 180–182, 198–200, 202–205
Karin Hochstatter, Köln   p. 168
Hubert P. Klotzeck, Eichstätt   pp. 189–191, 193
Carsten Riedl, Kirchheim unter Teck   pp. 194–197

ISBN: 978-3-7419-2152-0

Printed in China by Shenzhen Hua Xin Colour-printing & Platemaking Co., Ltd

Contents　Sommaire　Inhalt　Índice　Indice　Inhoud

Clamp stands and box houses

Supports avec sangle de serrage et maisons de boîtes en carton

Klemmständer und Schachtelhäuser

Soportes de abrazadera y casas de caja

Supporti di fissaggio e case scatola

Klemmenstandaards en doosjeshuizen

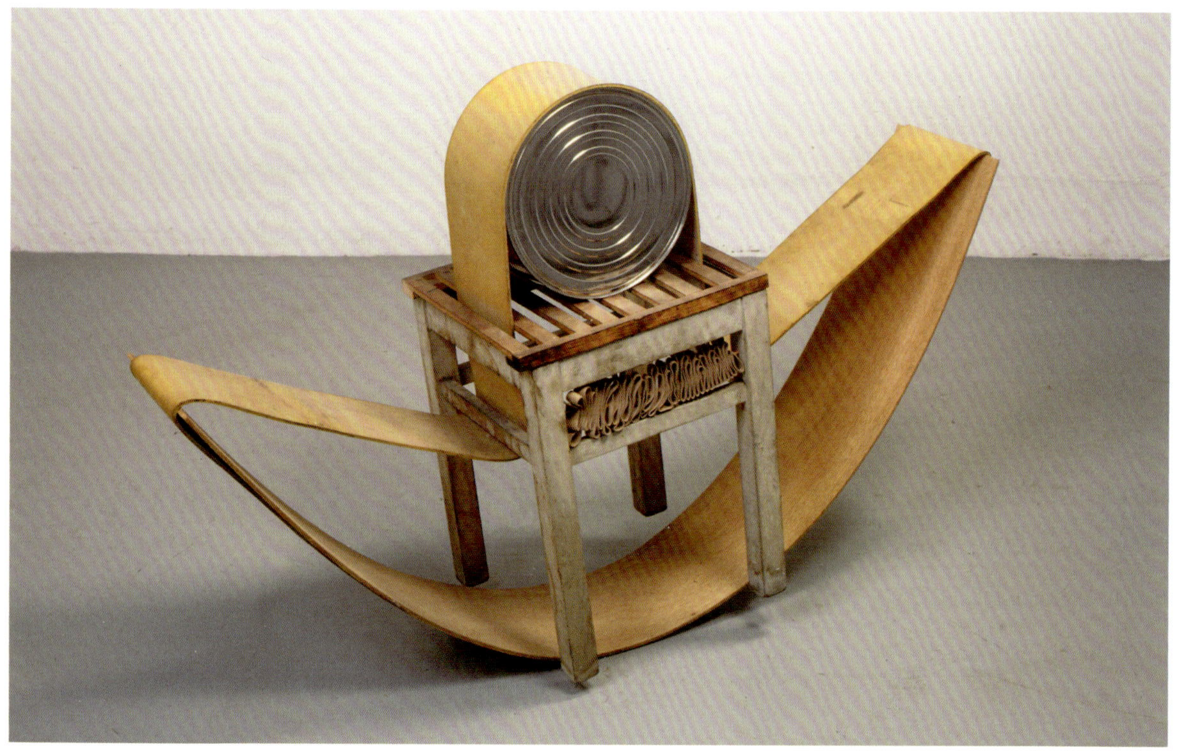

o.T.

1989, Sheet metal, wood, textile strip, 80 × 130 × 30 cm

o.T.

1991, Table trestles, steel, Private collection

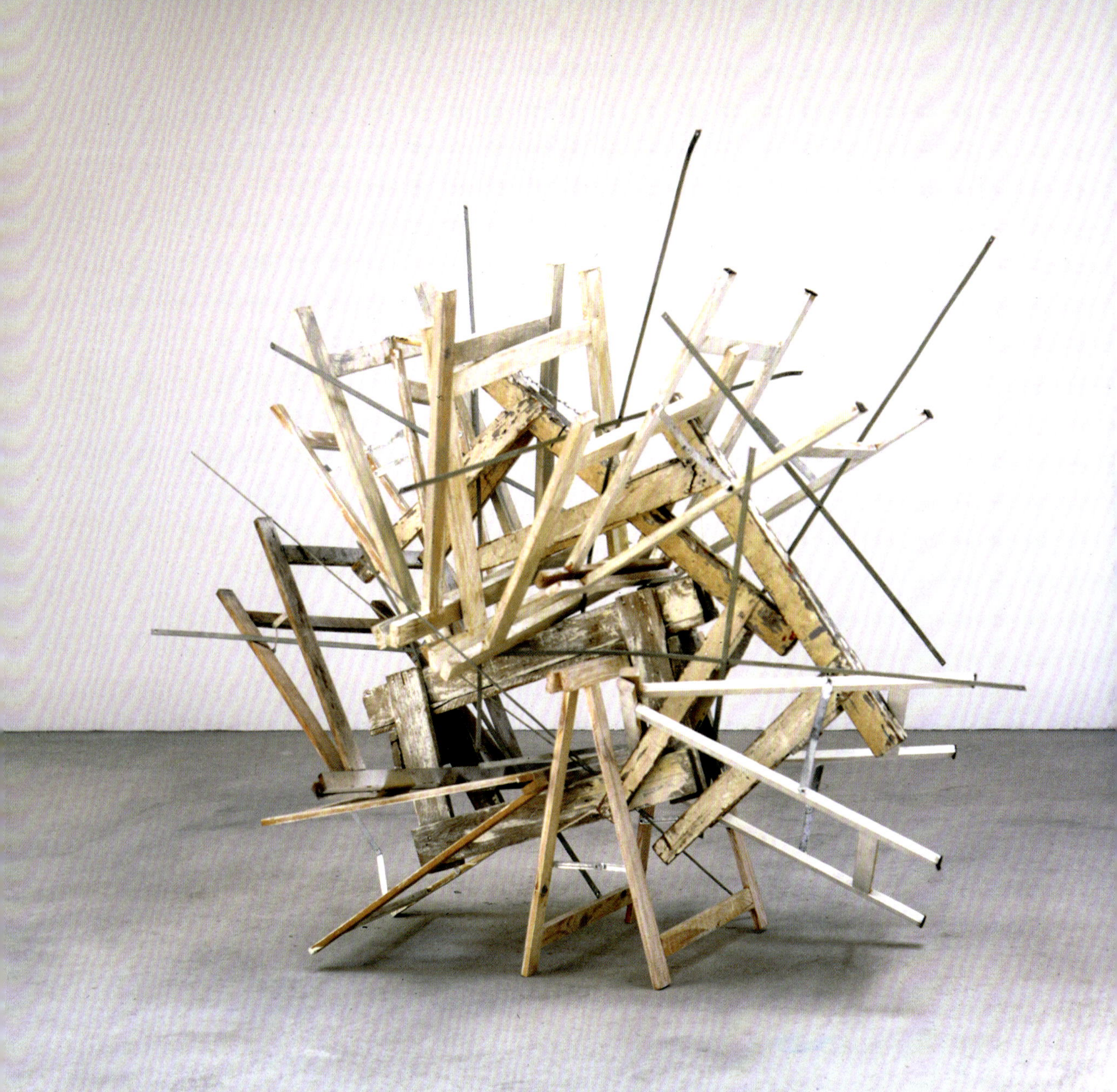

Instructions for use —
Please read carefully!

Application: free in the room, possibly with base, wall
Contents: leftovers in general, discarded products from DIY stores, high-quality laboratory supplies
Appearance: braids, plugs, clamps, rows
Side effects: astonishment, amusement, occasional confusion, dizziness, doubts about allocation, lack of ease
Dosage: if possible from all sides
Mode of action: Functional infiltration, eroticization of the used, accelerated discovery of joy about combinations
Long-term effect: rebalancing, lucid standstill
Dosage form: 10 × 7.3 × 12 cm to 300 × 300 × 120 cm, large packs on request
Consumation: insert through the eyes into the head
Storage: dust-free at room temperature, protect from darkness
Composition: general residues
Constitution: Jens Peter Koerver
Manufacturer: Tina Haase Werke, Cologne

Mode d'emploi – À lire attentivement

Méthode d'utilisation : seul dans une pièce, éventuellement avec socle, mur.
Composition : restes en en tout genre, rebuts de magasins de bricolage, fournitures de laboratoire de haute qualité.
Aspect : tressé, bouché, en étau, en rangées.
Effets secondaires : étonnement, gaieté, dans certains cas isolés confusion, étourdissements, doutes du positionnement, poids en rapport à la légèreté.
Dosage : si possible de tous les côtés.
Mode d'action : infiltration du fonctionnement, érotisation de de tout ce qui est usé, accélération de la combinaison de la découverte de la joie.
Effet à long terme : rééquilibrage, immobilisation lucide.
Posologie : 10 × 7,3 × 12 cm à 300 × 300 × 120 cm, emballages grands formats sur demande.
Méthode d'utilisation : à prendre par les yeux et laisser agir dans la tête.
Stockage : conserver à température. ambiante, à l'abri de la poussière et de l'obscurité.
Composition : en grande partie de résidus.
Constitution : Jens Peter Koerver
Fabricant : Tina Haase Werke, Cologne

Gebrauchsinformation – Bitte aufmerksam lesen!

Anwendungsgebiet: frei im Raum, u.U. gesockelt, Wand
Inhaltsstoffe: Reste allgemein, Verachtetes aus Baumärkten, hochwertiger Laborbedarf
Erscheinungsform: Flechten, Stopfen, Klemmen, Reihen
Nebenwirkungen: Frappierung, Heiterkeit, im Einzelfall Verwirrung, Schwindelgefühle, Sortierungszweifel, Leichtigkeitsschwere
Dosierung: nach Möglichkeit von allen Seiten
Wirkungsweise: Funktionsunterwanderung, Erotisierung des Verbrauchten, beschleunigte Kombinationsfreudenentdeckung
Langfristige Wirkung: Umordnung ins Gleichgewicht, luzider Stillstand
Darreichungsform: 10 × 7,3 × 12 cm bis 300 × 300 × 120 cm, Großpackungen auf Anfrage
Einnahme: über die Augen in den Kopf einführen
Lagerung: bei Zimmertemperatur staubfrei, vor Dunkelheit schützen
Zusammensetzung: Reste allgemein
Verfassung: Jens Peter Koerver
Hersteller: Tina Haase Werke, Köln

Instrucciones de uso –
Por favor, lea atentamente!

Aplicación: libre en la habitación, con basamento, pared
Ingredientes: restos en general, productos que las tiendas de bricolaje han desechado, material de laboratorio de alta calidad.
Aspecto: trenzas, tapones, abrazaderas, series
Efectos secundarios: asombro, alegría, confusión en casos aislados, mareos, dudas sobre la clasificación, severidad de la ligereza
Dosificación: si es posible en todos los lados
Modo de acción: Infiltración funcional, erotización de lo utilizado, alegría combinada y acelerada por el descubrimiento
Efecto a largo plazo: equilibrio, parada lúcida
Tipo de dosificación: 10 × 7,3 × 12 cm hasta 300 × 300 × 120 cm, embalajes grandes a petición
Administración: visual, en la cabeza
Almacenamiento: libre de polvo a temperatura ambiente, proteger de la oscuridad
Composición: residuos generales
Constitución: Jens Peter Koerver
Fabricante: Tina Haase Werke, Colonia

Istruzioni per l'uso –
Leggere attentamente!

Impiego: in posizione libera nella stanza, possibilmente su una base, alla parete
Componenti: resti in generale, prodotti non utilizzati nei negozi per il fai da te, forniture da laboratorio di alta qualità
Aspetto: intrecci, otturamenti, fissaggi, file
Effetti collaterali: stupore, allegria, occasionalmente confusione, vertigini, dubbi sulla collocazione, mancanza di leggerezza
Dosaggio: possibilmente da ogni lato
Effetto: infiltrazione funzionale, erotizzazione dell'usato, rapida scoperta della gioia nel combinare
Effetto a lungo termine: riequilibrio, stasi lucida
Forma di dosaggio: 10 × 7,3 × 12 cm a 300 × 300 × 120 cm, su richiesta confezione grande
Consumazione: inserire nella testa attraverso gli occhi
Posizionamento: in luogo privo di polvere e a temperatura ambiente, al riparo dall'oscurità
Composizione: residui in generale
Creazione: Jens Peter Koerver
Produttore: Tina Haase Werke, Colonia

Gebruiksaanwijzing –
a.u.b. aandachtig lezen!

Toepassing: vrij in de kamer, eventueel met sokkel, muur
Bestanddelen: restanten in het algemeen, afgekeurde producten uit bouwmarkten, hoogwaardige laboratoriumbenodigdheden
Verschijningsvorm: strengen, pluggen, klemmen, reeksen
Bijwerkingen: verwondering, amusement, af en toe verwarring, duizeligheid, twijfels over de sortering, gebrek aan gemak
Dosering: indien mogelijk van alle kanten
Werkwijze: functionele infiltratie, erotisering van het gebruikte, versnelde ontdekking van plezier met combinaties
Langetermijneffect: vernieuwd evenwicht, lucide stilstand
Doseringsvorm: 10 × 7,3 × 12 cm tot 300 × 300 × 120 cm, grote verpakkingen op aanvraag
Inname: via de ogen het hoofd binnenlaten
Bewaren: stofvrij bij kamertemperatuur, beschermen tegen duisternis
Samenstelling: algemene restanten
Constitutie: Jens Peter Koerver
Fabrikant: Tina Haase Werke, Keulen

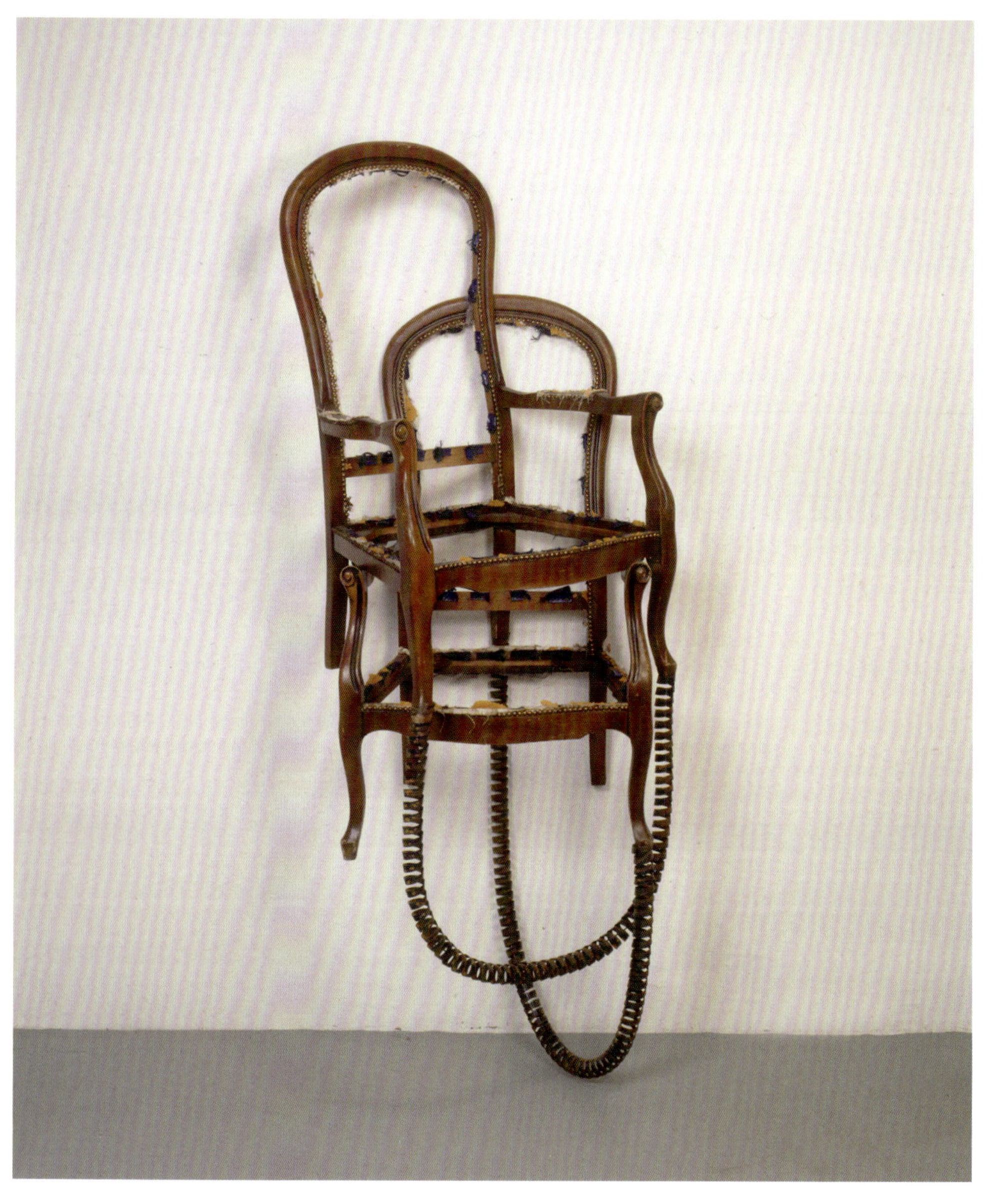

Besitzung

*1991, Chair frames,
steel, 150 × 70 × 60 cm*

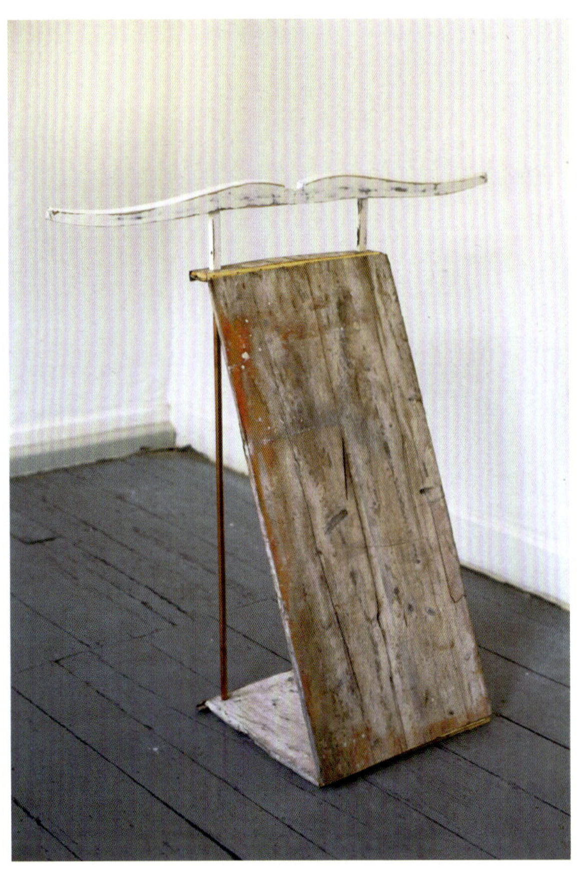

Über die einfache Standfreude aus der Serie der drei Chinesen

1988, Wood, copper, 120 × 108 × 36 cm, Private collection,
Courtesy Galerie Ulrich Mueller

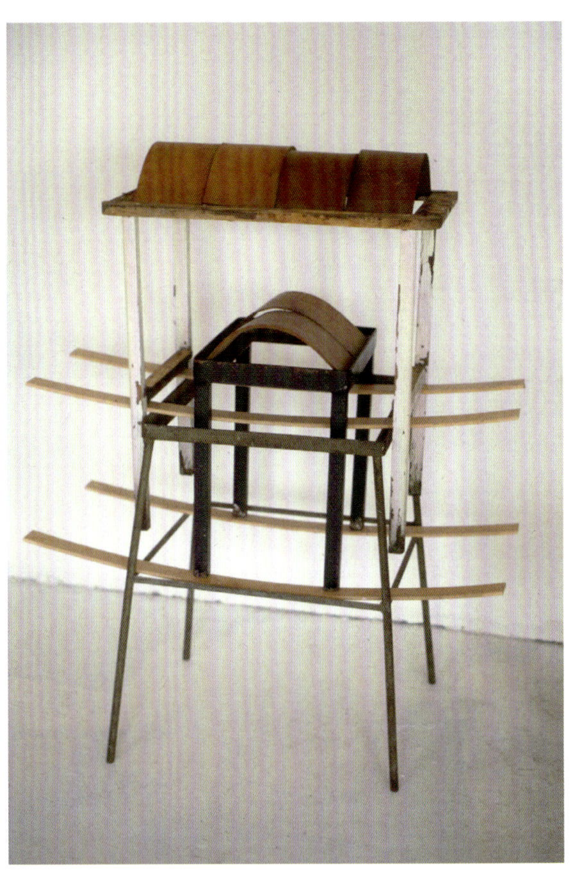

Aus der Serie der Chinesen

1989, Table frames, steel, leather, 115 × 80 × 38 cm

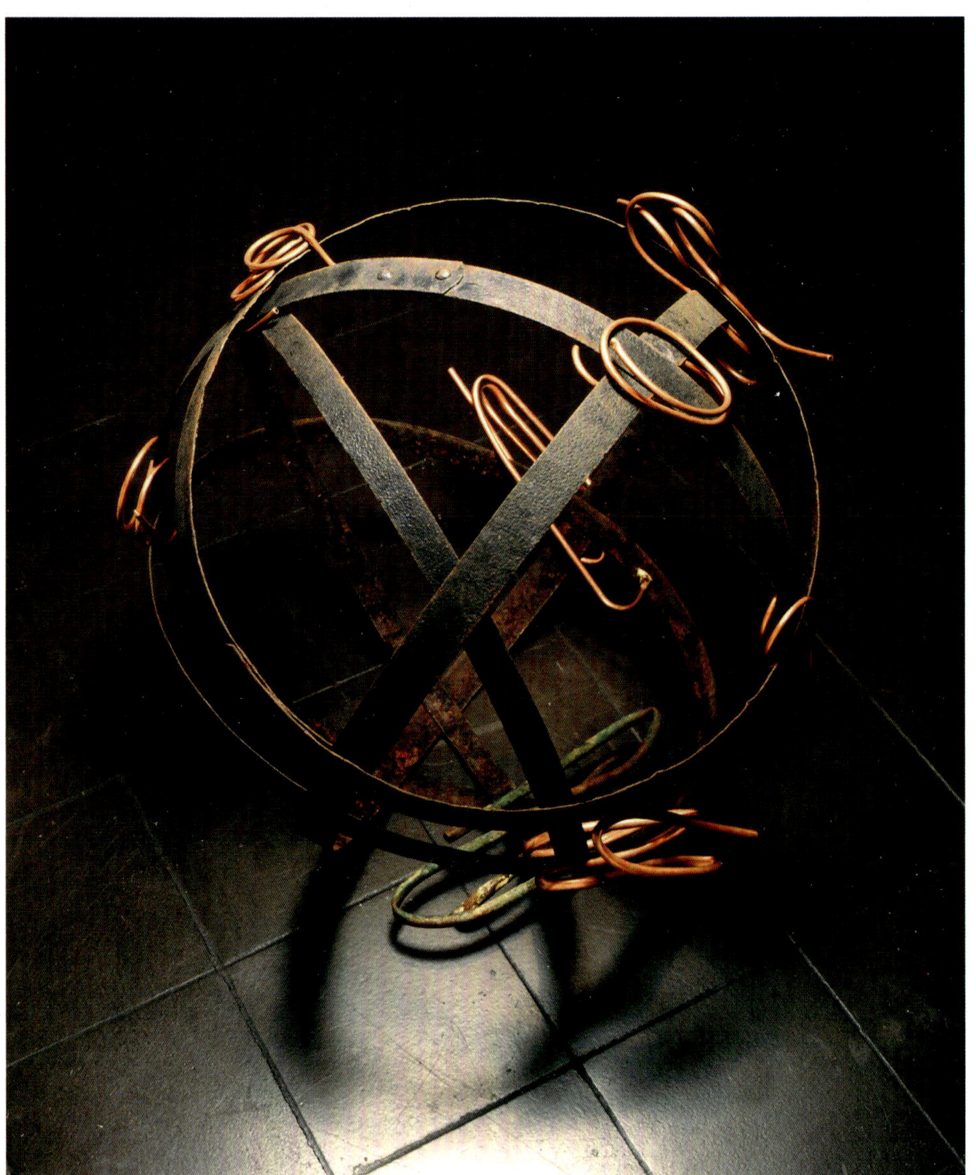

o.T.

*1988, Copper, steel,
Ø c. 60 cm*

o.T.

*1988, Wood, rubber,
210 × 180 × 65 cm*

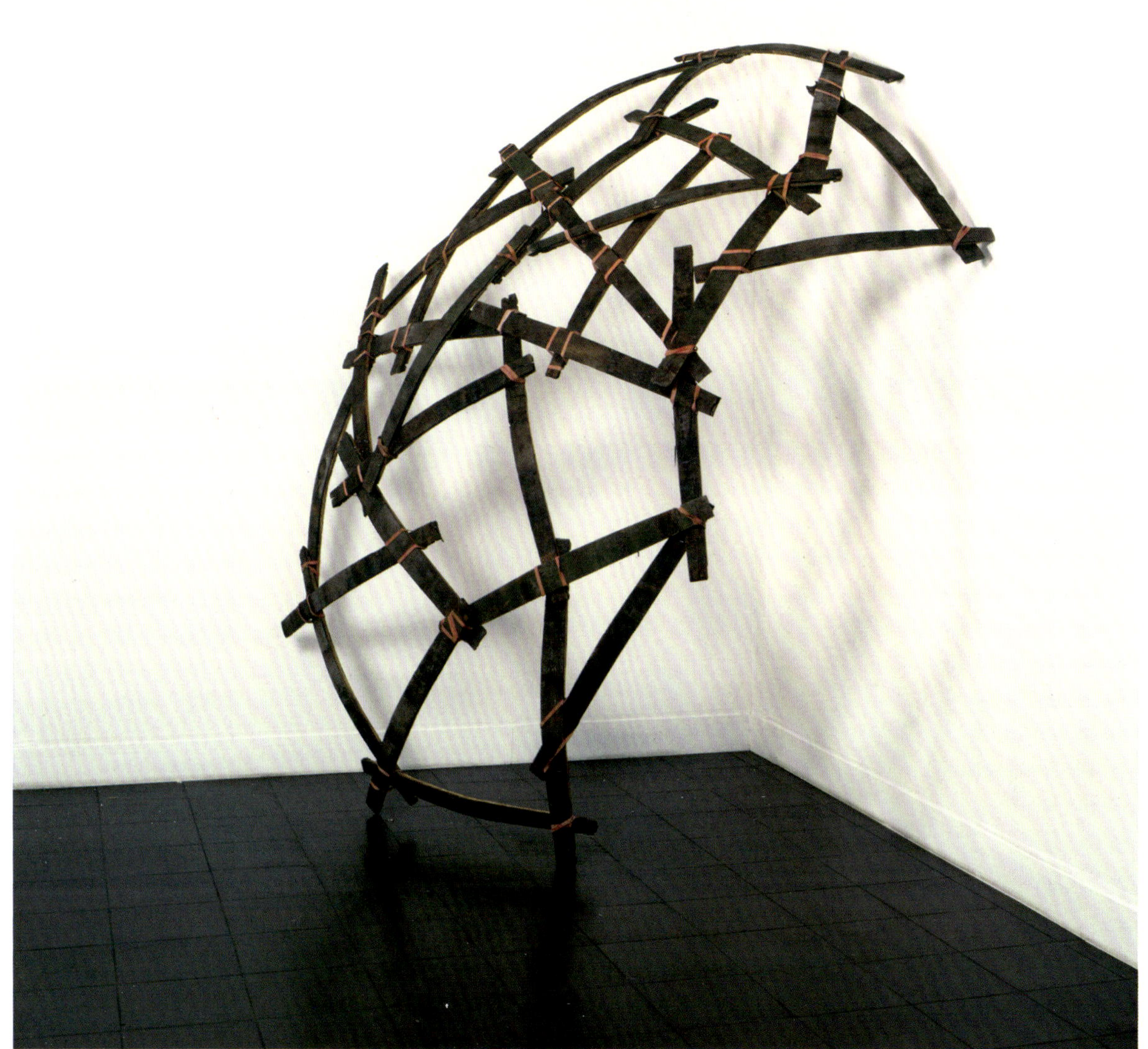

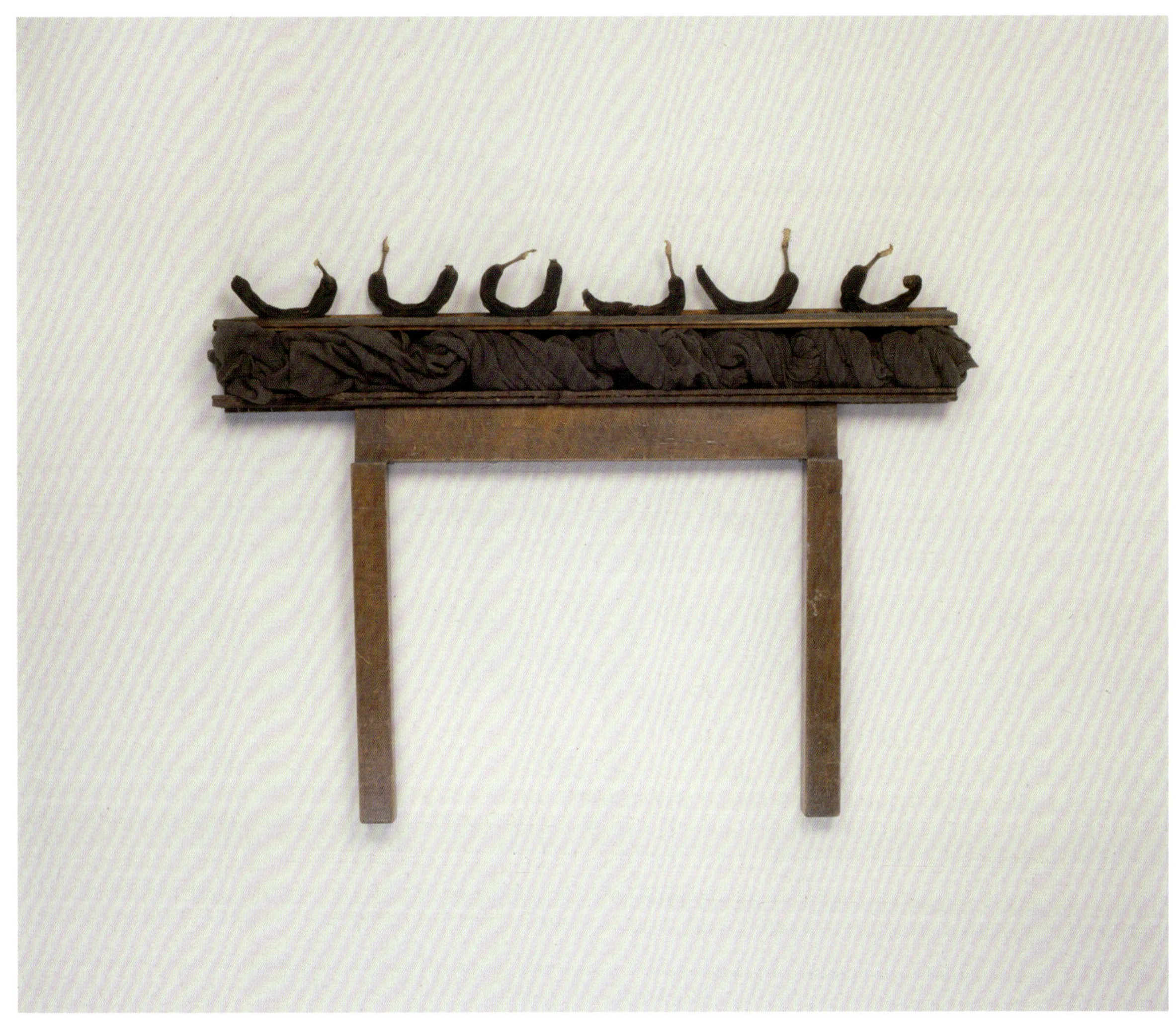

o.T.

1989, Wood, polyurethane foam, bananas, 57 × 80 × 12 cm, Private collection,
Courtesy Galerie Ulrich Mueller

o.T.

1989, Wood, 78 × 40 × 40 cm

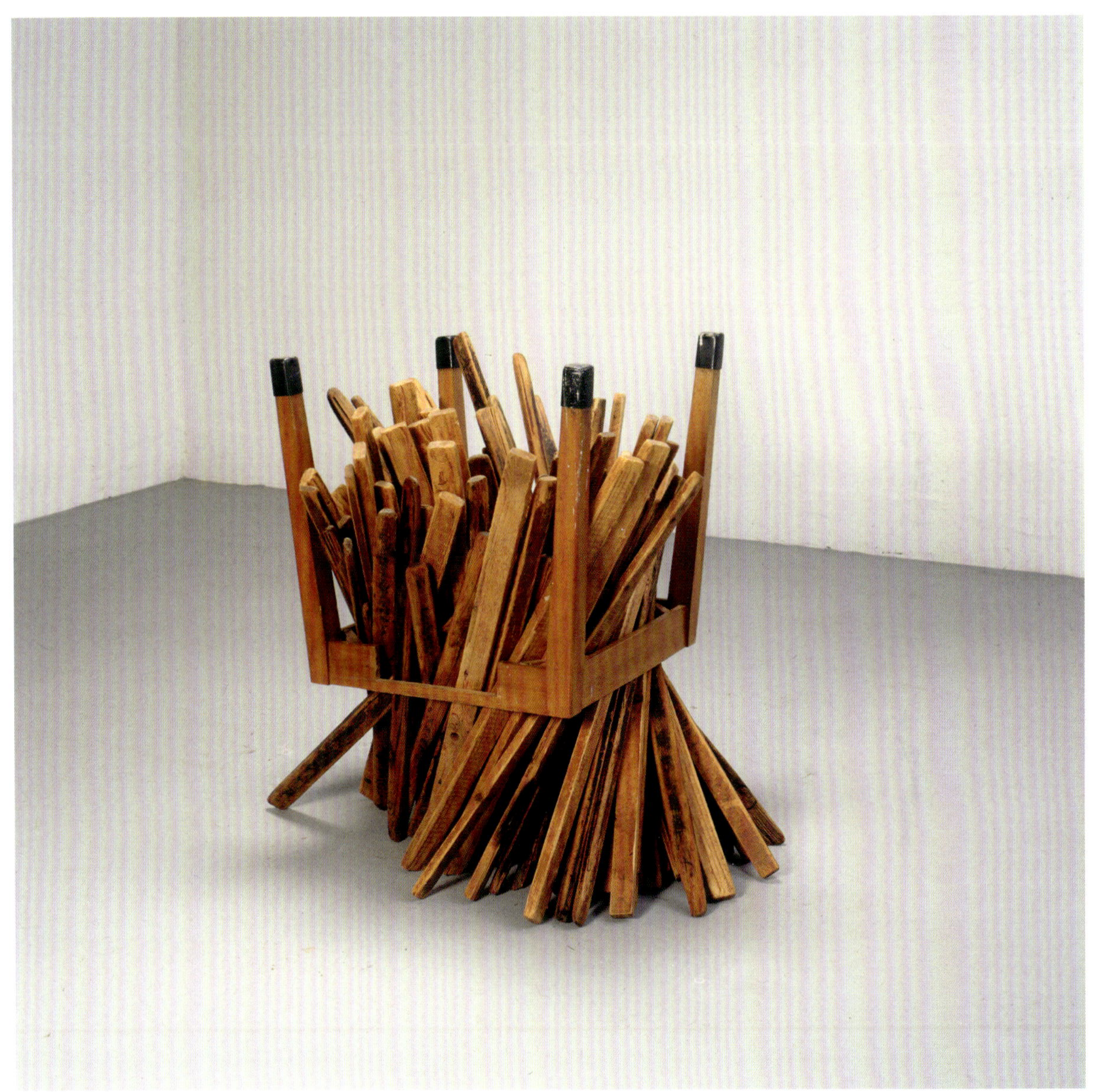

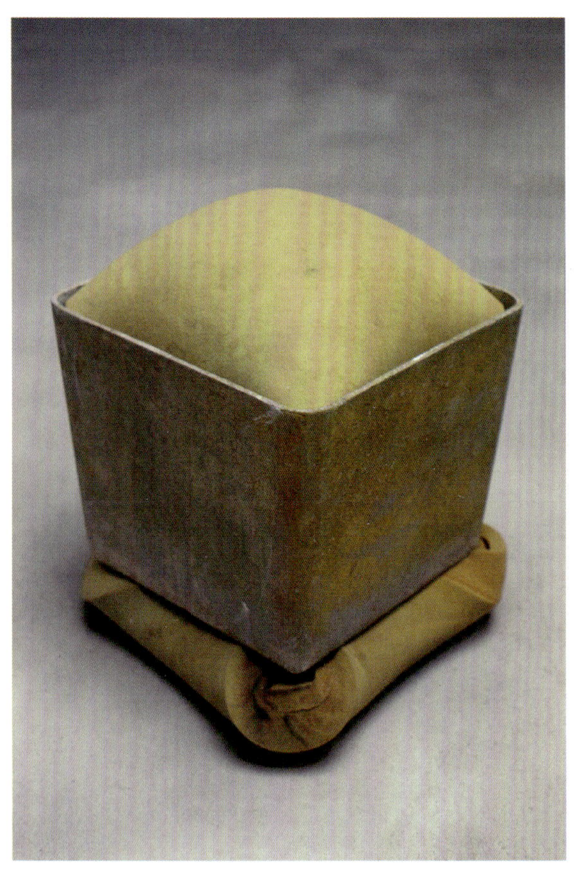

Klemmstück

1990, Polyurethane foam, fibre cement, 50 × 40 × 40 cm

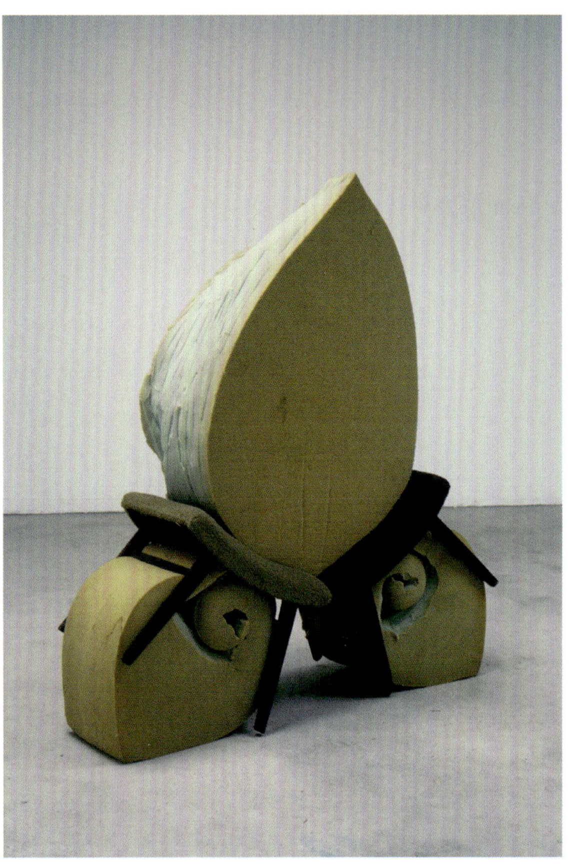

o.T.

1990, Polyurethane foam, stools, 165 × 40 × 11 cm

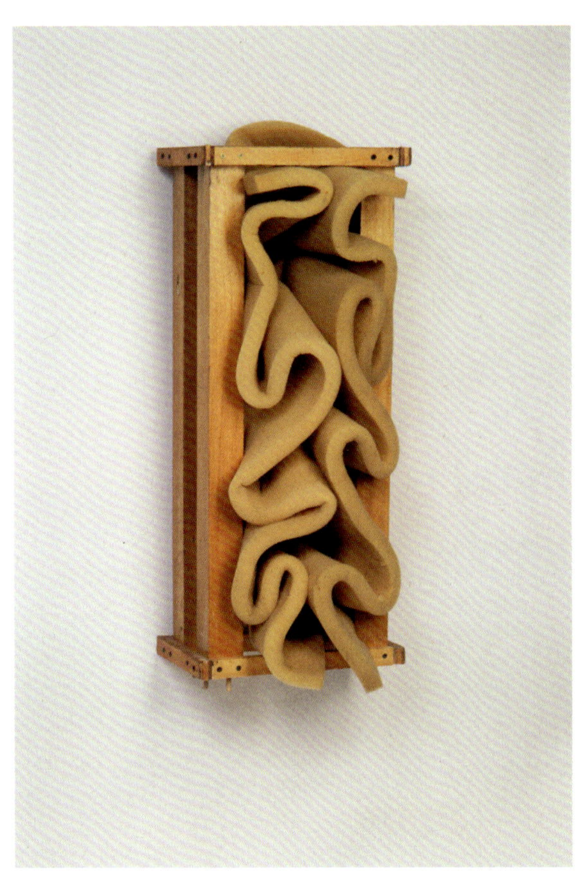

Gefüge

1990, Polyurethane foam, wood, 75 × 25 × 23 cm

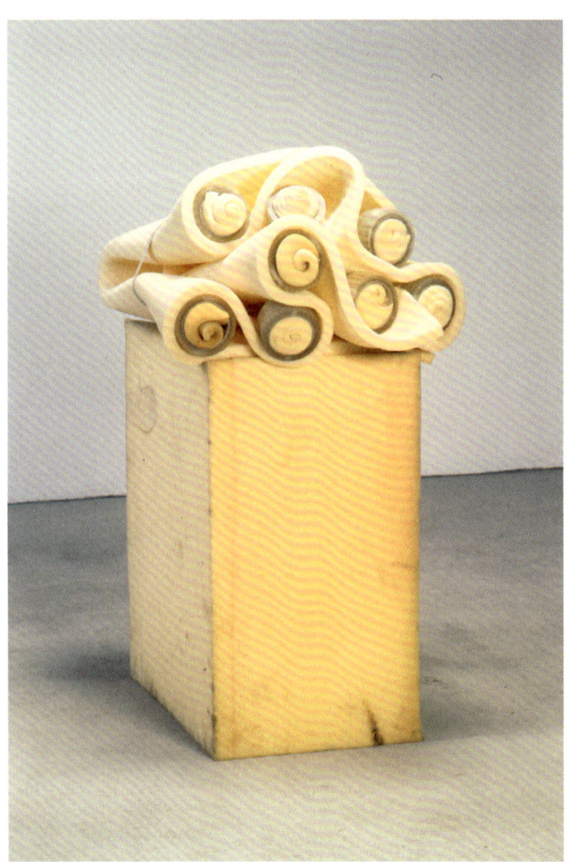

o.T.

1991, Polyurethane foam, adhesive rolls, 110 × 25 × 48 cm

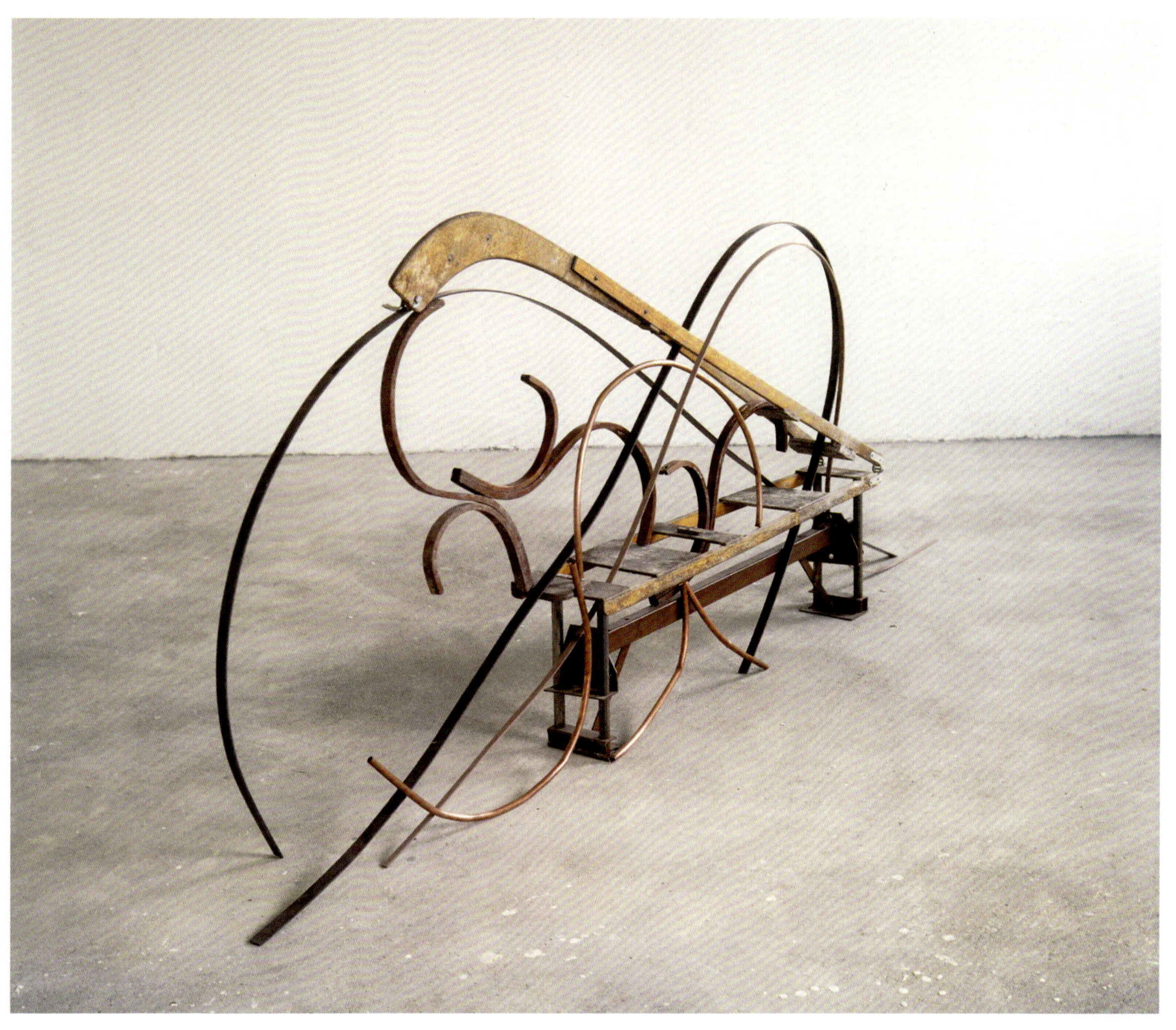

o.T.

1990, Wood, plastic, copper, 80 × 210 × 25 cm

o.T.

1990, Wood, rubber, copper, 180 × 150 × 40 cm

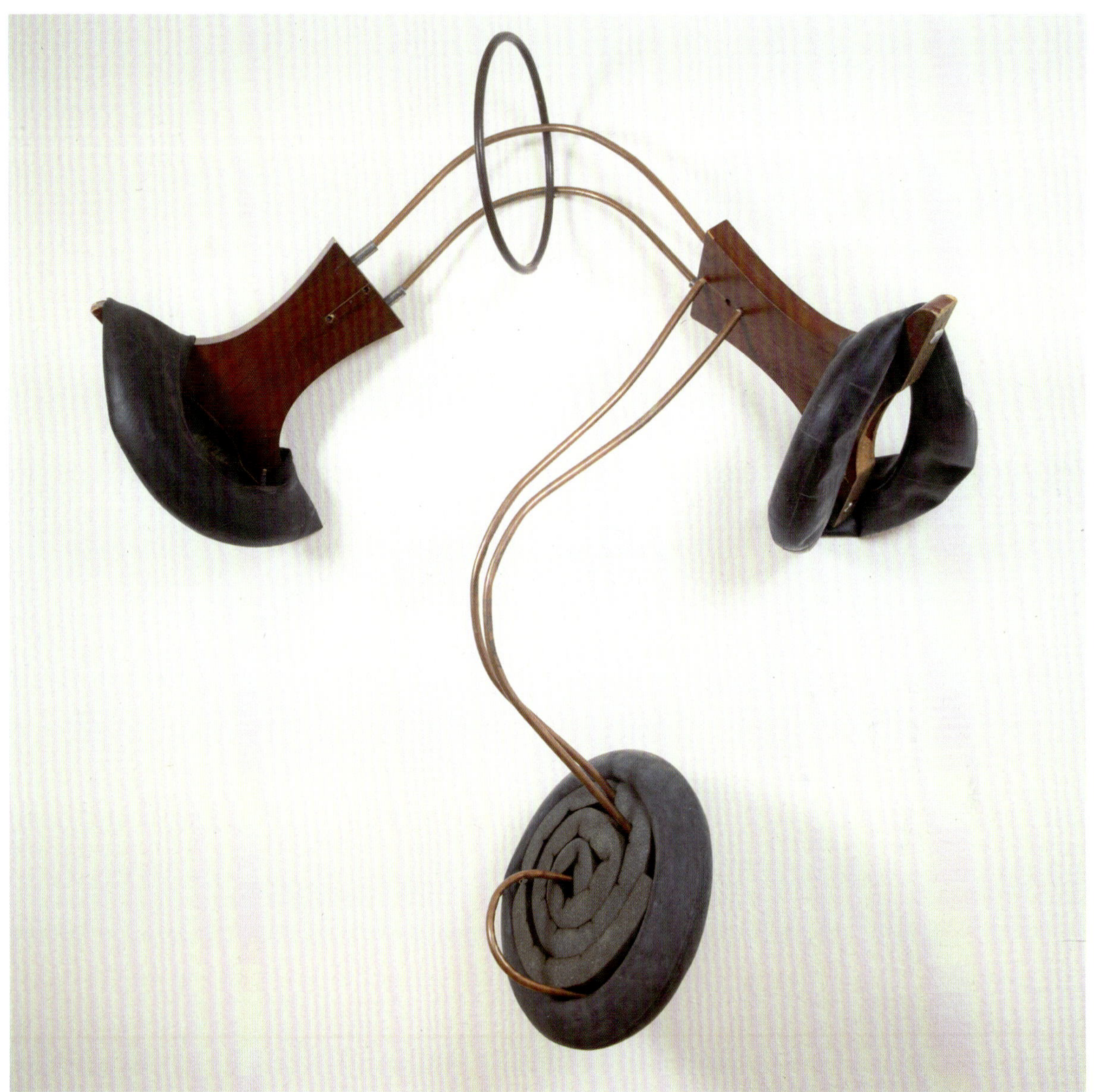

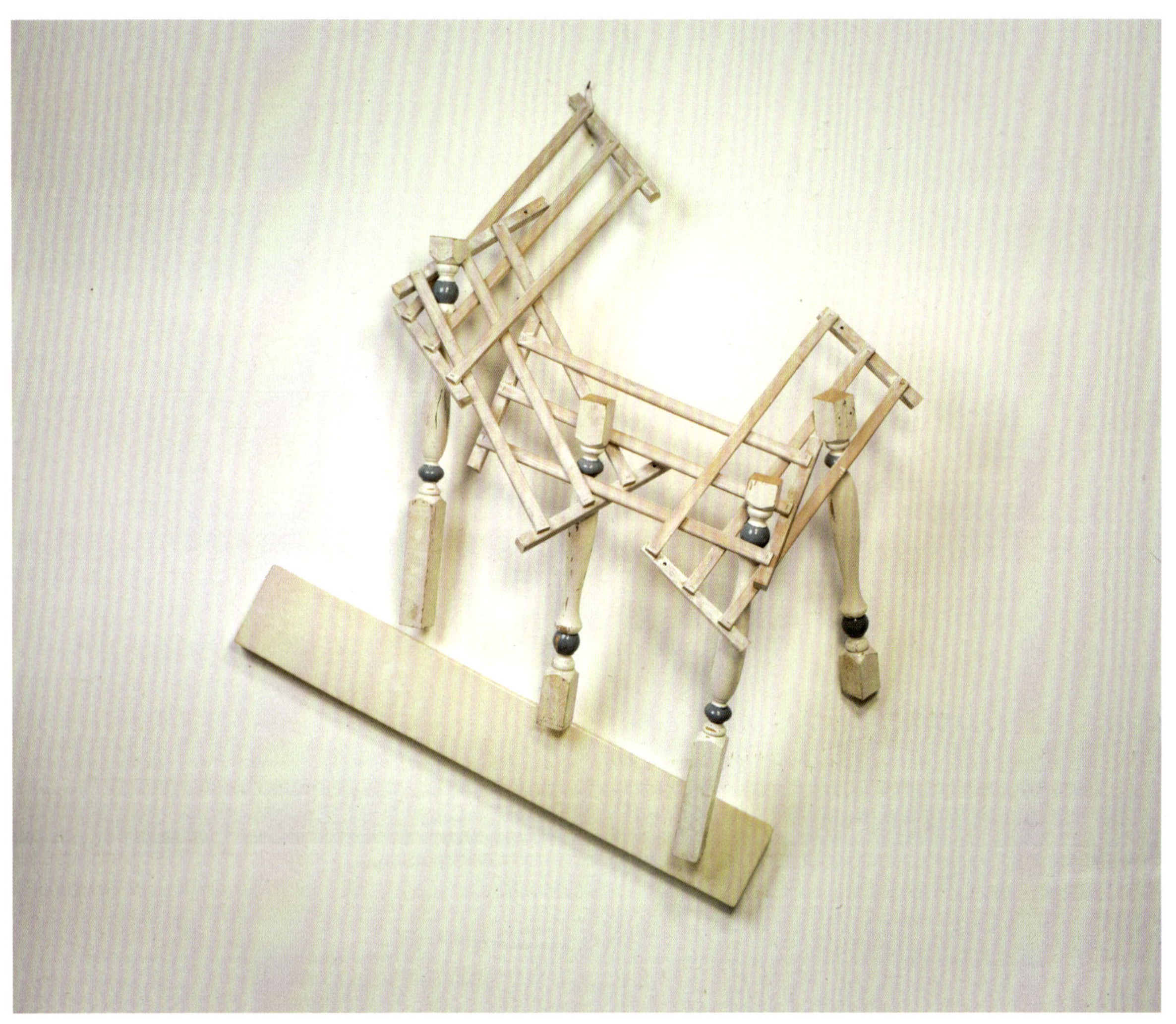

Verkantet

1991, Wood, plastic, 170 × 140 × 50 cm, Private collection

Lehnstück

1991, Steel, roofing felt, 210 × 110 × 110 cm

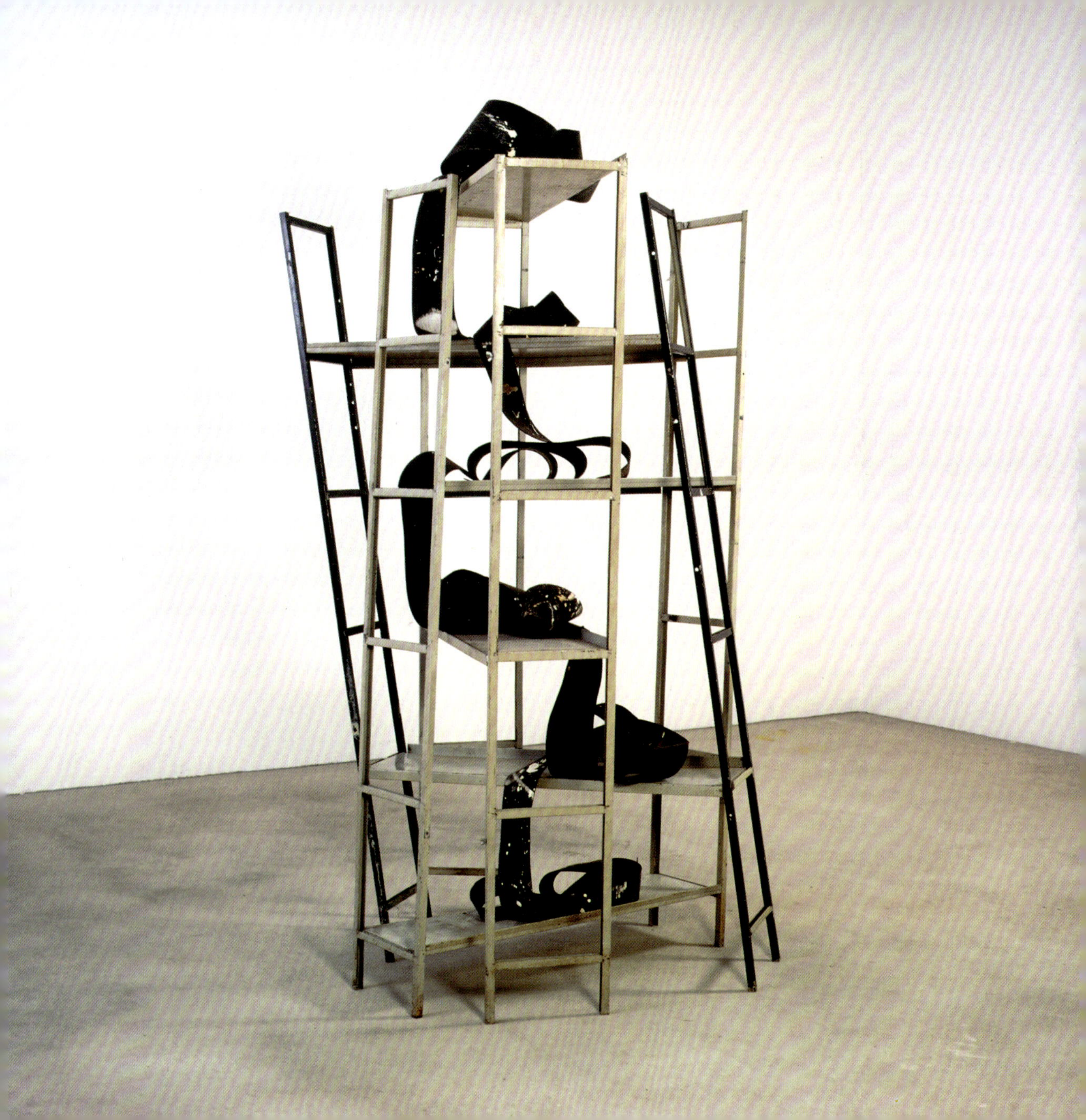

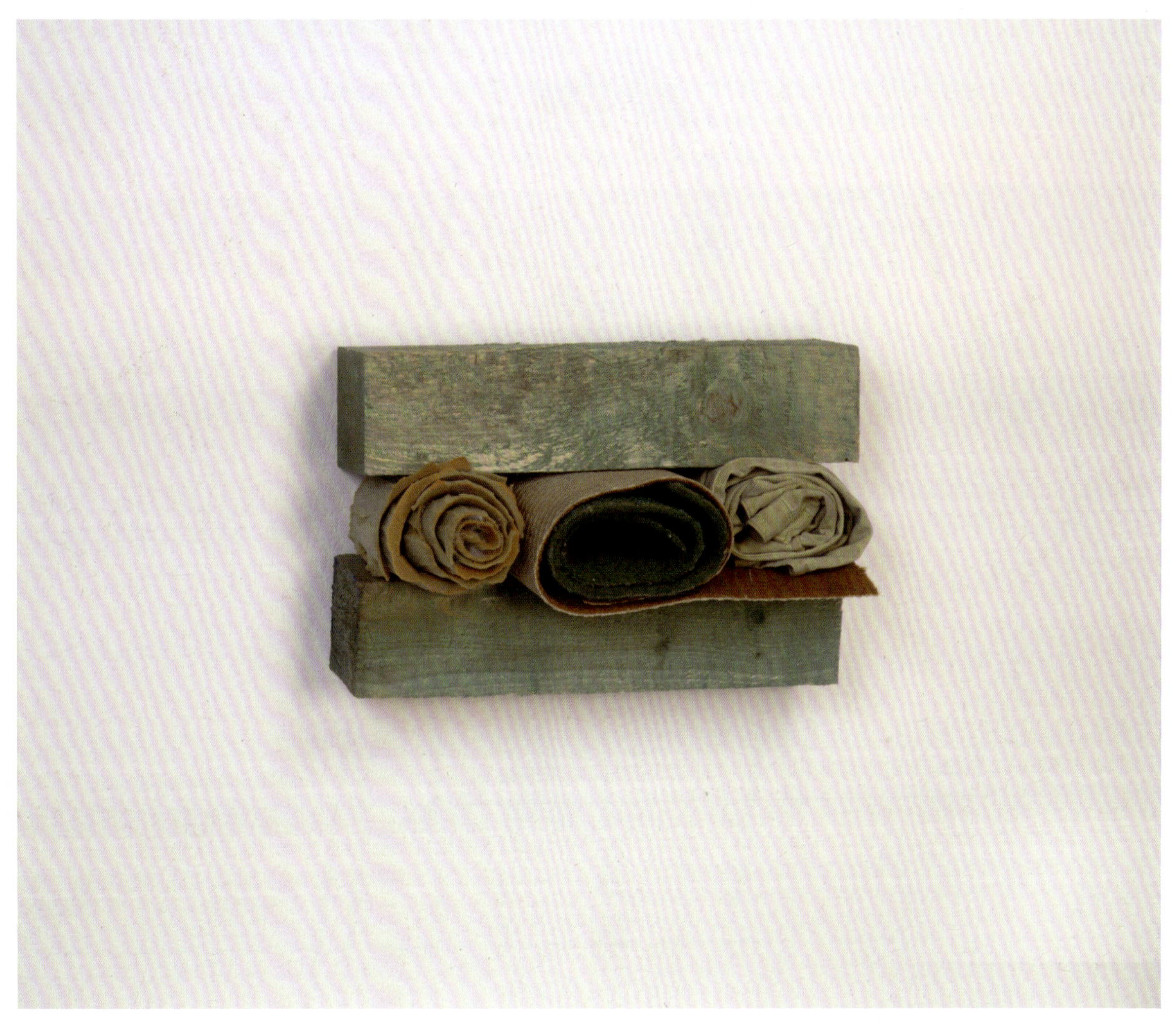

o.T.

1991, Wood, fabric, polyurethane foam, 40 × 50 × 15 cm, Private collection

o.T.

1991, Fabric, wood, steel

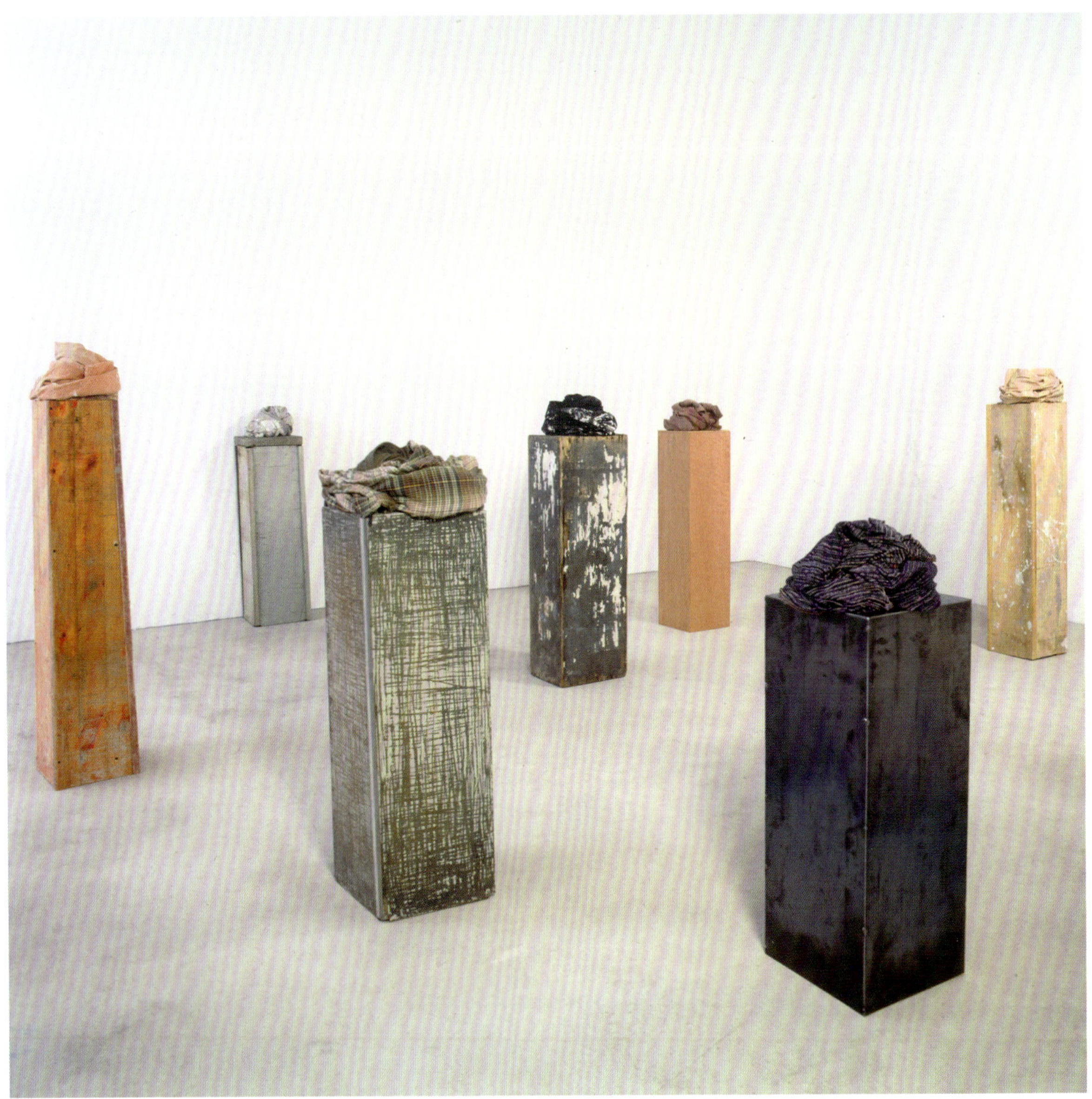

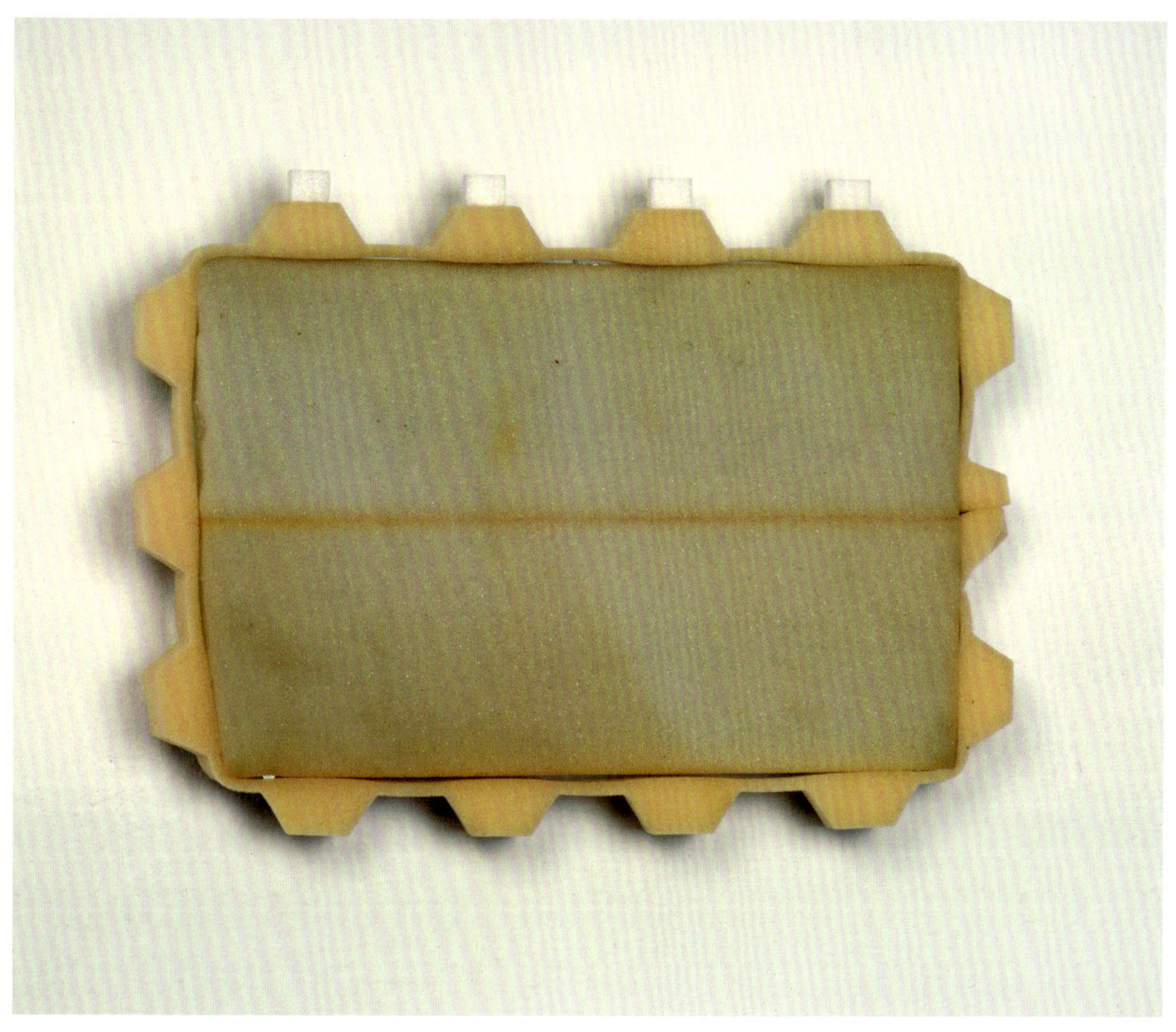

o.T.

1991, Sugar, polyurethane foam, 22 × 18 × 2 cm, Private collection

Schneckenburger

1992, Polyurethane foam, plastic, wood, leather, 75 × 180 × 40 cm

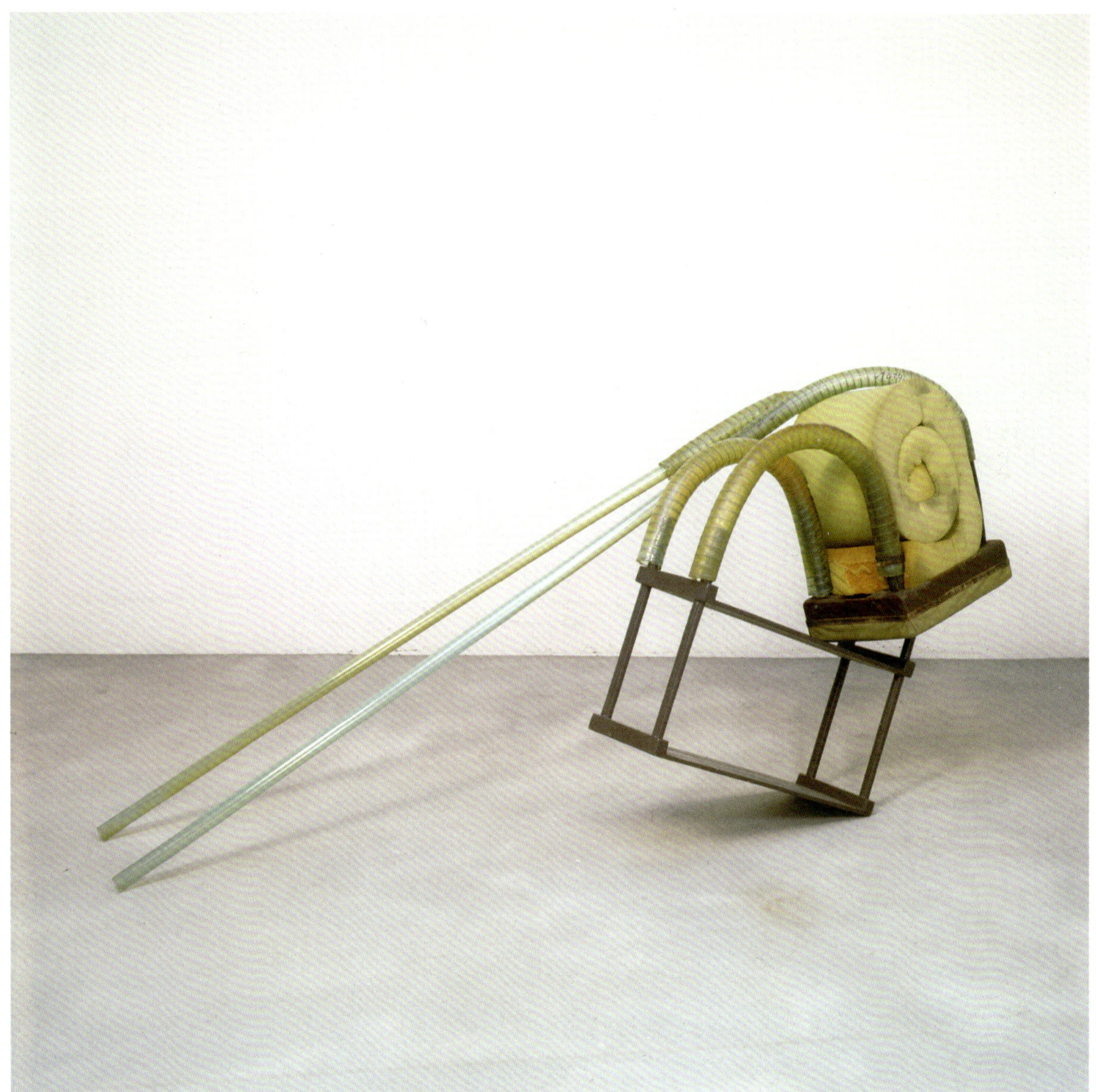

The shape that comes into being as if by itself

La forme qui naît comme d'elle-même

Die Form, die wie von selbst entsteht

La forma que nace como de sí misma

La forma che si crea come da sola

De vorm die haast vanzelf ontstaat

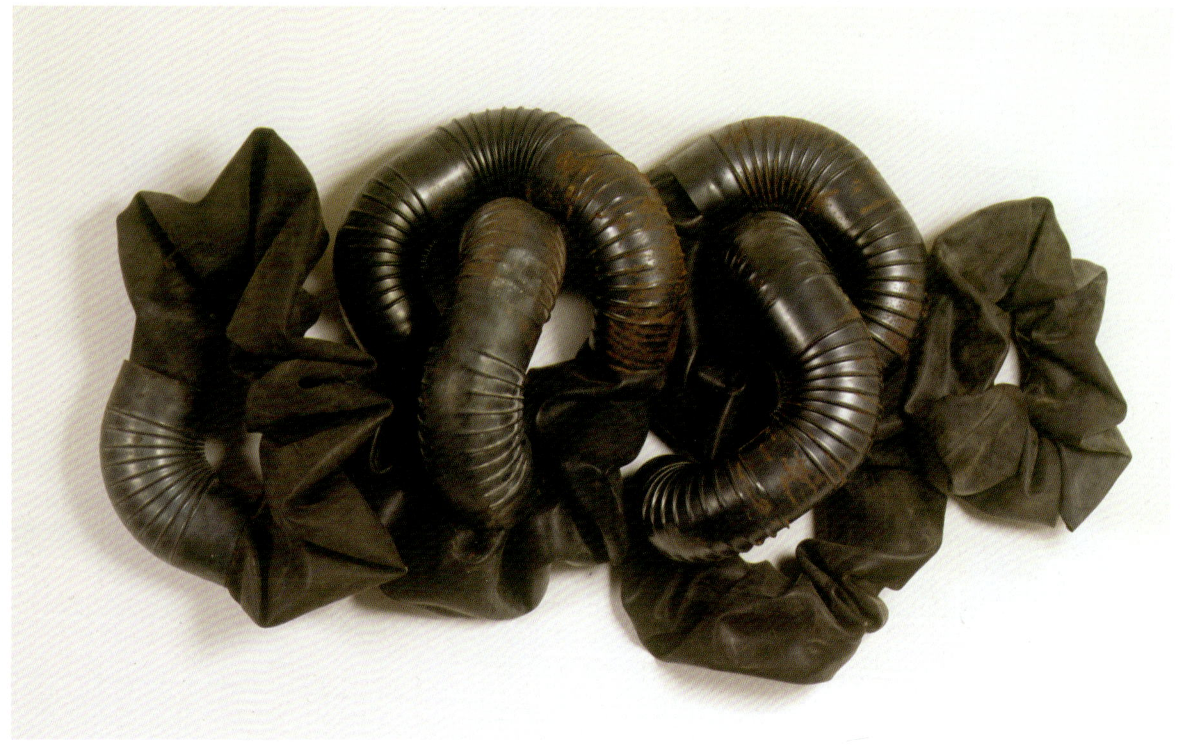

o.T.

1994, Tyre tubes, stovepipes, 85 × 160 × 38 cm

Dicke Luft

1993, Tyre tubes, Private collection

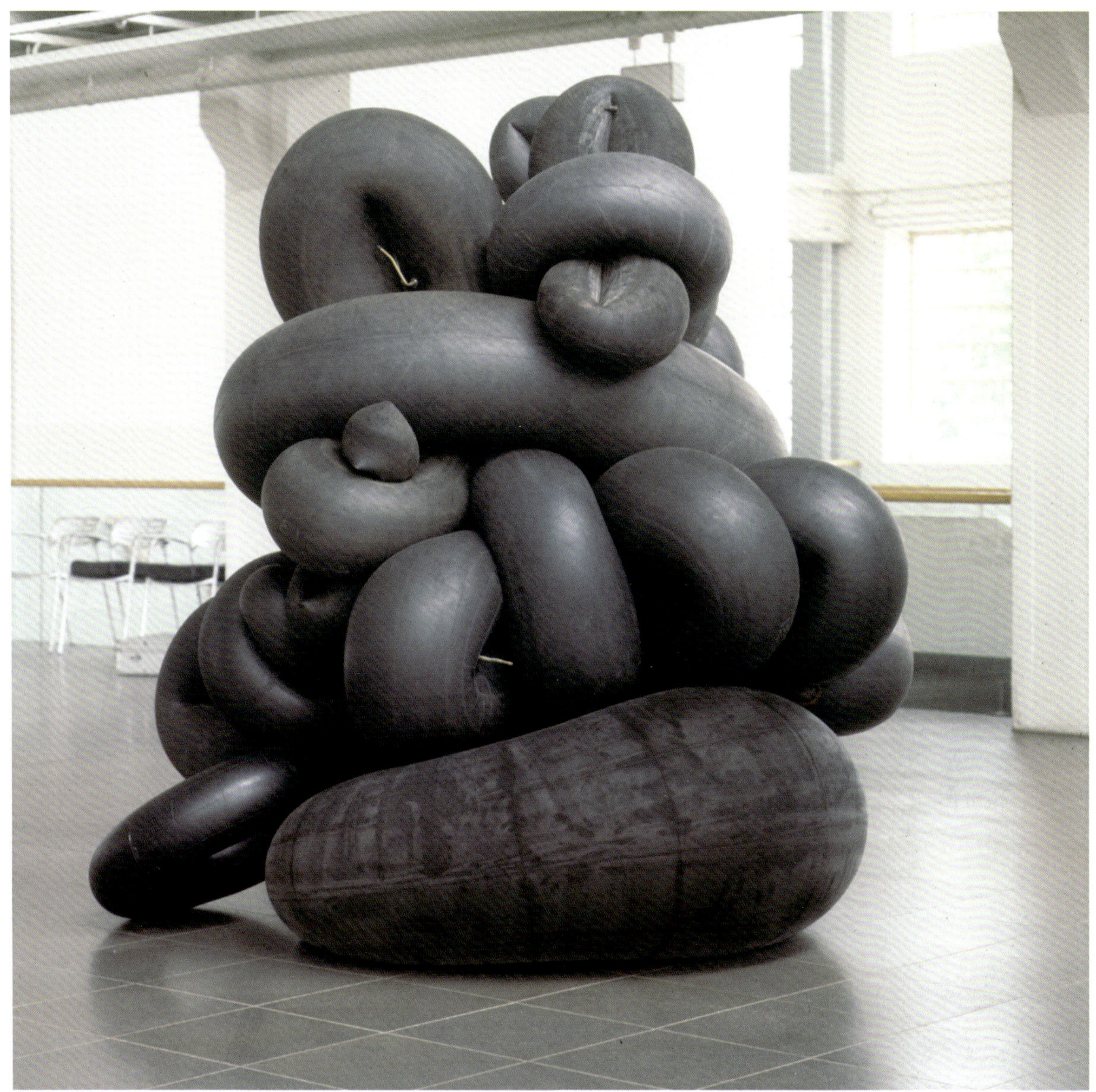

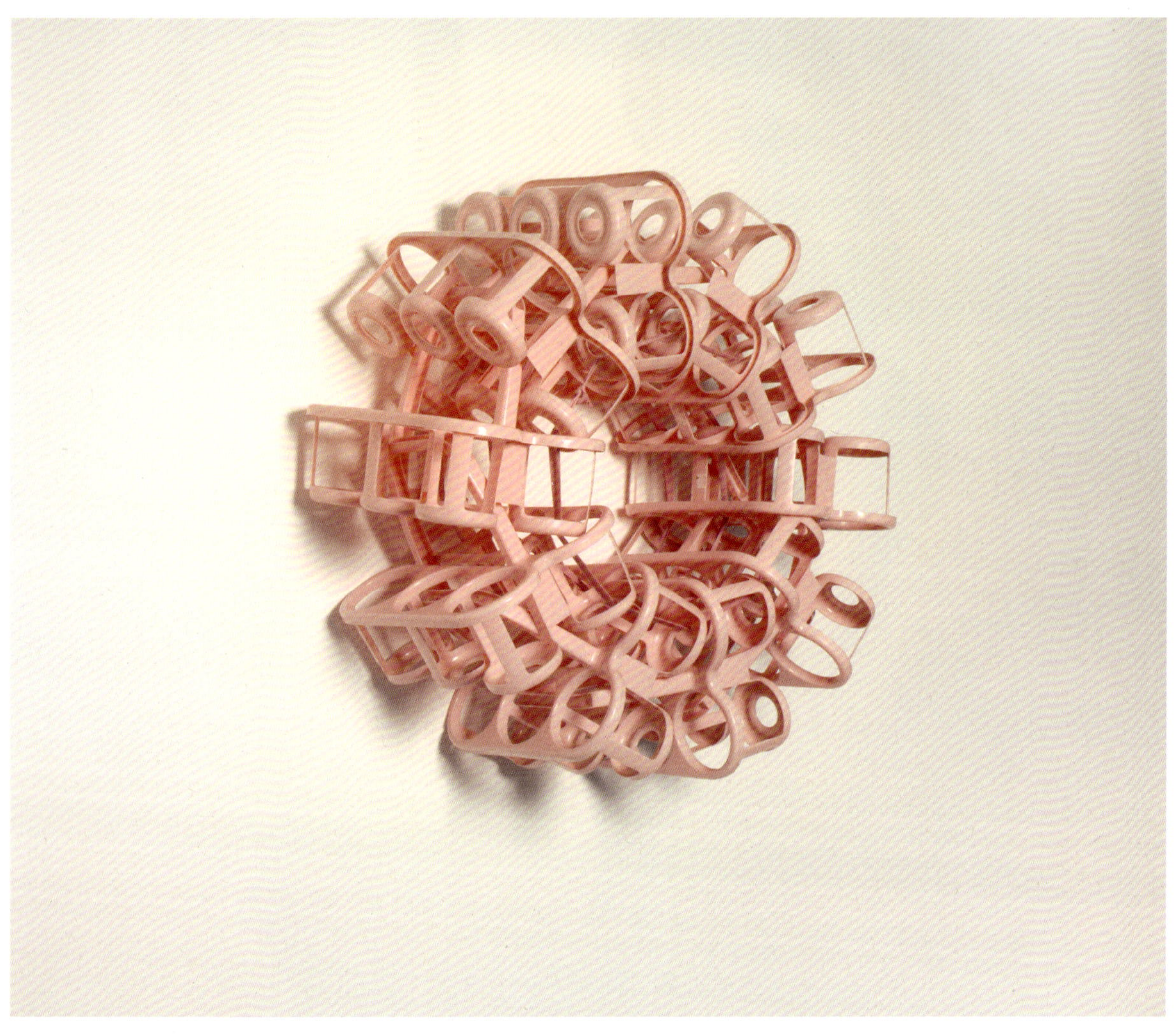

o.T.

1993, Plastic, textile tape

Auf der Kippe

1992, Copper, wood

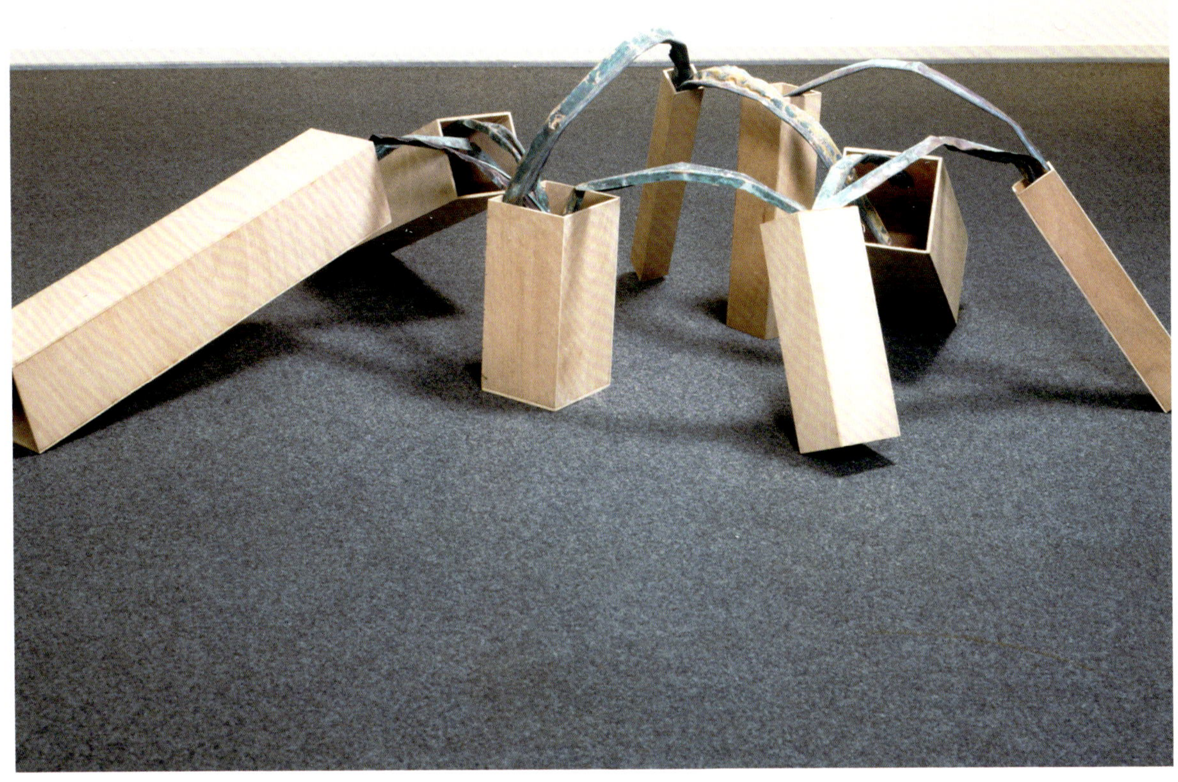

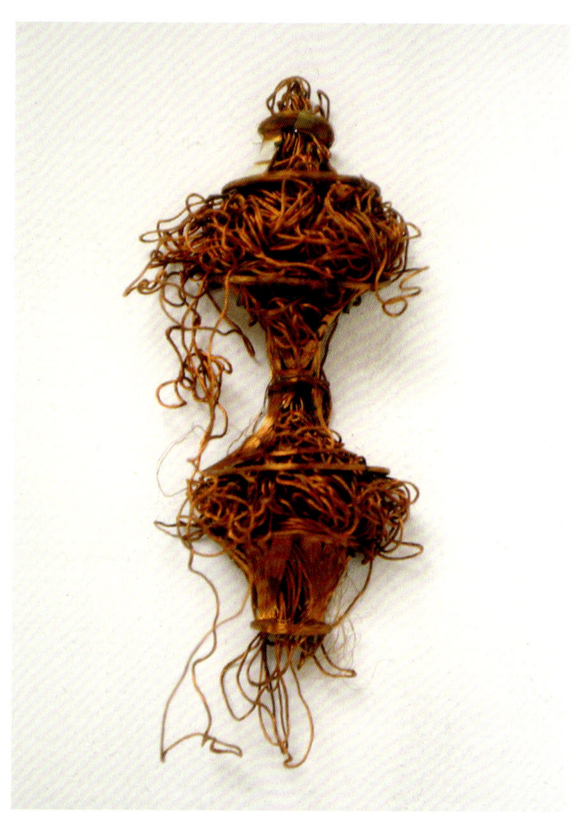

o.T.

1992, Copper, 48 × 18 × 10 cm

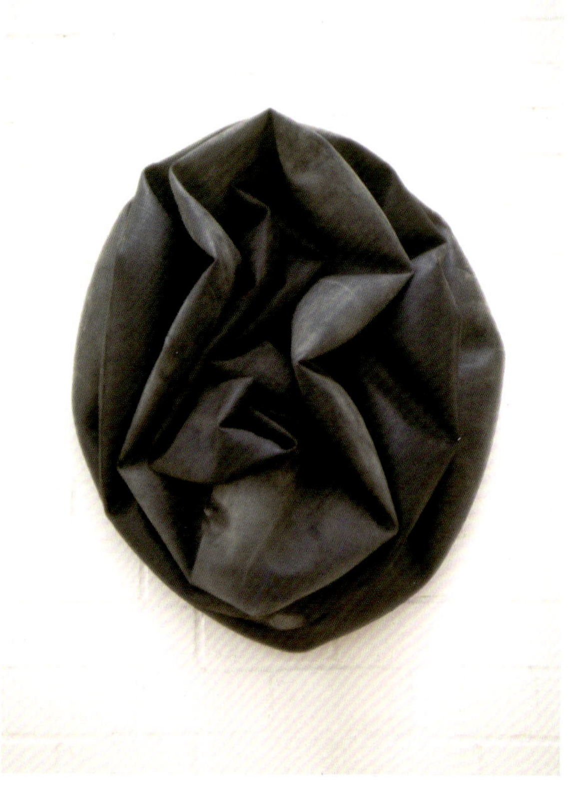

o.T.

1992, Rubber, 52 × 18 × 40 cm

Heraklith

1993, Cement-bonded wood fibre boards, fur, shuttlecocks, 60 × 46 × 13 cm, Private collection

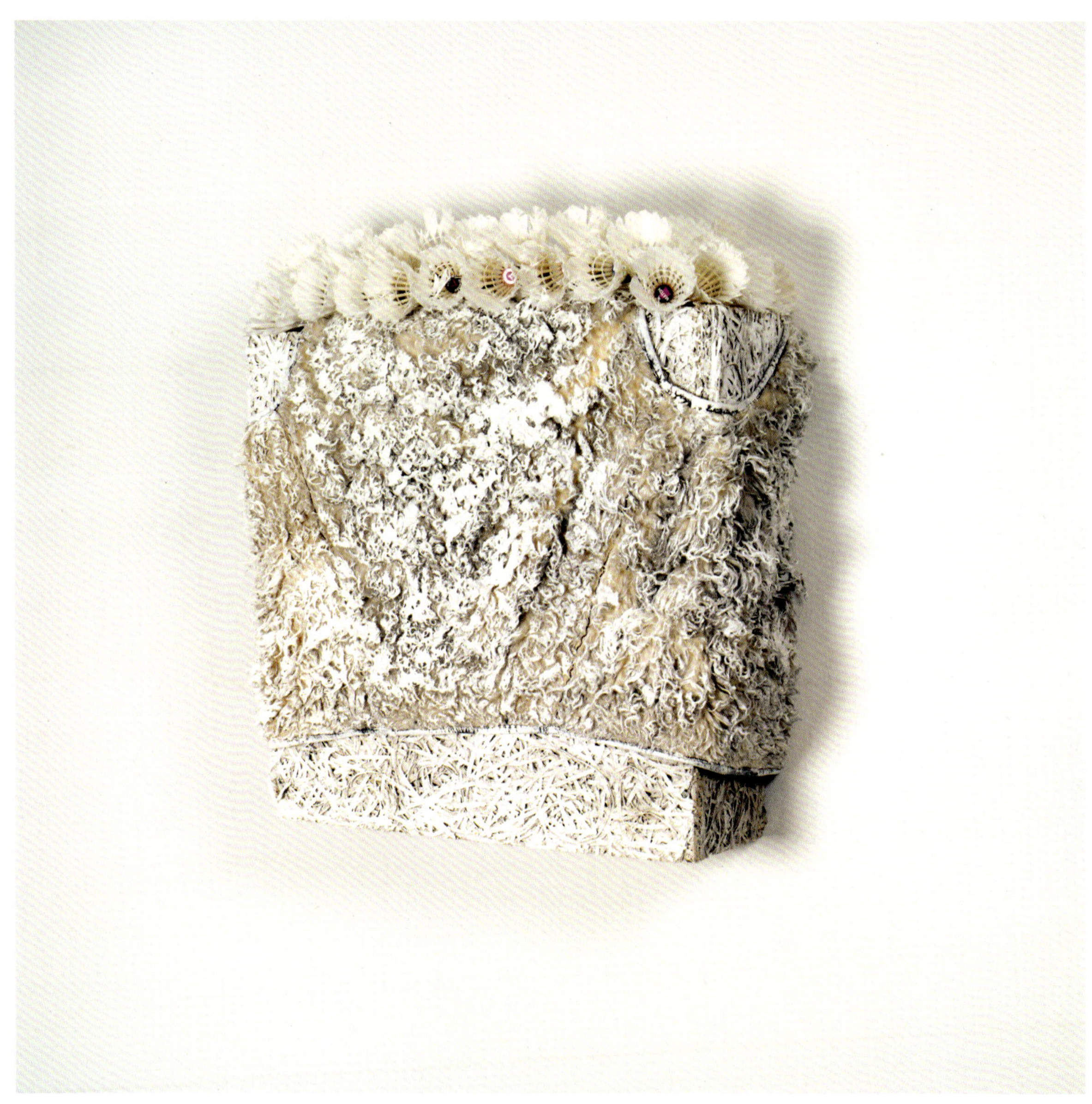

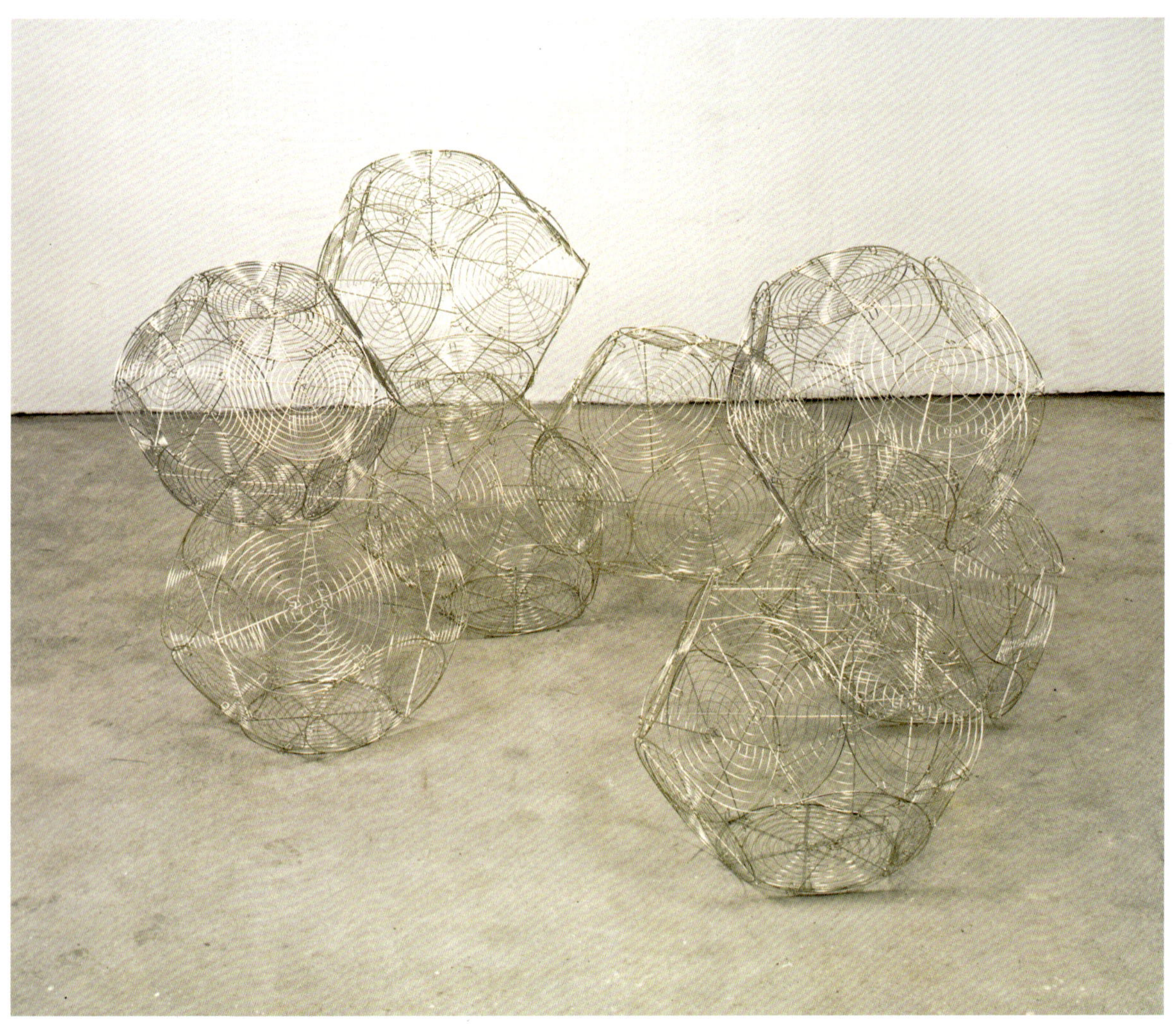

o.T.

1994, Iron wire

o.T.

1993, Aluminium, polyurethane foam, copper, brass, 80 × 65 × 75 cm, Private collection, Courtesy Galerie Ulrich Mueller

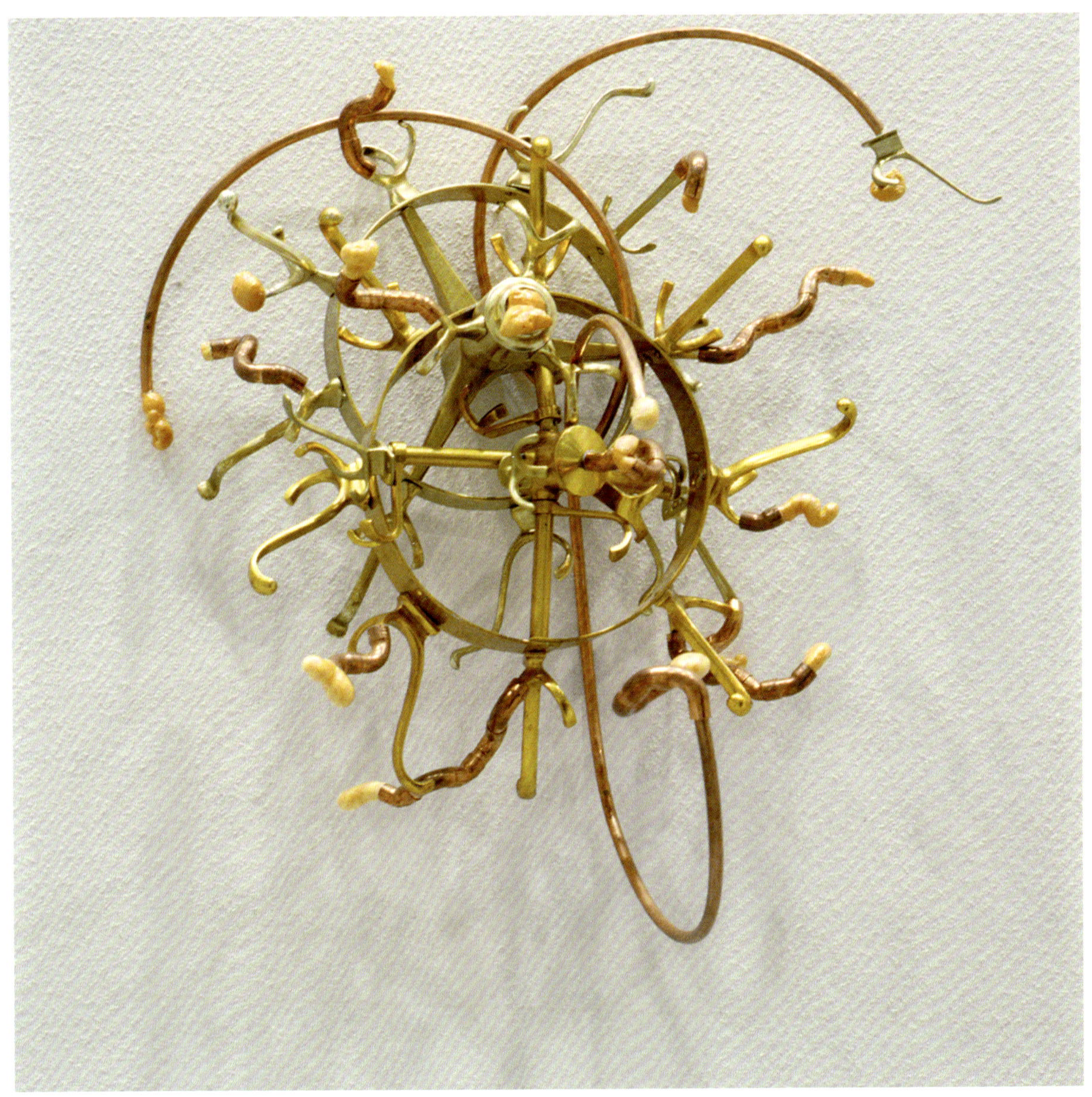

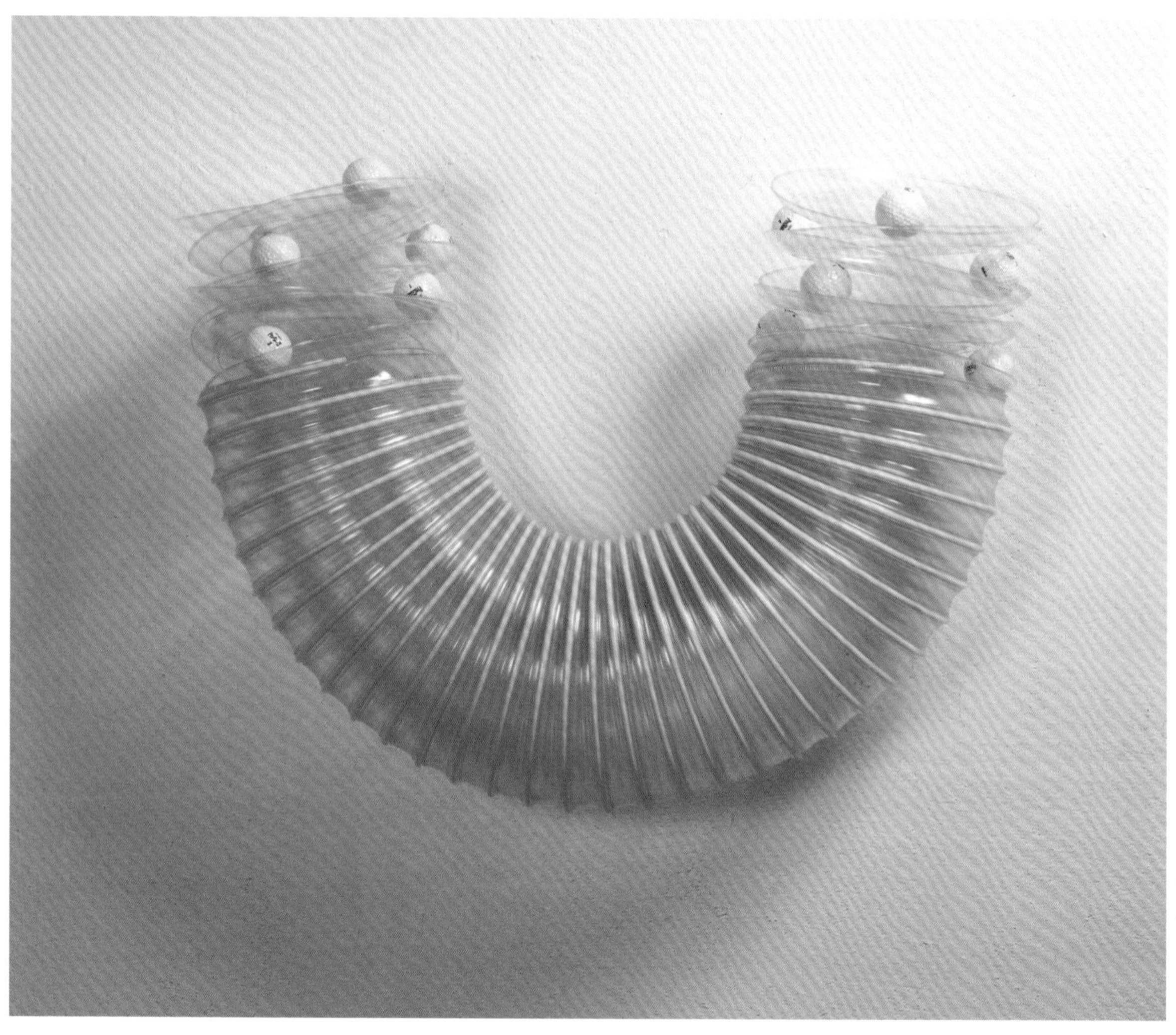

o.T.

1994, Plastic, 64 × 68 × 20 cm

o.T.

1994, Light bulbs, chicken wire, silicone, 42 × 90 × 100 cm, Private collection

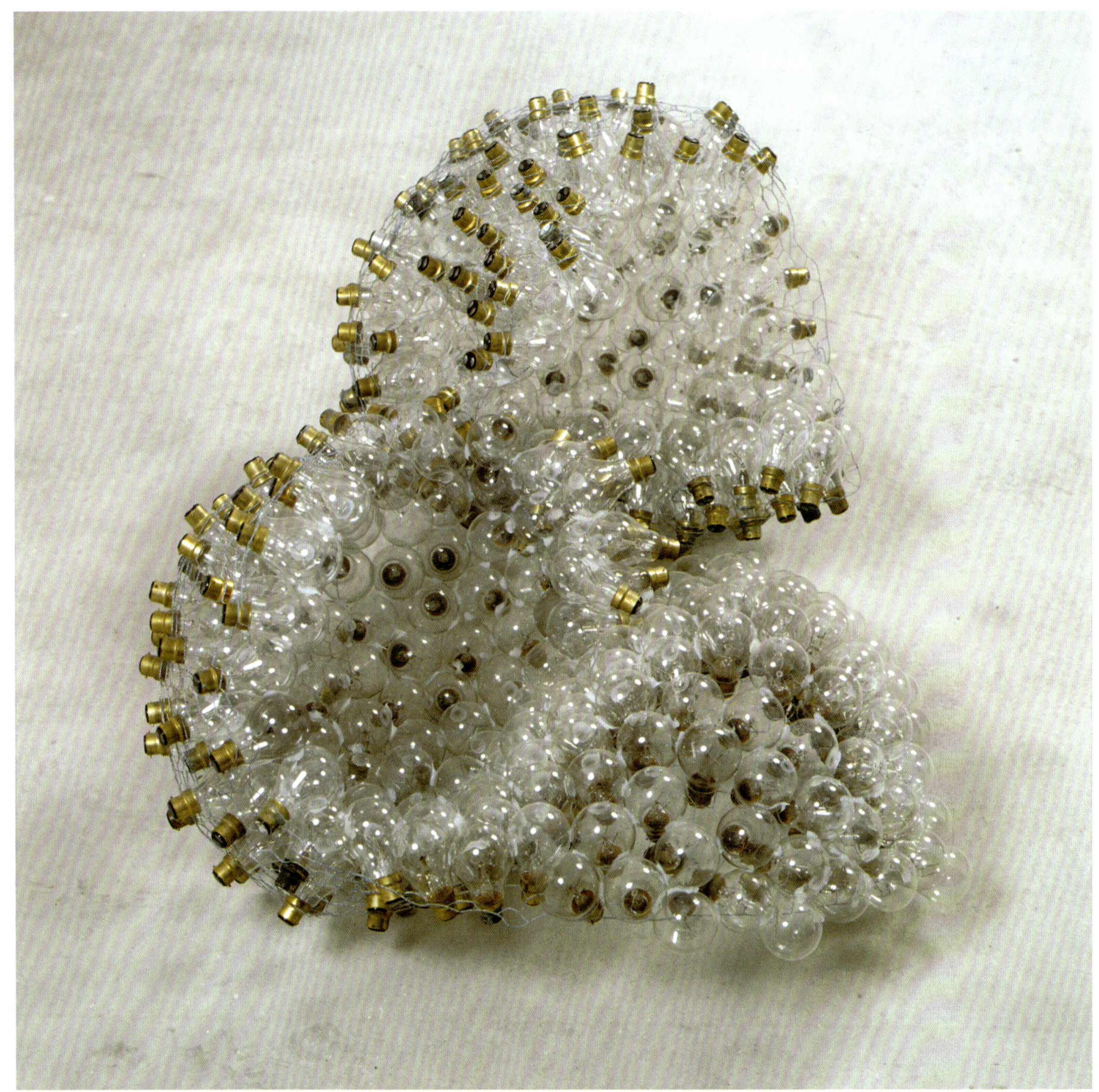

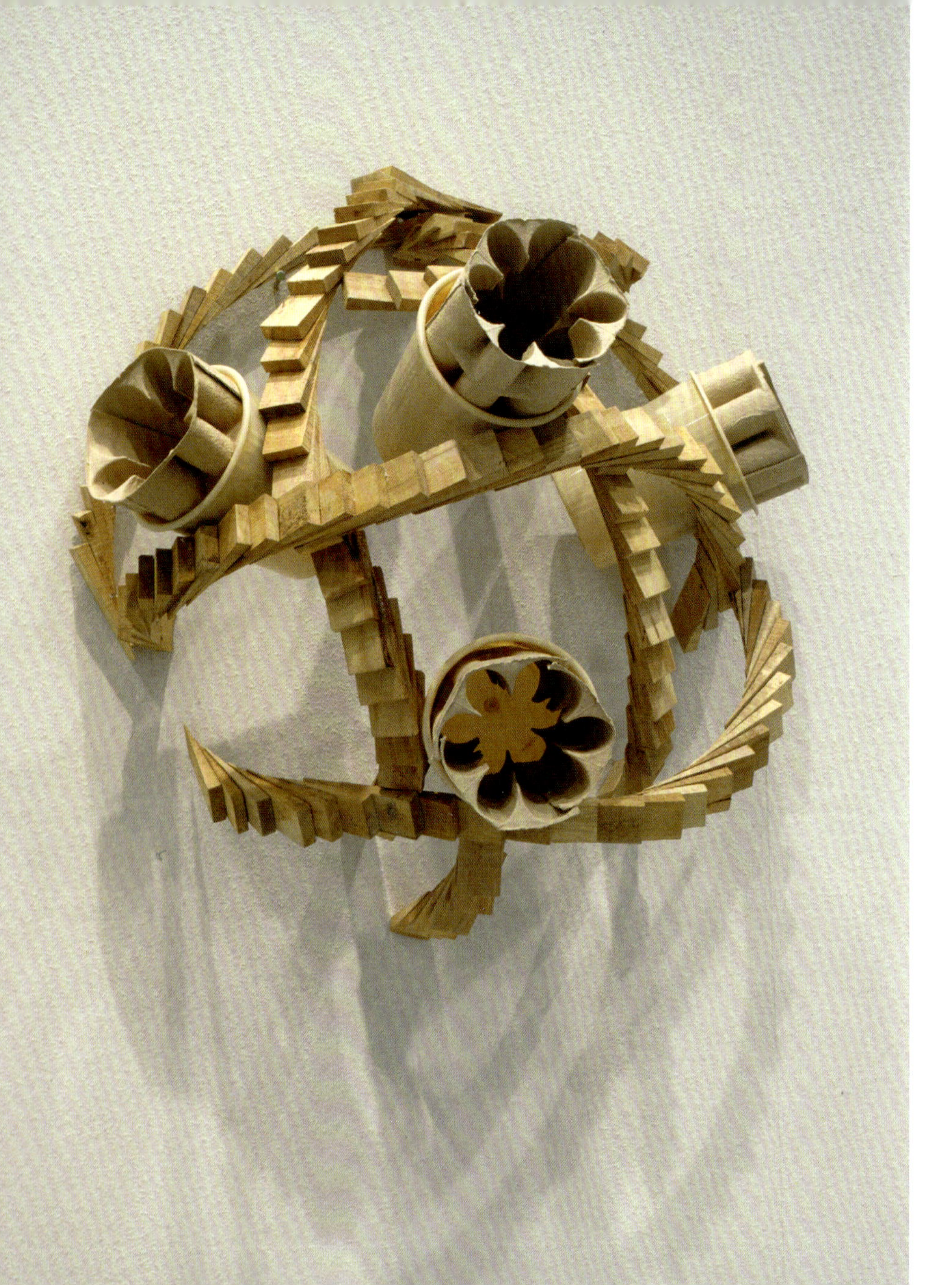

o.T.

*1994, Wood, plastic, cardboard,
105 × 110 × 52 cm, Private
collection*

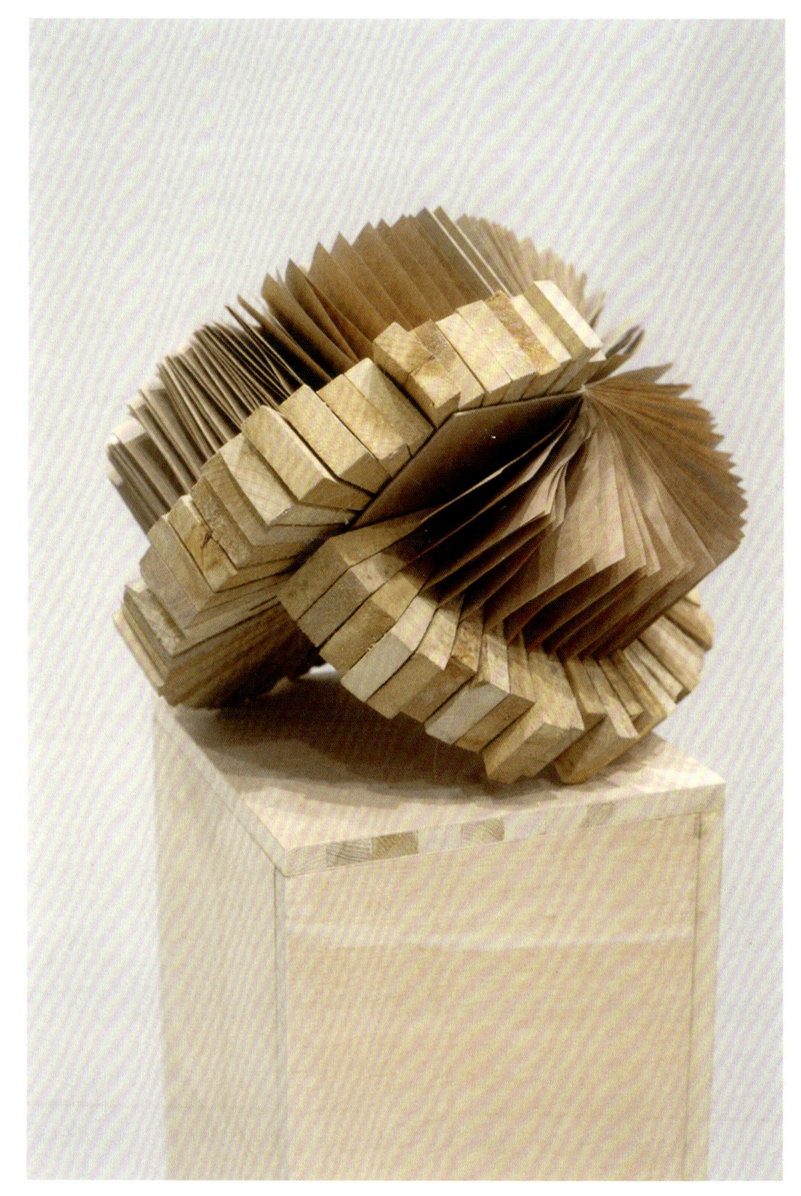

Bücherwurm

1994, Wood, paper, cardboard

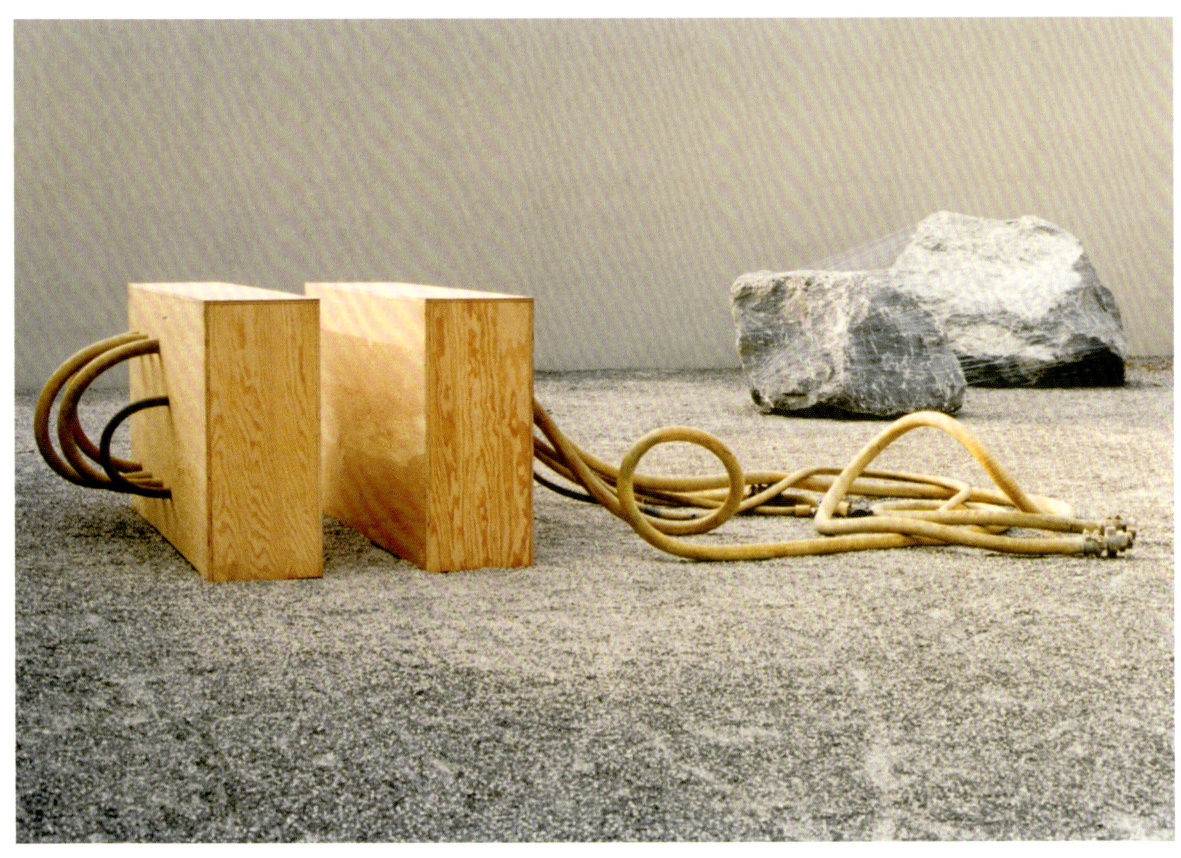

Zwischenraum

1994, Wood, PVC, 107 × 240 × 320 cm, Birmingham Museum of Art, Birmingham AL

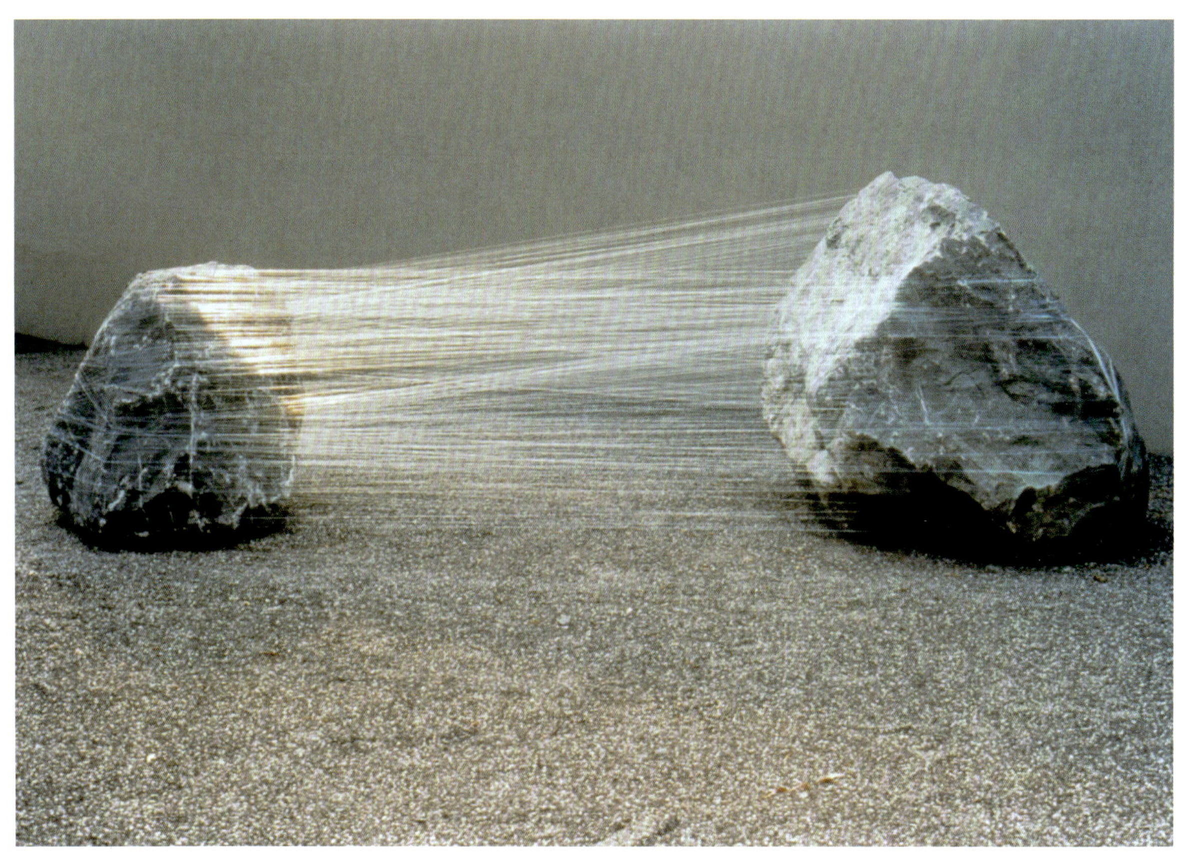

Hook, Line & Sinker

1994, Fluorescent nylon, sandstone, 110 × 130 × 420 cm, Birmingham Museum of Art, Birmingham AL

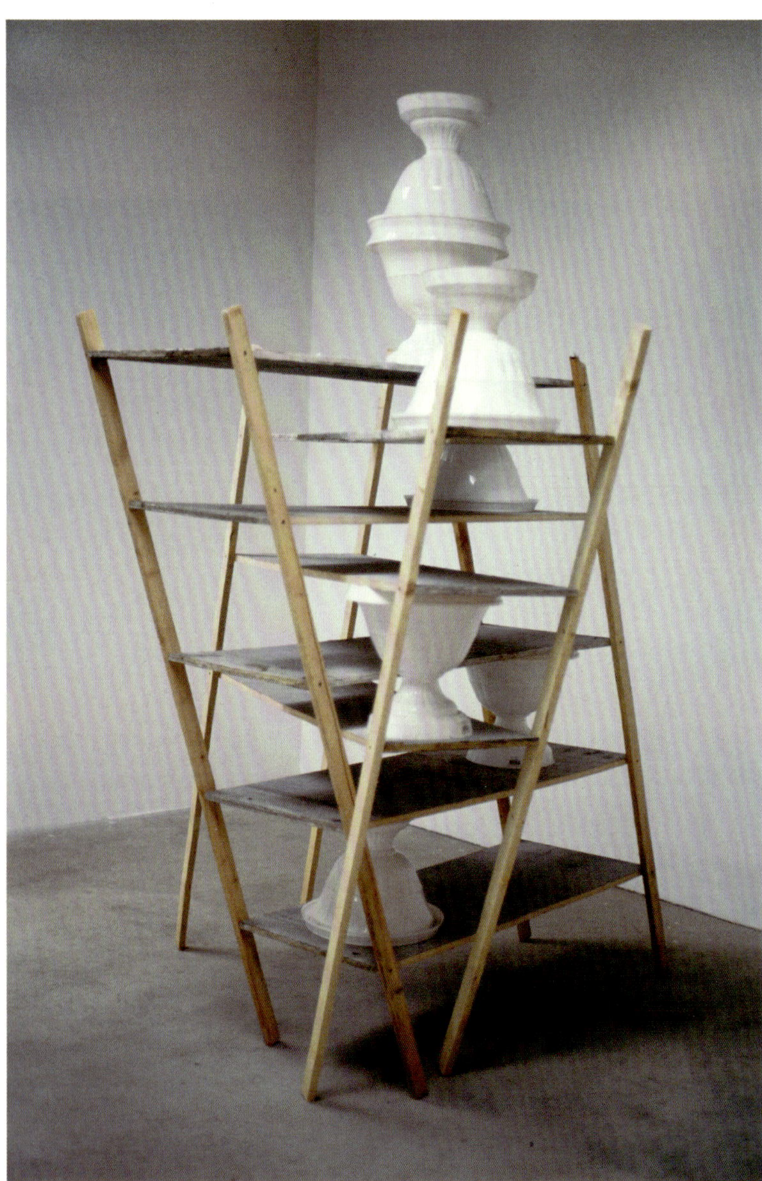

o.T.
1993, Wood, plastic, 220 × 190 × 190 cm

Mambo I
1994, Monobloc plastic chairs, screws,
140 × 110 × 39 cm

40

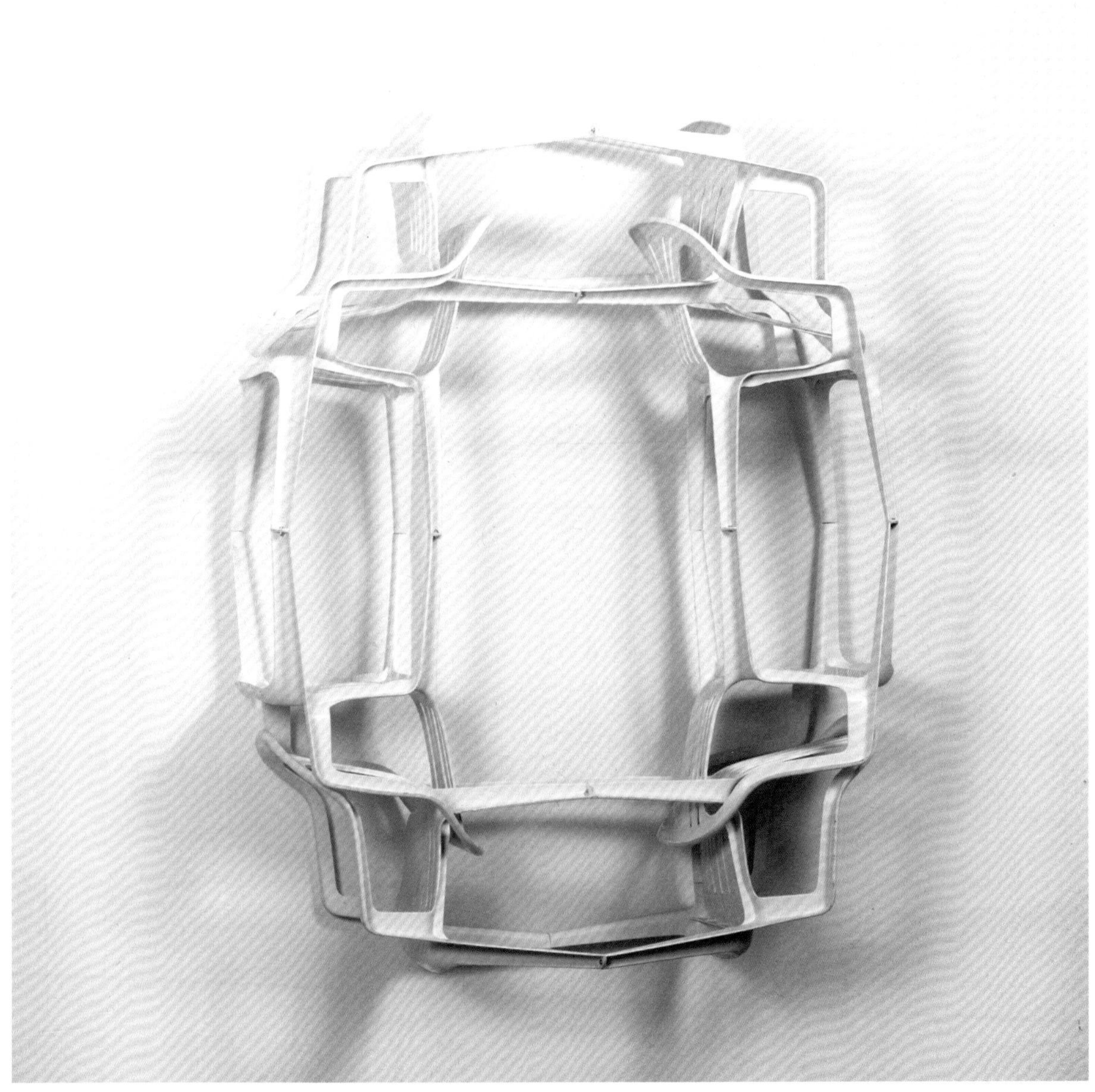

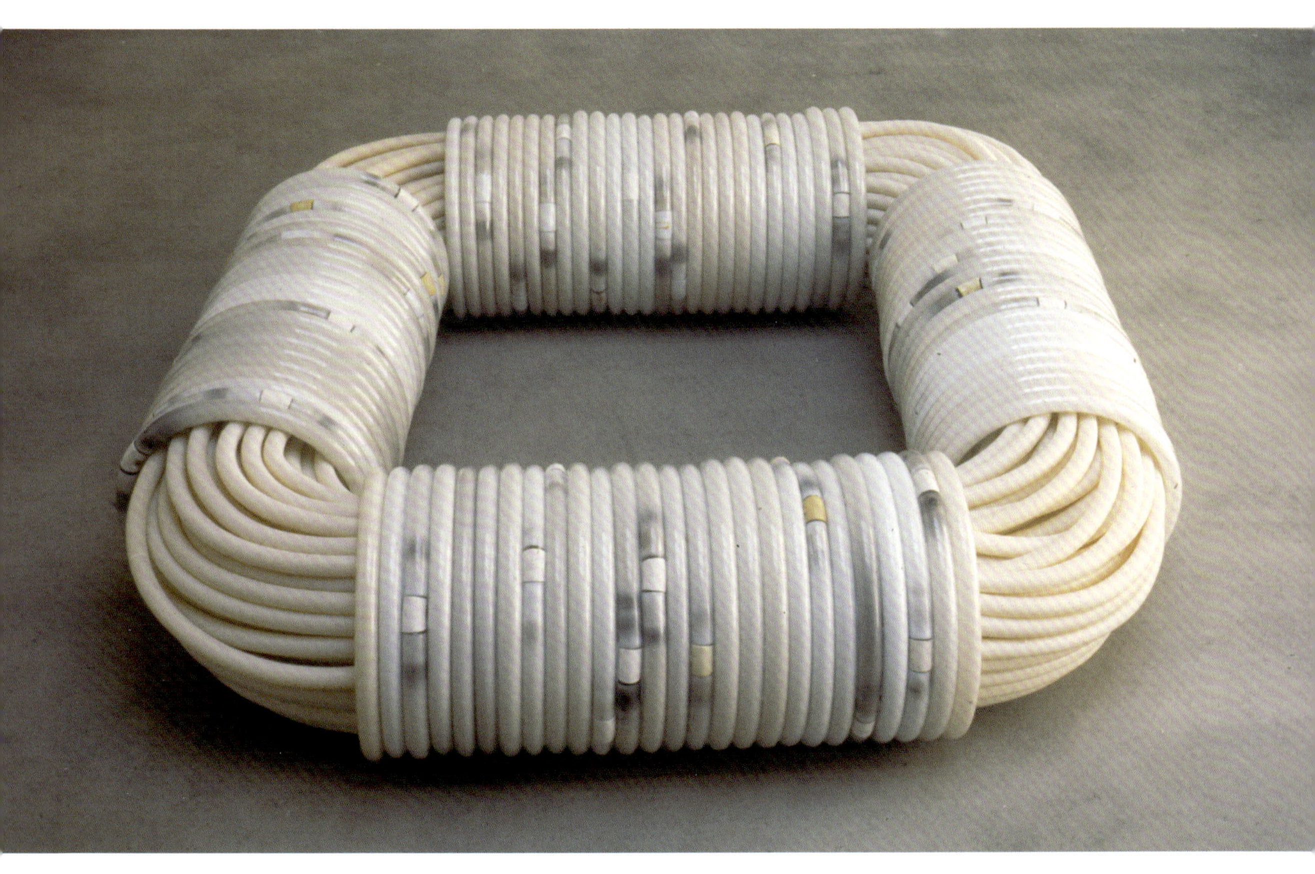

o.T.

1995, Glass, rigid PVC, silicone, 40 × 150 × 150 cm

o.T.

1995, Concrete, glass, 70 × 80 × 70 cm

42

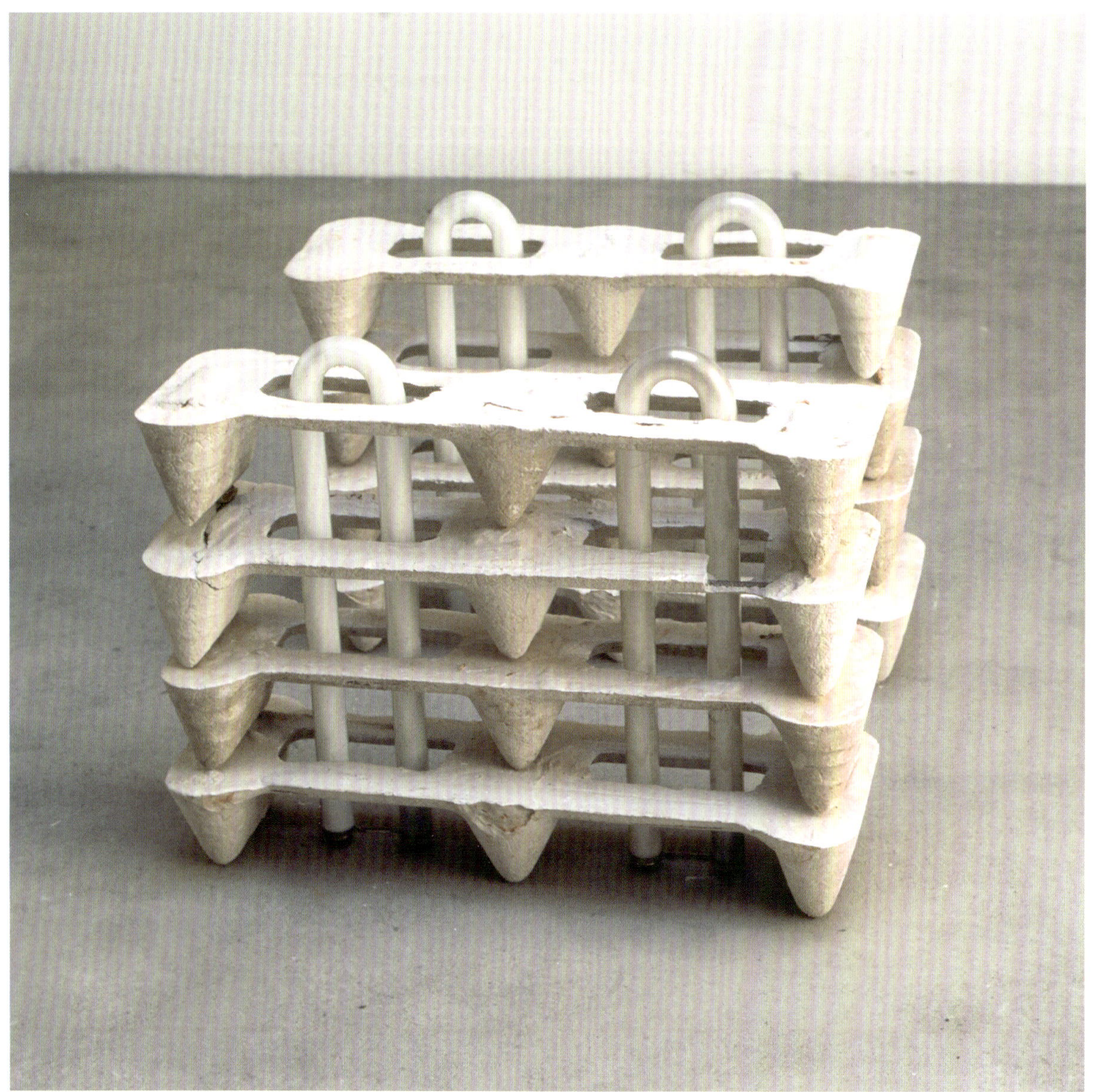

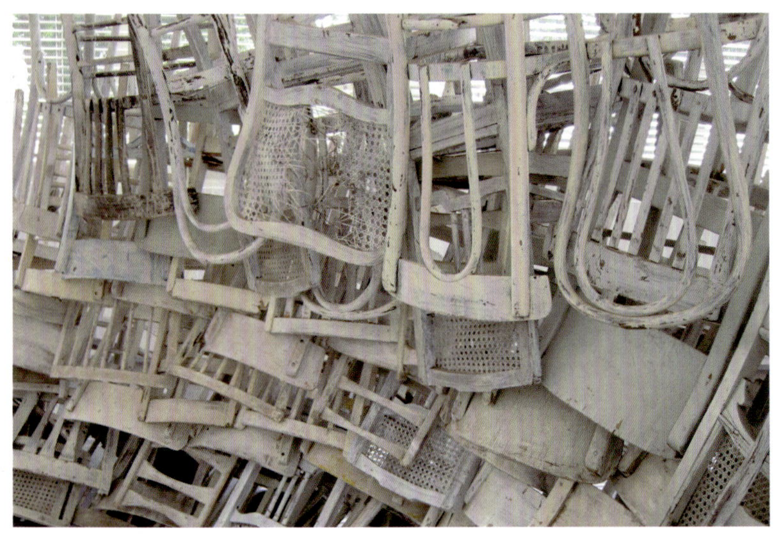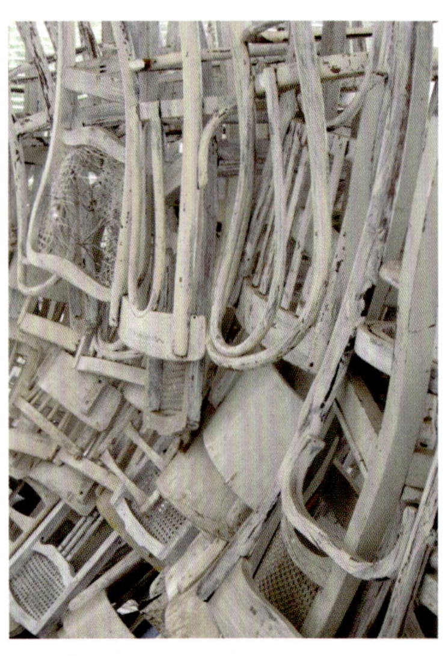

o.T.

1994, Wooden chairs, 180 × 380 × 280 cm

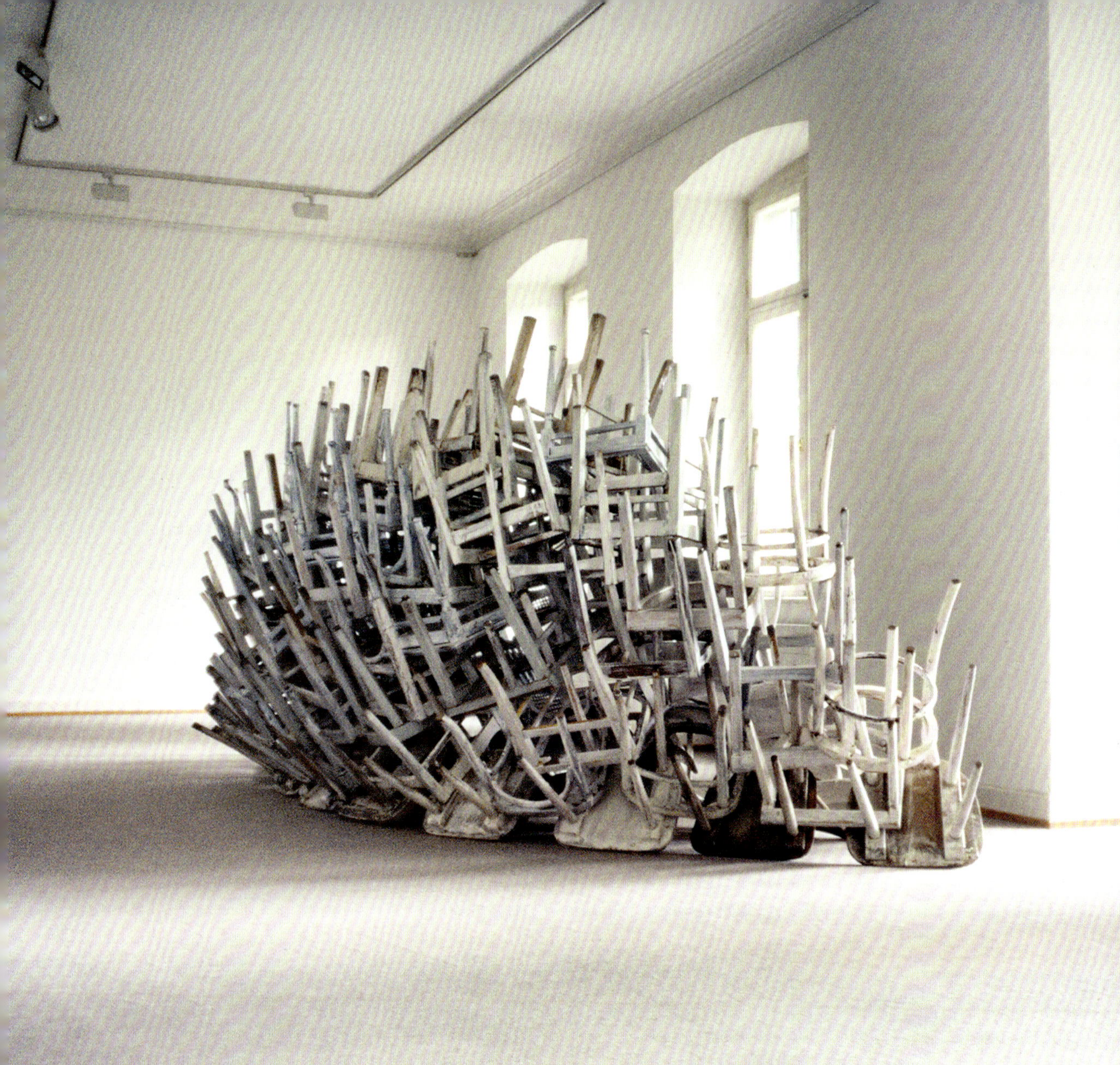

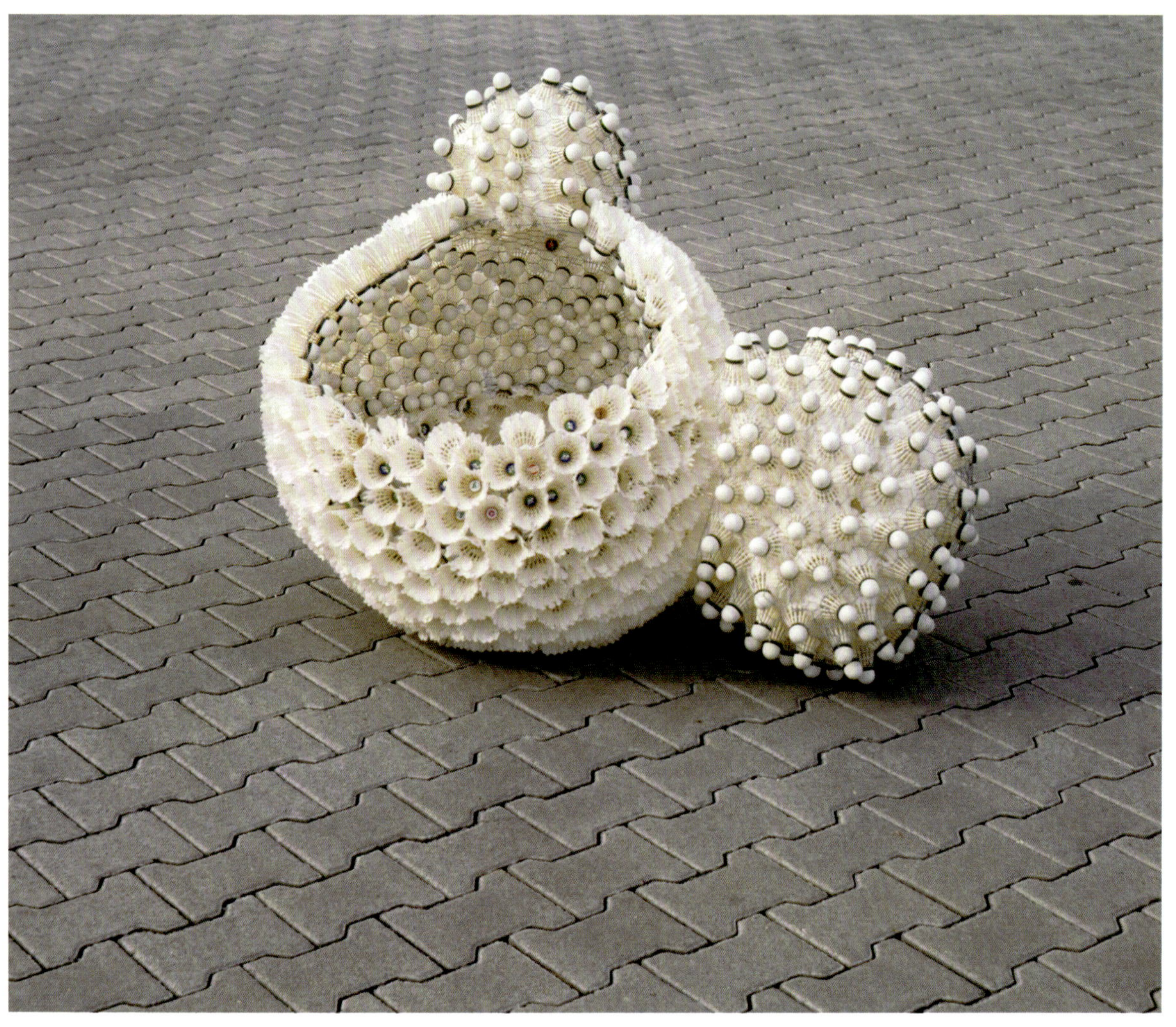

o.T.

1995, Wire, shuttlecocks, cork, 82 × 70 × 65 cm, Private collection

o.T.

1995, Wood, 70 × 120 cm

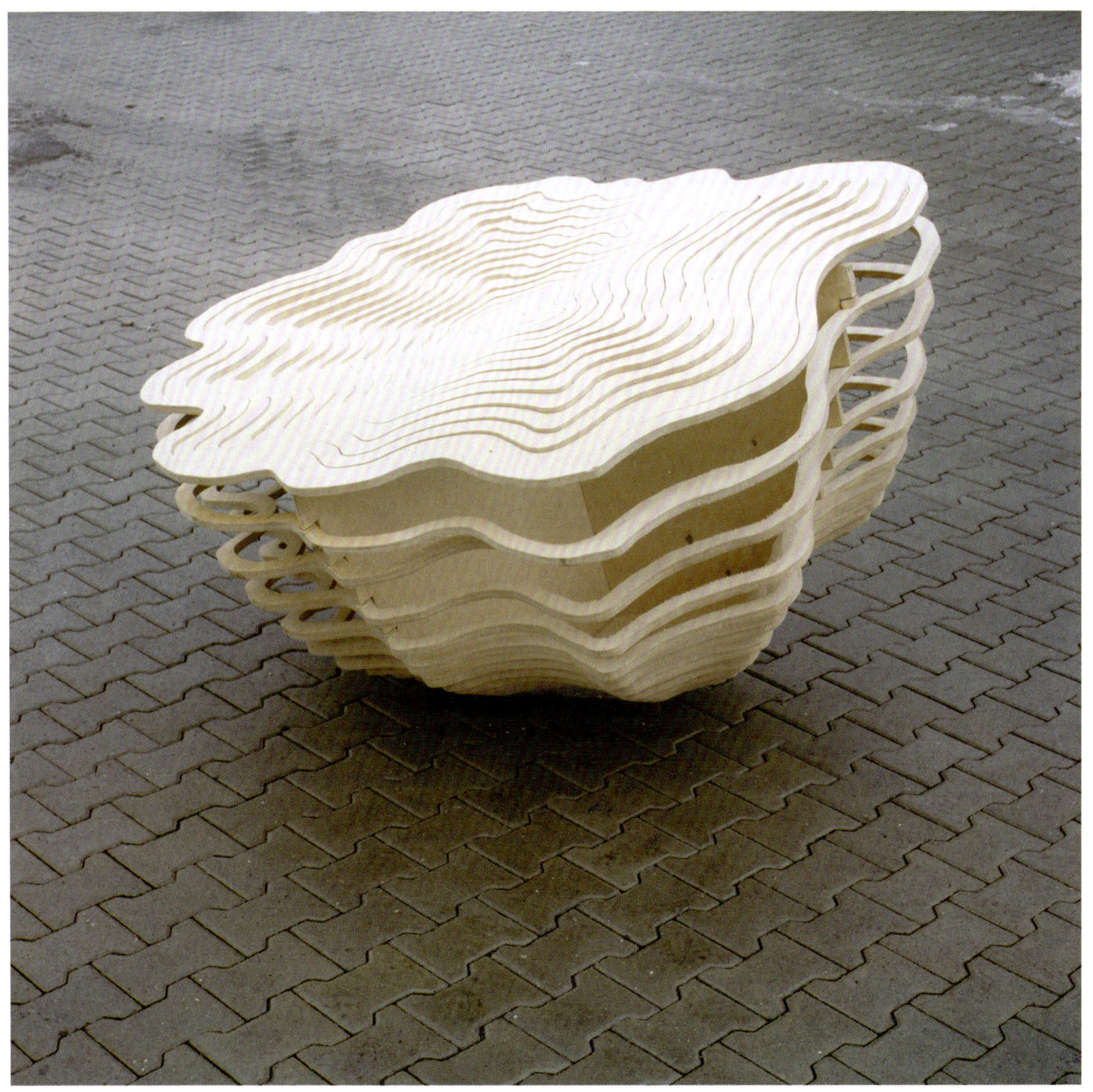

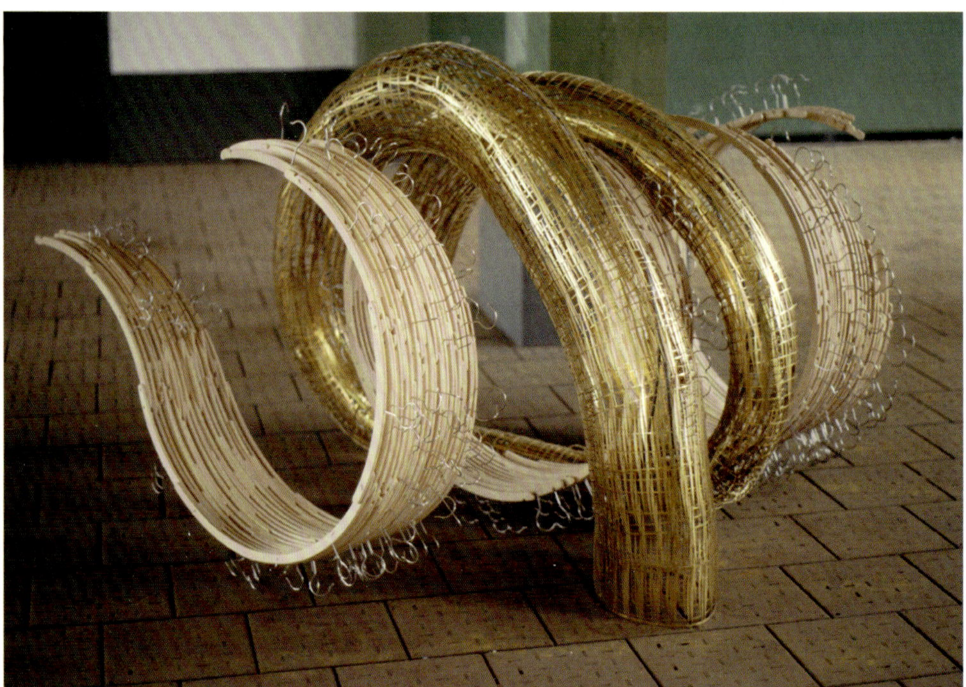

o.T.

*1998, Brass,
clothes hangers,
130 × 150 × 210 cm,
Colosseum Art
Collection, Essen*

What comes between

Everything is already there, nothing is being reinvented, DIY megastores with garden centres, shopping zones, everyday life and its remnants offer enough raw materials. Many of these can be utilised, transformed. Through rearrangement and relocation, sculptures emerge from used and new goods. Their sphere is simple. Objects or places open up for them. The artist helps them with rigour and precision. She creates what chairs, lamps, buckets, bottles and coat hangers, for example, have always wanted, been capable of doing and arranges the sculptural interplay of these commonplace things, thus enabling

L'inattendu

Tout existe déjà, rien ne s'invente, les magasins de bricolage et les jardineries, les zones commerciales, le quotidien et ses résidus offrent suffisamment de matières premières. Certains peuvent être réutilisées, transformées. Par un jeu de réorganisation et de recoupements, des sculptures naissent à partir d'objets vieux et neufs. Leur champ d'action est la simplicité. Lui, ce sont les objets eux-mêmes ou le lieu où ils se trouvent qui l'ont activé. Pour cela, l'artiste les aide avec rigueur et précision. Elle réalise ce que par exemple les chaises, les lampes, les seaux, les bouteilles et les cintres auraient toujours voulu devenir, auraient

Was dazwischen kommt

Alles ist schon da, nichts wird neu erfunden, Bau- und Gartenmärkte, Einkaufszonen, der Alltag und seine Reste bieten Rohstoffe genug. Davon kann manches verwandt, verwandelt werden. Durch Umordnung und Deplatzierung wachsen aus Verbrauchtem und Neuwaren Skulpturen heran. Deren Spielraum ist das Einfache. Den öffnen die Dinge oder der Ort. Dabei hilft ihnen die Künstlerin mit Strenge und Präzision. Sie realisiert, was zum Beispiel Stühle, Lampen, Eimer, Flaschen und Kleiderbügel immer schon gewollt, gekonnt hätten und arrangiert das plastische Zusammenspiel dieser

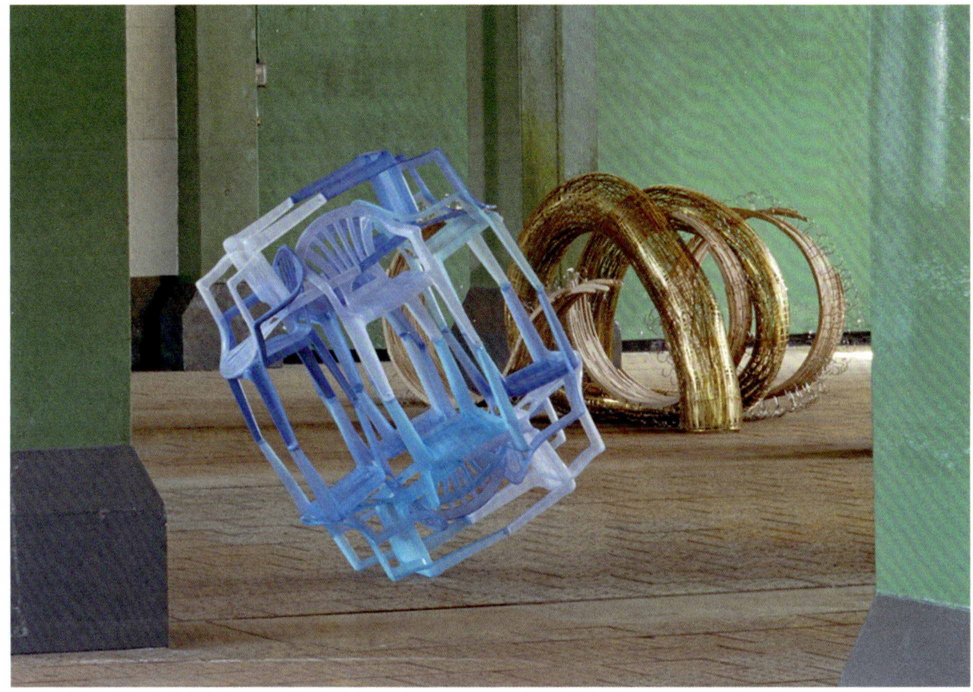

Lo que se interpone

Todo ya está ahí, nada se está reinventando, los almacenes gigantesncos de bricolaje con centros de jardinería, zonas comerciales, la vida cotidiana y sus residuos ofrecen materia prima suficiente. algunos de ellos pueden utilizarse, transformarse. A través de la reordenación y la reubicación, las esculturas crecen a partir de mercancía nuevas y usada. Su margen de maniobra es sencillo. Las esculturas inauguran los objetos o el espacio. La artista les ayuda con rigor y precisión,se da cuenta de lo que las sillas, lámparas, cubos, botellas y perchas, por ejemplo, siempre han querido, han sido capaces

Ciò che sta in mezzo

Tutto esiste già, niente è stato reinventato, megastore per il fai da te con centri per il giardinaggio, zone commerciali, la vita quotidiana e tutto ciò che rimane inutilizzato offrono materie prime a sufficienza. Molte di queste possono essere utilizzate, trasformate. Le sculture vengono create a partire da prodotti nuovi e usati, riordinati e ricollocati. Il loro contesto è semplice. Le cose o il luogo lo dischiudono. L'artista li aiuta in questo con rigore e precisione. Lei crea ciò che per esempio sedie, lampade, secchi, bottiglie e appendiabiti hanno sempre voluto o saputo fare e organizza l'interazione plastica di questi

Wat ertussen komt

Alles is er al, niets wordt opnieuw uitgevonden, grote bouwmarkten met tuincentrum, winkelcentra, het dagelijks leven en de overblijfselen ervan bieden voldoende grondstoffen. Veel daarvan kunnen worden gebruikt, getransformeerd. Door herinrichting en verplaatsing ontstaan sculpturen uit gebruikte en nieuwe goederen. Hun speelruimte is eenvoudig. Objecten of plaatsen openen zich ervoor. De kunstenaar helpt ze met uiterste nauwkeurigheid. Ze creëert wat bijvoorbeeld stoelen, lampen, emmers, flessen en kleerhangers altijd al gewild hebben, in staat waren om

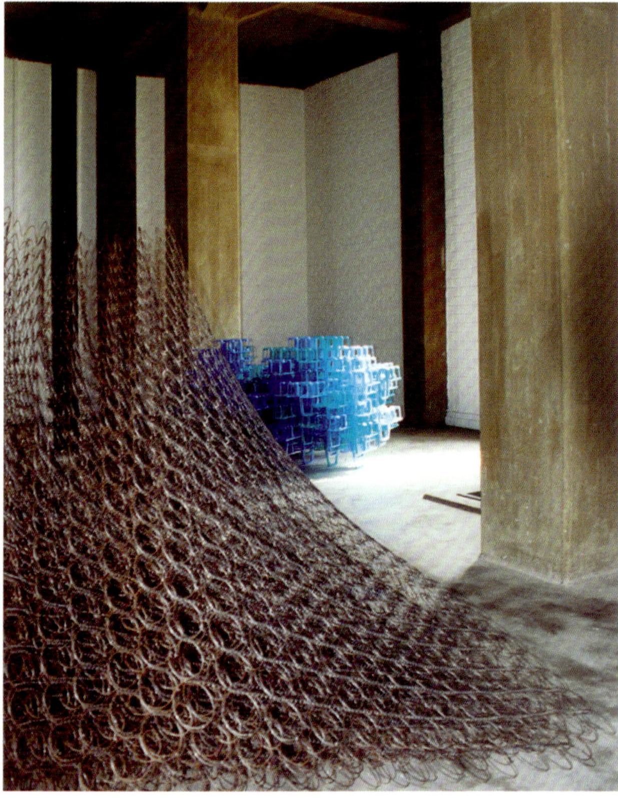

Vielfall

1999, Mattress springs, wire, 195 × 250 × 350 cm

everyone involved to gain prestige and knowledge, also astonishment and—not insignificant—amusement.

Through their form things themselves are the driving force behind everything else. They make suggestions for the course of events—for example by the curvature of a clothes hanger, its connection, insertion and hanging possibilities. Working with these offers without further changing the objects leads to immediately obvious solutions; the peculiar "logic" of the sculpture is

été capables de faire, et organise le jeu plastique de ces choses ordinaires, faisant ainsi naître chez chacun prestige et révélation, y compris l'étonnement et – ce qui n'est pas sans importance – l'amusement.

Les objets sont par leur forme la source même de l'inspiration. Ce sont eux qui suggèrent – par exemple par le biais d'une courbure de cintre, les possibilités qu'il offre à la liaison, l'insertion et l'accrochage – l'évolution plastique de l'œuvre. Travailler avec ces options sans

Allerweltsdinge, ermöglicht damit Ansehens- und Erkenntnisgewinne bei allen Beteiligten; Erstaunen und – nicht unwichtig – Erheiterung mit eingeschlossen.

Die Dinge selbst stiften durch ihre Form zu allem Weiteren an. Sie machen – etwa durch die Krümmung eines Kleiderbügels, seine Anschluss-, Einsteck- und Aufhängemöglichkeiten – Vorschläge für den Gang der plastischen Dinge. Mit diesen Angeboten zu arbeiten ohne die Gegenstände dabei weiter zu verändern

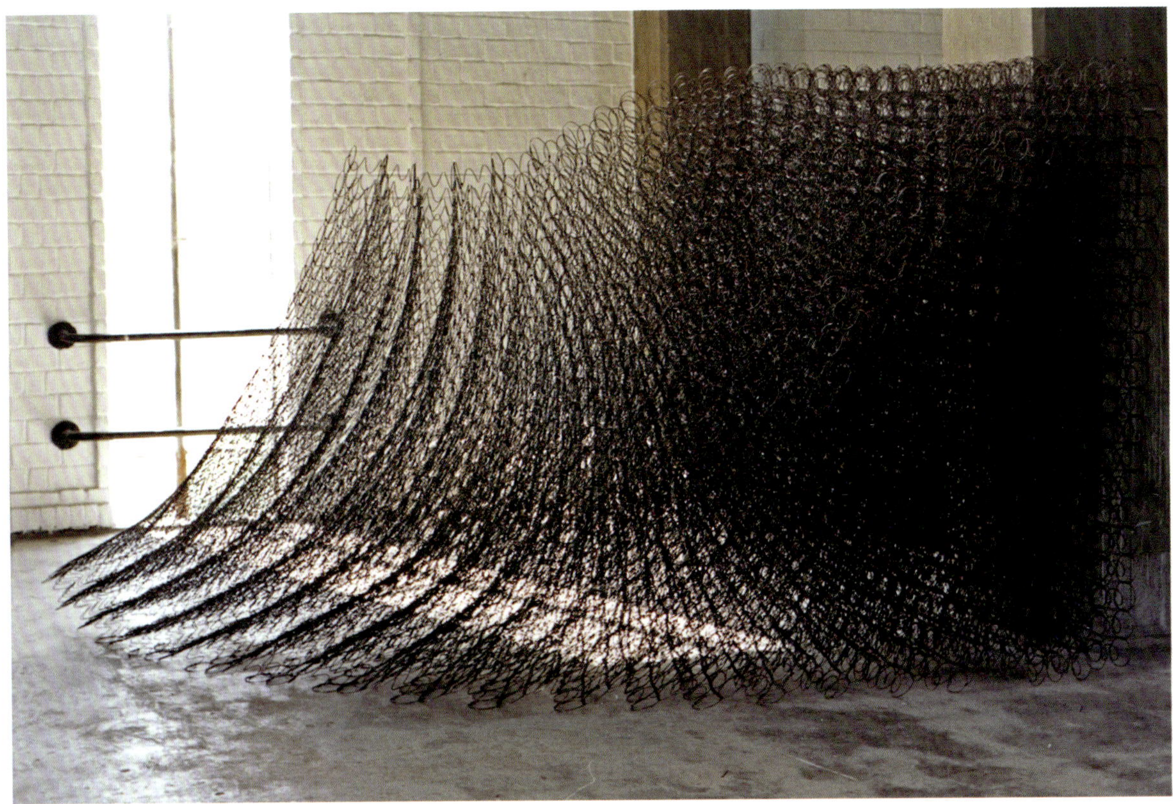

de organizar la interacción plástica de estos objetoscomunes, permitiendo así a todos los participantes ganar en prestigio y conocimiento, incluyendo el asombro y, no por ello menos relevante, la diversión.

Las cosas mismas incitan por su forma a todo lo demás. Hacen sugerencias,por ejemplo, con la curvatura de una percha, su conexión, inserción y posibilidades de suspensión. Trabajar con estas opciones sin seguir modificando los objetos conduce a soluciones de lógica

oggetti quotidiani, permettendo così a chi o cosa ne entra a far parte di acquisire prestigio e conoscenza, ma anche stupore e – non meno importante – divertimento.

Tramite la loro forma, sono le cose stesse a essere la forza trainante di ciò avverrà. Esse danno suggerimenti su quello che può essere il corso delle cose di plastica – per esempio a partire dalla curvatura di un appendiabiti, dalle possibilità che offre di congiungere, inserire e appendere. Lavorare con queste possibilità senza modificare

te doen, en regelt het sculpturale spel van deze alledaagse dingen, waardoor alle betrokkenen prestige en kennis kunnen opdoen, verwonderd en – niet onbelangrijk – vermaakt worden.

Door hun vorm zijn dingen zelf de drijvende kracht achter al het andere. Ze doen suggesties voor de gang van zaken – bijvoorbeeld door de kromming van een kleerhanger, de aansluit-, insteek- en ophangmogelijkheden. Het werken met het gebodene zonder de objecten verder te veranderen leidt tot

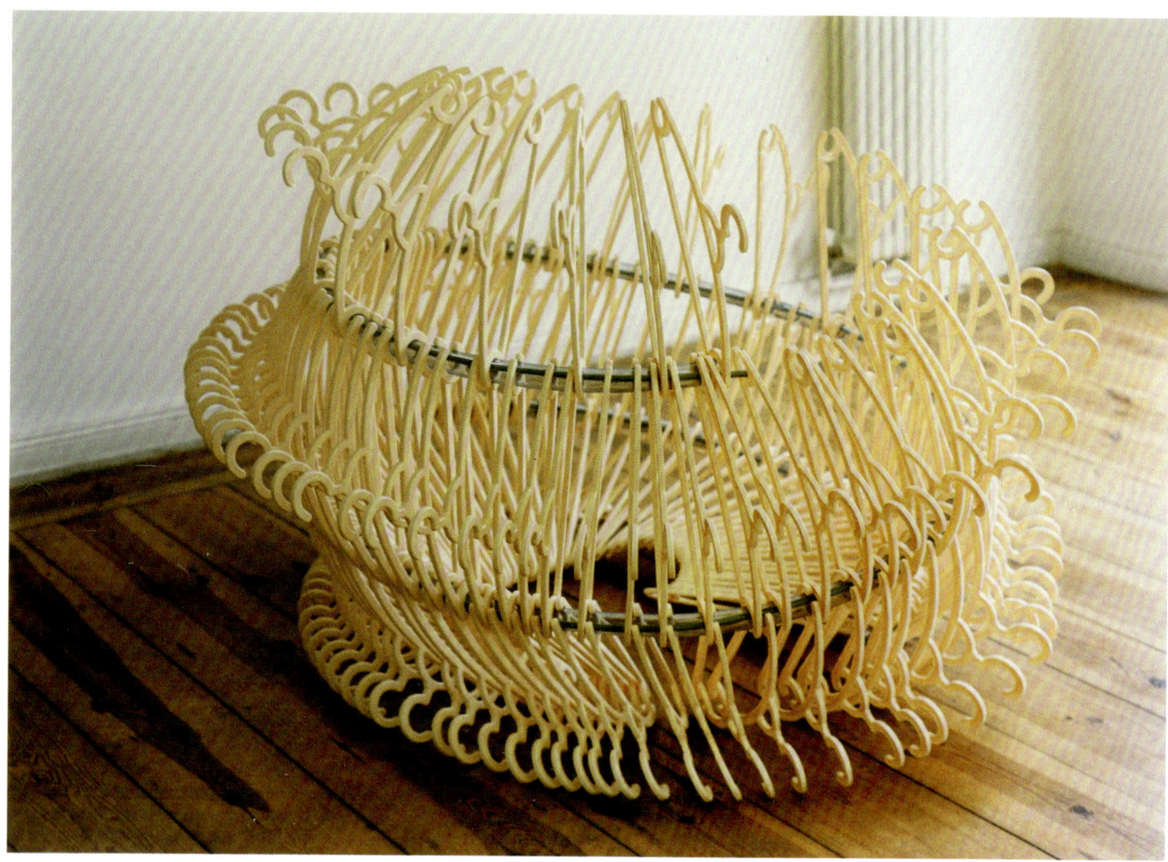

the result of the options inherent in the material.

What does the initial glance see? Is the plastic structure in space noticed first and then its components? Or is the focus initially on things from the large, familiar realm of the useful, a view of a detail that is then replaced by the perception of the sculptural presence that is characteristic of the work as a whole? Nevertheless, things never completely with draw, they

transformer les objets, conduit à des solutions immédiatement évidentes ; la « logique » propre à la sculpture résulte des options qui sommeillent dans la matière.

Que remarque le premier coup d'œil ? Perçoit-on en premier l'œuvre plastique dans l'espace où elle se trouve, puis les éléments qui la composent ? Ou est-ce que notre attention se porte plutôt sur les choses de ce monde vaste et familier

führt zu unmittelbar einleuchtenden Lösungen; die eigentümliche Logik der Skulptur ist Resultat der im Material schlummernden Optionen.

Was sieht der Anfangsblick? Wird erst das plastische Gebilde im Raum registriert und dann seine Bestandteilen? Oder gilt das Augenmerk zunächst den Dingen aus dem großen, vertrauten Reich des Nützlichen, einer Detailsicht, die abgelöst wird von der Wahrnehmung der

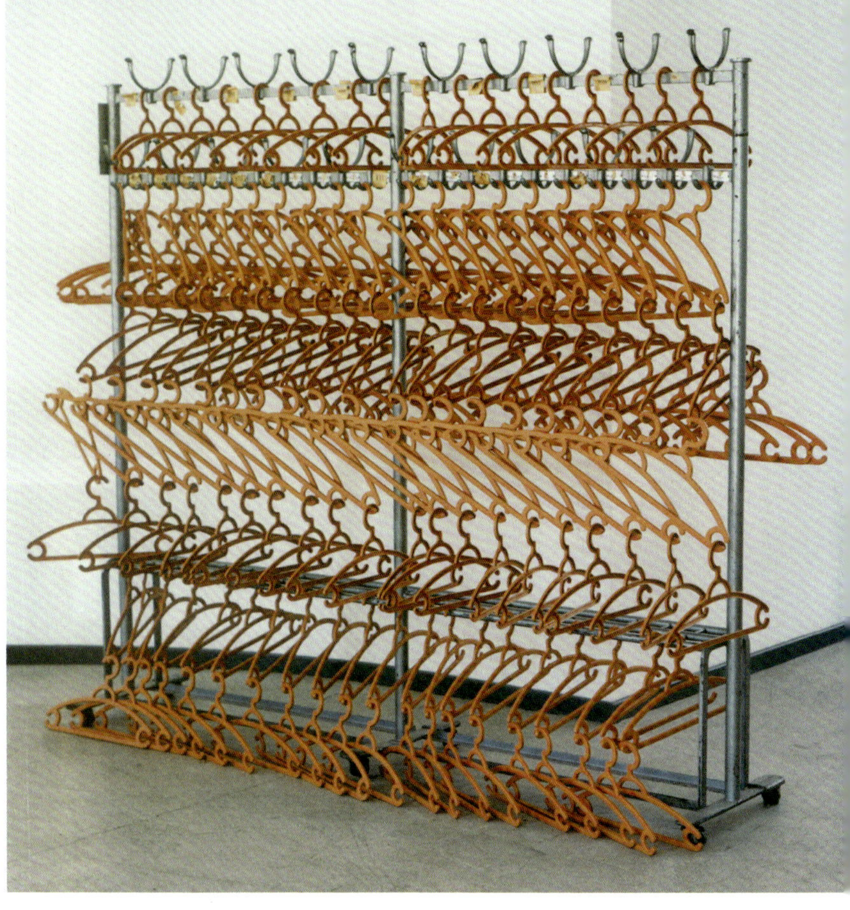

inmediata; la lógica peculiar de la
escultura es el resultado de las opciones
que se ocultan en el material.

   ¿Qué ve la mirada inicial? ¿Se registra
primero la creación plástica en el espacio
y luego sus componentes? ¿O es el
enfoque inicial de las cosas desde el
ámbito amplio y familiar de lo útil, una
visión del detalle que se despega de la
percepción de la presencia escultórica
característica de la obra en su conjunto?

ulteriormente gli oggetti porta a soluzioni
subito evidenti; la peculiare "logica" della
scultura è il risultato delle opzioni insite
nel materiale.

   Che cosa vede lo sguardo iniziale?
La struttura in plastica viene registrata
prima nello spazio circostante e poi nei
suoi componenti? Oppure l'attenzione
viene puntata inizialmente sulle cose
appartenenti al grande e familiare regno
dell'utile, una visione del dettaglio che

direct voor de hand liggende oplossingen;
de merkwaardige 'logica' van de sculptuur
is het resultaat van de opties die inherent
zijn aan het materiaal.

   Wat ziet de eerste blik? Wordt eerst de
plastic structuur in de ruimte opgemerkt
en daarna de componenten? Of is de
focus in eerste instantie op dingen uit
de grote, vertrouwde sfeer van het
nuttige, een kijk op details die vervolgens
wordt vervangen door de perceptie

53

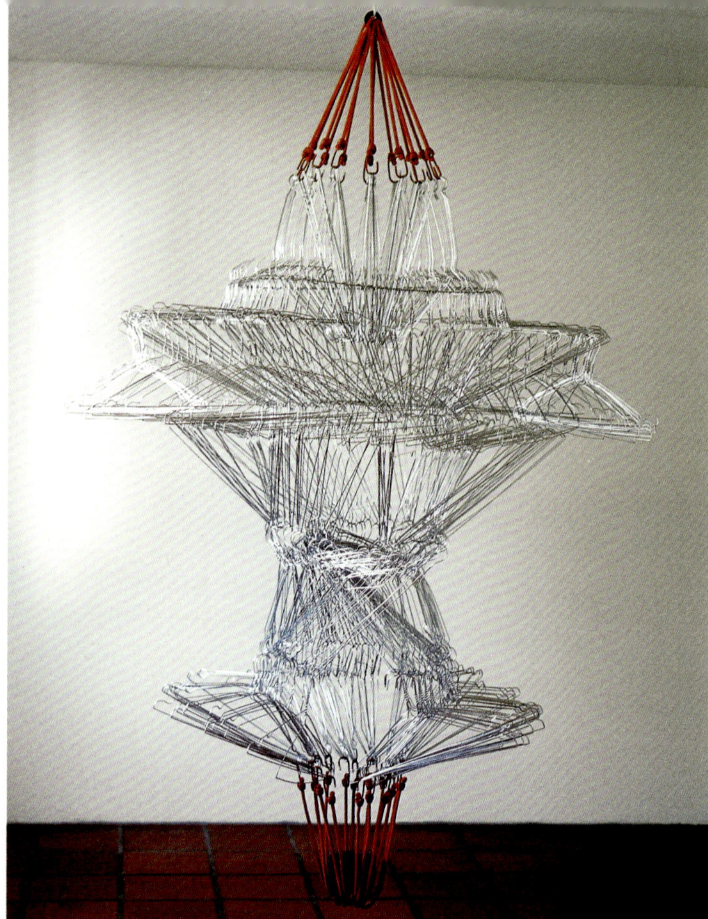

do not completely cast off their origin and their original purpose, they lead a double life as a utility tool (which they could become again) and as art material.

de l'utile, une perception du détail qui est remplacée par la vision de la présence sculpturale, caractéristique propre à l'œuvre dans son ensemble ?

Néanmoins, les choses ne sont jamais totalement dénaturées, ne sont jamais complètement dépouillées de leur origine et de leur fonction initiale, elles mènent une double vie comme un outil, mais aussi comme matériau d'art.

skulpturalen Präsenz, die der Arbeit im Ganzen eigen ist?

Gleichwohl ziehen sich die Dinge nie vollständig zurück, ihre Herkunft und ihren ursprünglichen Zweck streifen sie nicht ganz ab, sie führen ein Doppelleben als Nutzzeug (zu dem sie wieder werden könnten) und Kunst-Stoff.

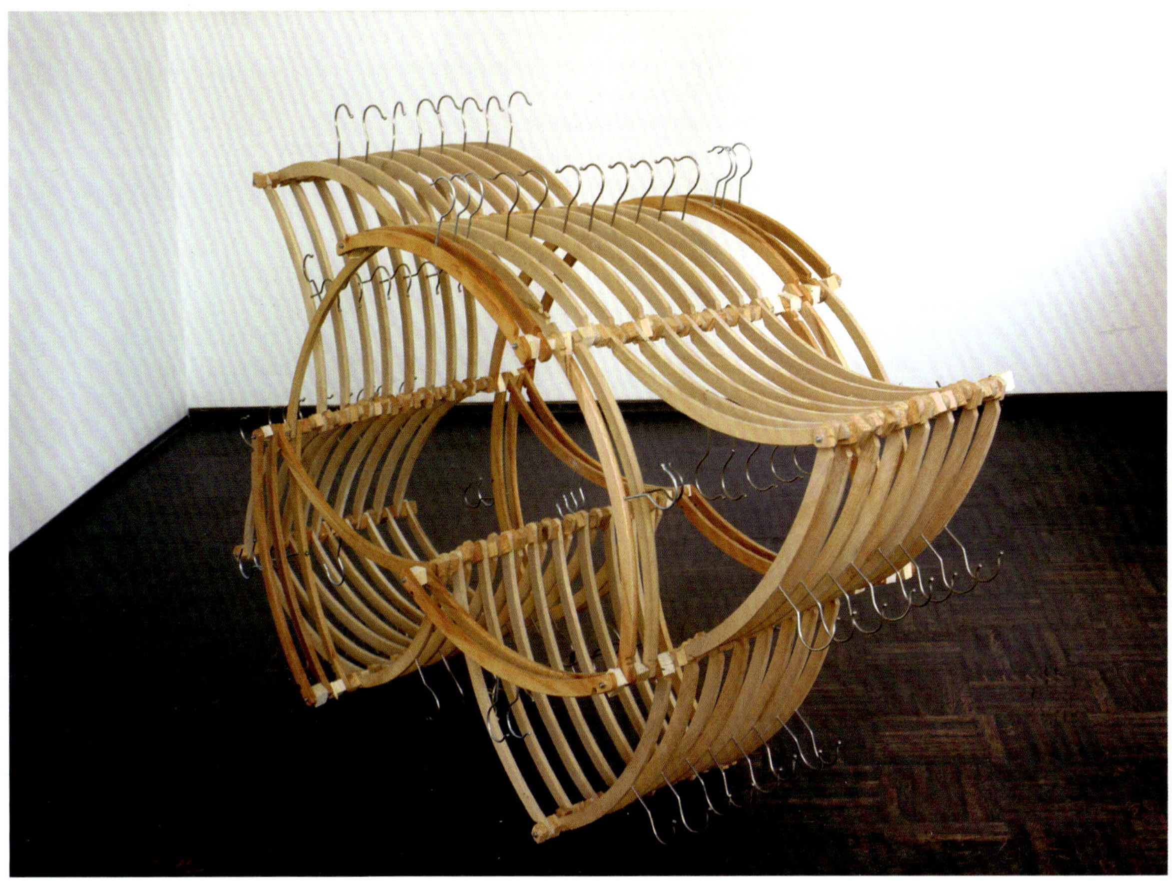

Sin embargo, las cosas nunca retroceden del todo, su origen y su propósito original no se despojan del todo, llevan una doble vida como herramienta de utilidad (en la que podrían volver a convertirse) y material artístico.

viene poi sostituita dalla percezione della presenza scultorea che caratterizza l'opera nel suo complesso?

Tuttavia, le cose non scompaiono mai completamente, non abbandonano mai completamente la loro origine e il loro scopo originale, conducono una doppia vita, al contempo oggetto funzionale (che potrebbero tornare a essere) e materiale artistico.

van de sculpturale aanwezigheid die kenmerkend is voor het werk als geheel?

Toch trekken dingen zich nooit volledig terug, ze werpen hun oorsprong en hun oorspronkelijke doel niet volledig af, ze leiden een dubbelleven als hulpmiddel (dat ze weer zouden kunnen worden) en kunstmateriaal.

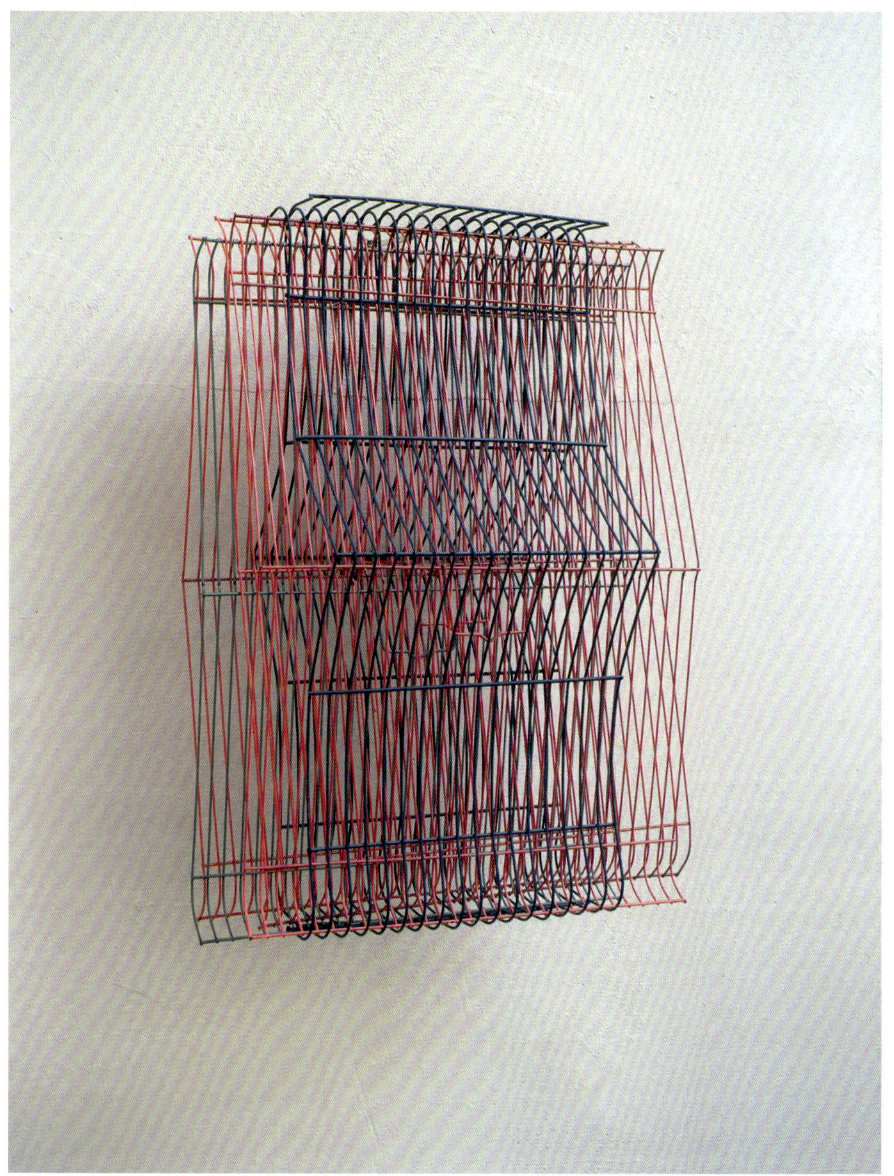

Flimmerblick

2002, Lacquered iron wire,
55 × 35 × 16 cm, Private collection

o.T.

1997, Mattress springs,
175 × 200 × 180 cm

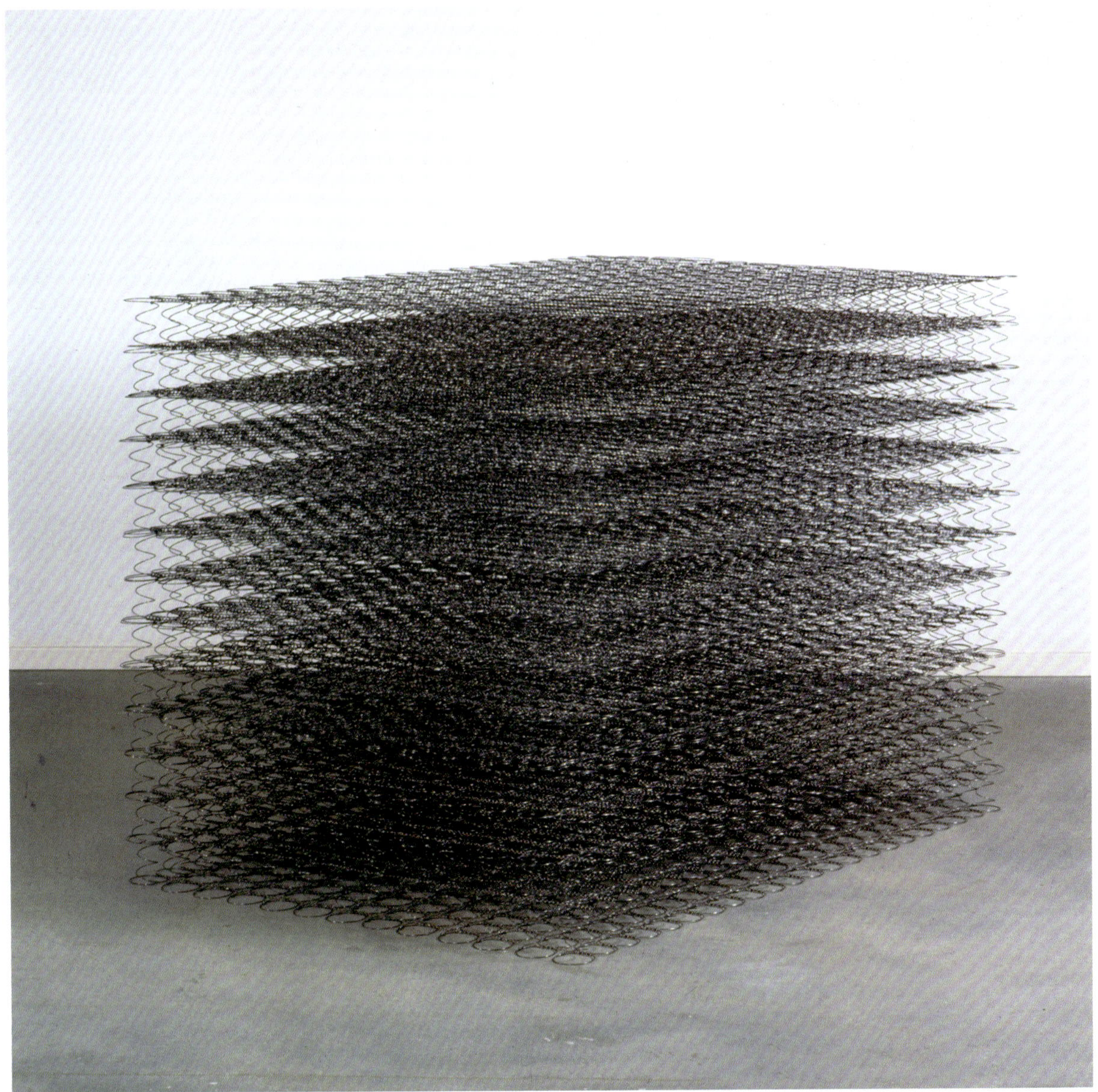

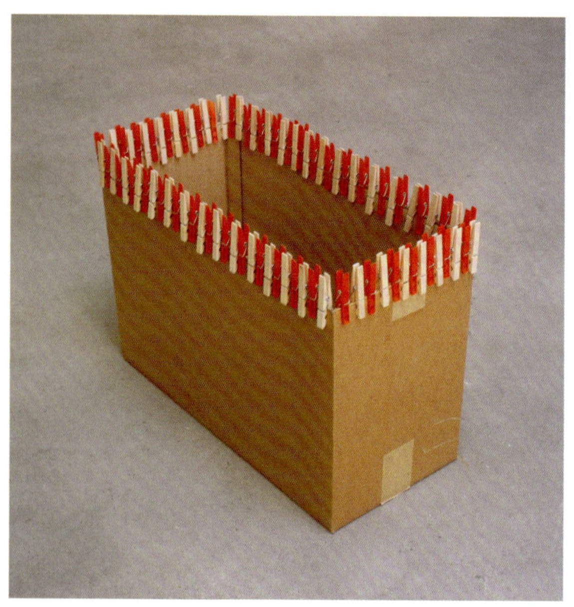

Indivisionell

2002, Clothes pegs, cardboard box, 40 × 58 × 30 cm

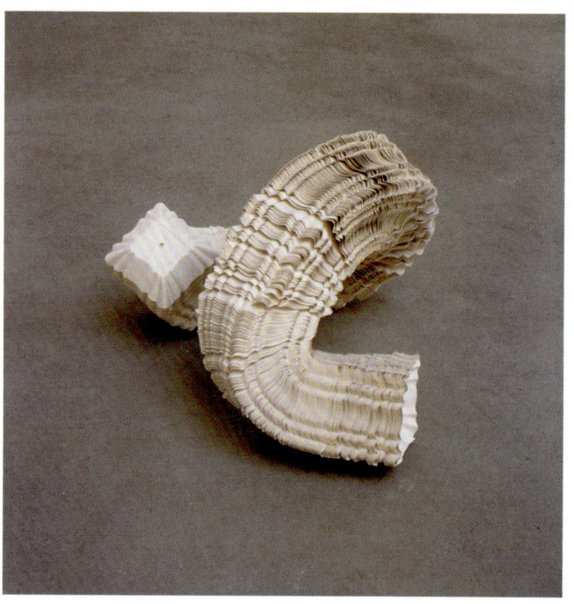

Cecile n'aime pas les frites

2002, Cardboard, iron wire, 30 × 58 × 35 cm

Dreigestirn

2002, Clothes pegs, plastic planters, 72 × 80 × 70 cm

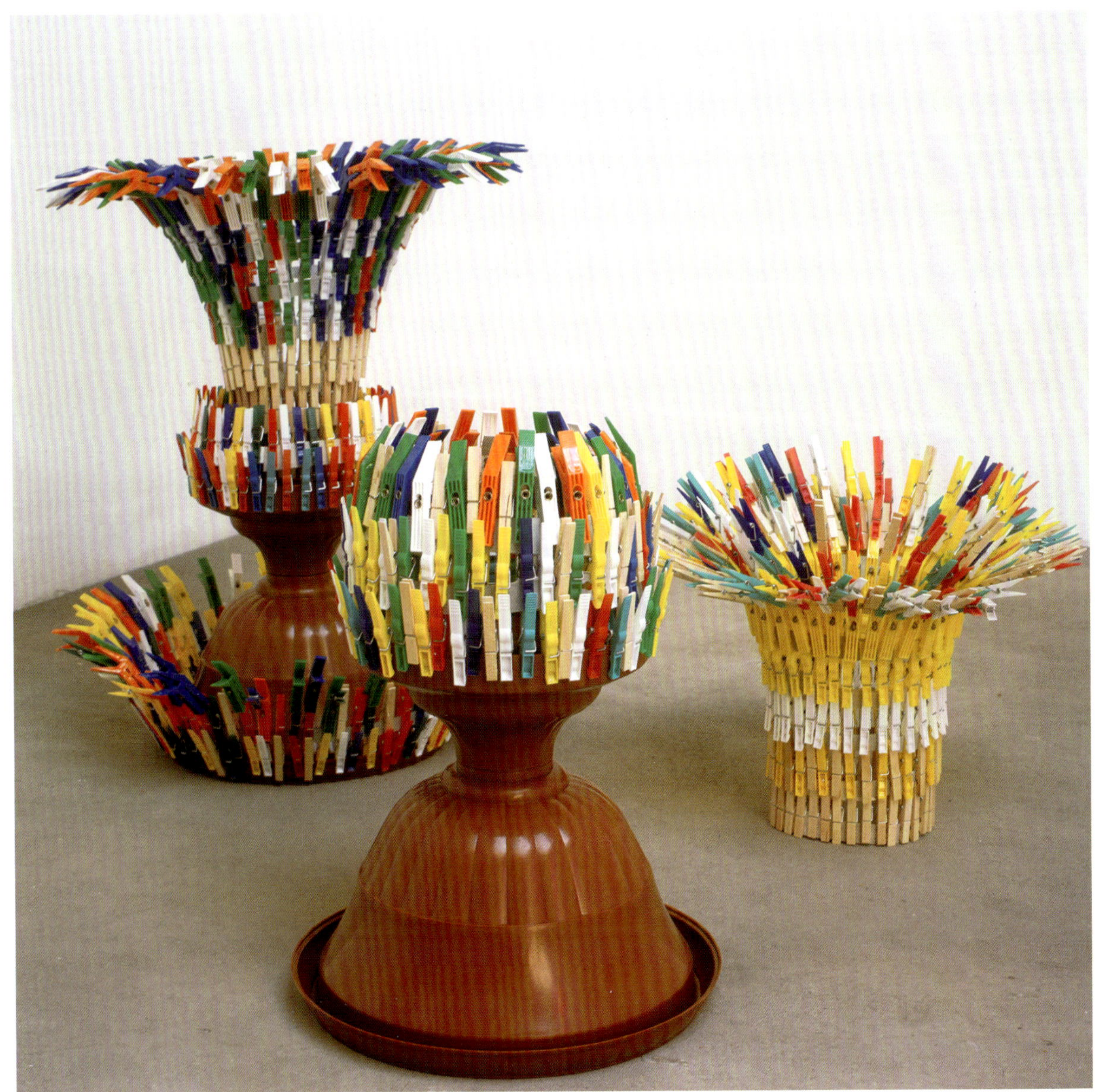

Spatial works

Installations

Raumbezogene Arbeiten

Obras espaciales

Lavori in un contesto spaziale

Ruimtelijke werken

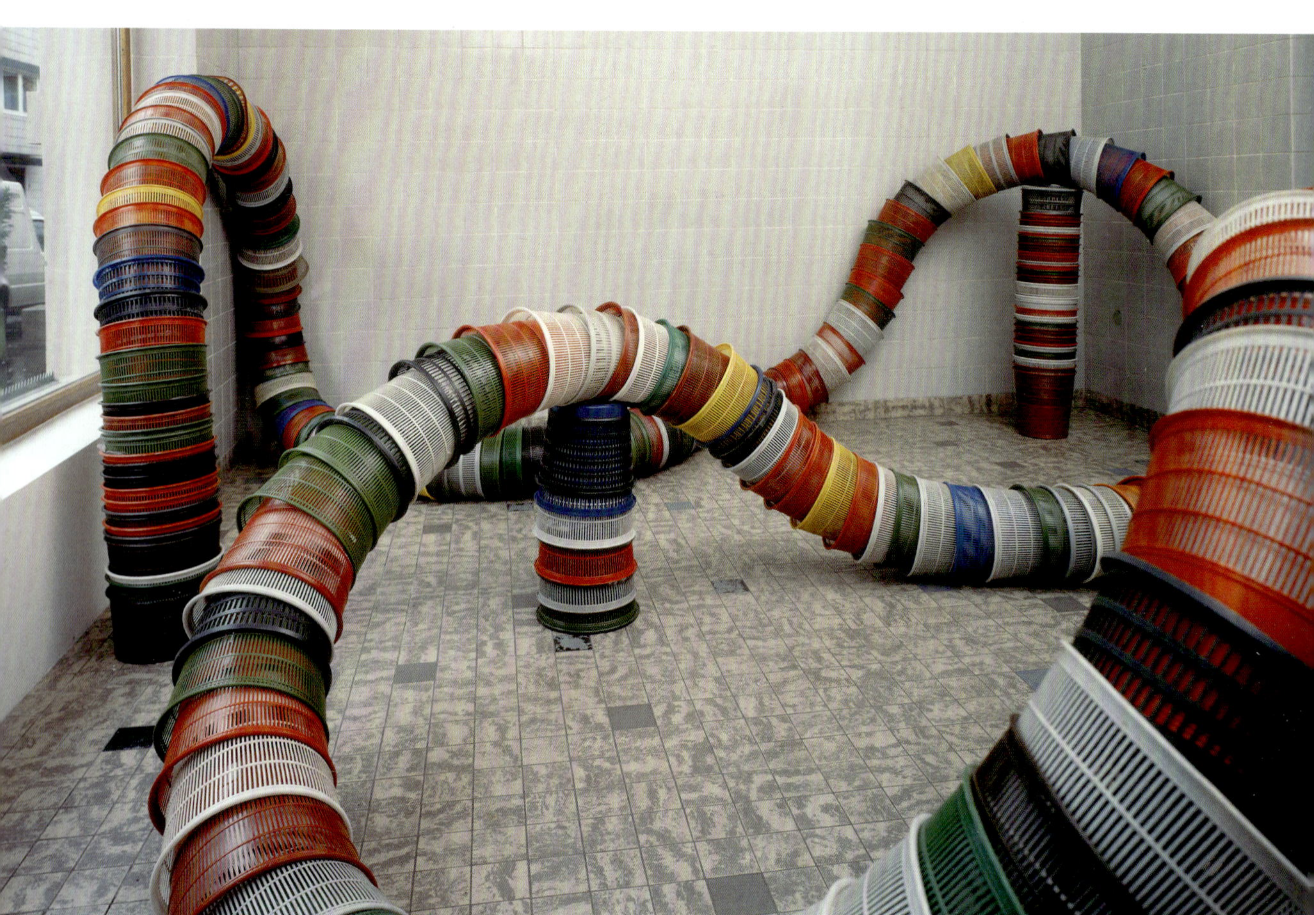

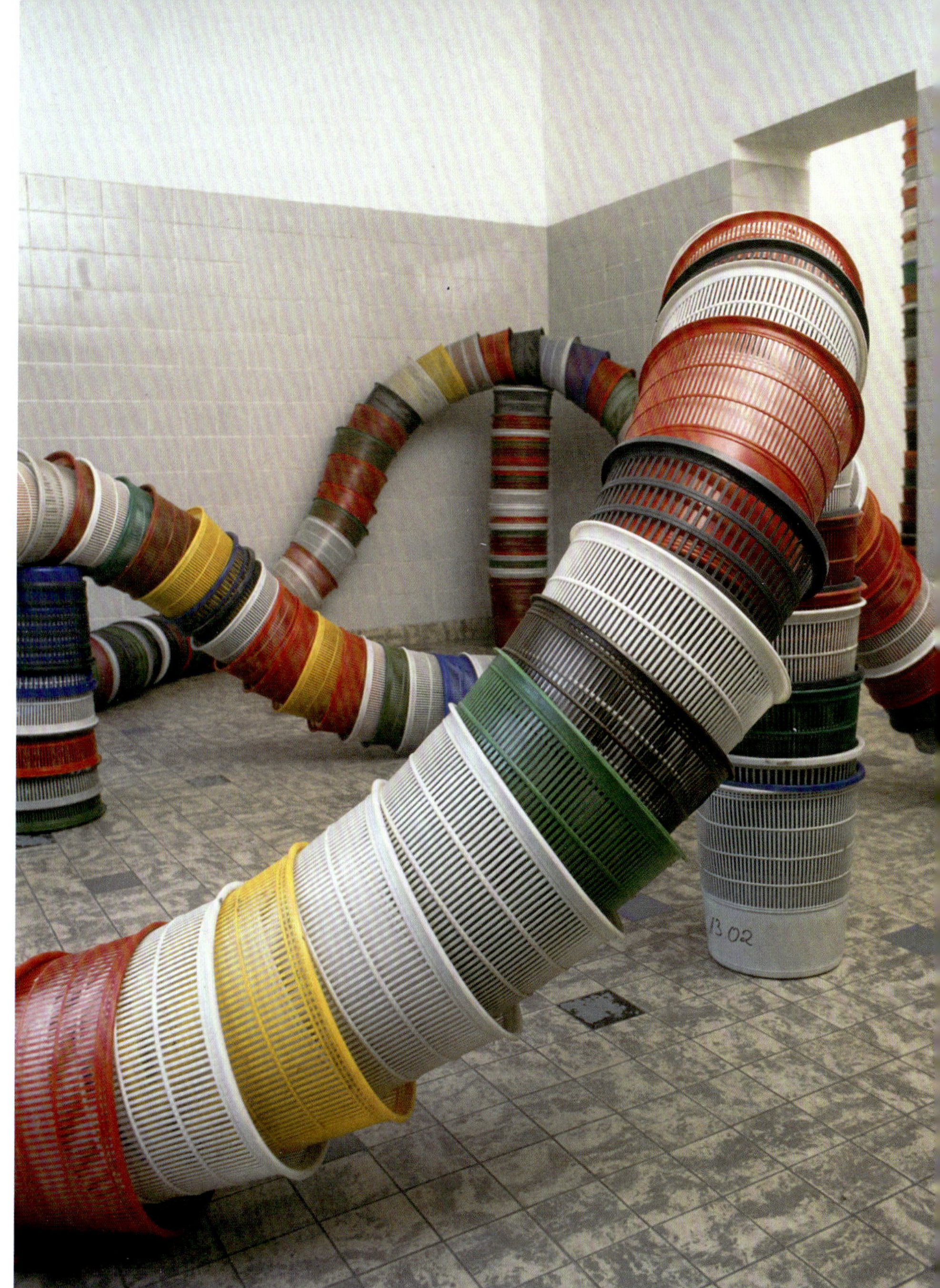

Full House

1999, Plastic (2007, 2009)

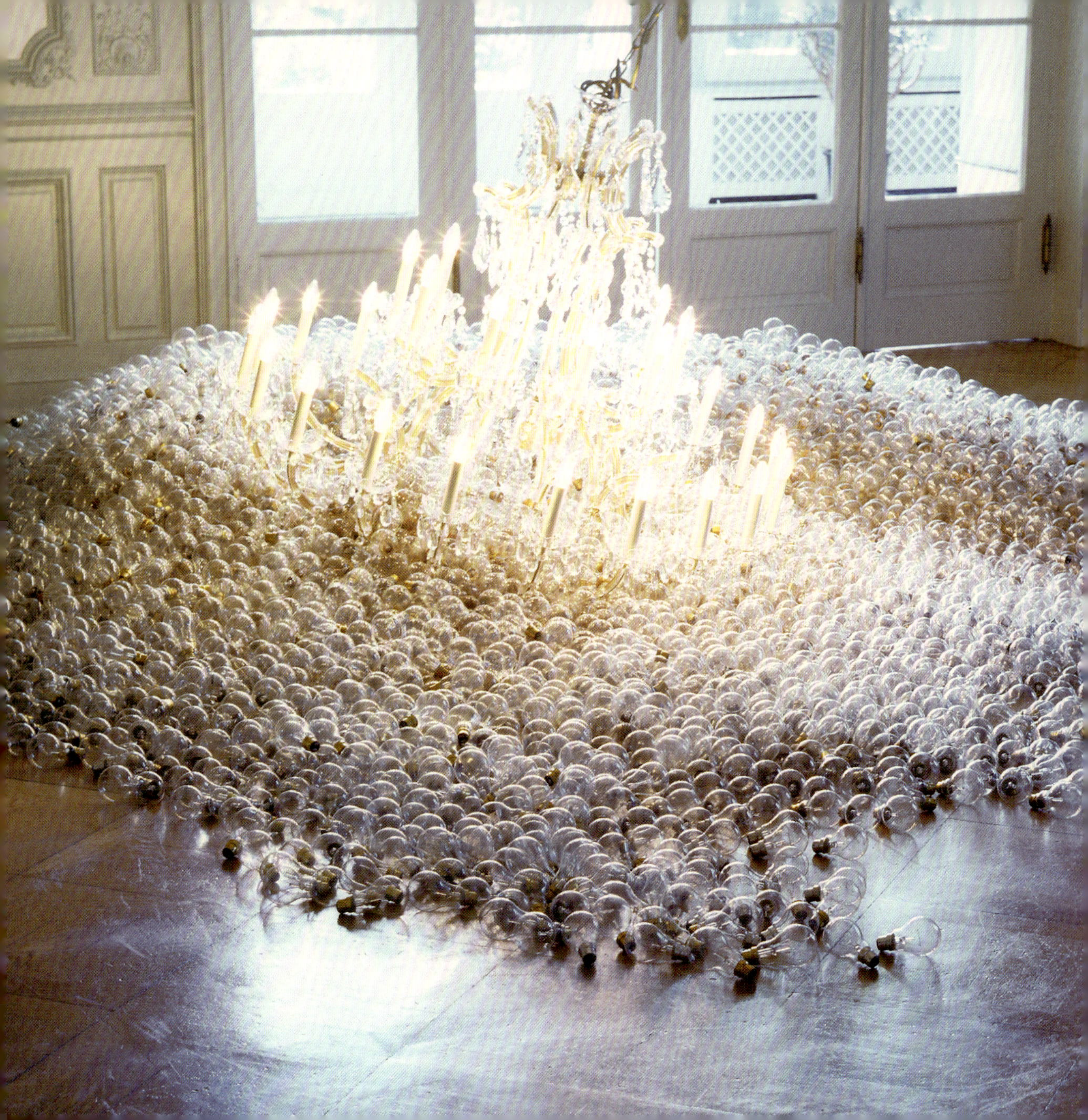

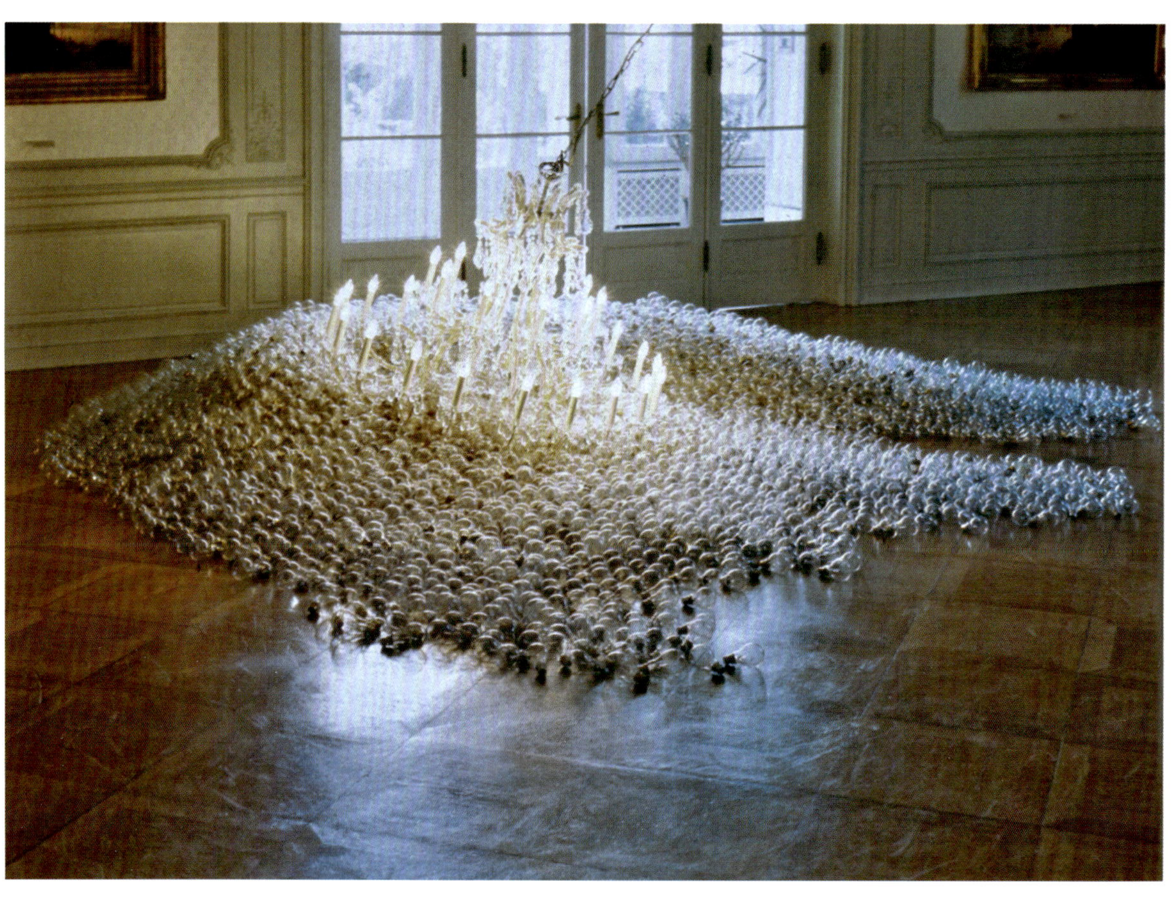

Salonstück

1995, Light bulbs, chandeliers, Kunstmuseum Villa Zanders, Bergisch Gladbach

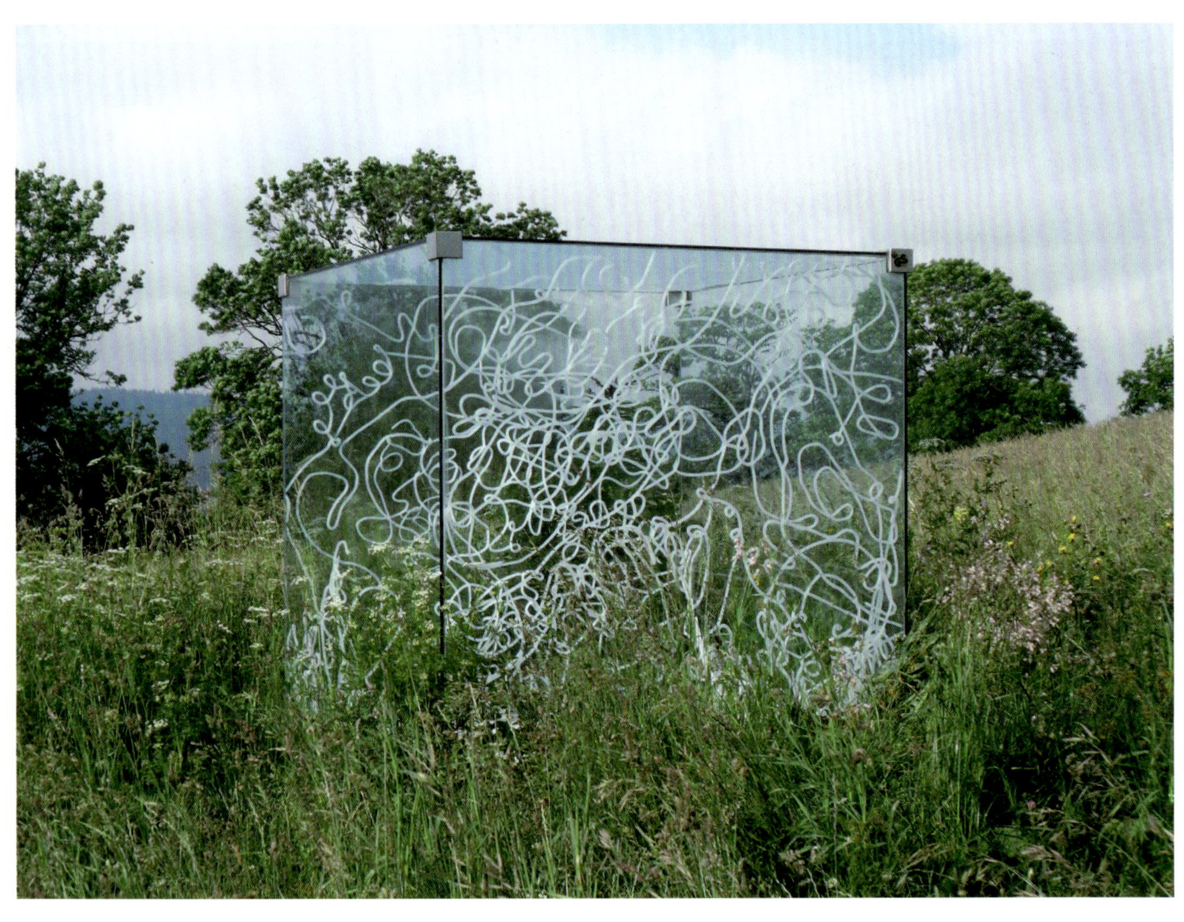

Flimmerkiste, Skulptur für einen Berg

1996, Glass, silicone, 160 × 150 × 150 cm, Hohenkarpfen, Trossingen

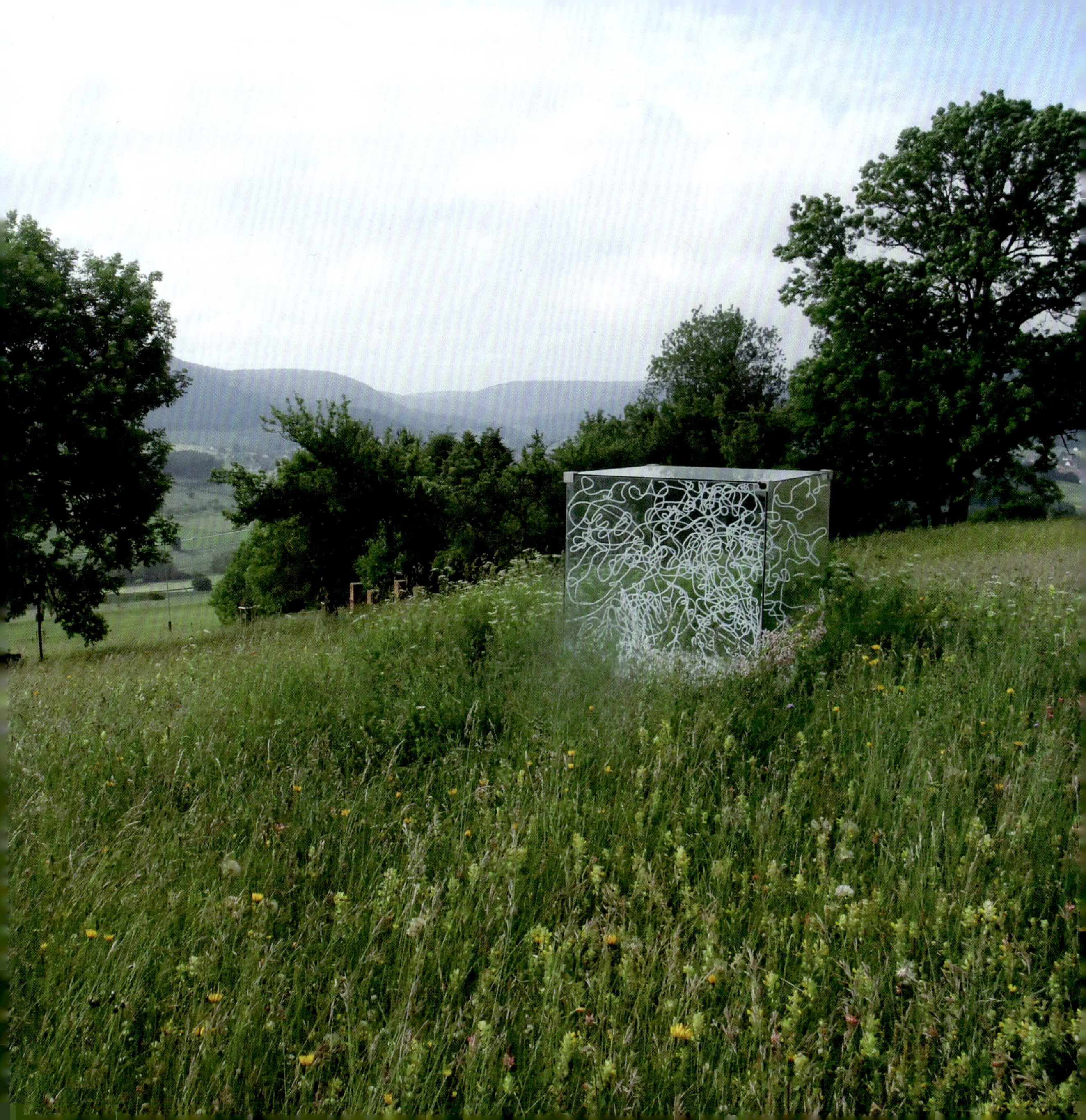

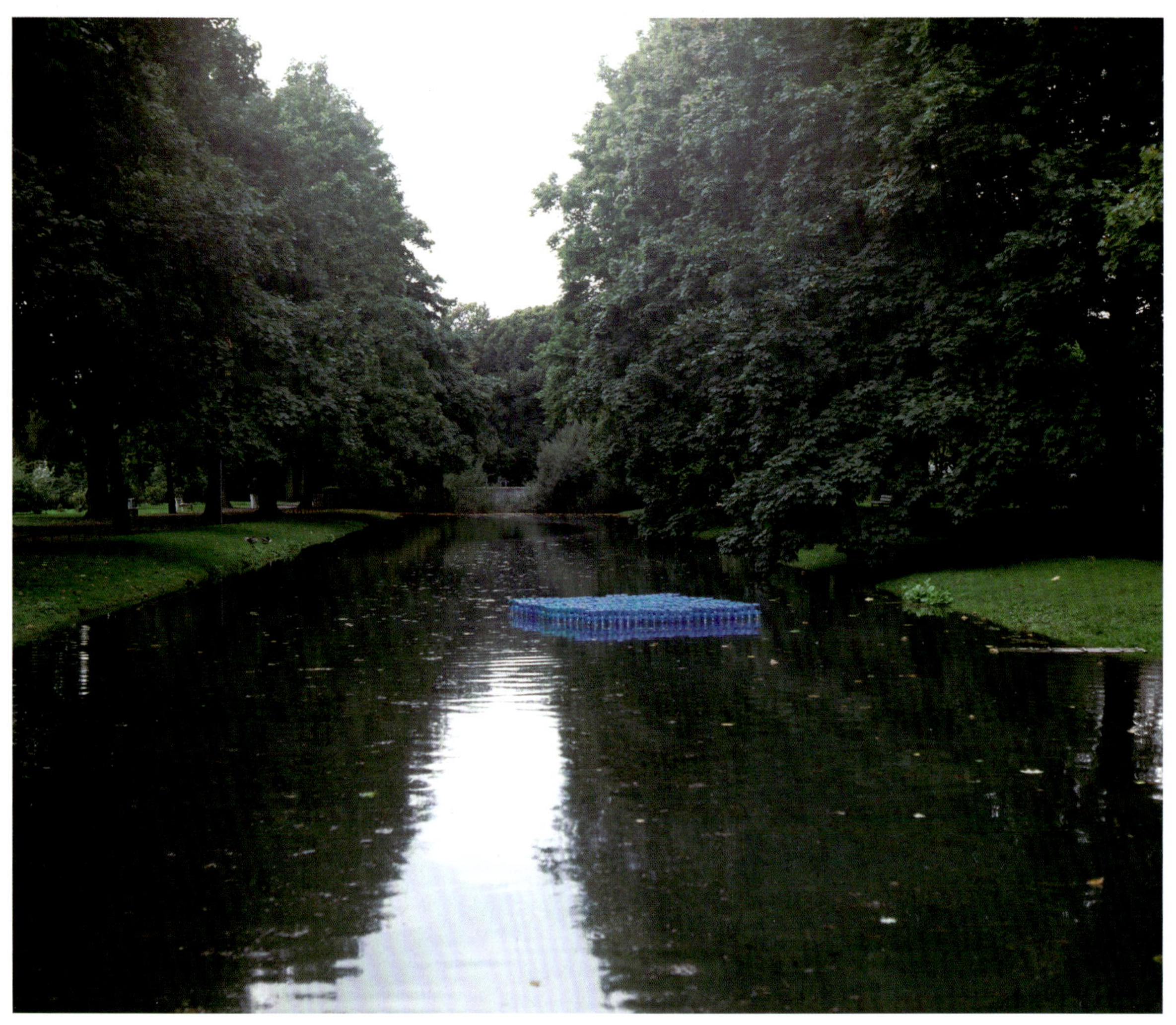

Gegen den bösen Blick

1998, Plastic, 45 × 250 × 230 cm

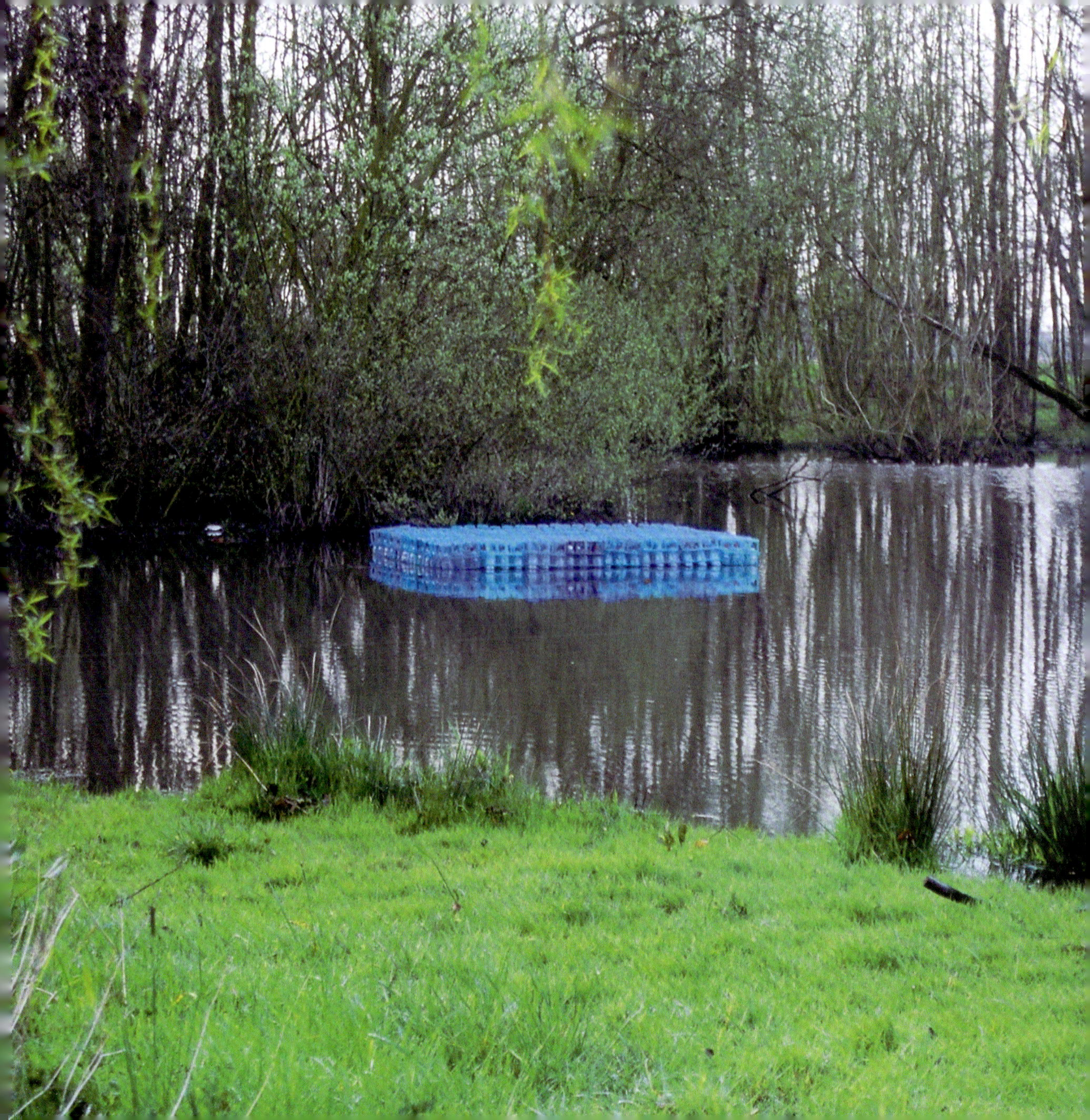

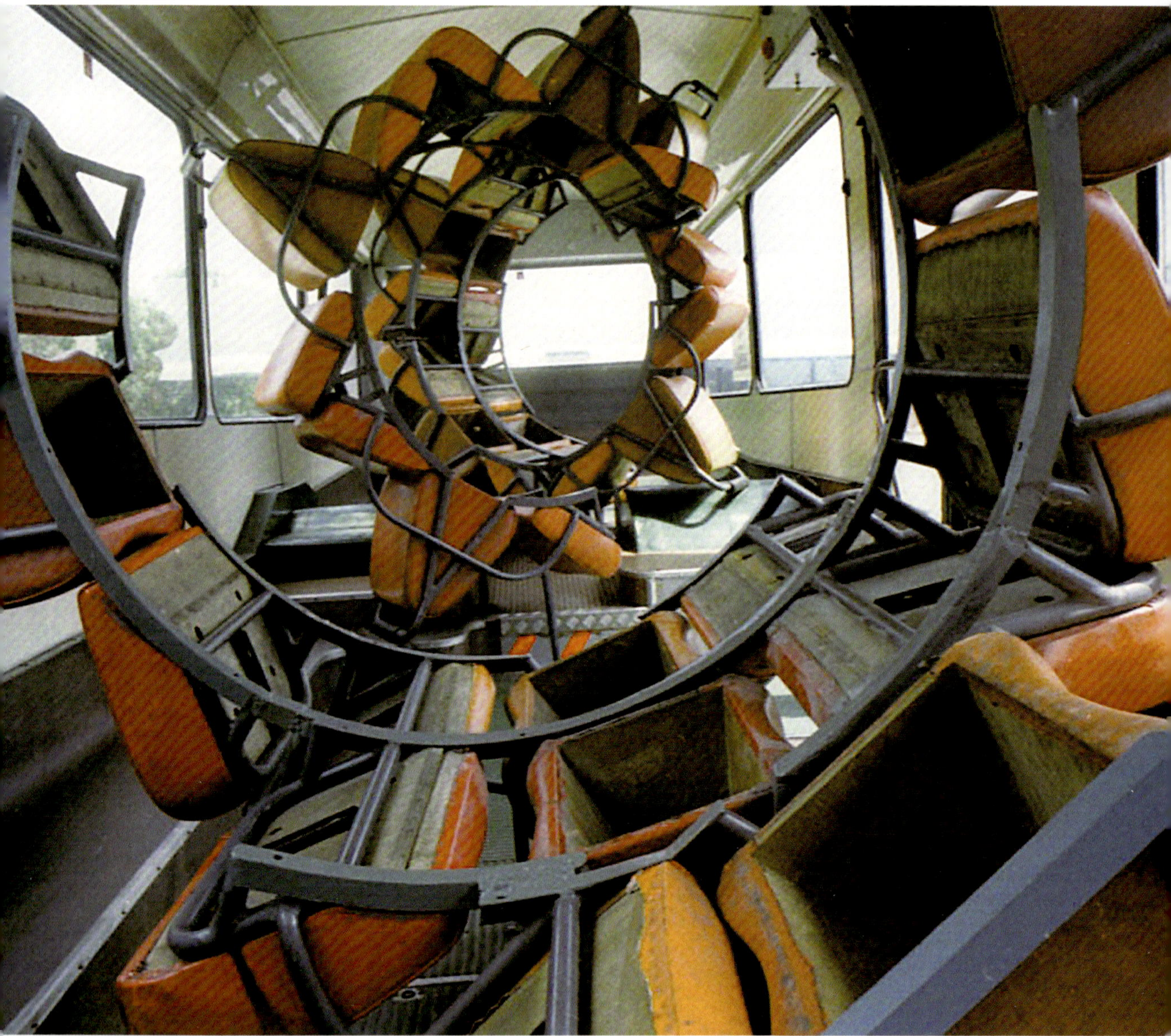

Installation für einen Linienbus

1999, Steel, plastic, wood, Gynaika, Antwerpen

The comprehensible and yet unforeseen interplay between one section and the whole of the work is astonishing, for bus seats had never been seen to have a life of their own before. Now they twist and turn in the narrow interior of the vehicle. By adding several identical elements, the rounding of the seat frames originally placed above the wheel arches has been closed to form a circle on the inside, resulting in a kind of star shape on the outside. Three of these structures are mounted one behind the other in a former bus; the installation was part of a mobile art project in Belgium. Whether the seating circles interlock, are connected with each other or are separated is only clear when climbing through them; only the body understands the space of this sculpture, to the eye it remains unclear.

Le jeu autant prévisible que surprenant entre l'élément indépendant et l'ensemble créé par accumulation est époustouflant, car jamais on aurait pu s'attendre à tant de vitalité de la part de sièges de bus. Maintenant, ils se retournent et virevoltent dans l'intérieur étroit du véhicule. Le châssis des sièges, dont la courbe se love à l'origine sur la tôle protectrice des roues du bus, forment, mis bout à bout, au centre une structure circulaire, tout en créant à l'extérieur une sorte d'étoile. Trois de ces structures ont été montées l'une derrière l'autre dans un vieux bus ; l'installation faisait partie d'un projet artistique itinérant présenté en Belgique. Est-ce que les structures circulaires des sièges sont encastrées l'une dans l'autre, est-ce qu'elles sont reliées ou sont-elles séparées ? Ces questions ne trouvent de réponses que si l'on y pénètre ; seul le corps peut assimiler l'espace créé par cette sculpture, pour l'œil, elle demeure incompréhensible.

Das nachvollziehbare und doch unvorhergesehene Wechselspiel von Teilstück und dem Ganzen des Werks verblüfft, denn dergleichen Eigenleben war Bussitzen zuvor nie anzumerken. Jetzt winden und drehen sie sich im schmalen Innenraum des Fahrzeugs. Die Rundung der ursprünglich über den Radkästen platzierten Sitzrahmen ist durch Addition mehrerer gleicher Elemente zu einem Kreis nach innen geschlossen worden, wodurch sich nach außen eine Art Sternform ergab. Drei dieser Gebilde sind hintereinander in einem ehemaligen Linienbus montiert; die Installation war Teil eines mobilen Kunstprojekts in Belgien. Ob die Sitzzirkel ineinander greifen, miteinander verbunden oder doch getrennt sind, klärt sich erst, wenn sie durchstiegen werden; der Körper erst begreift den Raum dieser Skulptur, dem Auge allein bleibt er unklar.

La interacción comprensible y a la vez imprevista entre la pieza y el conjunto de la obra es asombrosa, ya que nunca antes, los asientos de un autobús habían visto una vida tan propia. Ahora giran y giran en el estrecho interior del vehículo. El curvatura de los bastidores de los asientos, colocados originalmente por encima de los compartimentos de ruedas, se ha completado añadiendo varios elementos idénticos para formar un círculo hacia el interior, dando como resultado una especie de estrella hacia el exterior. Tres de estas estructuras están montadas una detrás de la otra en un antiguo autobús. La instalación formaba parte de un proyecto de arte móvil en Bélgica. Si los círculos de asiento se entrelazan, están conectados entre sí o están separados solo queda claro cuando se atraviesan. El cuerpo solo entiende el espacio de esta escultura cuando todo sigue siendo confuso a la vista.

Nel contesto dell'opera, l'interazione, imprevista per quanto comprensibile, tra la parte e il tutto è stupefacente, poiché sedili per autobus non erano mai stati considerati prima come capaci di vita propria. Ora girano e si ruotano nel piccolo spazio all'interno del veicolo. Con l'aggiunta di più elementi identici tra di loro, la linea curva formata dai telai dei sedili, un tempo posti laddove la carrozzeria si incurvava a seguire la forma delle ruote sottostanti, si è conchiusa a formare un cerchio all'interno, mentre sul lato esterno ne è derivata una sorta di forma a stella. Tre di queste strutture sono state montate una dietro l'altra in un vecchio autobus; l'installazione faceva parte di un progetto di arte mobile in Belgio. Se i cerchi dei sedili si incastrino, siano collegati tra loro oppure siano rimasti separati diventa chiaro solo passandoci dentro. Solo il corpo capisce la spazialità di questa scultura, cosa che l'occhio da solo non riesce a cogliere.

De begrijpelijke en toch onvoorziene wisselwerking tussen een onderdeel en het geheel van het werk is verbluffend, want nooit eerder was zo'n eigen leven van busstoelen te zien geweest. Nu wenden en draaien ze in het smalle interieur van het voertuig. De ronding van de oorspronkelijk boven de wielkasten geplaatste stoelframes is door toevoeging van enkele identieke elementen tot een cirkel gesloten, waardoor aan de buitenkant een soort stervorm is ontstaan. Drie van deze structuren zijn achter elkaar gemonteerd in een voormalige bus; de installatie maakte deel uit van een mobiel kunstproject in België. Of de zittingencirkels in elkaar grijpen, met elkaar verbonden zijn of van elkaar gescheiden zijn, is pas duidelijk als je er doorheen klimt; alleen het lichaam begrijpt de ruimte van deze sculptuur, voor het oog blijft die onduidelijk.

Modell Mambo IV

2000, Plastic, screwed, Colosseum Art Collection, Essen

The Mambo 1 monoblock chair also remains a chair in the *Mambo 1* sculpture, especially when plastic garden chairs of the same type are standing in the background of the cafeteria of the Rheine Technology Centre waiting for visitors, while the other chairs, which have become sculptures, show what else they can do; thus two forms of existence meet. The contrast makes the chair-work seem like a circus act. Artfully legs cross over each other, are surrounded by backrests, everything interlocks and forms a strictly symmetrical structure, systematically interwoven and crossed to ensure the cohesion of the large volume. Inherently stable, the complex penetration of surface forms and empty spaces is balanced on a very small area.

La chaise monobloc Mambo 1 garde avant tout sa nature de chaise dans la sculpture *Modèle Mambo 1,* tout particulièrement si l'on considère le contexte dans lequel elle est mise en scène, dans les locaux de la cafétéria du Centre Technologique de Rheine, au milieu des chaises de jardin en plastique du même type qui invitent les spectateurs à venir s'assoir, tandis que les autres sièges, transformés en sculptures, montrent ce dont ils sont capables ; ainsi deux formes d'existence se rencontrent. Le contraste fait ressembler l'œuvre à un numéro de cirque. Les pieds s'emmêlent artistiquement, se lovent dans les dossiers, le tout se mélange et forme une composition strictement symétrique, comme tissée et entrecroisée avec soin, afin d'assurer la cohésion de l'ensemble. Sur la plus petite base permise, naît un équilibre parfait de surfaces et de vides entrecroisés.

Der Monoblockstuhl Mambo 1 bleibt auch in der Skulptur *Modell Mambo 1* noch Stuhl, vor allem, wenn im Hintergrund der Cafeteria des Technologiezentrums Rheine Plastikgartenstühle gleichen Typs wie auf Zuschauer wartend stehen, während die anderen, zur Skulptur gewordenen Sitzmöbel zeigen, was sie sonst noch können; so begegnen sich zwei Existenzformen. Der Kontrast lässt die Stuhlarbeit wie einen zirzensischen Akt erscheinen. Kunstvoll treffen Beine aufeinander, werden von Lehnen umfasst, greift alles ineinander und formt ein streng symmetrisches Gebilde, planvoll verwoben und gekreuzt, um den Zusammenhalt des großen Volumens zu gewährleisten. In sich stabil balanciert die komplexe Durchdringung von Flächenformen und Leerräumen auf geringster Standfläche.

La silla monobloque Mambo 1 sigue siendo también una silla en la escultura *Mambo 1,* sobre todo cuando al fondo de la cafetería del Centro Tecnológico de Rheine hay sillas de jardín de plástico del mismo tipo que esperan a los espectadores, mientras que las otras sillas, convertidas en esculturas, muestran lo que pueden hacer; así se encuentran dos formas de existencia. El contraste hace que el trabajo en la silla parezca un acto de circo. Las piernas se encuentran artísticamente, están rodeadas de respaldos, todo se entrelaza y forma una figura estrictamente simétrica, tejida y cruzada de manera metódica para asegurar la cohesión del gran volumen. En un equilibrio estable, la compleja penetración de las formas planas y los espacios vacíos se equilibran en una superficie muy pequeña.

La sedia monoblocco Mambo 1 rimane una sedia anche nella scultura *Mambo 1,* soprattutto quando sedie da giardino in plastica dello stesso tipo sono dislocate sullo sfondo della caffetteria del Rheine Technology Centre in attesa di visitatori, mentre le altre sedie, diventate sculture, mostrano di cos'altro sono capaci. In questo modo si incontrano due forme di esistenza. Il contrasto fa apparire il lavoro con le sedie come un'acrobazia da circo. Le gambe si incrociano ad arte, sono circondate da schienali residui, tutto si incastra e forma una struttura rigorosamente simmetrica, intrecciata in maniera sistematica e incrociata a garantire coesione alla forma voluminosa. In equilibrio stabile, la complessa compenetrazione di forme e superfici e di vuoti trova bilanciamento in uno spazio molto ridotto.

De monoblockstoel Mambo 1 blijft ook een stoel in de sculptuur *Modell Mambo 1,* vooral als op de achtergrond van de kantine in het Technologiecentrum Rheine plastic tuinstoelen van hetzelfde type staan te wachten op toeschouwers, terwijl de andere stoelen, die sculpturen zijn geworden, laten zien wat ze nog meer kunnen; zo ontmoeten twee bestaansvormen elkaar. Door het contrast lijkt het stoelwerk een circusact. Kunstig kruisen poten elkaar, worden omringd door rugleuningen, grijpt alles in elkaar om een strikt symmetrische structuur te vormen, systematisch geweven en gekruist om de samenhang van het grote volume te verzekeren. Op zich stabiel balanceert de complexe penetratie van oppervlaktevormen en lege ruimtes op een zeer klein oppervlak.

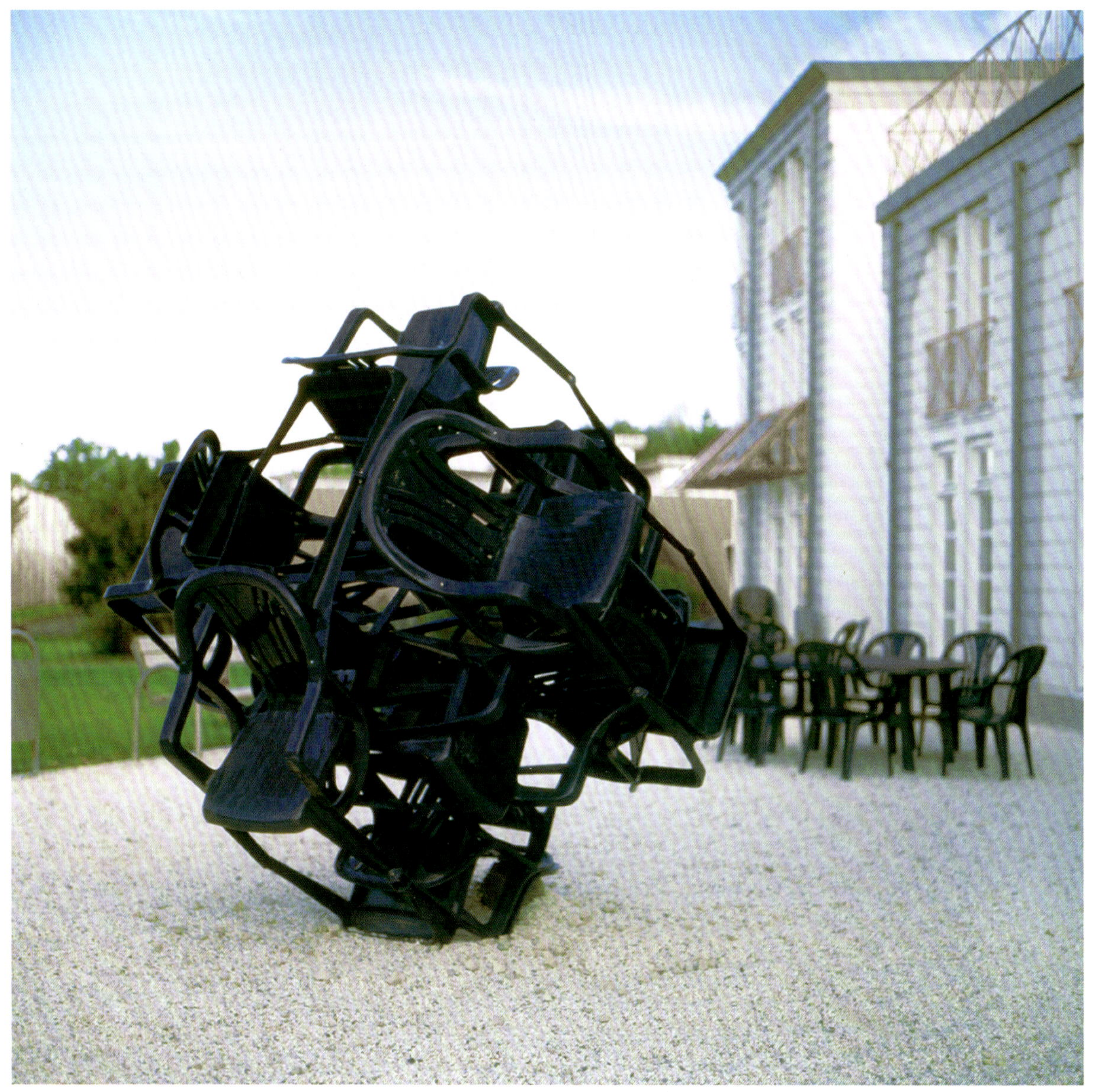

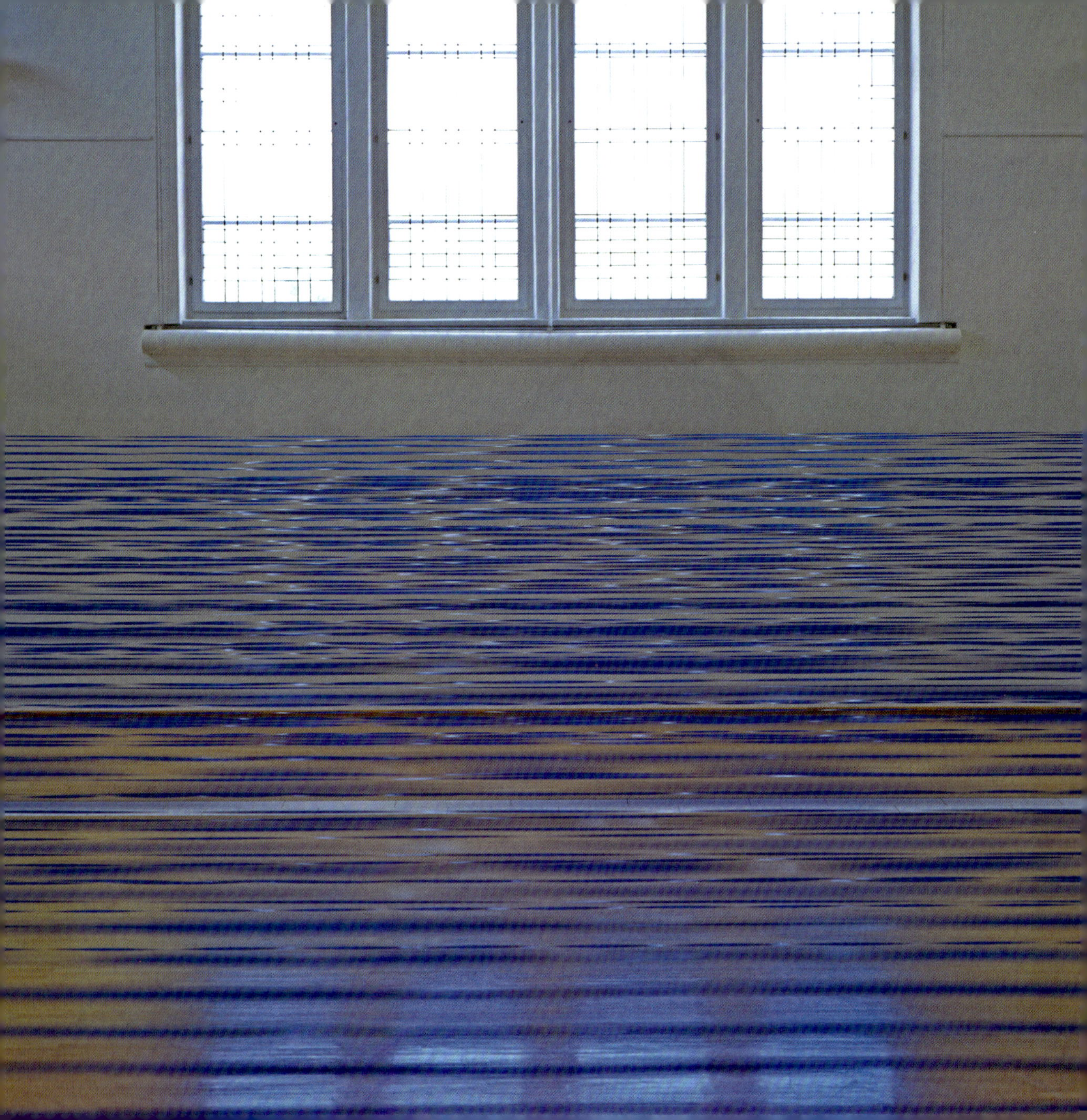

Streifenweise (Detail)

2000, Artificial bast, wrapped

Titled *Streifenweise* ("stripewise"), the intervention in the Heidenheim Art Museum, a former swimming pool, seems at first objective, almost simple. The impetus for this work came essentially from its location: Several layers of blue ribbon were placed around three opposing pairs of pillars structuring the room, so that a total of six permeable layers of twisted lines stretch through the room. To the eye, they appear to be inextricable, like floating, placeless superimposed blue, shimmering in the light like a ruffled water surface with every movement in front of or between the layers of ribbon. Everything that comes between them, that is behind them, dissolves, becomes diffuse. In the otherwise clearly structured hall, an area without spatial shape is created, where the near and the far collapse into slightly unsettling vagueness. These and other visual facets of the *stripewisely* absorbed space were demonstrated and explored in several performances.

L'installation intitulée *Streifenweise* (« en bandes ») réalisée au Musée d'Art de Heidenheim, une ancienne piscine reconvertie, semble objective, presque simple à première vue. Ce travail a essentiellement été inspiré par la nature du lieu où il a été réalisé: Les piliers qui ordonnent visuellement la salle, trois de chaque côté, ont été reliés sur différentes hauteurs par de longs rubans bleus pour papier cadeau, découpant ainsi la pièce à six niveaux par des rideaux transparents, composés de rangées de lignes torsadées. À chacun de nos mouvements devant ou au milieu de l'installation, l'œil les assimile à un mirage bleuté, superposition de lignes inextricables, flottantes et sans attaches, luminosité vacillante comme la surface de l'eau dans la lumière. Tout ce qui ce qui apparaît entre ou derrière les rideaux de rubans semble se dissoudre, devient diffus. Un espace atemporel naît dans cette salle, à l'origine clairement structurée, les distances deviennent irréelles. Ces facettes et autres effets optiques de l'espace reformaté *en bandes* ont été démontrés et testés, lors d'une performance en trois parties.

Sachlich, fast simpel mutet zunächst der *Streifenweise* betitelte Eingriff im Kunstmuseum Heidenheim, einem ehemaligen Schwimmbad an. Der Anstoß für diese Arbeit ging wesentlich vom Ort aus, der in die Arbeit verwickelt wird: Um drei einander gegenüberstehende, den Raum gliedernde Pfeilerpaare wurden jeweils mehrere Lagen blaues Geschenkband gelegt, so dass sich insgesamt sechs durchlässige Schichten aus in sich gedrehten Linien durch den Raum spannen. Dem Blick erscheinen sie als unentwirrbares, wie schwebendes, ortloses Überlagerungsblau, flirrend wie eine bewegte Wasseroberfläche im Licht bei jeder Bewegung vor oder zwischen den Bänderschichten. Alles, was zwischen sie gerät, was hinter ihnen ist, löst sich auf, wird diffus. In der sonst klar strukturierten Halle entsteht ein enträumlichter Bereich, dort fallen Nahes und Fernes zu etwas verunsichernd Vagem zusammen. Diese und andere visuelle Facetten des *streifenweise* verschluckten Raumes wurden in mehreren Performances demonstriert und ausgelotet.

La intervención en el Museo de Arte de Heidenheim, titulada *Streifenweise* ("por tiras"), parece objetiva, casi simple en un principio. El acicate para este trabajo llegó esencialmente del lugar en que el se enzarza este trabajo: Se colocaron varias capas de cinta azul alrededor de tres pares de pilares opuestos que estructuraban la habitación, de modo que un total de seis capas translúcidas de líneas trenzadas se tensan a través de la habitación. Para el ojo, parecen ser inextricables, como suspendidas, un solapamiento azul desubicado, brillando como una superficie de agua que se mueve ala luz con cada movimiento delante de las capas de cinta o entre estas. Todo lo que se interpone entre ellas, lo que está detrás de ellas, se disuelve, se difumina. En la sala, que por lo demás está claramente estructurada, se crea un área clara donde lo cercano y lo lejano coincidenen algo desconcertante. Estas y otras facetas visuales del espacio tragado *por tiras* fueron demostradas y exploradas en varias performances.

L'intervento all'ex piscina che oggi ospita il Museo d'arte di Heidenheim, intitolato *Streifenweise* ("a strisce"), appare sobrio, quasi semplice. L'idea per questo lavoro è venuta essenzialmente dal luogo stesso: diversi metri di nastro blu sono stati avvolti intorno a tre coppie di pilastri che si fronteggiano definendo lo spazio, in modo che un totale di sei strati di strisce di nastro rigirate su se stesse, che non bloccano del tutto la vista, si allungano attraverso la stanza. A occhio nudo, sembrano formare un blu inestricabile, come sospeso nell'aria, senza vera collocazione, e che risplende alla luce come una superficie d'acqua in movimento ogni volta che qualcosa si muove davanti o tra gli strati di strisce. Tutto ciò che finisce tra di loro, o che sta dietro di loro, si dissolve, assume contorni diffusi. Nella stanza, altrimenti chiaramente strutturata, viene a crearsi un'area come senza contorni, dove il vicino e l'estremo collassano in qualcosa di inquietante e vago. Queste e altre sfaccettature visive di uno spazio *a strisce* sono state dimostrate ed esplorate in diverse performance.

In eerste instantie doet de *Streifenweise* ("reepsgewijs") getitelde interventie in het Kunstmuseum Heidenheim, een voormalig zwembad, objectief, bijna eenvoudig aan. De impuls voor dit werk ging hoofdzakelijk uit van de locatie: rond drie tegenover elkaar staande zuilenparen die de ruimte opdeelden, werden meerdere lagen blauw cadeaulint gewikkeld, om in totaal zes doorlatende lagen gedraaide lijn in de ruimte te spannen. Op het oog lijken ze onontwarbaar, als zwevend, plaatsloos opgelegd blauw, glinsterend in het licht als een rimpelend wateroppervlak bij elke beweging voor of tussen de lagen. Alles wat ertussen komt, wat erachter zit, lost op, wordt diffuus. In de verder duidelijk gestructureerde hal is een gebied zonder ruimtelijke vorm gecreëerd, waar het nabije en het verre samenvallen in een iets verwarrende vaagheid. Deze en andere visuele facetten van de *reepsgewijs* ingeslikt ruimte werden in verschillende performances gedemonstreerd en verkend.

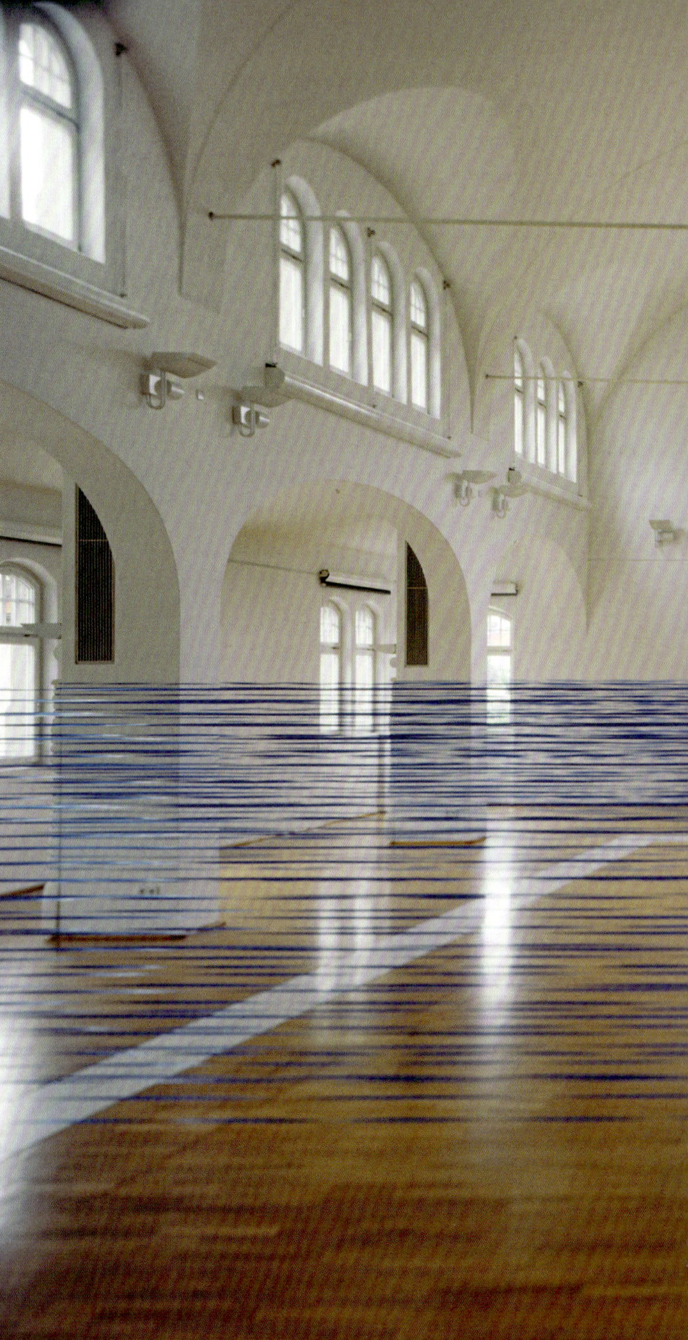

Streifenweise (Detail)

2000, Artificial bast, wrapped

The former Heidenheim swimming pool has been converted into an art museum. The architect wanted to retain the old condition with the white pool surround. This conflict is shown by the spatial intervention.

L'ancienne piscine de Heidenheim a été transformée en musée d'art. En conservant la limite du bassin, l'architecte a voulu conserver le caractère d'origine. Cette interférence est accentuée par l'installation.

Das ehemalige Schwimmbad von Heidenheim wurde in ein Kunstmuseum umgebaut. Der Architekt wollte mit der weißen Beckeneinfassung am alten Zustand festhalten. Diesen Konflikt zeigt die Raumintervention.

La antigua piscina de Heidenheim se ha convertido en un museo de arte. El arquitecto quiso conservar la antigua condición con el marco blanco de la piscina. Este conflicto se manifiesta en la intervención espacial.

L'ex piscina di Heidenheim è stata trasformata in un museo d'arte. L'architetto ha voluto mantenere la linea della vecchia vasca tracciandola in bianco. L'intervento in questo spazio vuole dimostrare il conflitto che ne deriva.

Het voormalige zwembad van Heidenheim is omgebouwd tot kunstmuseum. De architect wilde met de witte bak van het zwembad vasthouden aan de oude situatie. Dit conflict blijkt uit de ruimtelijke ingrepen.

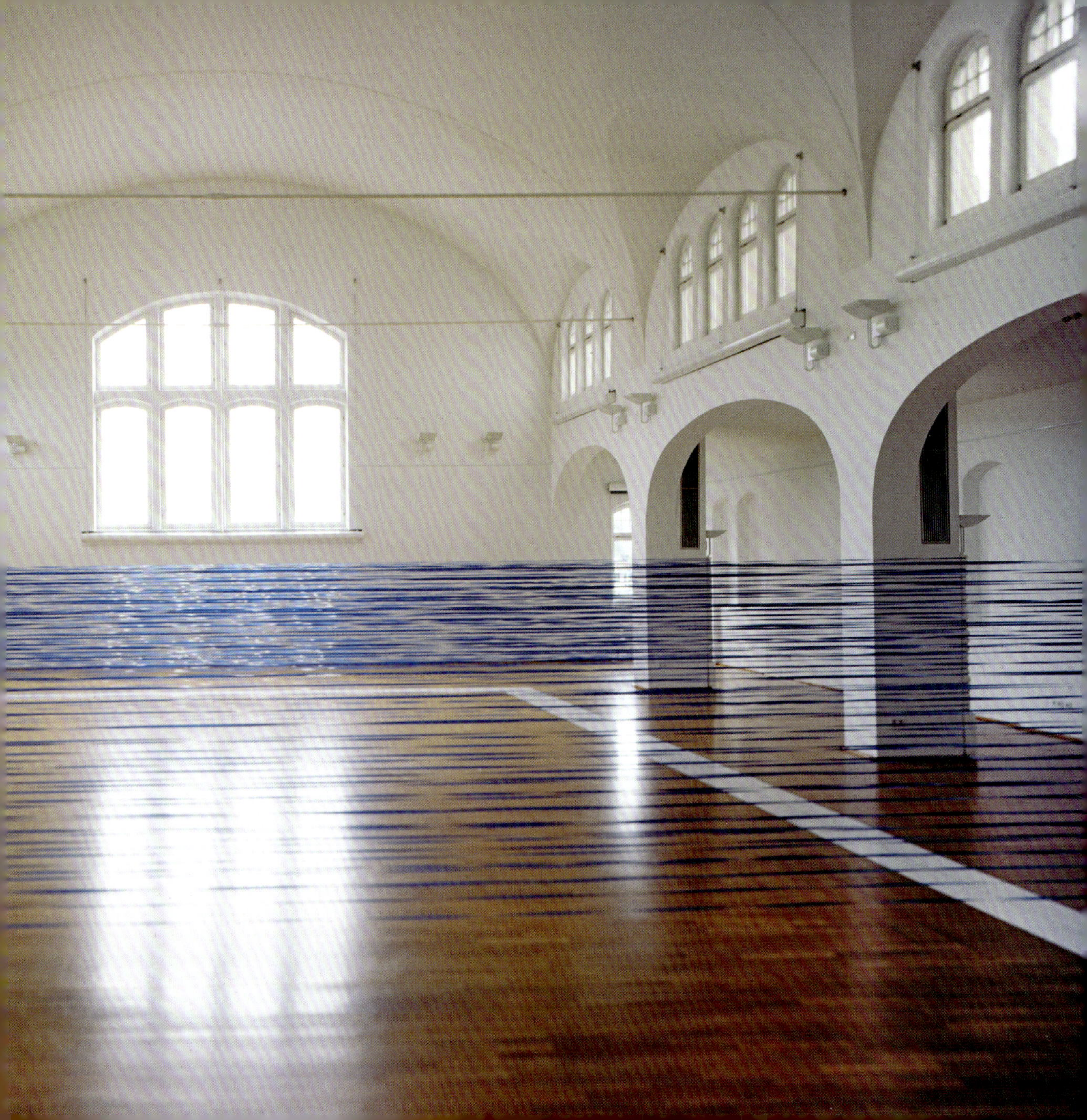

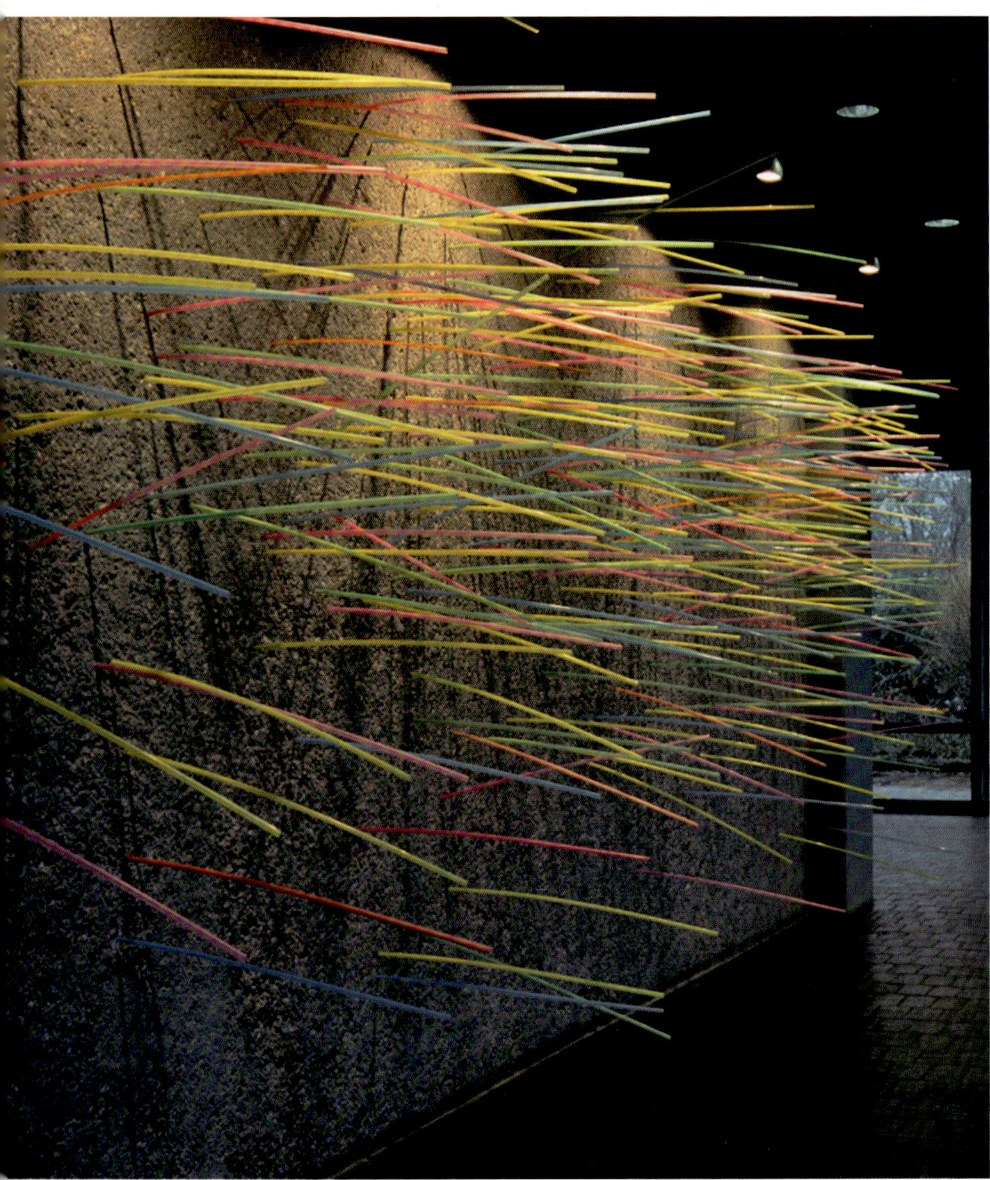

eingelocht

*2002, Fluorescent plastic
straws, 250 × 400 × 60 cm*

In the Japanese Cultural
Institute in Cologne you were
no longer allowed to drill
holes in the special plaster
in the exhibition area. So all
the old holes are the starting
point for this work.

À l'Institut Culturel Japonais
de Cologne, à cause de son
caractère très particulier,
on ne peut plus percer de
trou dans le plâtre de la salle
d'exposition. Les trous déjà
existants ont donc servi de
point de départ pour cette
œuvre.

Im Japanischen Kulturinstitut
in Köln durfte man im
Ausstellungsbereich
keine Löcher mehr in den
besonderen Putz bohren.
Also bilden alle alten Löcher
den Ausgangspunkt für diese
Arbeit.

Al Instituto Japonés de
Cultura de Colonia ya no se
le permitía perforar agujeros
en el yeso especial del área
de exposición. Así, todos los
viejos agujeros son el punto
de partida de este trabajo.

Nell'Istituto Giapponese
di Cultura in Colonia non
era possibile perforare lo
speciale intonaco dell'area
espositiva. Quindi tutti i
fori preesistenti sono stati
il punto di partenza per
questo lavoro.

In het Japans Cultuureel
Instituut in Keulen mocht
men geen gaten meer boren
in het speciale stucwerk in de
tentoonstellingsruimte. Alle
oude gaten vormen dus het
uitgangspunt voor dit werk.

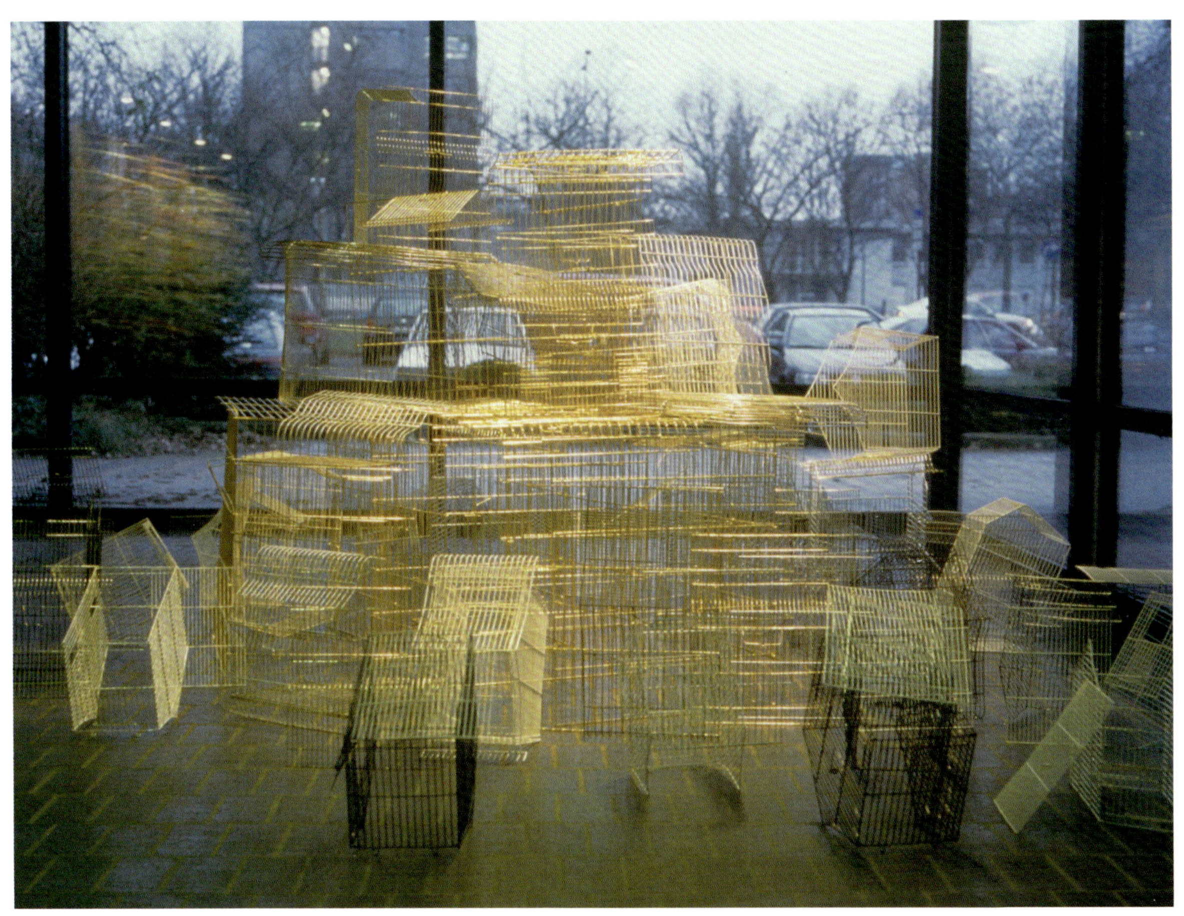

Mont sans victoire

2002, Metal, c. 165 × 280 × 300 cm

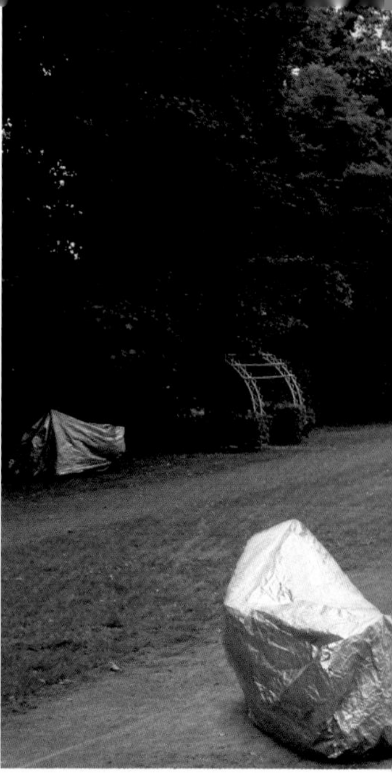

Verwechslung

2001, Tyvek tarpaulins, motorcycles

Twelve motorcycles stand under twelve shiny silver Tyvek tarpaulins for a day in a small park, nothing more. Arbitrarily placed as it seems, on paths and green spaces; ignoring the symmetry of the complex they are everywhere. Unevenly distributed elements—glittering chunks, still veiled sculptures, something sleeping, waiting, … an oversight, a "mistake"? Isolated, similar and yet not identical members of a form family. The wind changes the shape of the covers, reaches under them, expands the metallic, loose skin or models the bodies of the hidden machine more clearly through the tarpaulins. The light also plays with hollows and wrinkles, creases, lets everything glitter suddenly or recede drably; next morning the motorcycles disappeared again as if nothing had happened. What remains are pictures of an ambiguous, mysterious perforation of the contexts and the memory of previously unseen everyday sculptures.

Douze motos ont été tout simplement disposées, recouvertes de bâches en Tyvek argentées, pendant une journée entière, dans un petit parc. Disposées apparemment de façon aléatoire, soit sur les chemins, soit sur les pelouses ; ignorant totalement la symétrie de l'ensemble, elles sont partout. Éléments inégalement répartis – blocs scintillants, sculptures encore voilées, elles semblent somnoler, elles semblent attendre, … un oubli, une « confusion » ? Membres isolés, similaires, mais pas identiques d'une famille morphologique. Le vent modifie la forme des housses, s'y engouffre, dilate l'épiderme métallisé, dissocié de son corps ou accentue la morphologie des engins dissimulés sous leur bâche. La lumière joue aussi avec les creux et les plis et replis, fait étinceler les formes ou les laisse redevenir mat ; le lendemain matin, les motos ont disparues, comme elles n'avaient n'avait jamais existé. Il ne reste plus que les images d'une interférence ambiguë et mystérieuse d'une réalité relative et le souvenir de sculptures jamais vu auparavant dans un espace public.

Dann stehen zwölf Motorräder unter zwölf silberglänzenden Tyvekplanen für einen Tag in einem kleinen Park, mehr nicht. Willkürlich platziert wie es scheint, auf Wegen und Grünflächen; die Symmetrie der Anlage ignorierend sind sie überall. Ungleichmäßig verteilte Elemente – glitzernde Brocken, noch verhüllte Plastiken, etwas Schlafendes, Wartendes, … ein Versehen, eine „Verwechslung"? Vereinzelte, einander ähnliche und doch nicht identische Mitglieder einer Formfamilie. Der Wind verändert die Gestalt der Hüllen, greift unter sie, bläht die metallische, lose Haut oder modelliert die Körper der verborgenen Maschine deutlicher durch die Planen hindurch. Auch spielt das Licht mit Mulden und Falten, Knitterungen, lässt alles aufblitzen oder stumpf zurücktreten; am nächsten Morgen sind die Motorräder wieder verschwunden als sei nichts gewesen. Was bleibt sind Bilder einer vieldeutigen, rätselhaften Perforation der Zusammenhänge und die Erinnerung an zuvor so nicht gesehene Alltagsskulpturen.

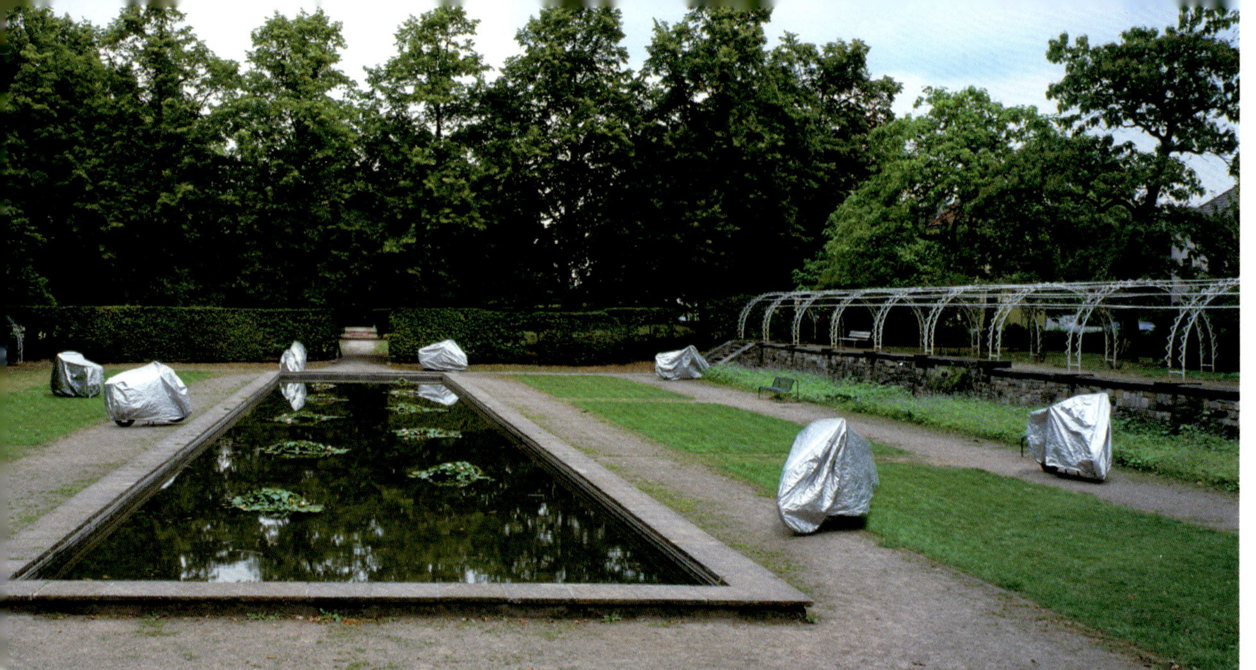

Después figuran doce motocicletas tapadas por doce lonas plateadas y brillantes durante un día en un pequeño parque, nada más. Están colocadas de manera arbitraria , como parece, en senderos y espacios verdes; ignorando la simetría del complejo en el que se encuentran, están por todas partes. Elementos distribuidos de manera desigual con pedazos brillantes, plásticos que disimulan, algo que dormita, espera, … un descuido, ¿una "confusión"? Miembros aislados, similares y, sin embargo, no son miembros idénticos, nacidos de una misma forma. El viento cambia el aspectode las fundas, entra por debajo, infla la piel metálica y flácida o modela los cuerpos de la máquina oculta con claridad a través de las lonas. La luz también juega con huecos y dobleces, pliegues, todo destellas o retrocede con indiferencia. A la mañana siguiente las motocicletas volvieron a desaparecer como si nada hubiera pasado. Lo que queda son imágenes de una perforación ambigua yenigmática de las relaciones y el recuerdo de esculturas cotidianas nunca vistas.

In un piccolo parco, dodici motociclette sono poste sotto dodici teloni in tessuto non tessuto Tyvek, argenteo e lucente, per l'arco di una giornata, niente di più. Disposte all'apparenza in maniera arbitraria, su sentieri e spazi verdi, si trovano un po' ovunque, senza tener conto della simmetria del complesso. Elementi distribuiti senza ordine – pezzi scintillanti, sculture ancora velate, qualcosa che dorme, aspetta… una svista, un "equivoco"? Membri isolati, simili ma non identici, appartenenti a un'unica famiglia di forme. Il vento cambia la forma delle coperture, si insinua sotto di esse, espande la pelle metallica distaccata o modella più chiaramente i corpi delle macchine nascoste sotto i teloni. La luce gioca anche con cavità e pieghe, increspature, fa sì che tutto luccichi all'improvviso o scompaia sfocato sullo sfondo; la mattina dopo le moto sono scomparse come se niente fosse accaduto. Rimangono le immagini di uno sfondamento ambiguo e misterioso dei contesti e la memoria di sculture quotidiane inedite.

Dan staan in een klein park twaalf motorfietsen een dag onder twaalf glanzend zilveren Tyvek-dekzeilen, meer niet. Schijnbaar willekeurig neergezet, op paden en gazons; ze zijn overal, terwijl ze de symmetrie van het park negeren. Ongelijkmatig verdeelde elementen – glinsterende hompen, nog verhulde sculpturen, iets slapends, wachtends, … een vergissing, een 'verwisseling'? Op zichzelf staande, op elkaar lijkende en toch niet identieke leden van een vormfamilie. De wind verandert de vorm van de hoezen, reikt eronderdoor, laat de metalige, losse huid opbollen of modelleert de lichamen van de verborgen machines duidelijker door de dekzeilen heen. Ook speelt het licht met plooien en vouwen, kreukels, laat alles oplichten of mat verdwijnen; de volgende ochtend zijn de motorfietsen weer verdwenen alsof er ze er nooit geweest zijn. Wat overblijft zijn beelden van een dubbelzinnige, mysterieuze perforatie van de contexten en de herinnering aan nog nooit eerder vertoonde alledaagse sculpturen.

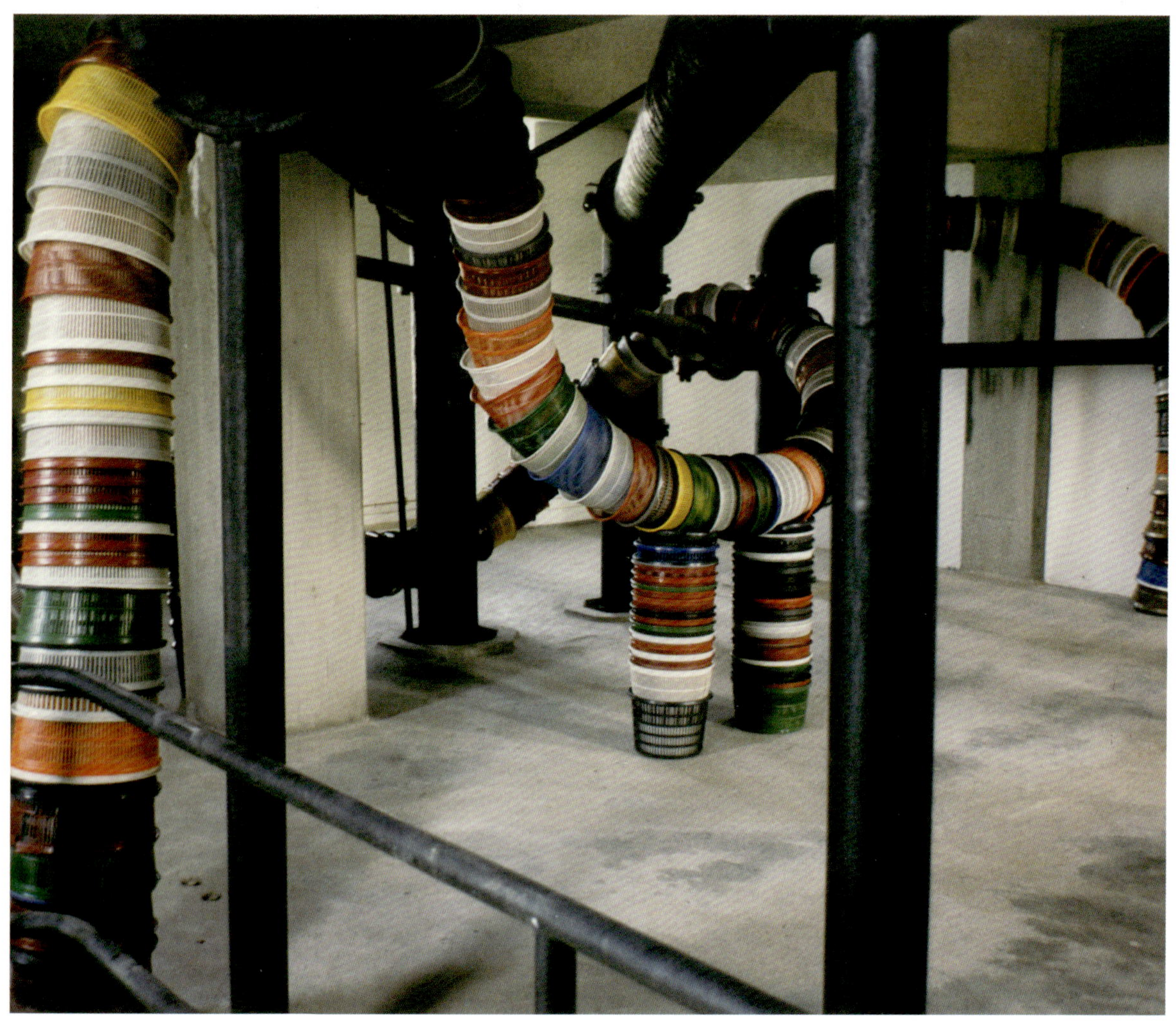

Installation

1999, Plastic, Watertoren, Vlissingen

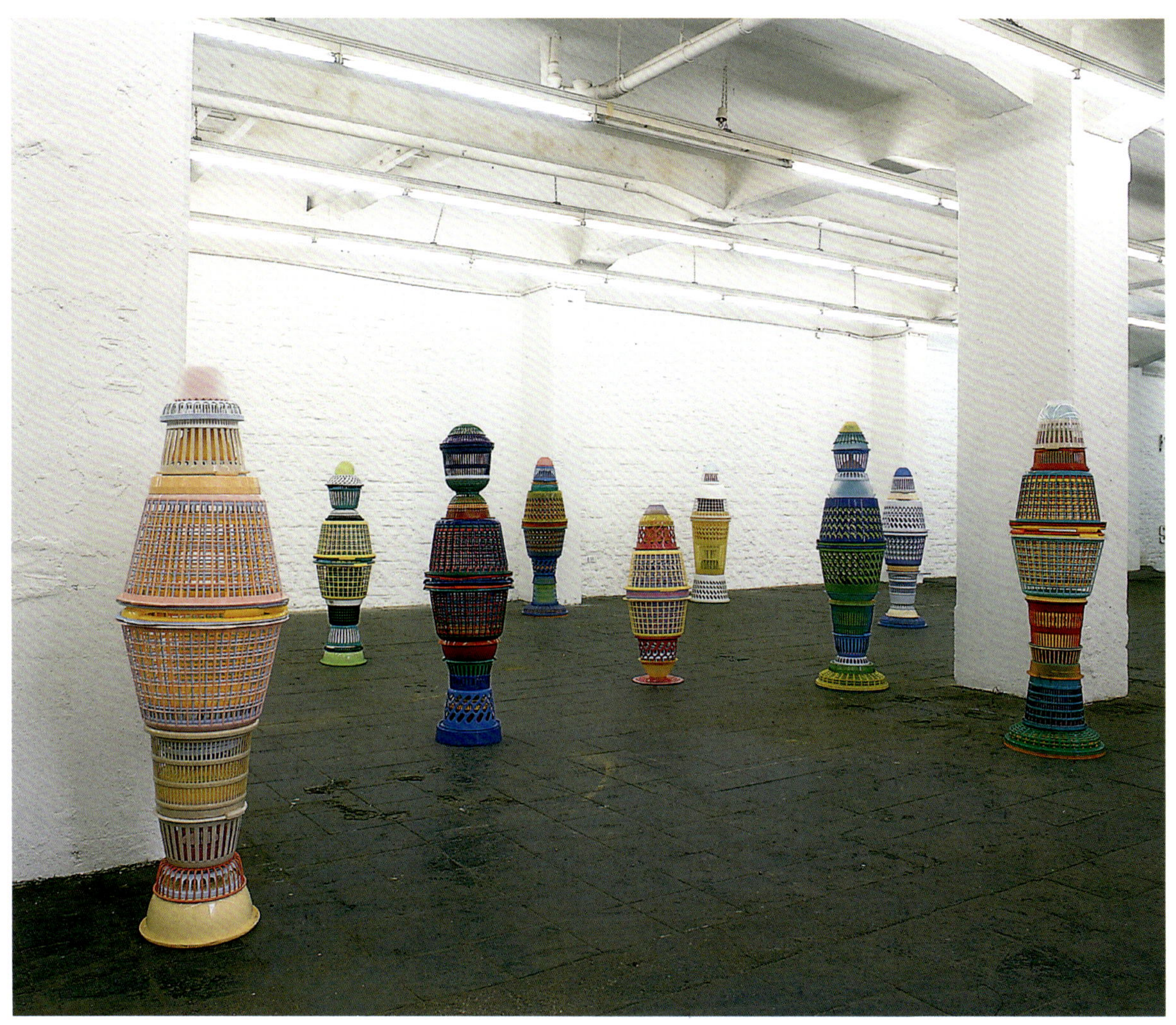

Liberos

1998, Plastic

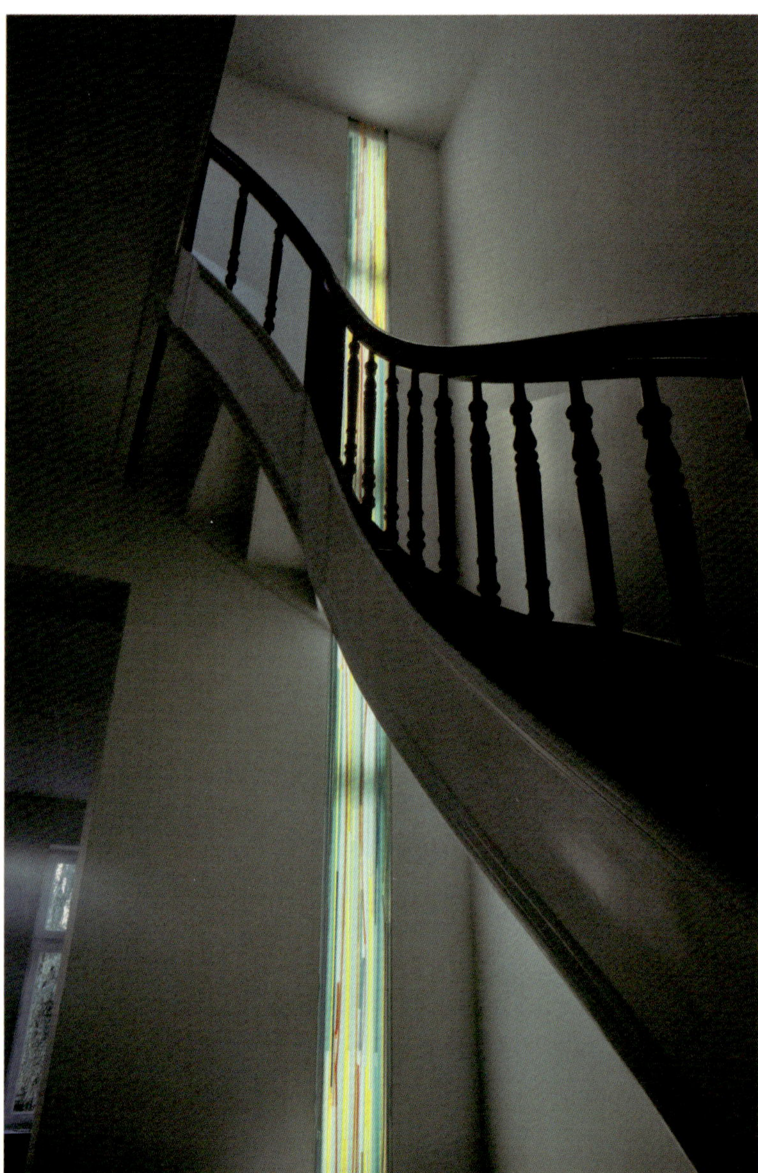

Treppenhausinstallation

2005, Plastic, 700 × 20 cm, Private collection

Information to get rid of

2002, Plastic, wire, motor, light, Hypokunsthalle,
München

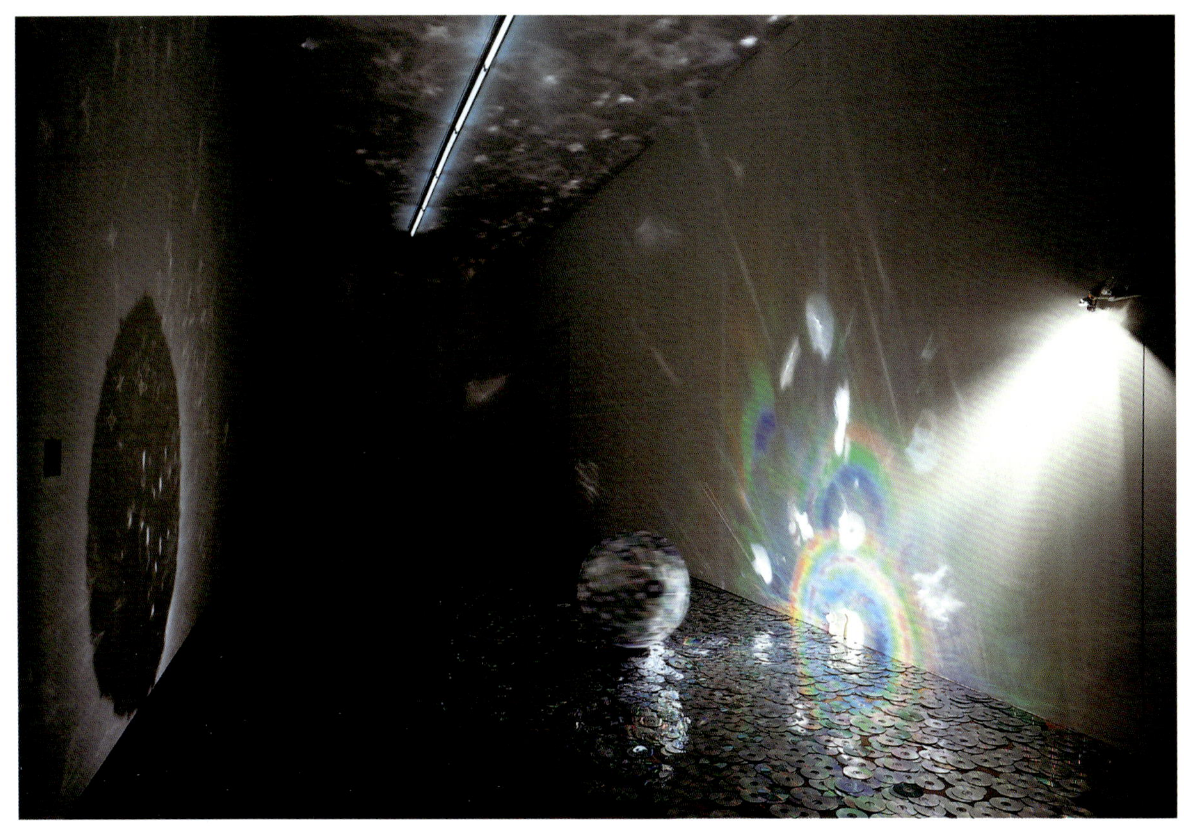

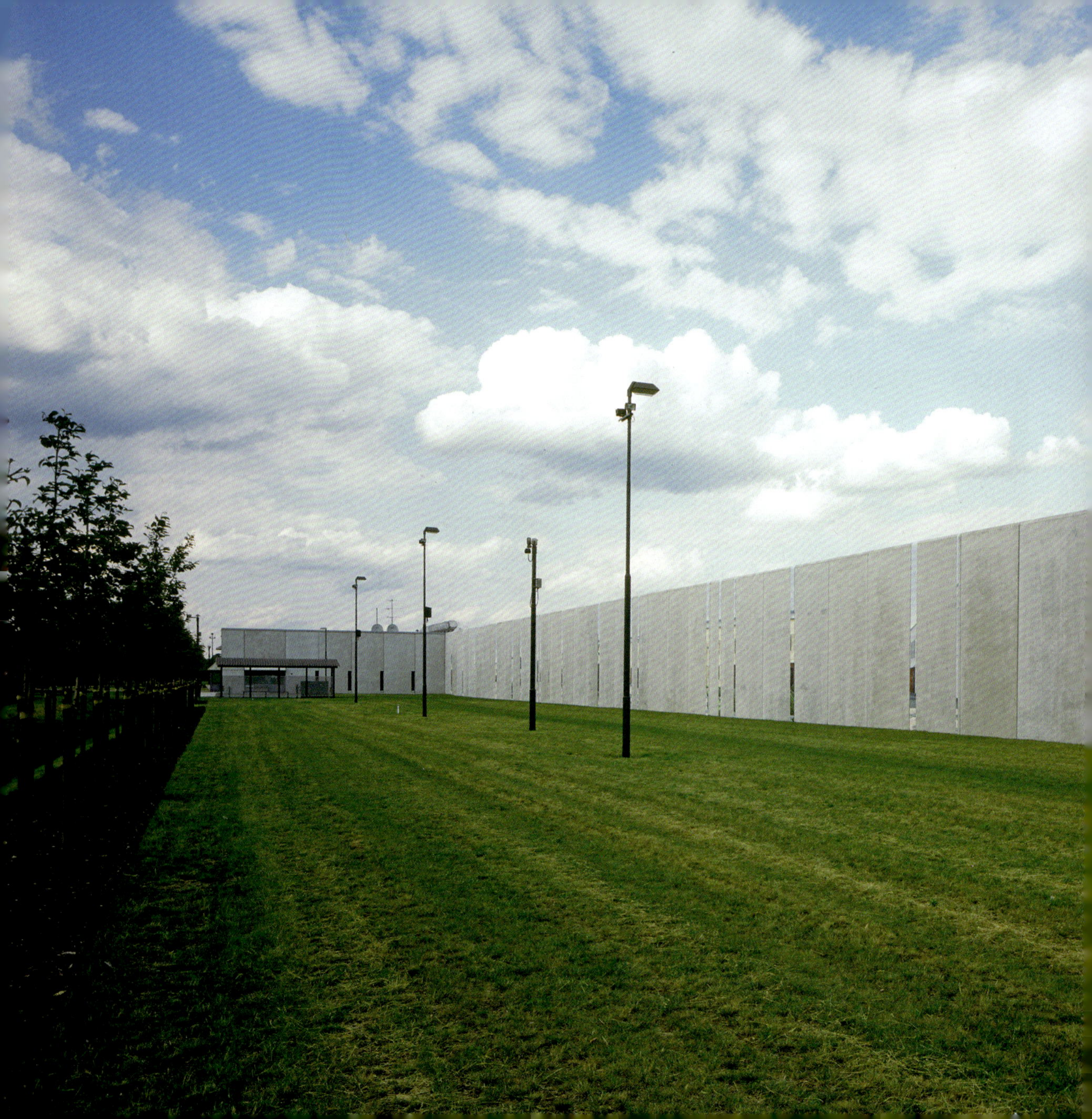

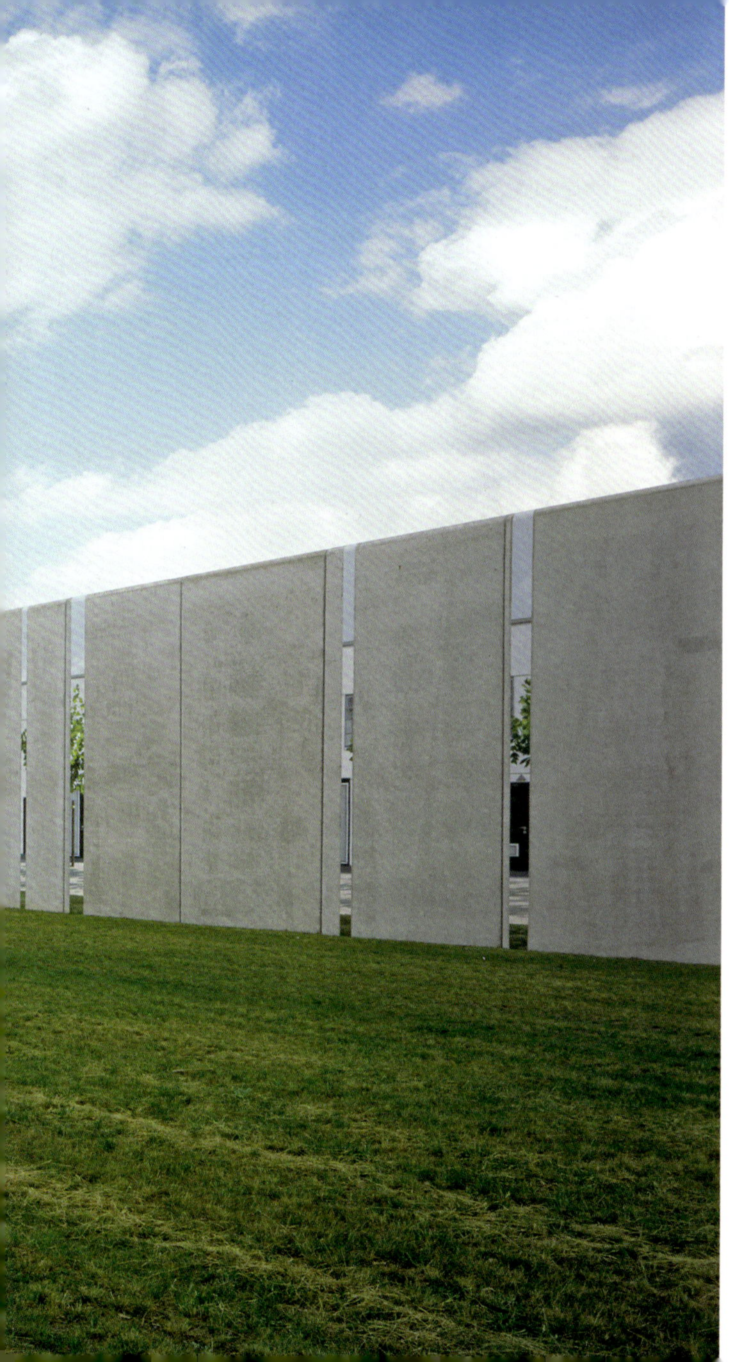

JVA Neuruppin-Wulkow

*2002, Mural painting, 650 × 15000 cm, Justizvollzugsanstalt
Neuruppin-Wulkow*

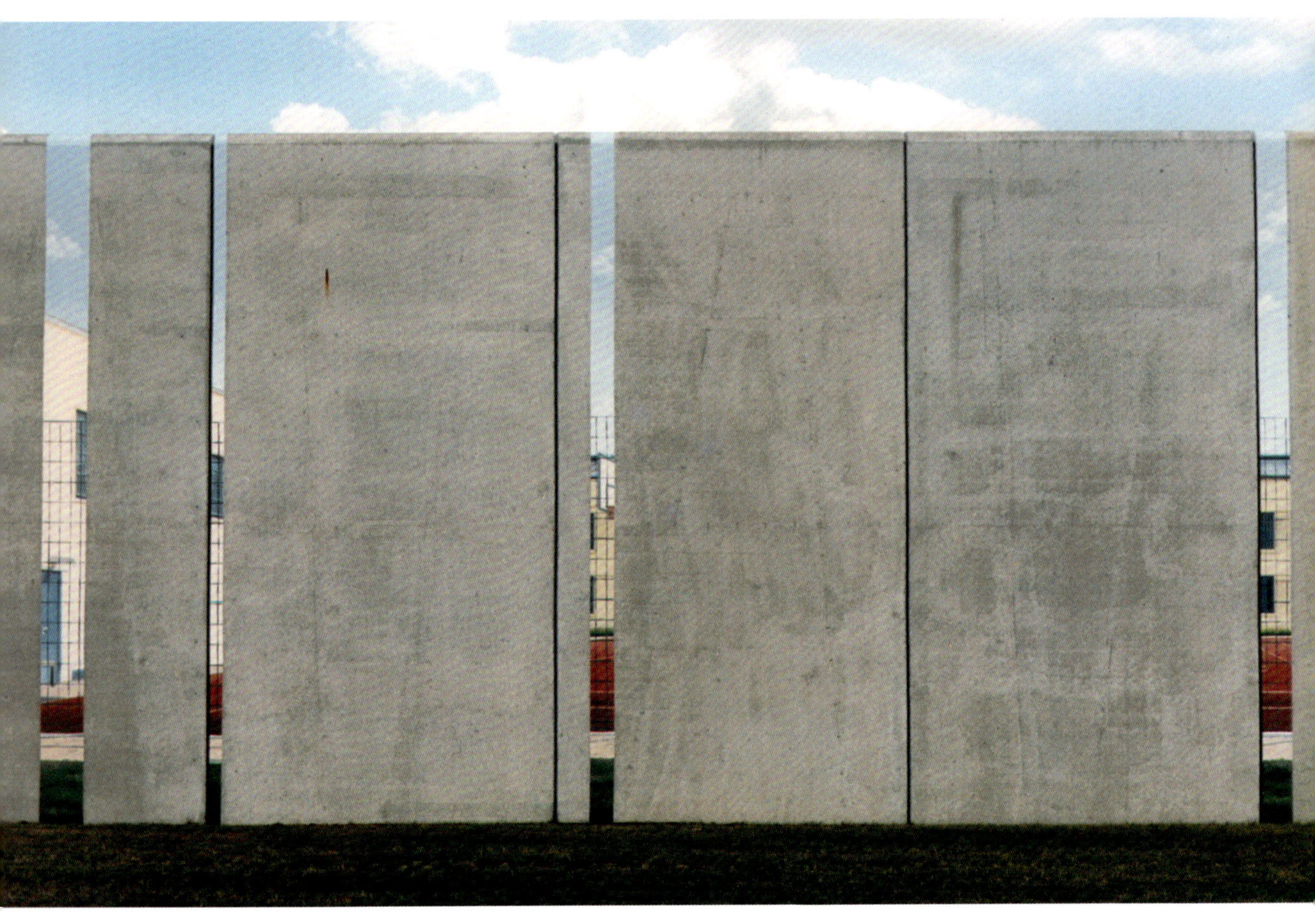

The 30 vertical stripes painted on the Neuruppin-Wulkow correctional facility look like slits. They show the view you would have if the stripes were actual wall openings. This work refers to the rumour that many citizens of Neuruppin queued for up to nine hours to see a prison from the inside on Open Day.

Les 30 bandes verticales peintes en trompe-l'œil sur le mur d'enceinte de la maison d'arrêt de Neuruppin-Wulkow ressemblent à des larges fentes. Elles offrent une vue que l'on aurait, si elles avaient été de véritables ouvertures murales. Cette œuvre se réfère à la réputation de l'établissement pénitentiaire, selon laquelle les habitants de Neuruppin pouvaient faire la queue près de neuf heures pour la visiter, lors des journées portes ouvertes.

Wie Sehschlitze wirken die 30 senkrechten, aufgemalten Streifen an der JVA Neuruppin-Wulkow. Sie geben den Blick frei, den man hätte, wenn die Streifen tatsächliche Maueröffnungen wären. Diese Arbeit bezieht sich auf das Gerücht, dass zahlreiche Neuruppiner Bürger am Tag der offenen Tür bis zu neun Stunden in der Warteschlange standen, um ein Gefängnis von innen zu sehen.

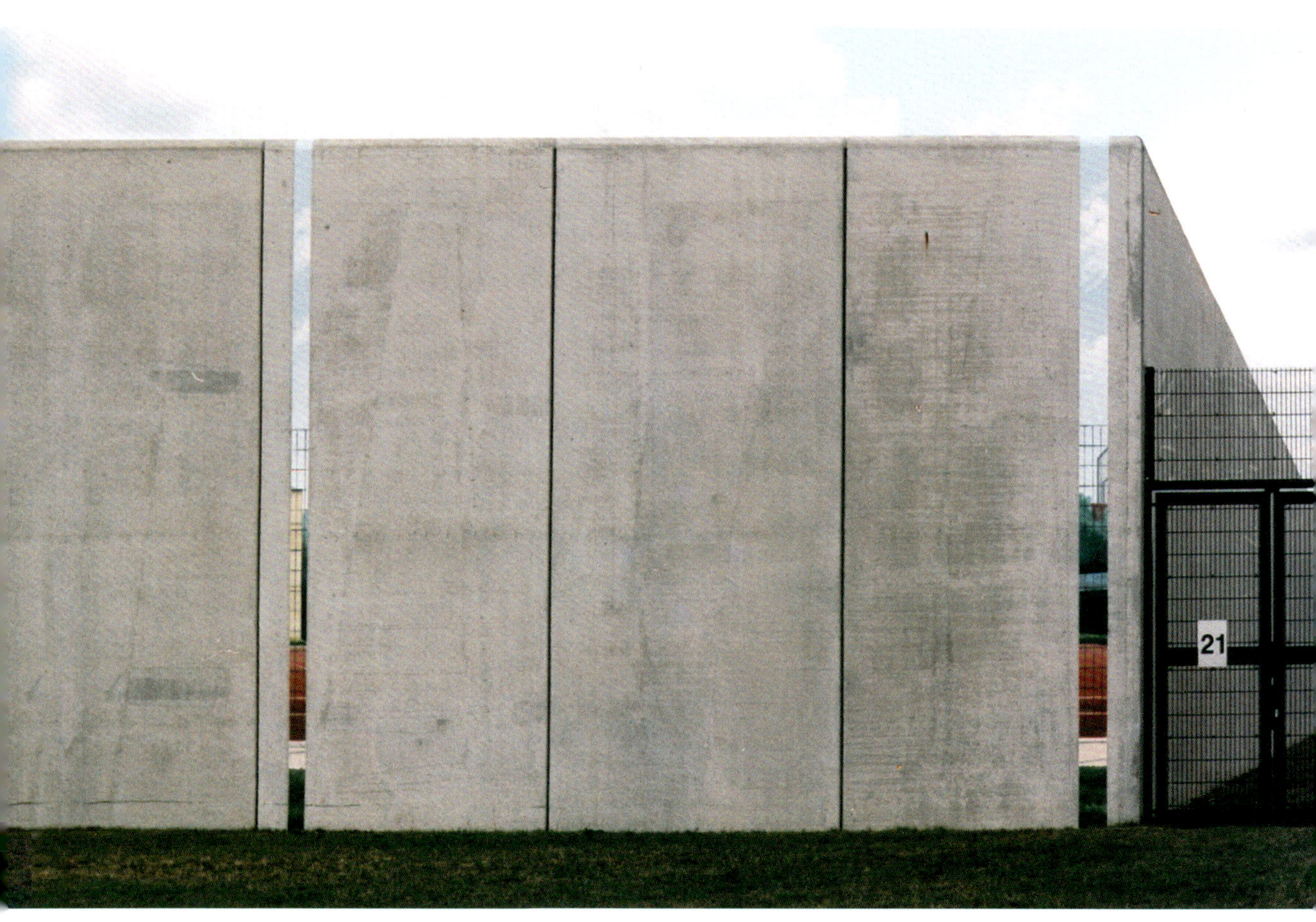

Las 30 franjas verticales pintadas en la cárcel de Neuruppin-Wulkow parecen hendiduras. Te dan la vista que tendrías si las rayas fueran aperturas de paredes reales. Este trabajo se refiere al rumor de que muchos ciudadanos de Neuruppin hacían cola hasta nueve horas para ver una prisión desde dentro en la jornada de Puertas Abiertas.

Le 30 strisce verticali dipinte sulla parete del carcere di Neuruppin-Wulkow fanno pensare a delle fessure. Grazie a loro è possibile godere della vista che si avrebbe se le strisce fossero vere e proprie aperture nel muro. Questo lavoro si riferisce alla voce che durante la giornata di apertura al pubblico molti cittadini di Neuruppin siano stati in coda fino a nove ore per vedere una prigione dall'interno.

De 30 verticale strepen die op de Neuruppin-Wulkow-gevangenis zijn geschilderd, lijken kijkspleten. Ze tonen het zicht dat je zou hebben als de strepen echte muuropeningen zouden zijn geweest. Dit werk verwijst naar het gerucht dat veel inwoners van Neuruppin wel negen uur in de rij stonden om op de open dag de gevangenis vanbinnen te bekijken.

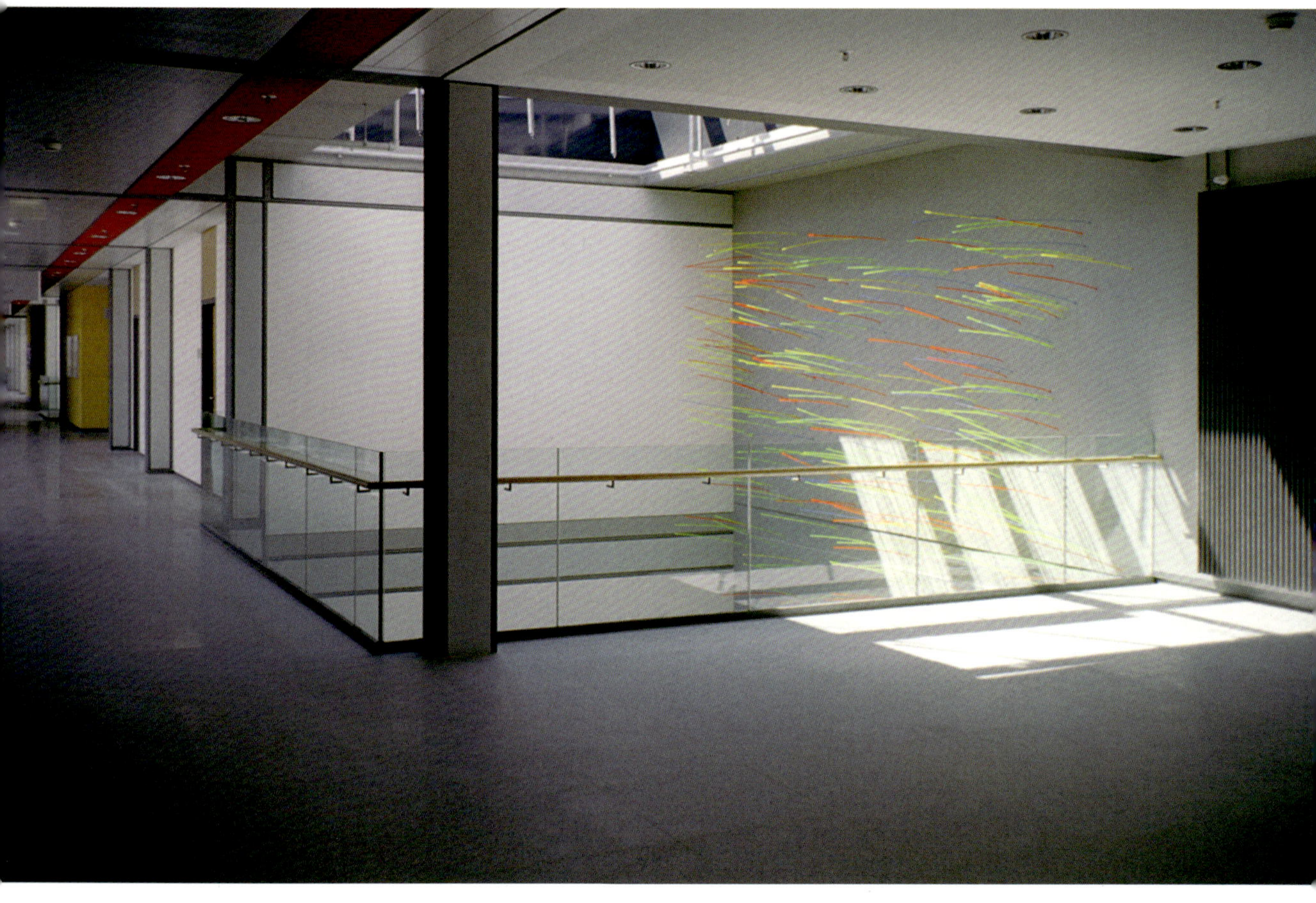

o.T.

2002, Fluorescent plastic rods, 1500 × 400 × 100 cm, Universitätsklinikum, Halle an der Saale

The pores of the exposed concrete provided the design proposal for the 14-metre high light shaft in the children's clinic of the university hospital in Halle.

Les pores du béton ont servi de point de départ à la métamorphose du puits de lumière de 14 mètres de haut, de la clinique pour enfants du centre hospitalier universitaire à Halle.

Die Poren des Sichtbetons lieferten den Gestaltungsvorschlag für den 14 Meter hohen Lichtschacht der Kinderklinik des Universitätsklinikums in Halle.

Los poros del hormigón visto aportaron la propuesta de diseño para el pozo de luz de 14 metros de altura de la clínica infantil de la clínica universitaria de Halle.

I pori del calcestruzzo a vista hanno fornito l'idea progettuale per il lucernario di 14 metri situato nella clinica pediatrica dell'ospedale universitario ad Halle.

De poriën van het kale beton vormden het ontwerpvoorstel voor de 14 meter hoge lichtschacht in de kinderkliniek van de universiteitskliniek in Halle.

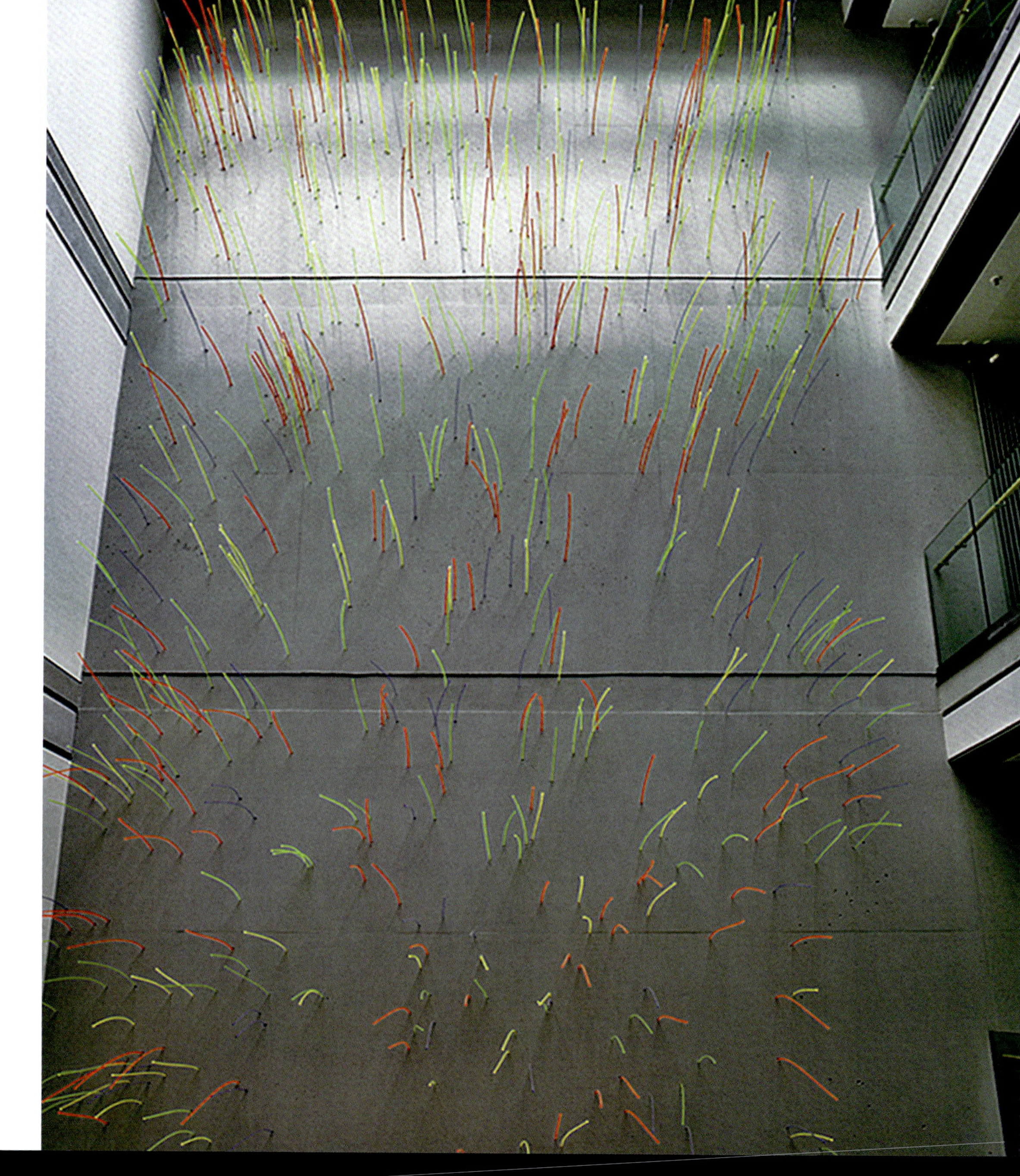

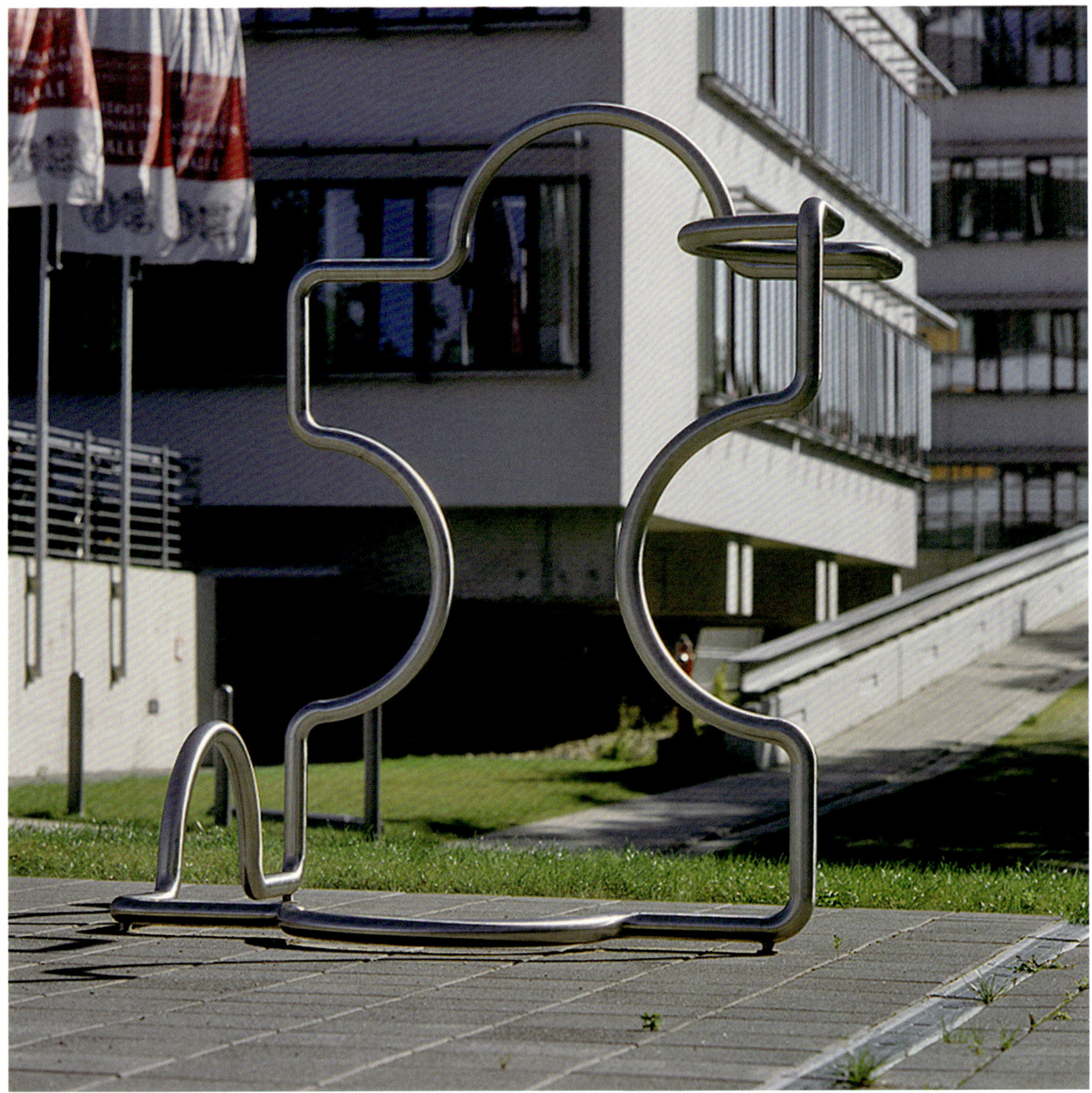

o.T.

2003, Stainless steel, polished, 165 × 165 × 165 cm,
Universitätsklinikum, Halle an der Saale

The steel sculpture takes up the forms of the
rectangle of the hospital and the large circle of
the helipad and plays with them.

La sculpture en acier se réfère à la forme
parallélépipédique de l'hôpital et à celle
circulaire de l'héliport et les décline.

Die Stahlskulptur greift das Eckige des
Krankenhauses und das große Rund des
Hubschrauberlandeplatzes auf und spielt damit.

La escultura de acero ocupa la plaza central del
hospital y la gran ronda del helipuerto juega
con ella.

La scultura in acciaio riprende le forme del
piazzale rettangolare dell'ospedale e del grande
cerchio dell'eliporto, giocando con loro.

De stalen sculptuur beslaat het plein
van het ziekenhuis en de grote ronde
helikopterlandingsplaats en speelt ermee.

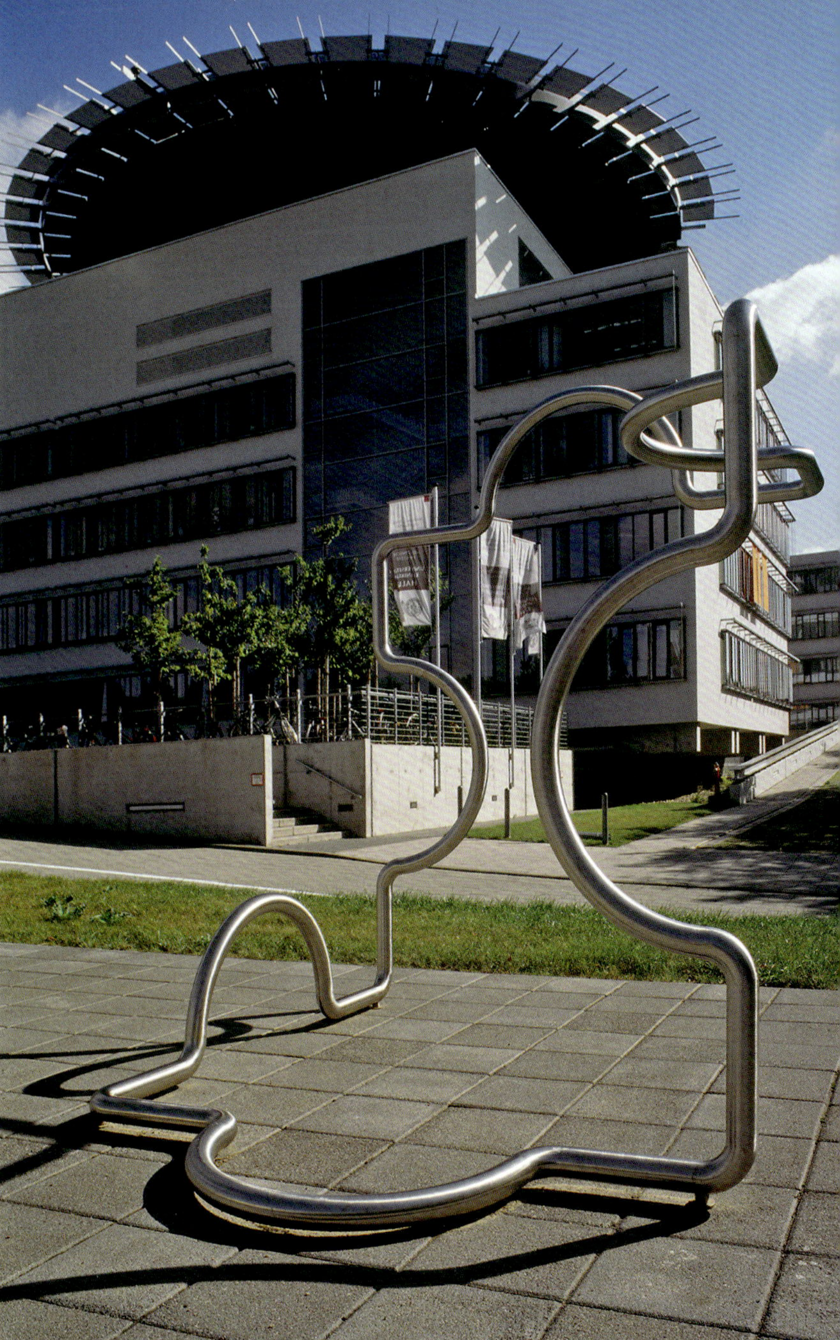

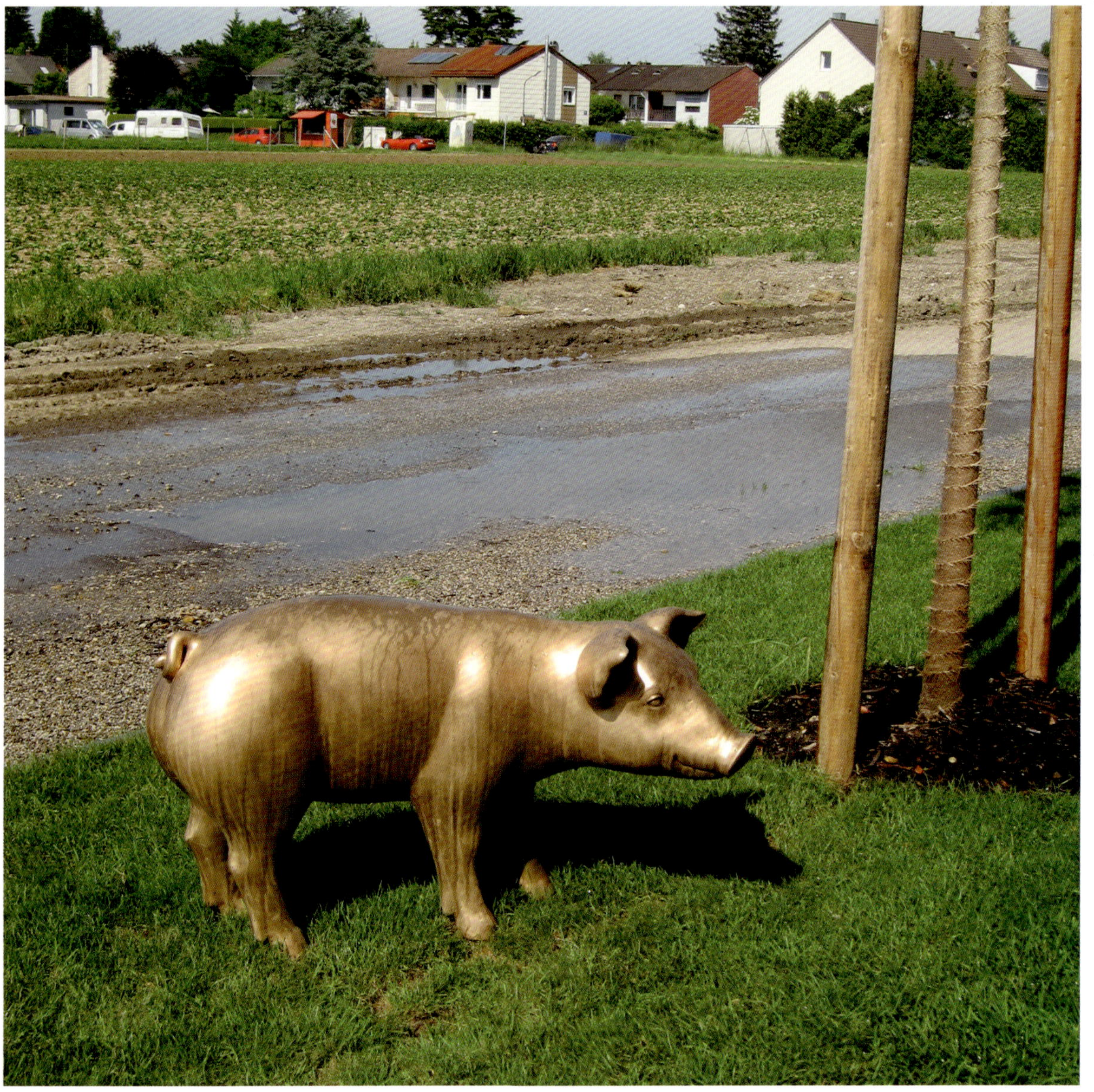

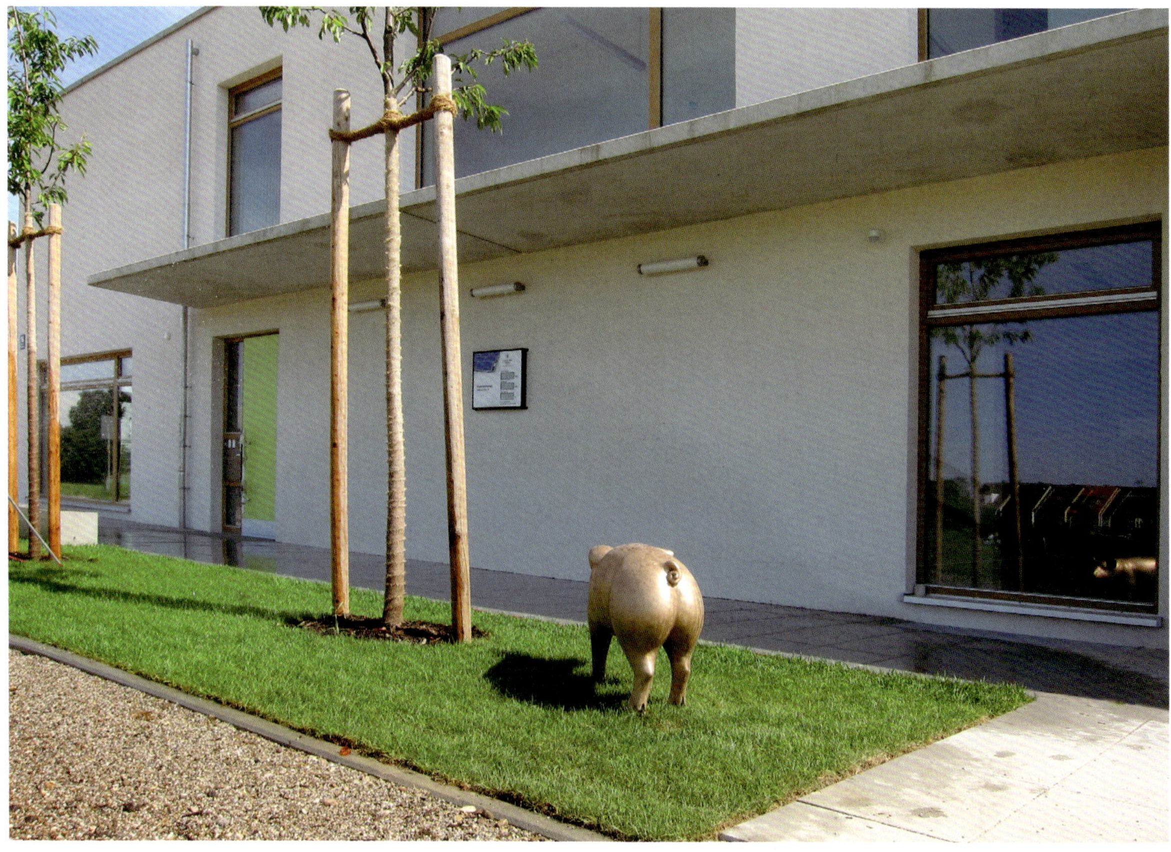

Gaby

2012, Bronze, 62 × 82 × 33 cm, Kita Ramersdorf, München

The golden bronze pig stands in front of the entrance to the day care centre. It marks the temporary city boundary, because opposite it there are still strawberry fields. It plays with the interior and exterior.

Le cochon en bronze doré se tient à l'entrée de l'école maternelle. Il marque la limite temporaire de la ville, parce qu'en face, il y a toujours des champs de fraises. Le cochon joue sur l'ambivalence de l'intérieur et l'extérieur.

Das goldene Bronzeschwein steht vor dem Eingang der Kindertagesstätte. Es markiert die temporäre Stadtgrenze, denn gegenüber befinden sich noch Erdbeerfelder. Es spielt mit dem Innen und Außen.

El cerdo de bronce dorado se encuentra frente a la entrada de la guardería. Marca el límite temporal de la ciudad, porque todavía hay campos de fresas enfrente. Juega con el interior y el exterior.

Il maiale di bronzo dorato si trova davanti all'ingresso dell'asilo nido. Esso segna il confine temporaneo della città, poiché nella zona di fronte alla struttura ci sono campi di fragole. La figura vuole interagire con l'interno e l'esterno.

Het goudkleurige bronzen varken staat voor de ingang van het kinderdagverblijf. Het markeert de tijdelijke stadsgrens, want ertegenover liggen nog aardbeienvelden. Het speelt met binnen en buiten.

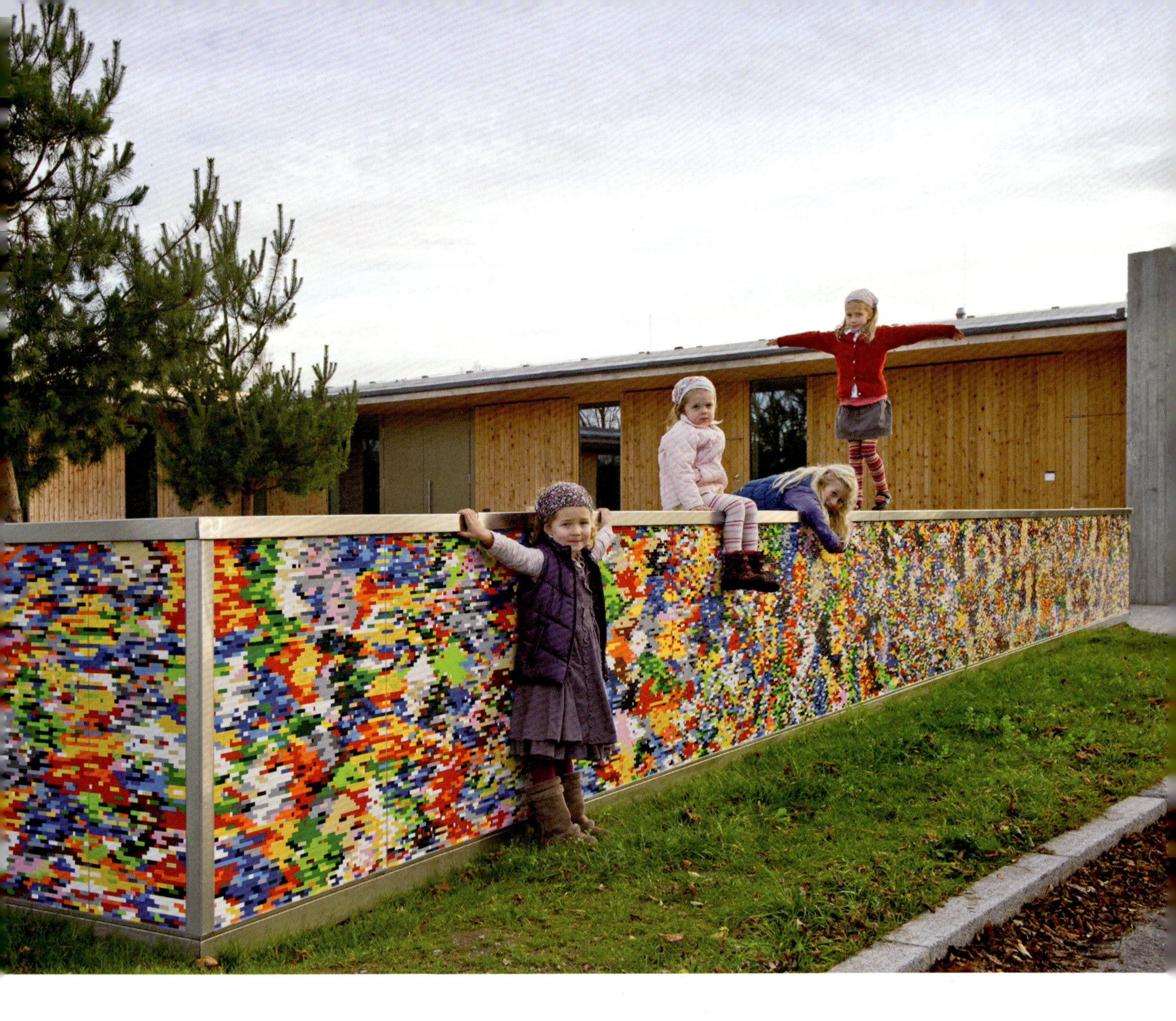

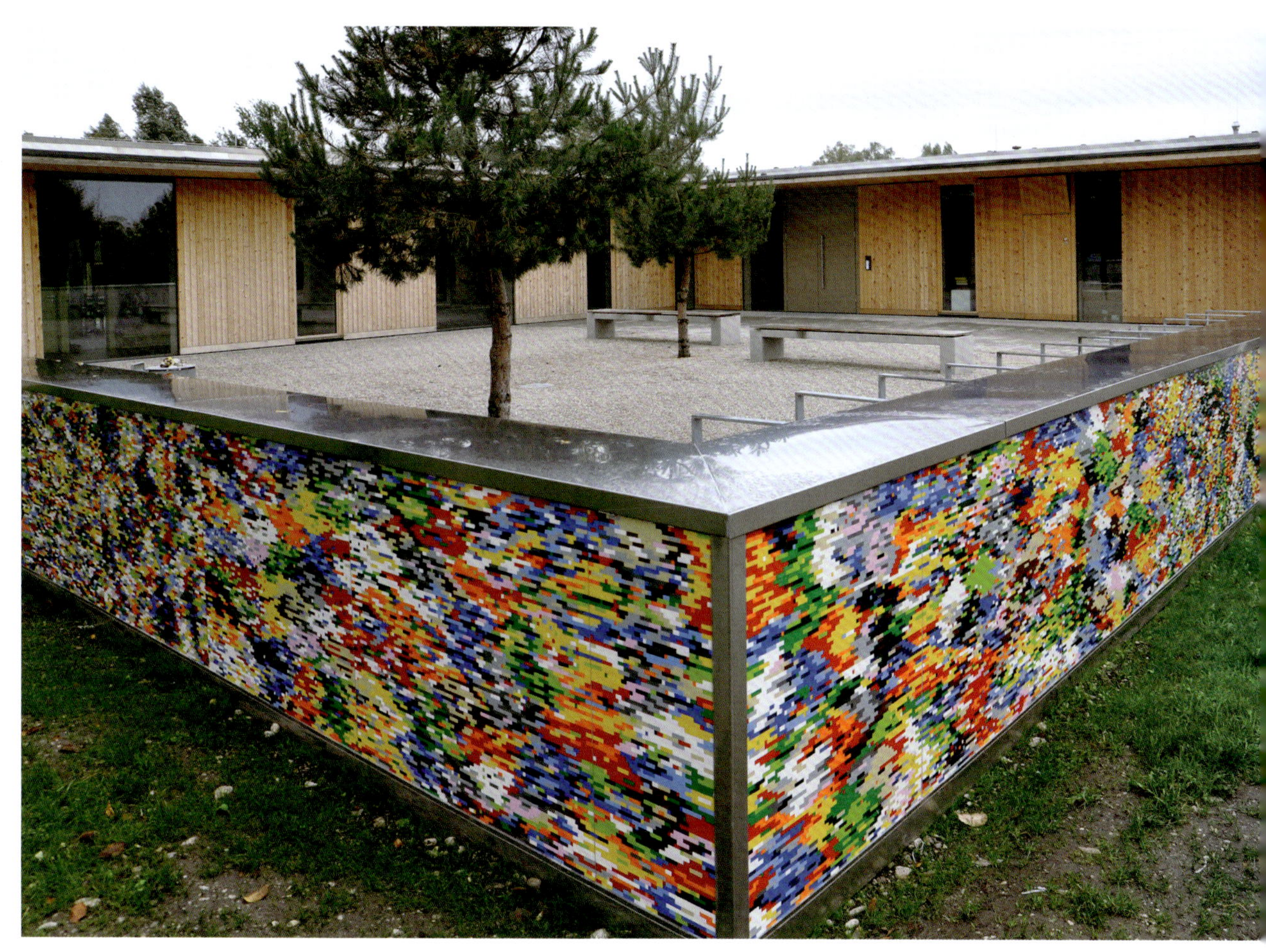

Realphantasierter Kindertraum

2010, ABS (Lego), 100 × 1300 × 130 cm, Ingeborg-Ortner-Kinderhaus, München

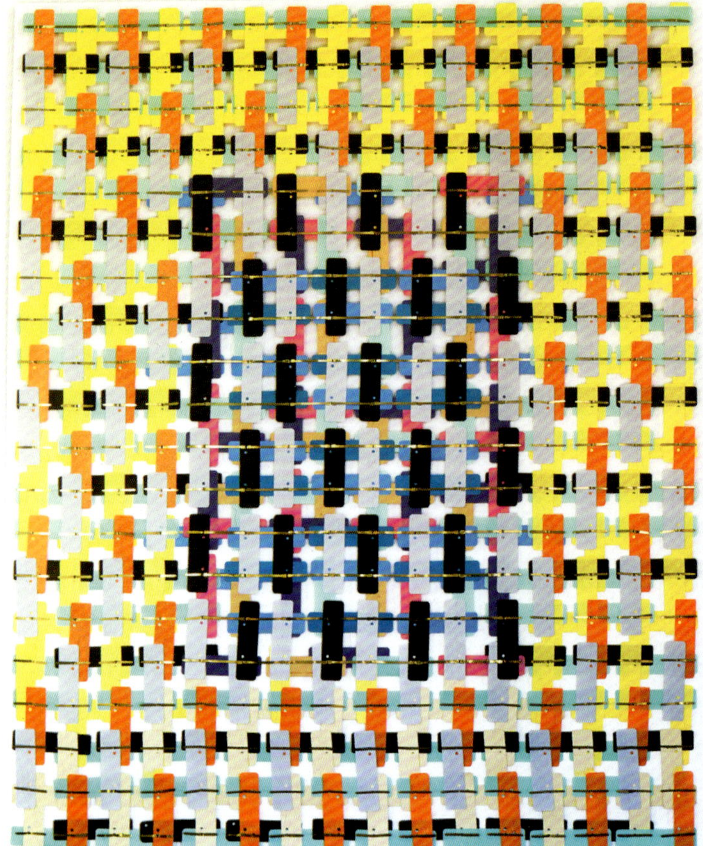

o.T.

2001, Filing strip fasteners, 150 × 180 cm,
Sammlung J.v.d. Ende

It is not so much an inventive look as an exploratory one. How can things be connected, hooked together and inserted? What unnoticed sculptural potential are the objects hiding? It is revealed in the constructions, where (if necessary) some screws, glue, a retracted metal ring, create stability. For others, simple setting, stacking or positioning is enough to initiate

Il s'agit moins d'un regard inventif, mais plutôt d'un regard explorateur. Comment les choses peuvent-elles être reliées, accrochées les unes avec les autres et insérées l'une dans l'autre ? Quel est le potentiel plastique insoupçonnable que cachent les objets ? Il est révélé par la construction, où (si nécessaire) quelques vis, de la colle, une bague métallique facilitent la stabilité. Dans

Es ist weniger ein erfinderischer als vielmehr ein entdeckender Blick. Wie lassen sich die Dinge verbinden, ineinander haken und stecken? Welches noch unbemerkte plastische Potential verbergen die Gegenstände? Es entbirgt sich in den Konstruktionen, denen (wenn es sein muss) einige Schrauben, Klebstoff, ein eingezogener Metallreif zu Stabilität verhelfen. Anderen genügt

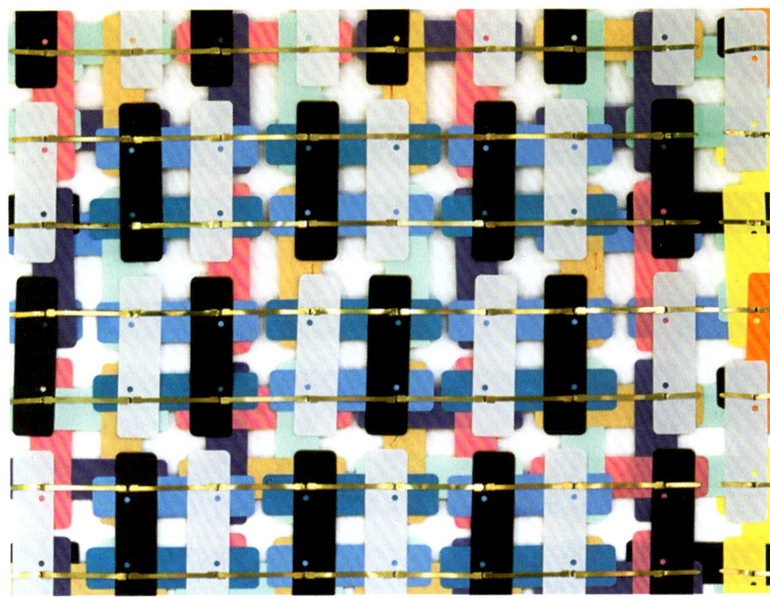

No es tanto una mirada inventiva como descubridora. ¿Cómo pueden conectarse, engancharse e insertarse las cosas? ¿Qué potencial plástico inadvertido ocultan los objetos? Este se revela en las construcciones, donde (si es necesario) se emplean algunos tornillos, pegamento, o un anillo metálico retraído para estabilizar. Para otros, un simple ajuste, apilamiento o colocación es suficiente

Non si tratta tanto di uno sguardo inventivo, quanto piuttosto di uno esplorativo. Come collegare, agganciare e inserire le cose tra di loro? Quale potenziale plastico si cela inosservato dentro di loro? Esso si rivela nelle costruzioni, dove (se necessario) alcune viti, il collante, un anello di metallo ritratto danno stabilità. In altri casi, un semplice inserimento, accatastamento o

Het is niet zozeer een inventieve als wel een verkennende blik. Hoe kunnen dingen met elkaar worden verbonden, in elkaar worden geklemd en gestoken? Wat zijn de onzichtbare plastische mogelijkheden van voorwerpen? Ze worden onthuld in de constructies, waar (indien nodig) enkele schroeven, lijm, een ingeschoven metalen ring stabiliteit verlenen. Bij andere is het

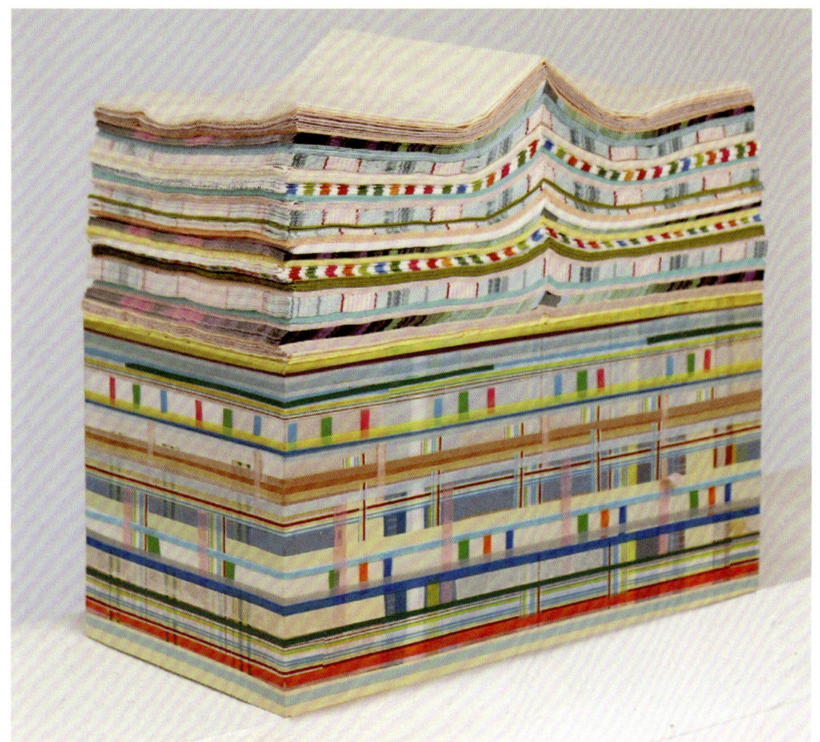

transformations and eye-opening alienation.

Tina Haase's works are the simple things that are difficult to do. But when they are there, it couldn't be any other way, because they show: nothing has to be the way it is, everything is full of alternative possibilities. With ease they create openings and through them something of the "back of things" can be envisaged.

d'autres cas, une simple mise en place, un empilage ou une autre disposition suffisent à initier la métamorphose et l'aliénation révélatrice.

Les œuvres de Tina Haase matérialisent la simplicité, celle qui est difficile à réaliser. Mais dès qu'elles sont là, on se rend bien compte qu'il ne peut plus en être autrement, alors elles nous montrent que : rien ne doit être tel qu'on le connaît, tout est ressource à une infinité de possibilités. Avec une facilité déconcertante, elles nous ouvre de nouvelles perspectives et nous laisse deviner un peu du « dos des choses ».

einfaches Setzen, Stapeln oder Stellen, um Verwandlungen und augenöffnendes Befremden in Gang zu setzen.

Die Arbeiten von Tina Haase sind das Einfache, das schwer zu machen ist. Wenn sie aber da sind, konnte es gar nicht anders kommen, dann zeigen sie: Nichts muss so sein wie es ist, alles steckt voll anderer Möglichkeiten. Mit Leichtigkeit schaffen sie Öffnungen und durch sie ist etwas vom „Rücken der Dinge" zu ahnen.

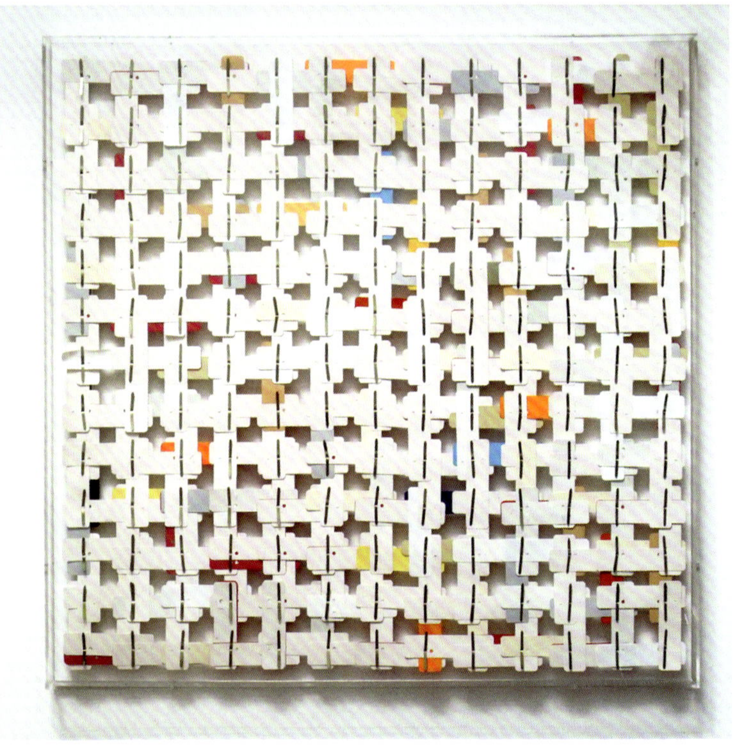

o.T.

2003, MDF, filing strip fasteners, 90 × 90 × 3 cm,
Private collection

para iniciar transformaciones y una extrañeza que abre los ojos.

Los trabajos de Tina Haase convierten en sencillo lo que es difícil de hacer. Pero una vez allí, no pudo ser de otra manera, entonces estos se muestran: nada tiene que ser como es, todo está lleno de otras posibilidades. Con facilidad crean aperturas y a través de ellas se puede sospechar algo del "dorso de las cosas".

posizionamento è sufficiente per mettere in moto trasformazioni e alienazioni che aprono gli occhi.

Il lavoro di Tina Haase consiste di cose semplici difficili da realizzare. Ma nel momento in cui vengono create, diventano ineluttabili poiché dimostrano che nulla deve essere per forza ciò che è, ogni cosa è ricca di possibilità alternative. Con leggerezza si creano aperture e attraverso di loro si lascia intravedere il "dorso delle cose".

eenvoudigweg neerzetten, stapelen of plaatsen voldoende om transformaties en ogen openende vervreemding in gang te zetten.

Het werk van Tina Haase is het eenvoudige dat moeilijk te maken is. Maar als de werken er eenmaal zijn, was dat de enige manier, omdat ze laten zien: niets hoeft te zijn zoals het is, alles zit vol andere mogelijkheden. Met gemak creëren ze openingen en door die openingen laat zich iets van de 'rug van de dingen' vermoeden.

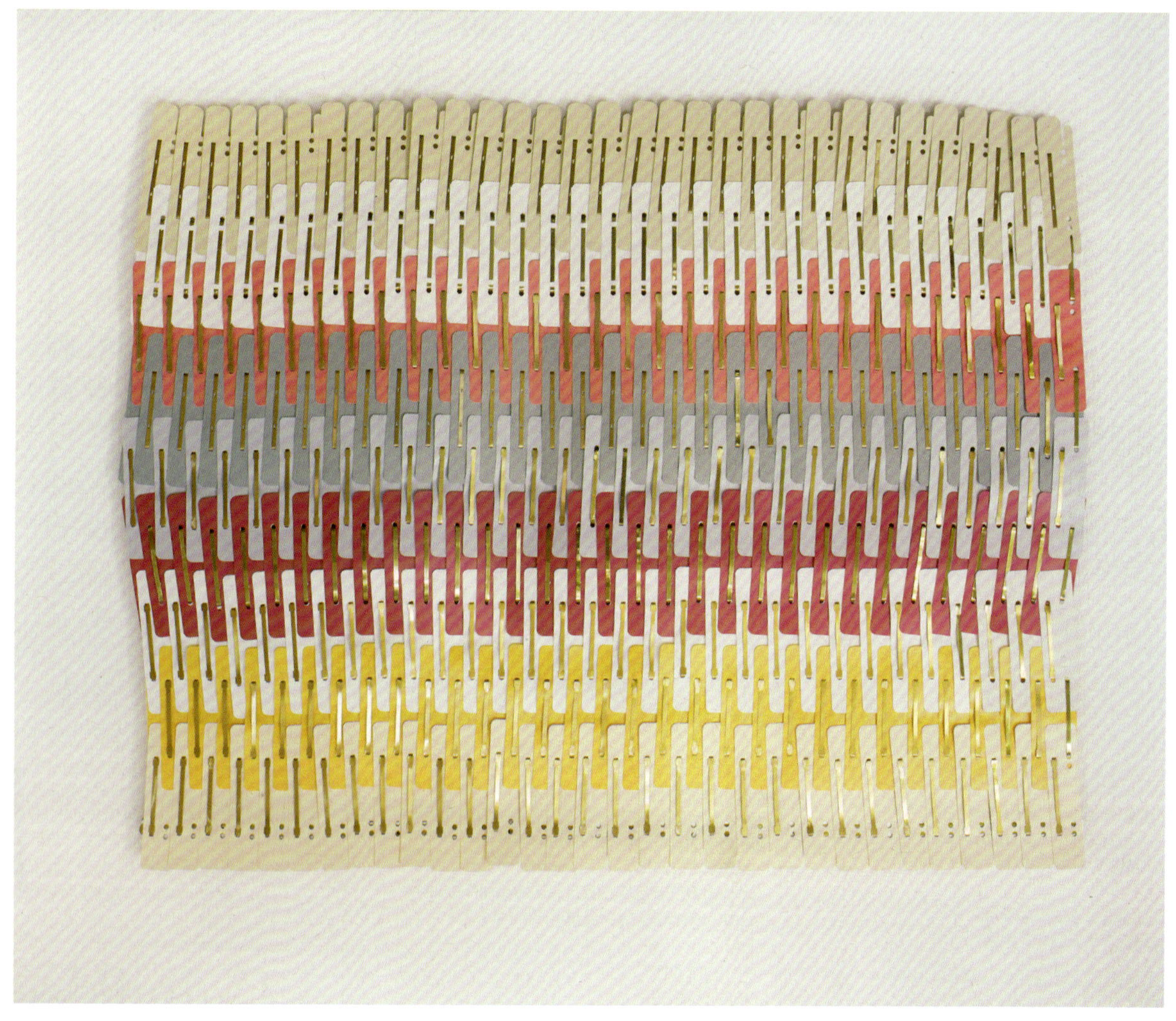

Heftstreifenweise

2002, Filing strip fasteners, 70 × 100 cm, Private collection

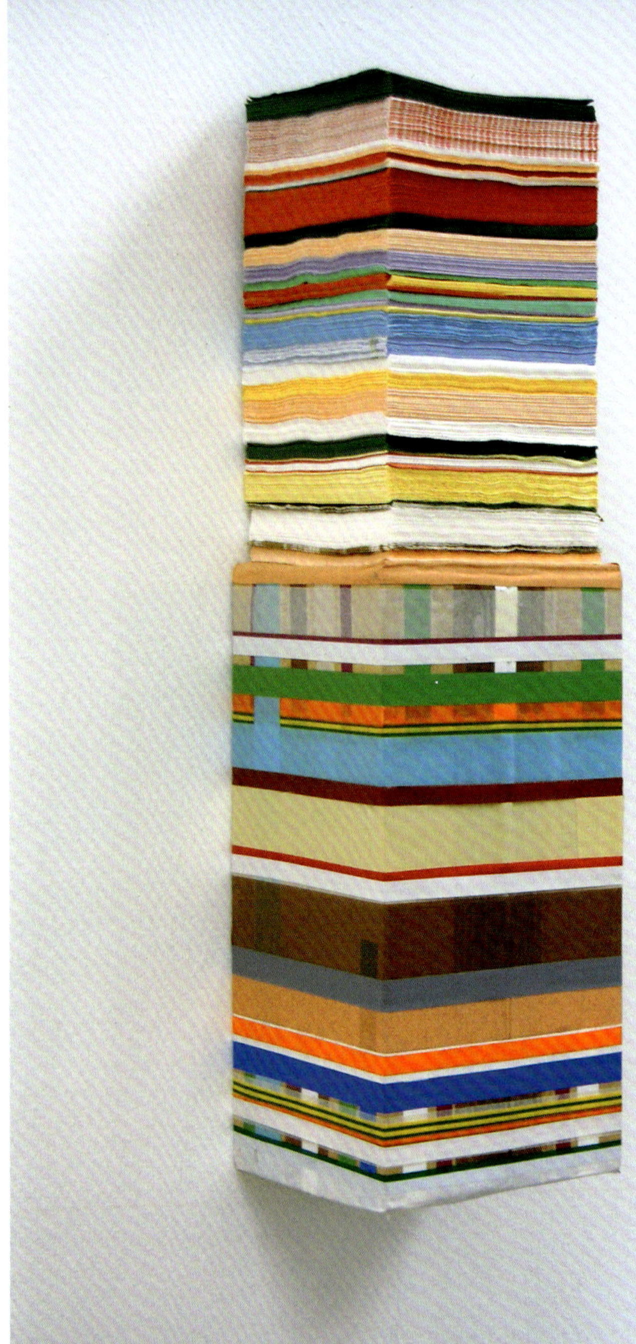

o.T.

2005, Cardboard, adhesive strips, napkins,
52 × 18 × 18 cm

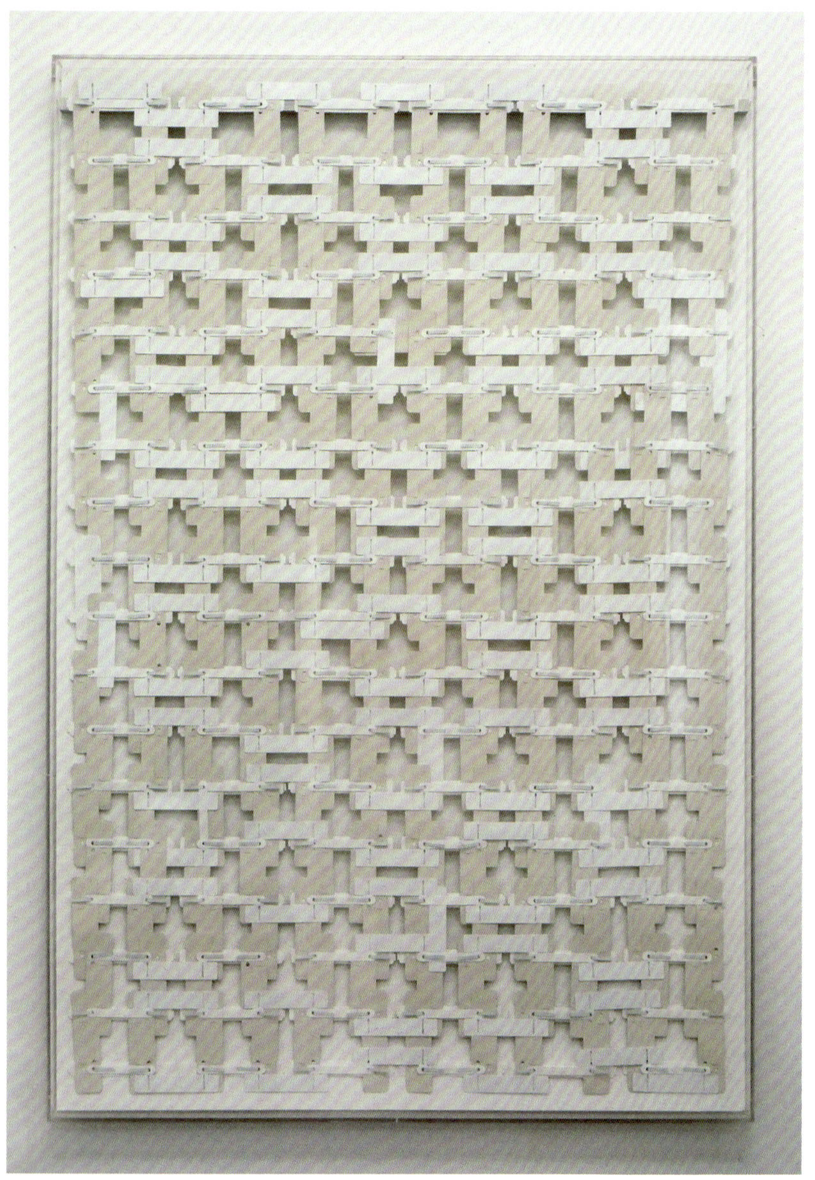

o.T.

*2009, MDF, filing strip fasteners,
165 × 85 × 3 cm, Courtesy Ulrich Mueller*

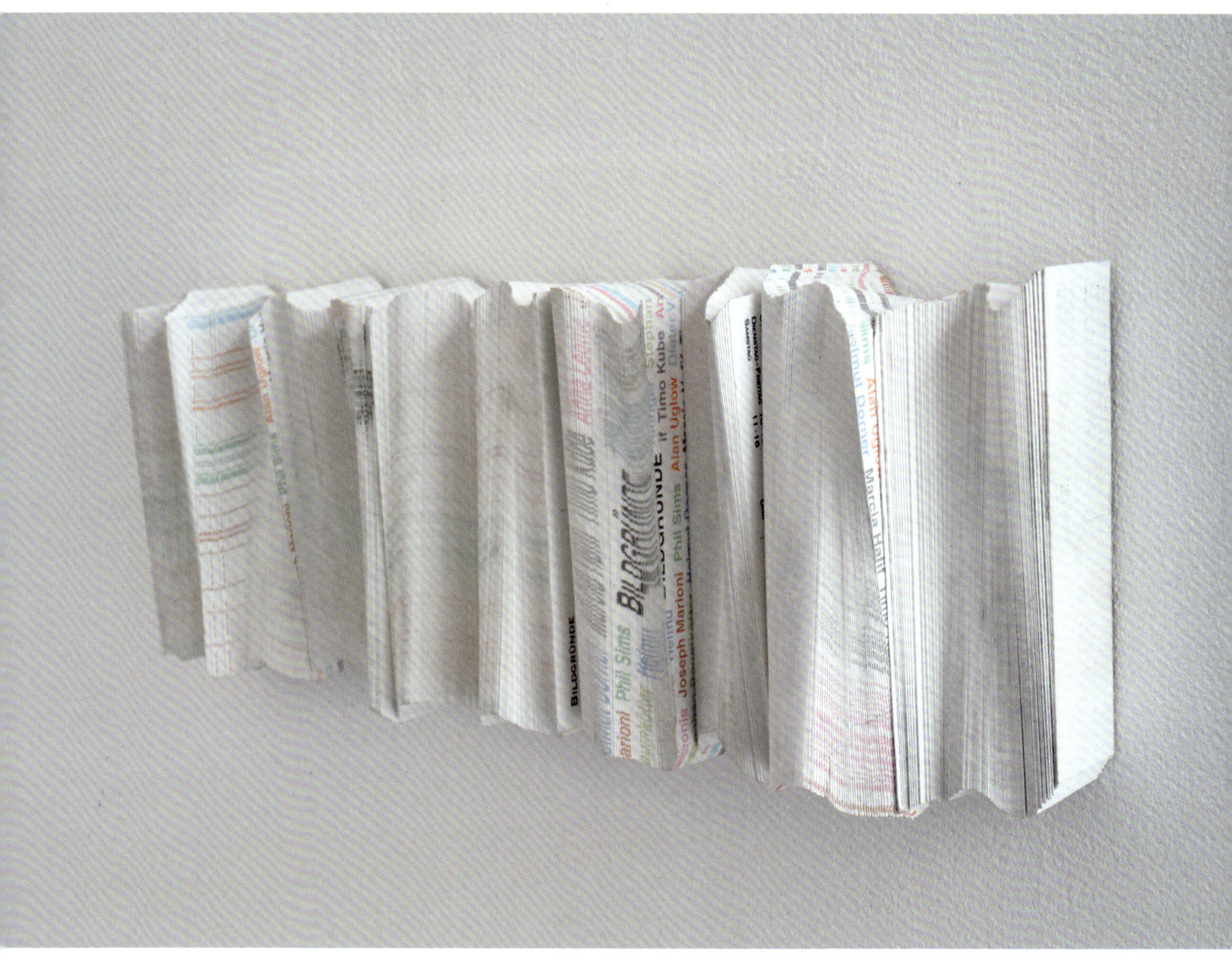

Bildgründe

2013, Cardboard, 20 × 32 × 12 cm, Private collection

o.T.

2015, Filing strip fasteners, 105 × 105 × 3 cm, Sammlung Joop v.d. Enden

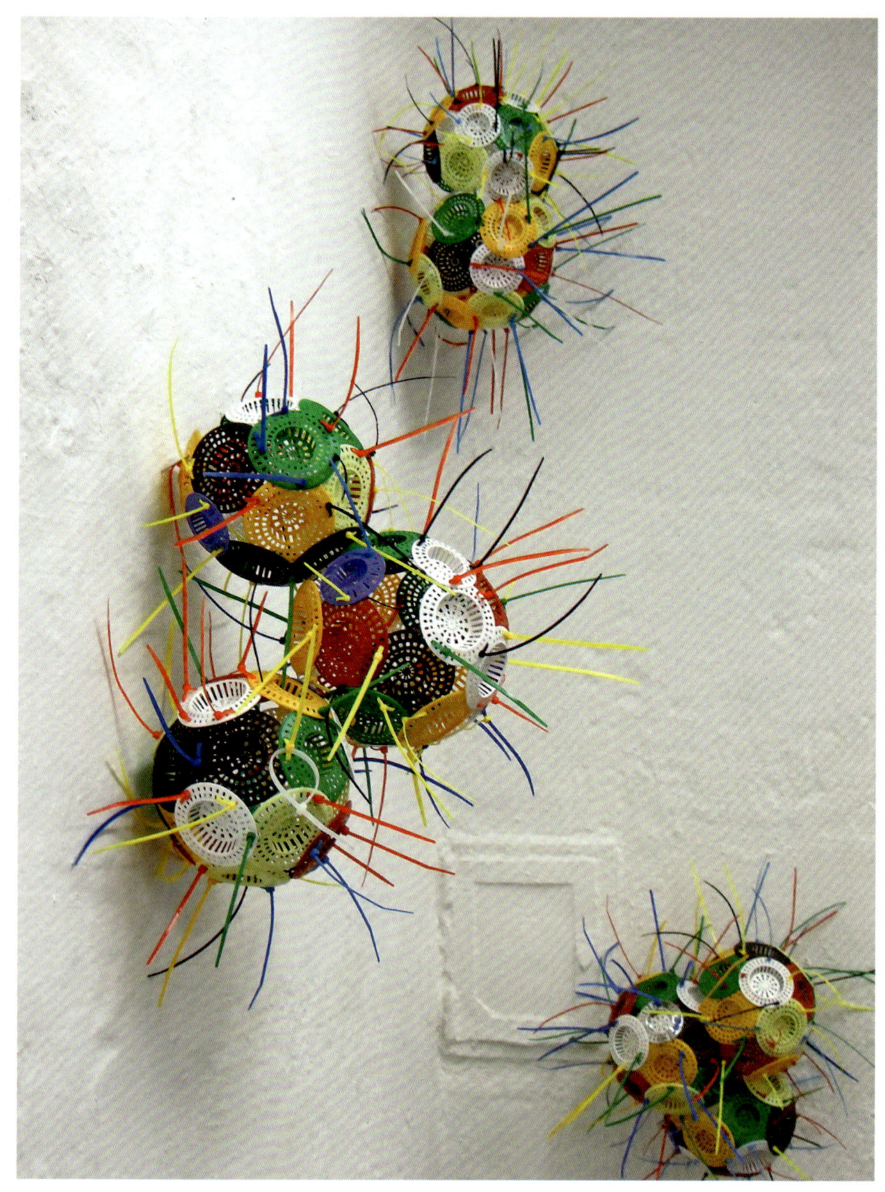

Virus

2008, Plastic

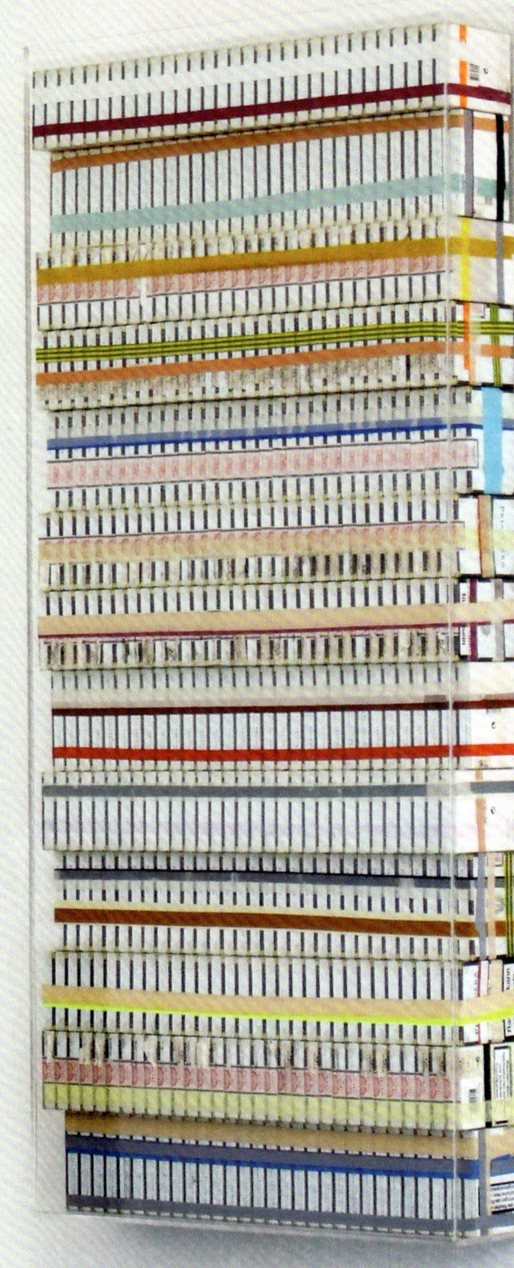

Prima Vera

2008, Cardboard, adhesive tape, acrylic glass,
152 × 60 × 9 cm, Private collection

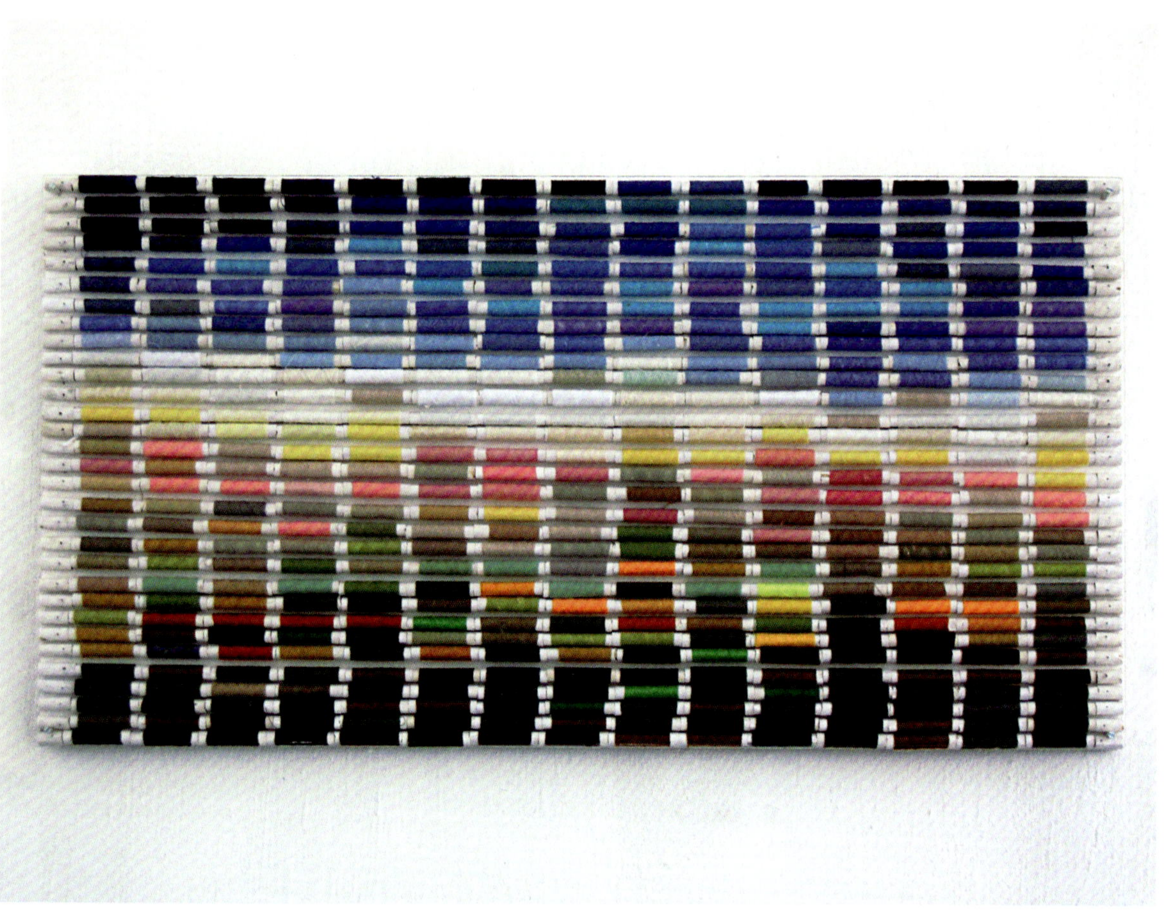

Gütermann

2005, Thread rolls, wood, acrylic glass, 38 × 58 × 2 cm

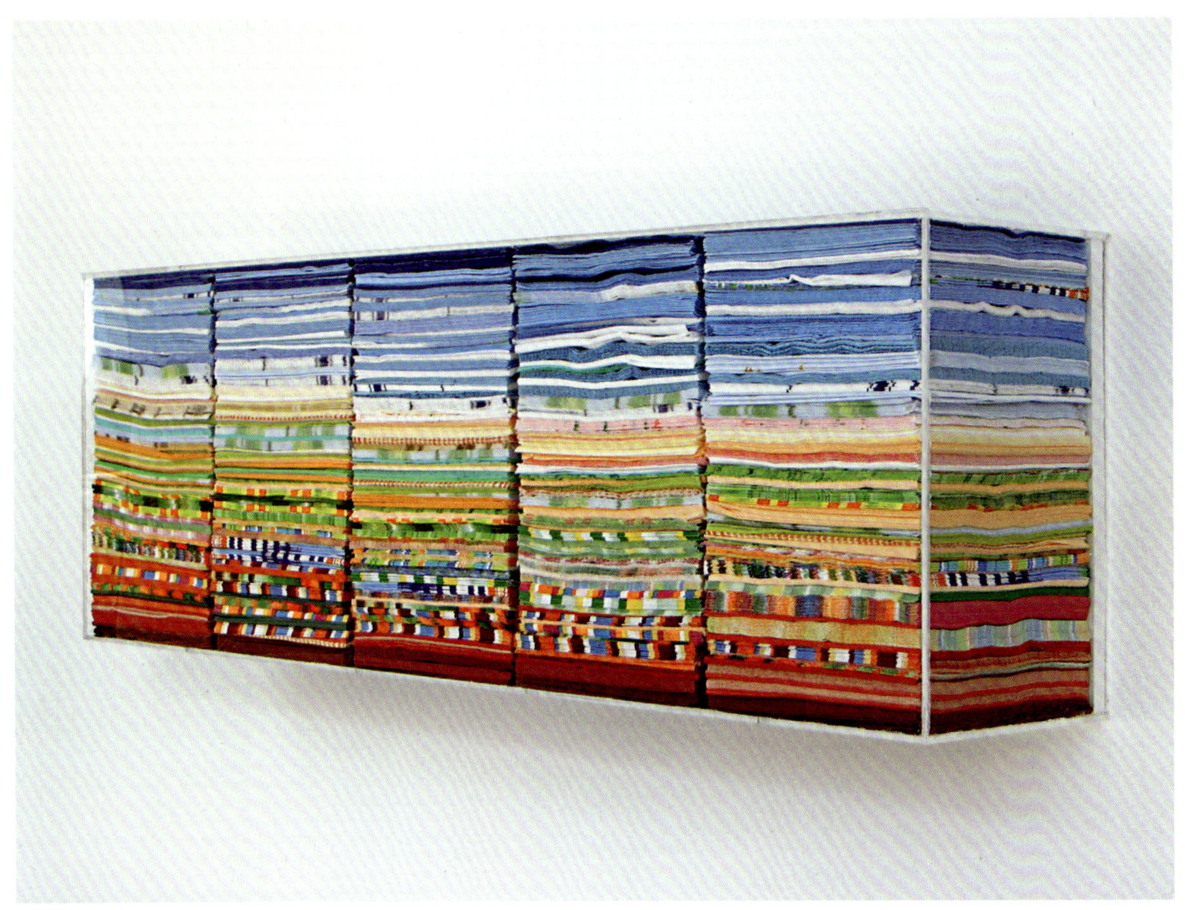

Worpswede

2005, Napkins, acrylic glass, 30 × 87 × 20 cm

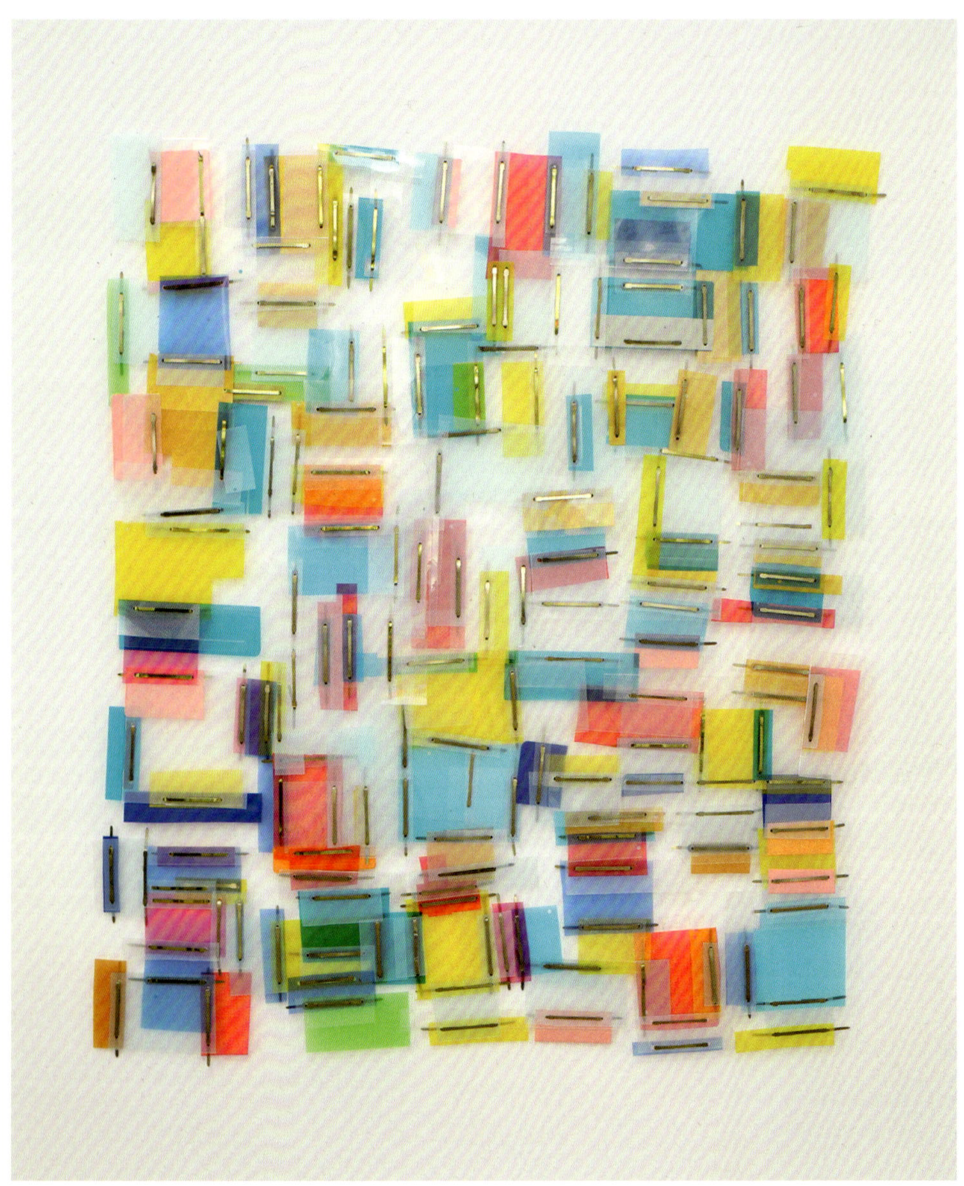

o.T.

2010, Plastic, metal,
120 × 78 cm

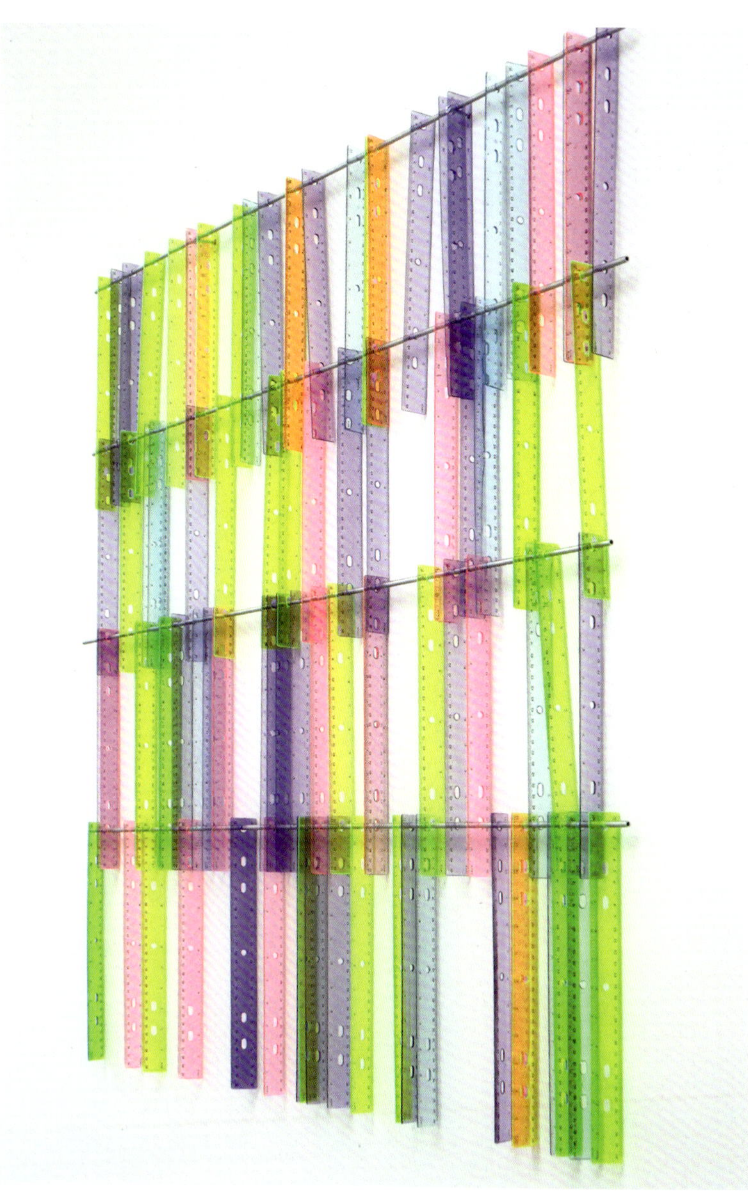

Zwischenmaß

2010, Plastic, aluminium, 115 × 95 × 3 cm

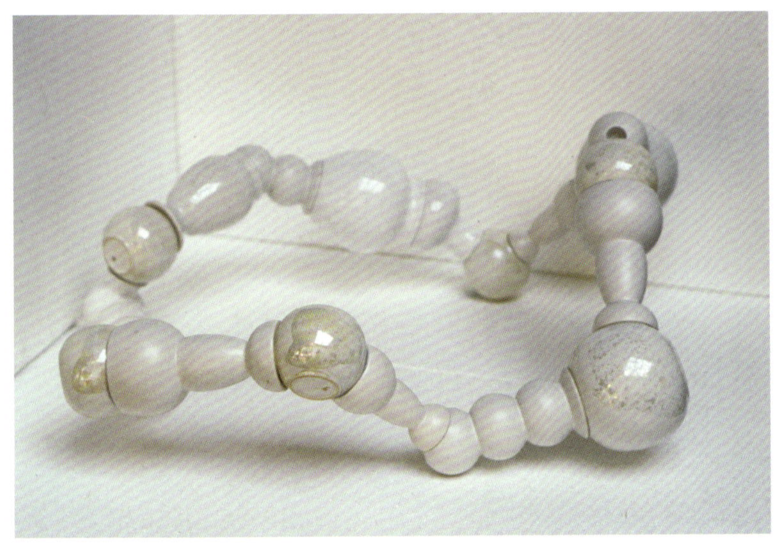

o.T.

2002, Porcelain, ceramics, silicone, 22 × 85 cm

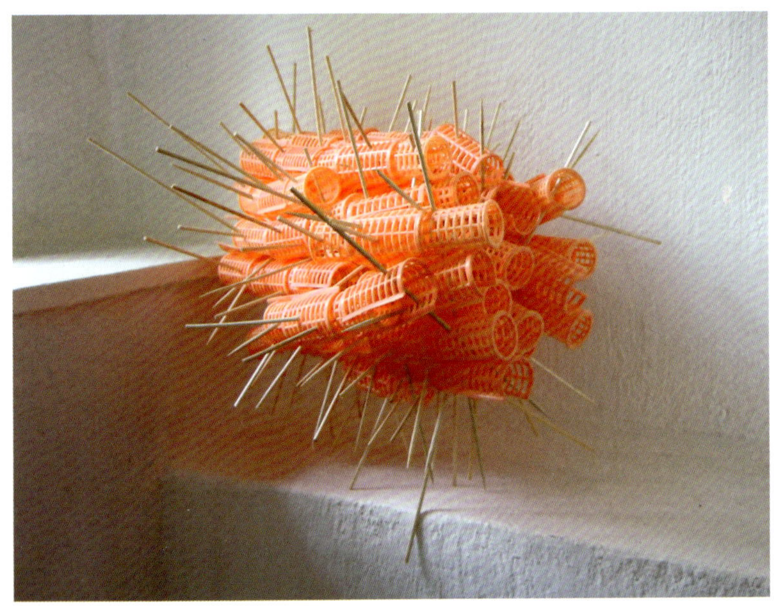

Stachelschwein

2007, Plastic, wood, 36 × 26 cm, Private collection
Courtesy Galerie Ulrich Mueller

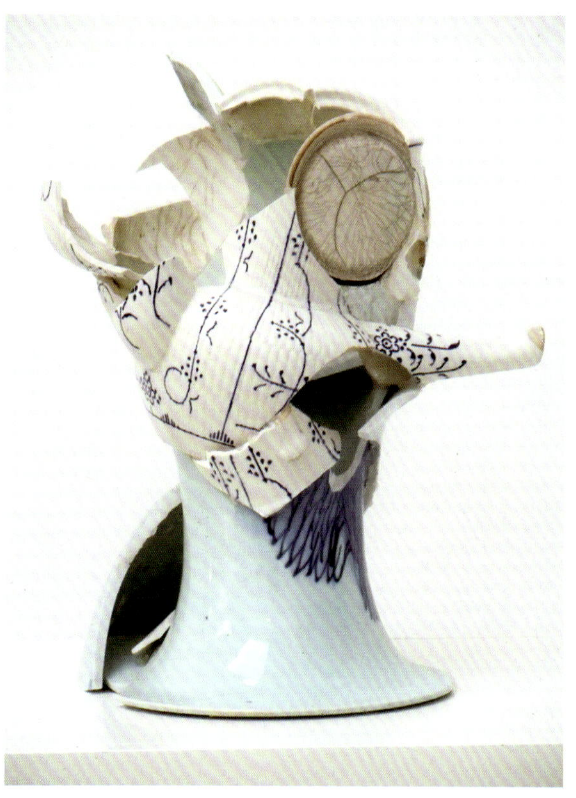

Picassos Aussteuer

2007, Porcelain, ceramics, silicone, 29 × 28 cm, Private collection Courtesy Galerie Ulrich Mueller

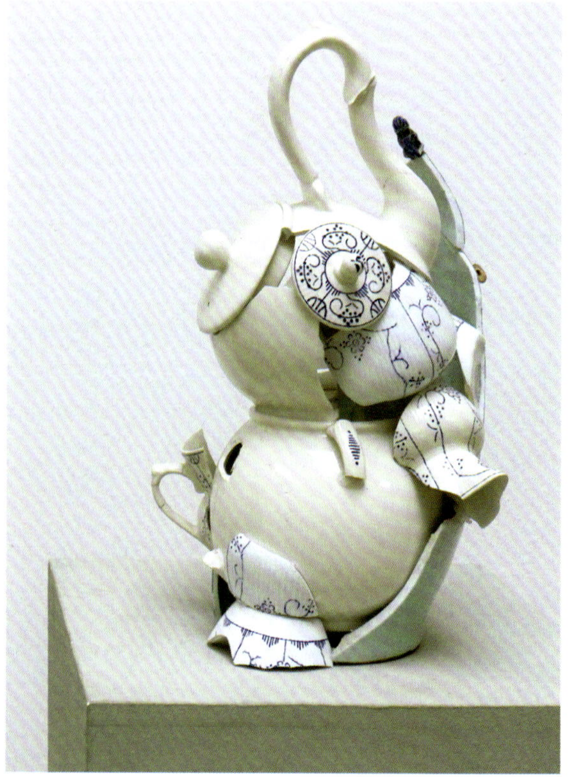

Schwanenburger Nymphe

2013, Porcelain, ceramics, silicone, 36 × 30 cm

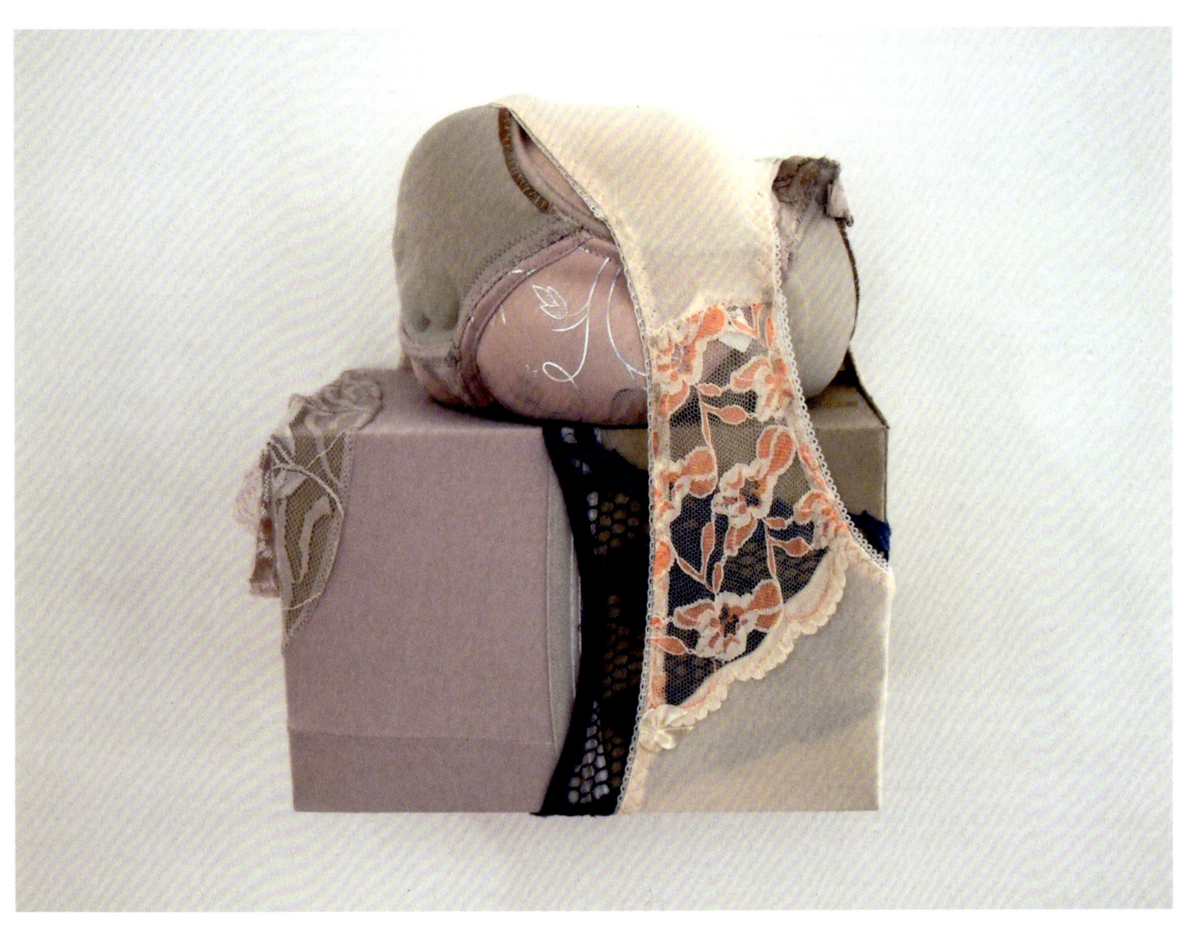

zunächst sachlich

2007, Textiles, cardboard, cotton wool, 28 × 28 × 20 cm

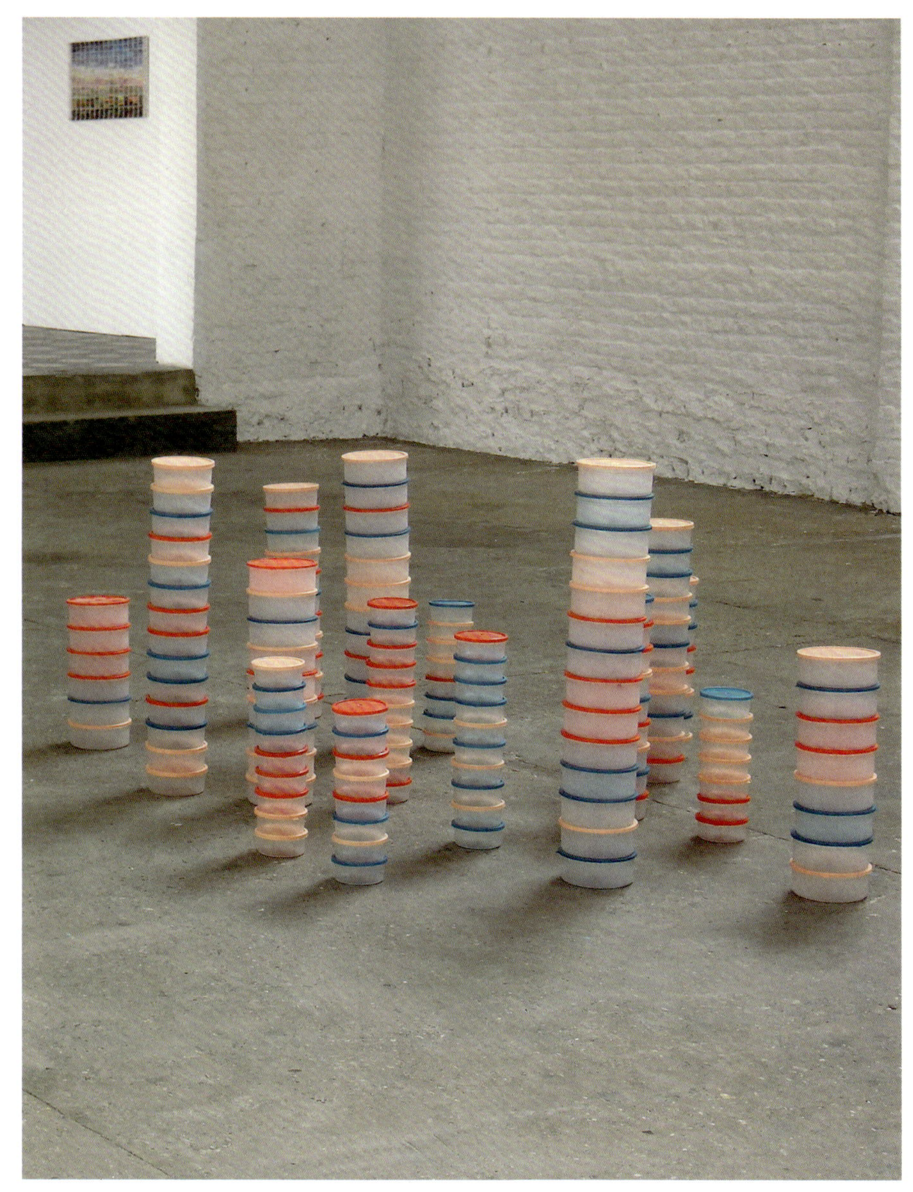

Der geringste Widerstand

2002, Plastic, 80 × 180 × 160 cm

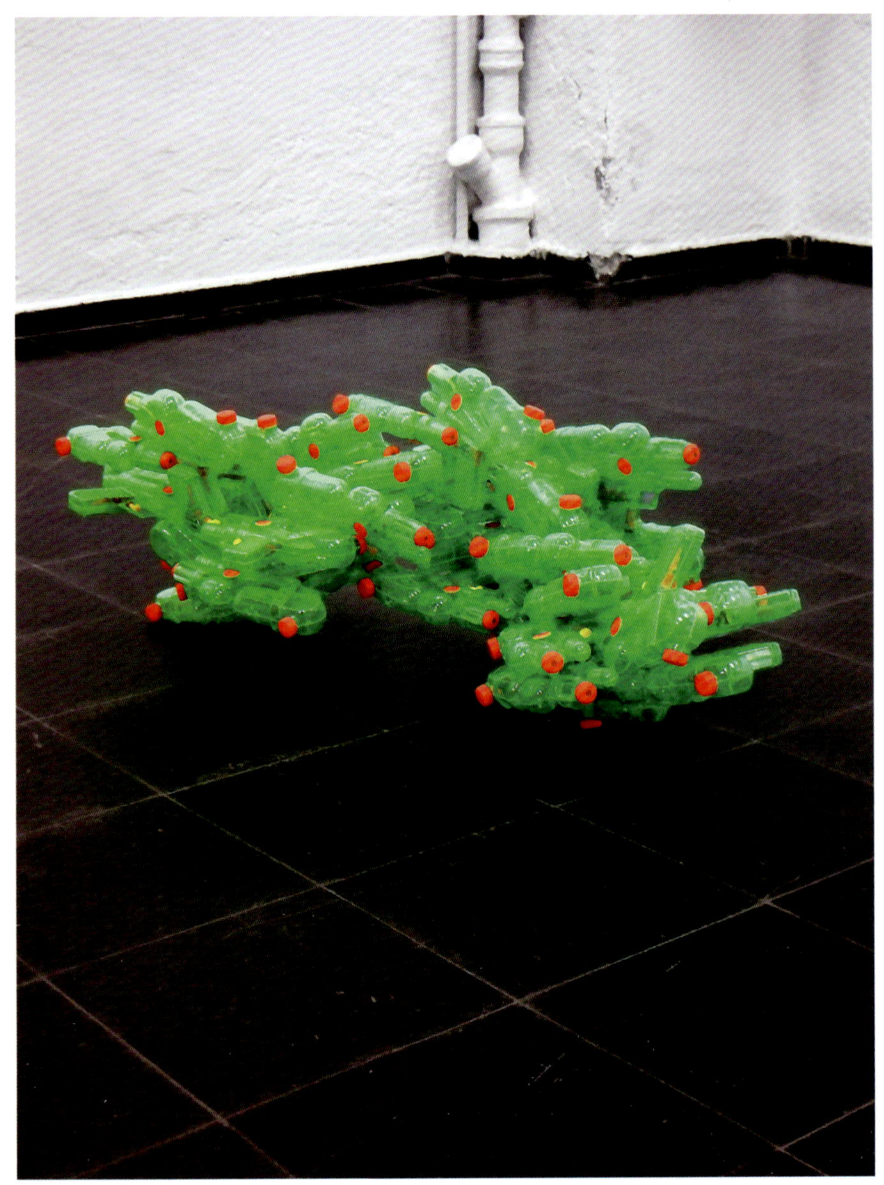

Shootingstar 2

2007, Plastic, glued, 40 × 110 × 40 cm,
Private collection

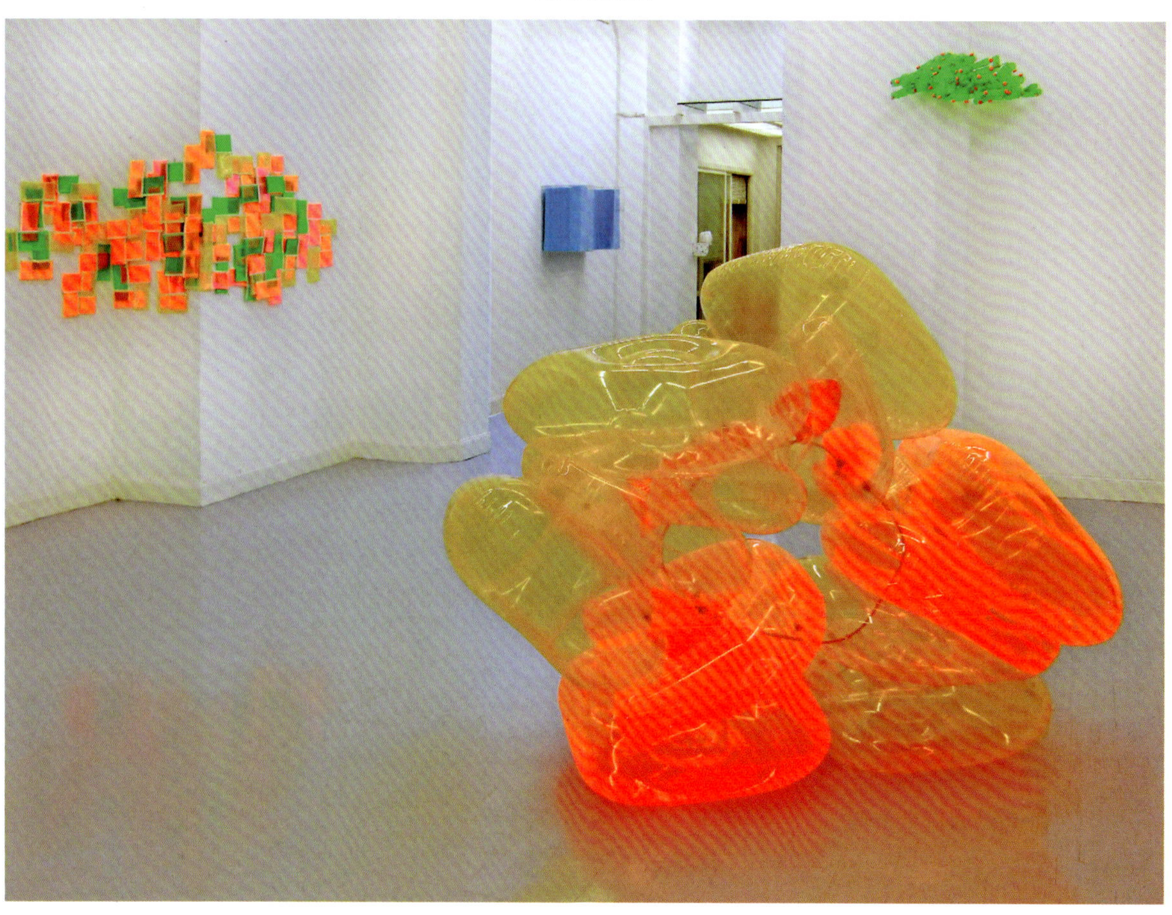

Mäppchenarbeit

2006, Plastic

Holiday Sculpture

2006, Plastic

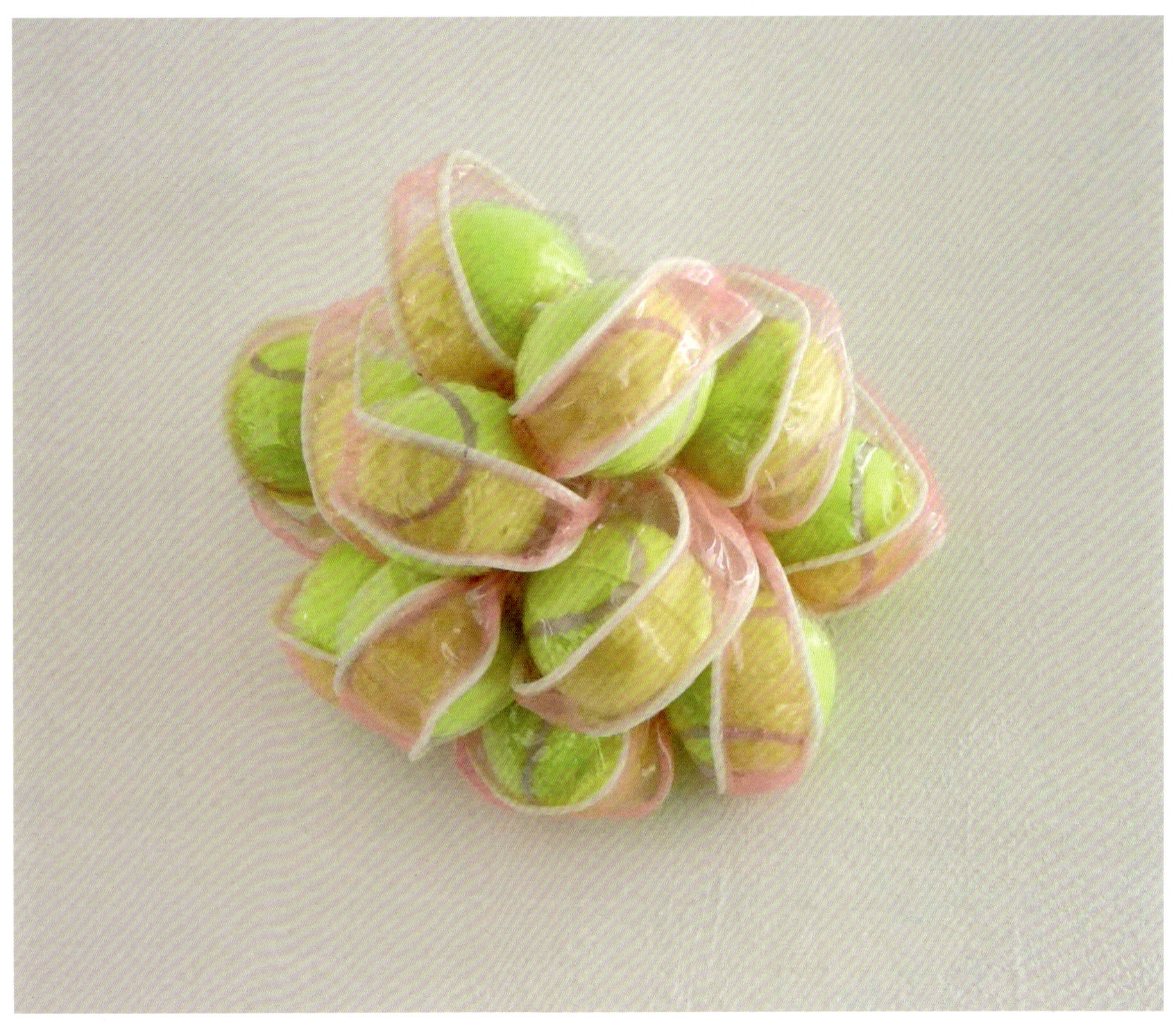

Seifenblick

2007, PVC, tennis balls

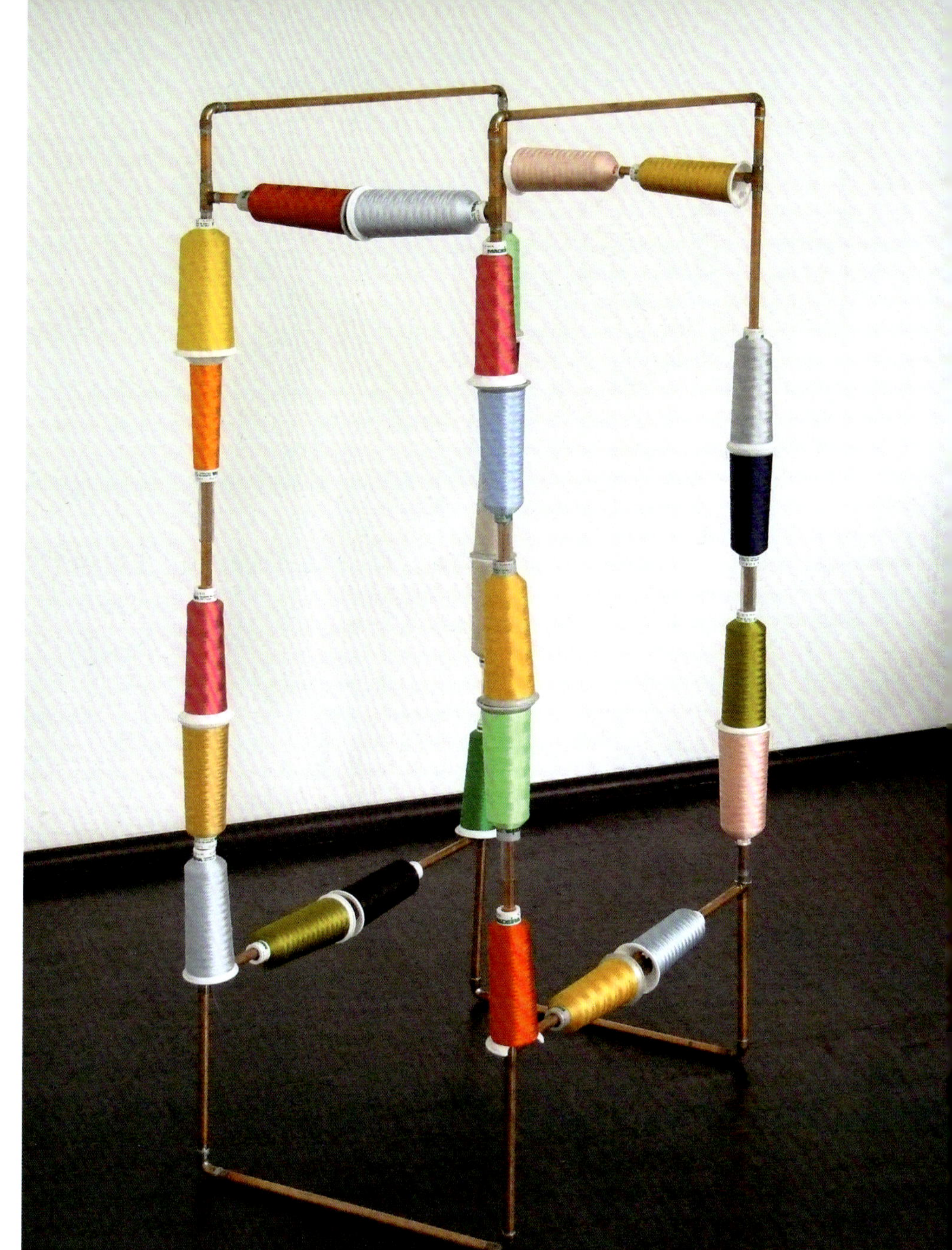

Alltagsmunition

2008, Thread reels, copper,
plastic, 130 × 45 × 67 cm

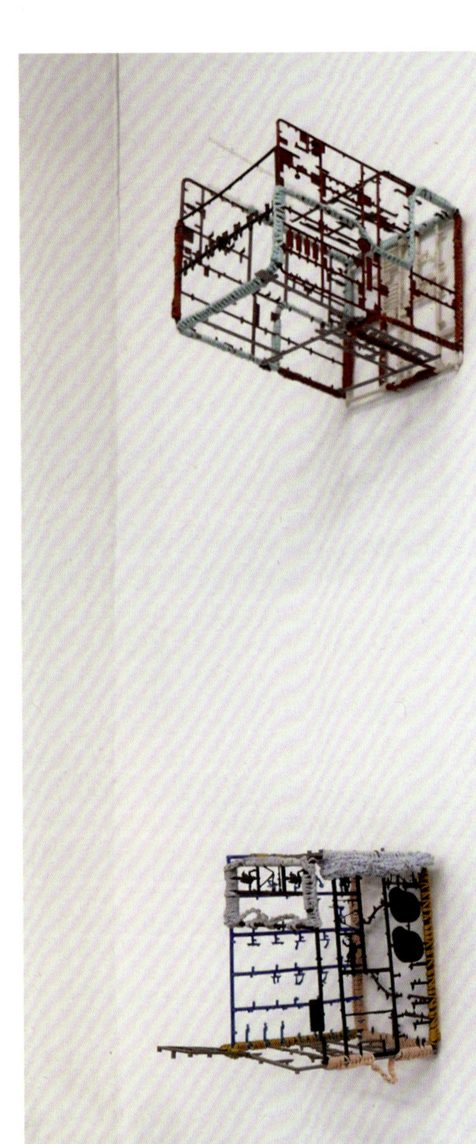
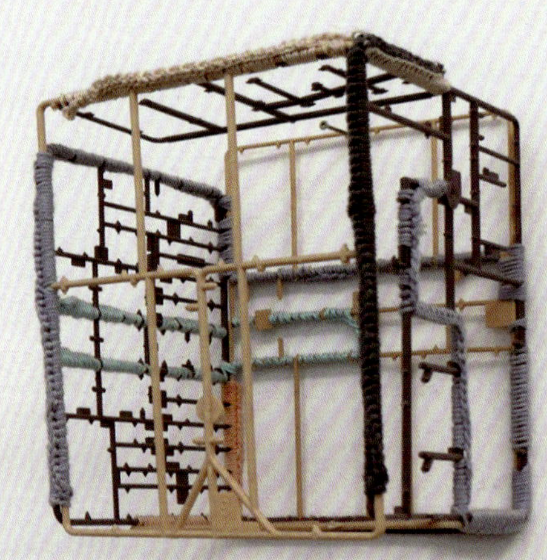

Aus der Serie der
Wendestücke
(ADSDW)

2001–2005, Plastic,
cotton

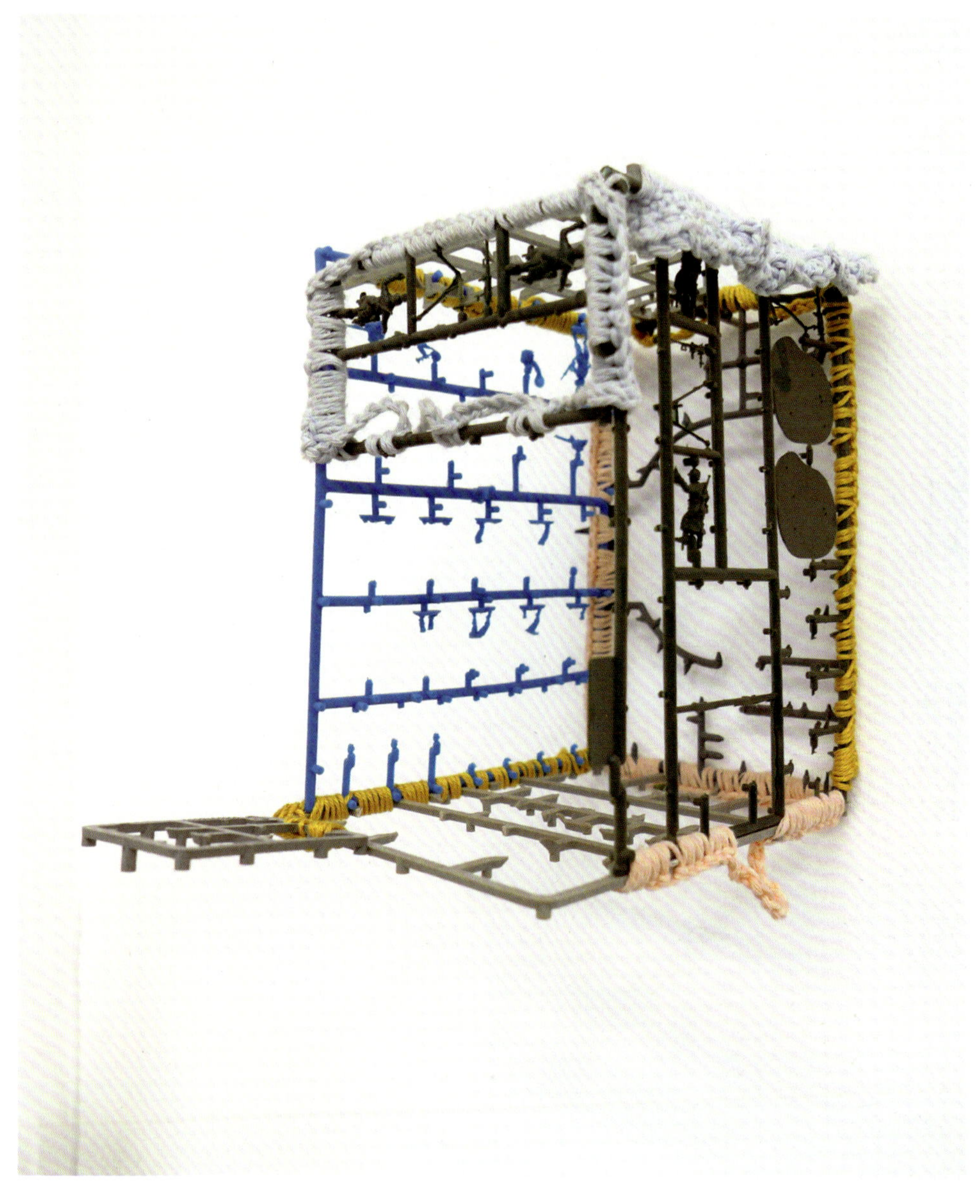

2005, Plastic, cotton,
18 × 12 × 10 cm

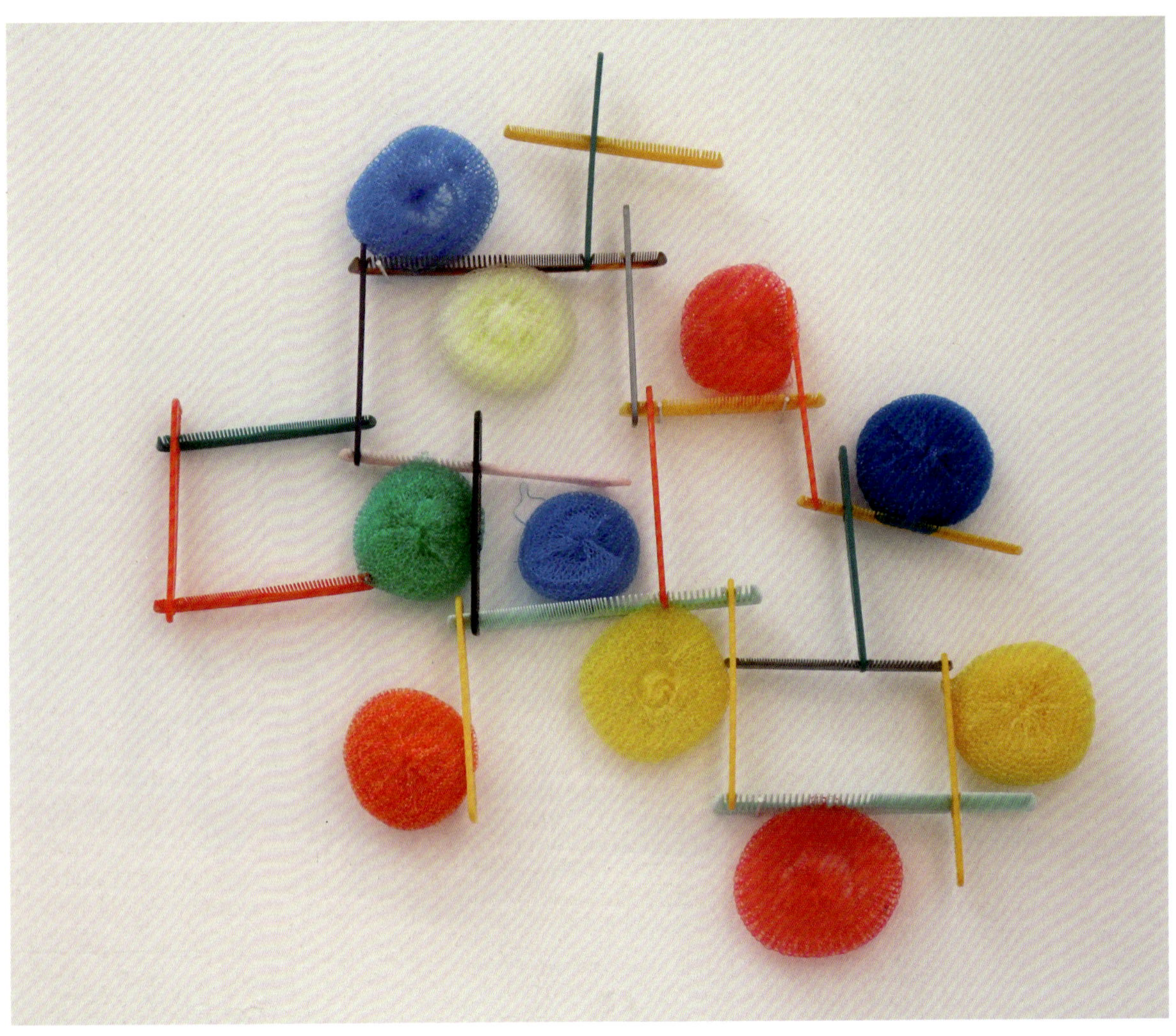

Kämme und Schwämme

2004, Plastic, 55 × 55 × 5 cm

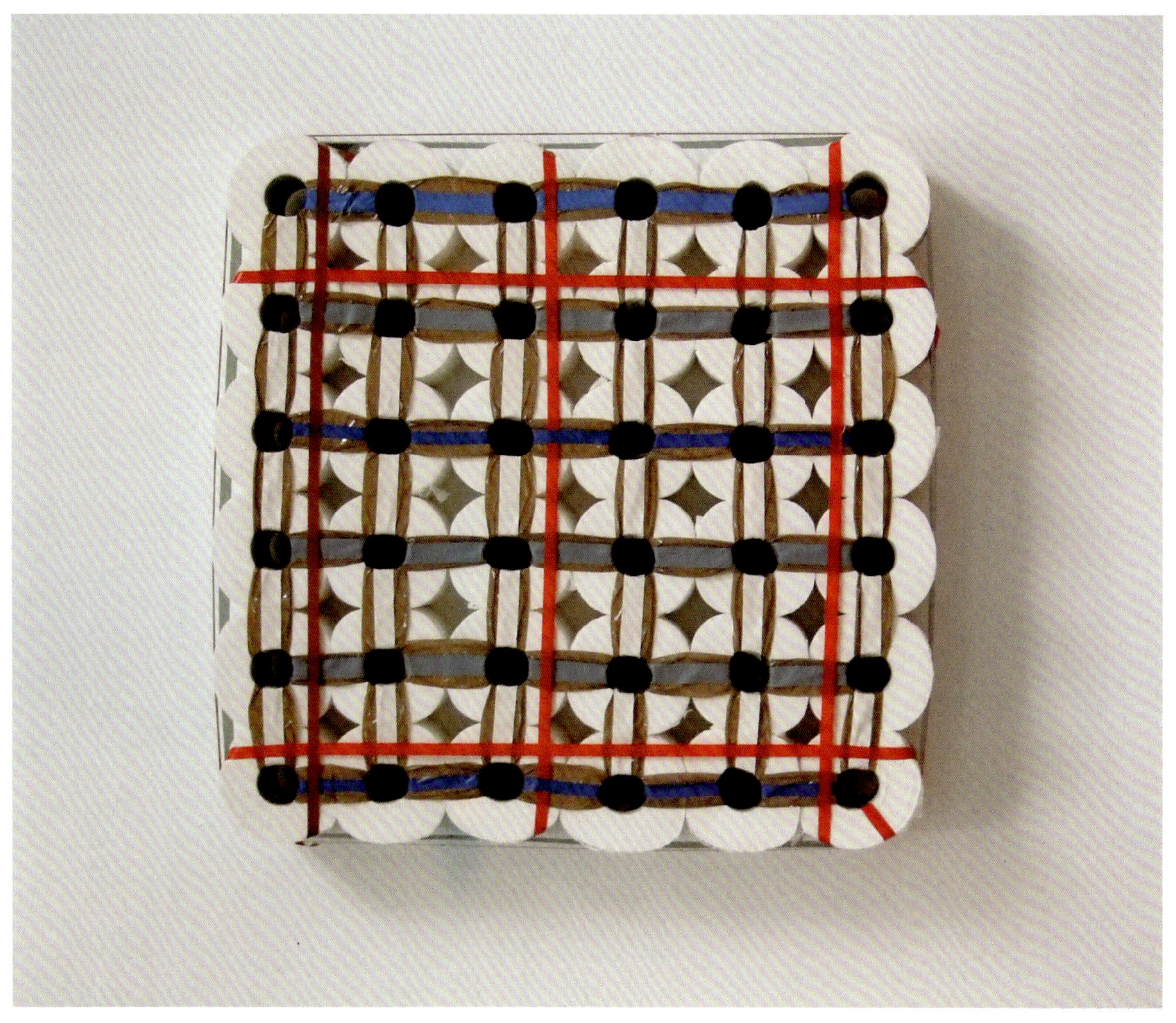

o.T.

2004, Toilet paper, adhesive tape, 100 × 100 × 12 cm

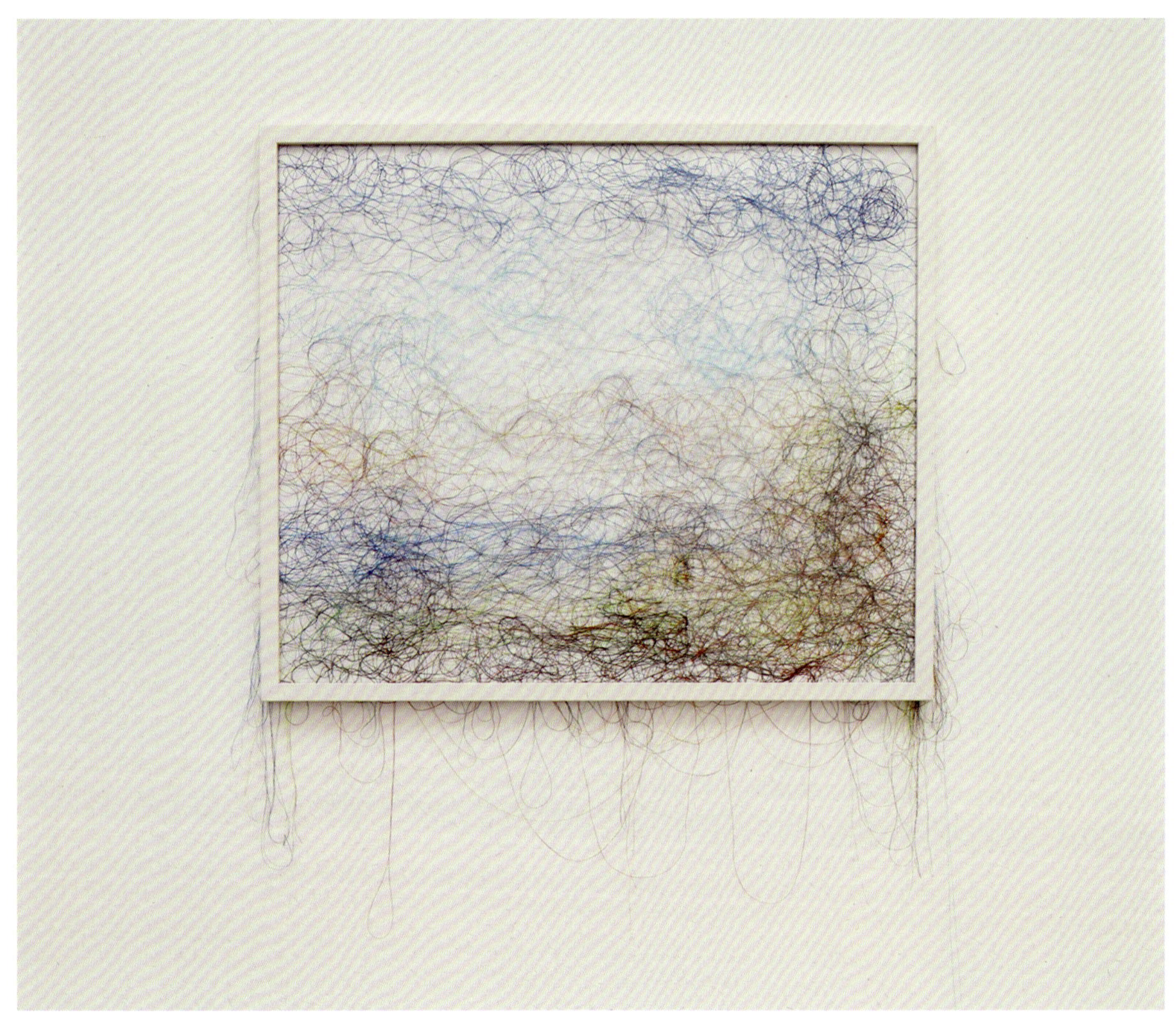

Landliebe

2009, Picture frame, yarn, 80 × 70 cm, Private collection

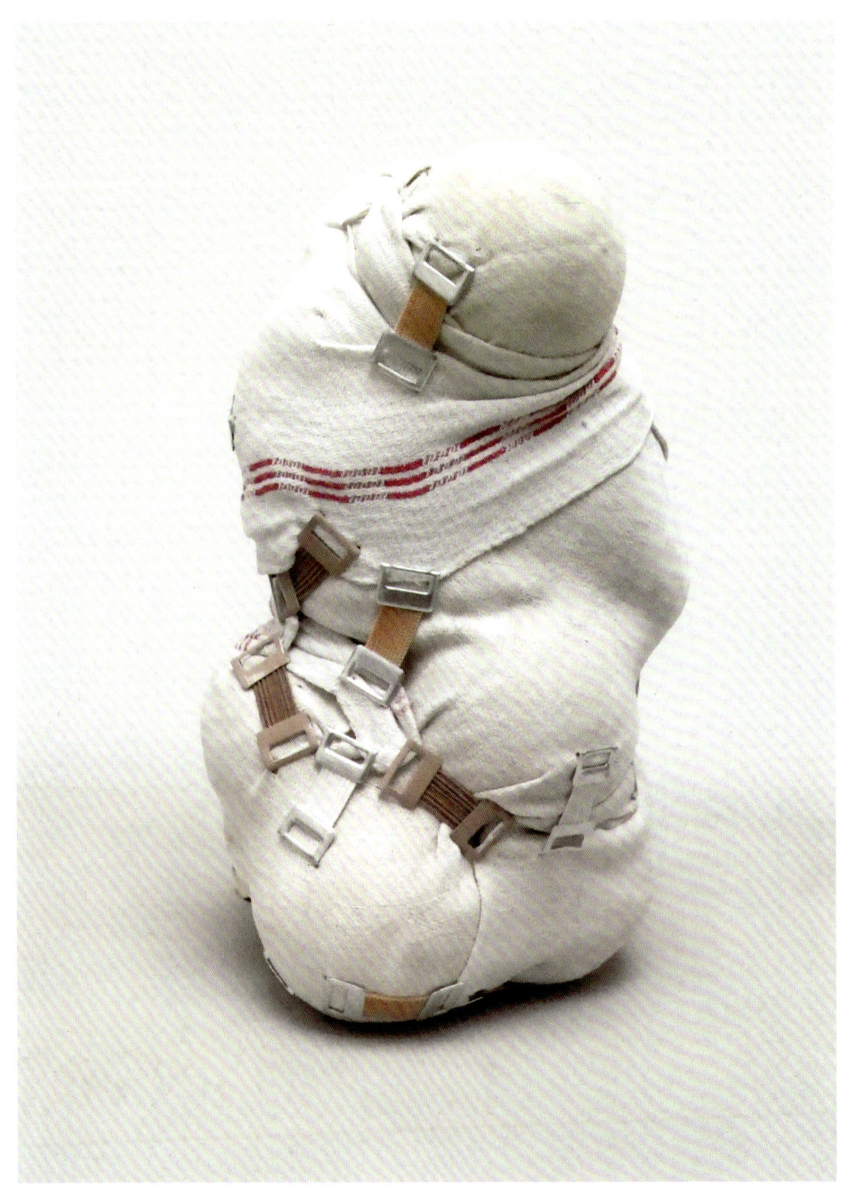

Schwiegermutter

2007, Textiles, elastic clips, 25 × 13 × 13 cm

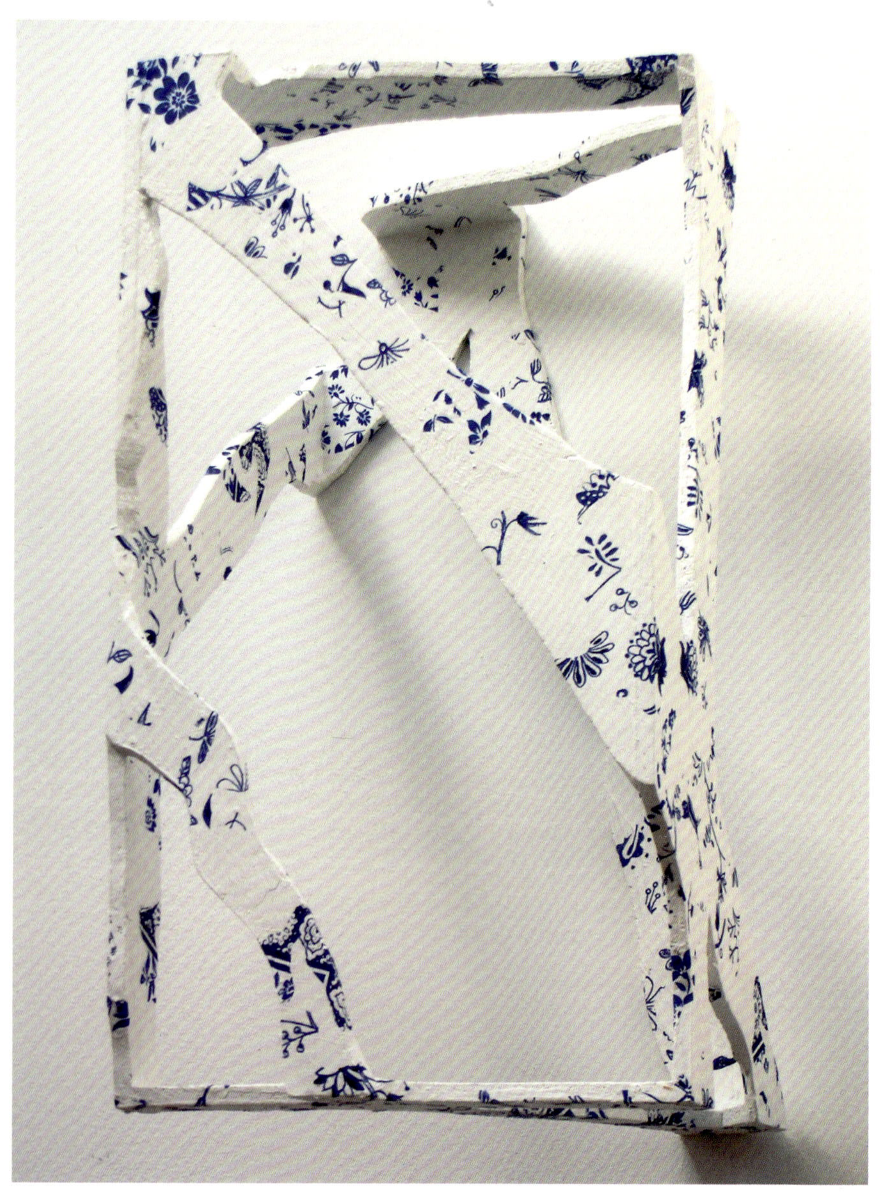

Delfter Gefühl

2008, MDF, mixed media,
62 × 25 × 25 cm

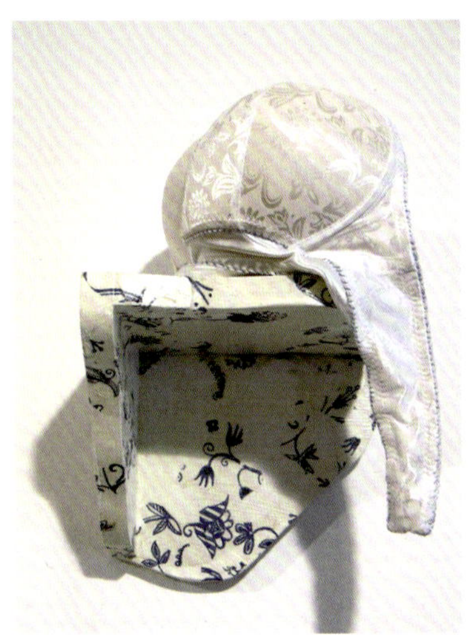

Delfter BHs 1

2006, MDF, mixed media

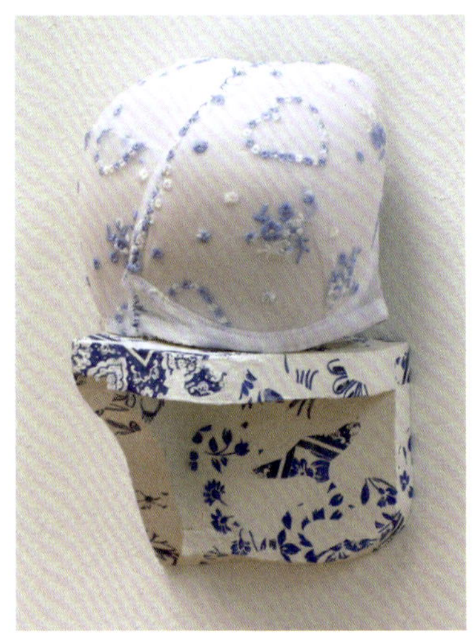

Delfter BHs 2

2006, MDF, mixed media

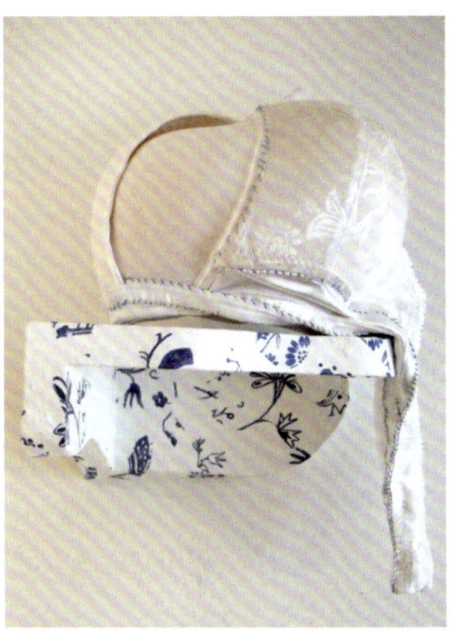

Delfter BHs 3

2006, MDF, mixed media

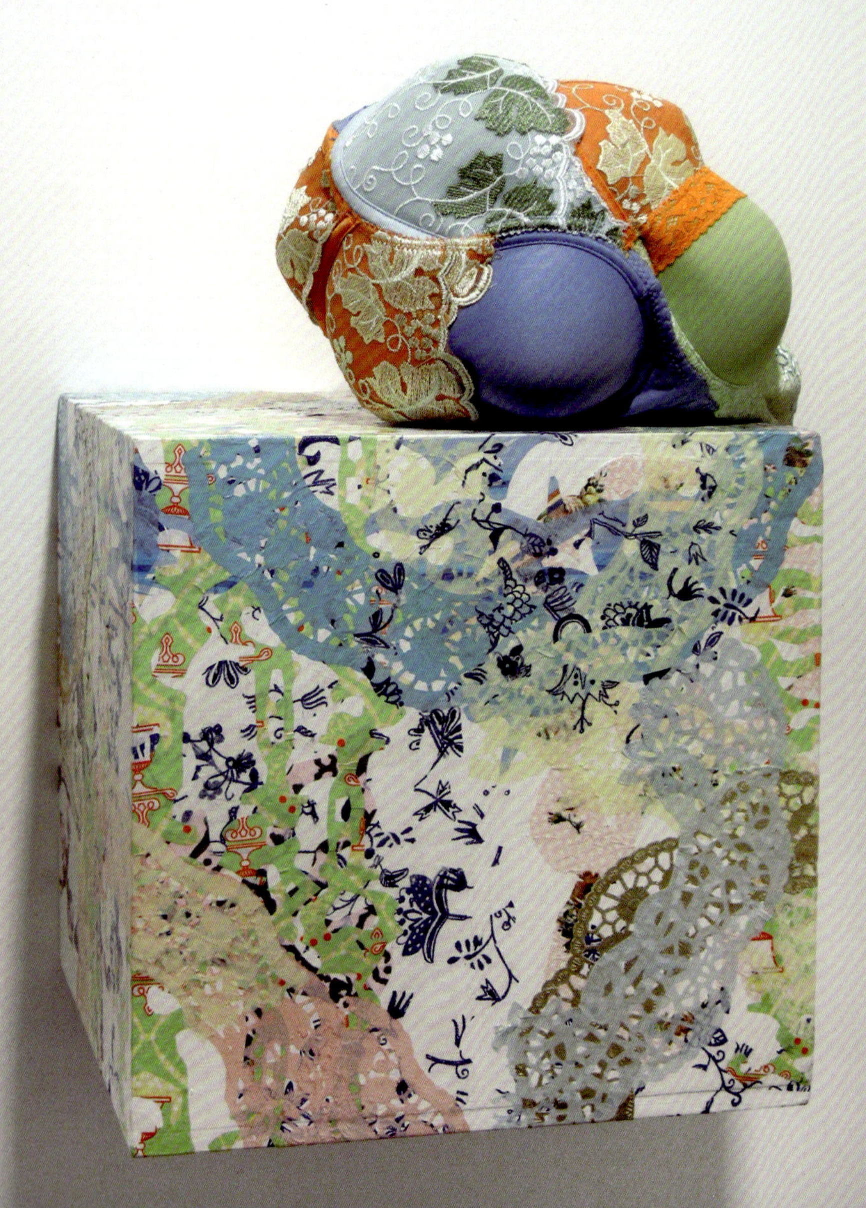

Spitzenteil

*2006, MDF, textiles, cotton
wool, 48 × 35 × 35 cm,
Private collection*

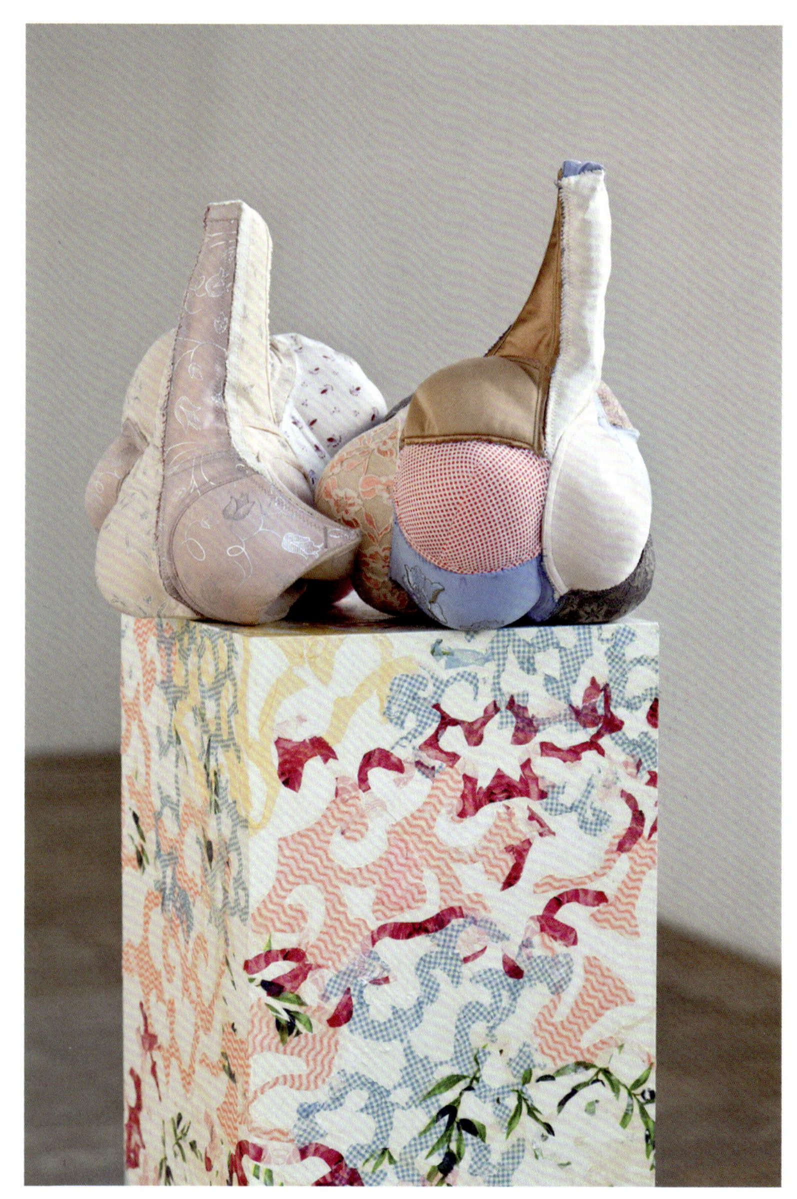

2 AKWs

2011, MDF, mixed media, textiles, cotton wool,
120 × 40 × 40 cm

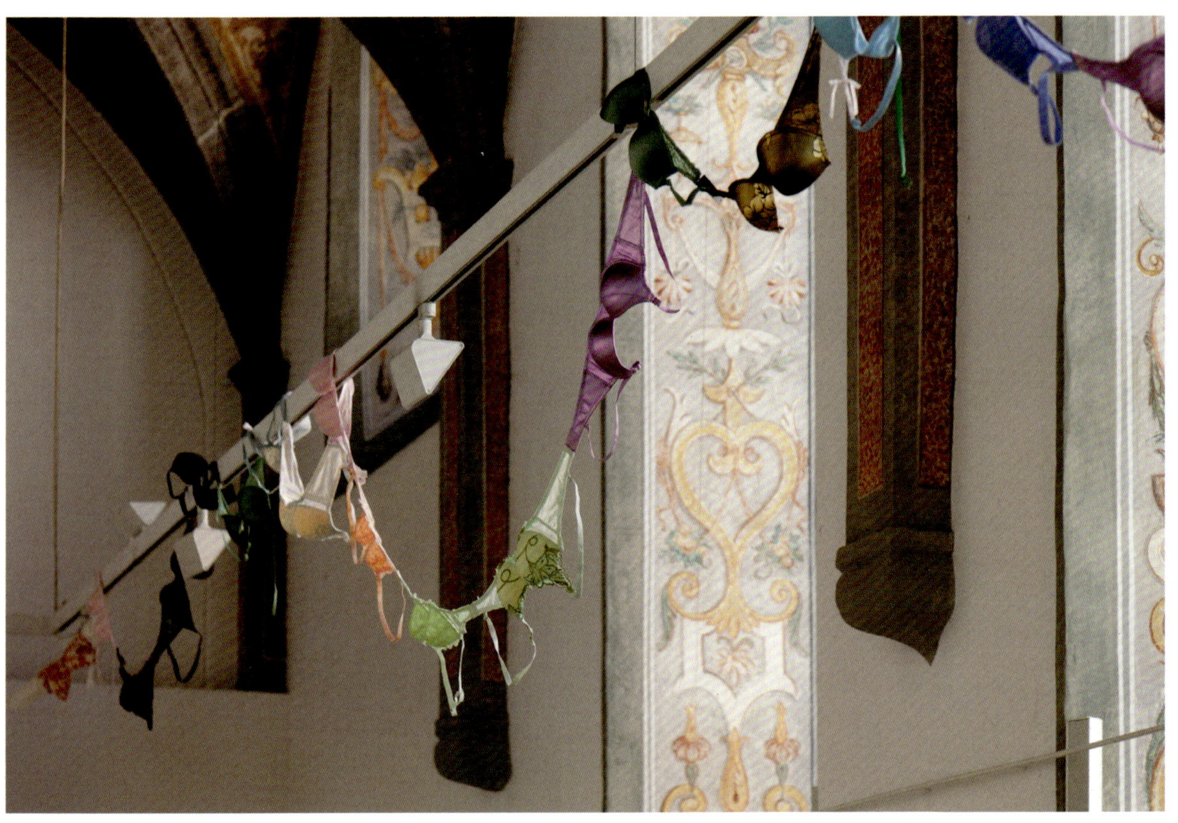

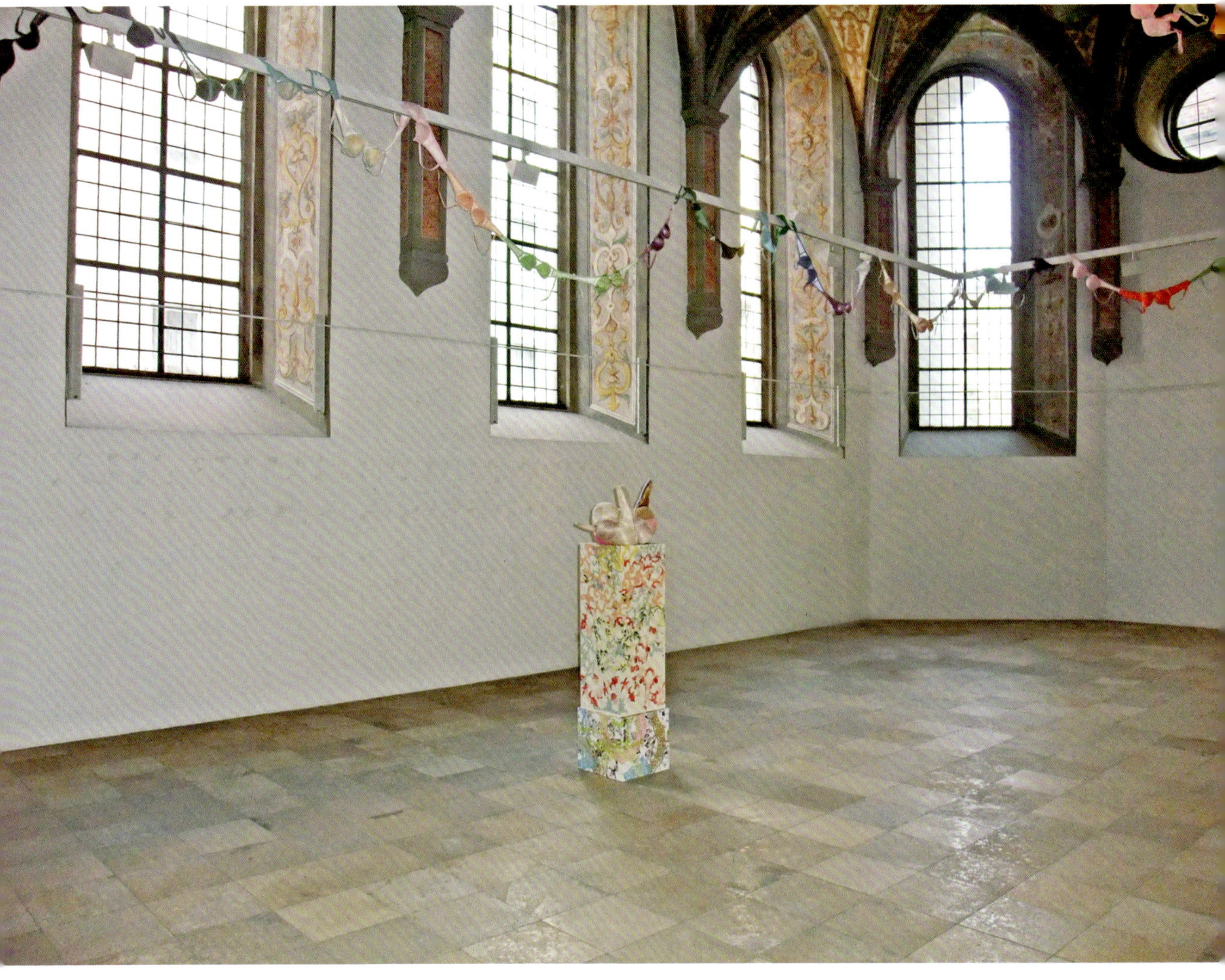

o.T.

2011, Textiles, cardboard, cotton wool, Sankt-Anna-Kapelle, Passau

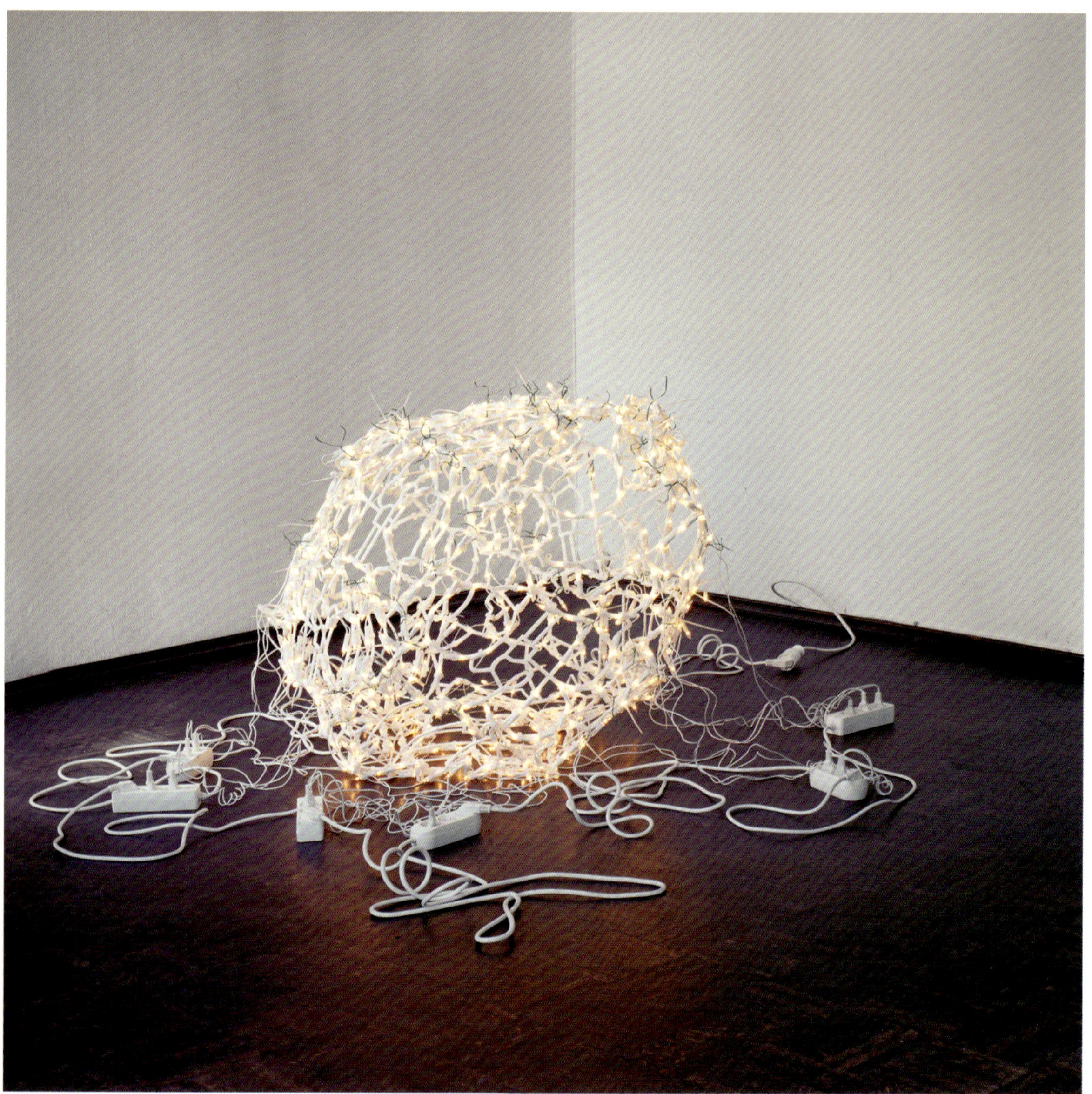

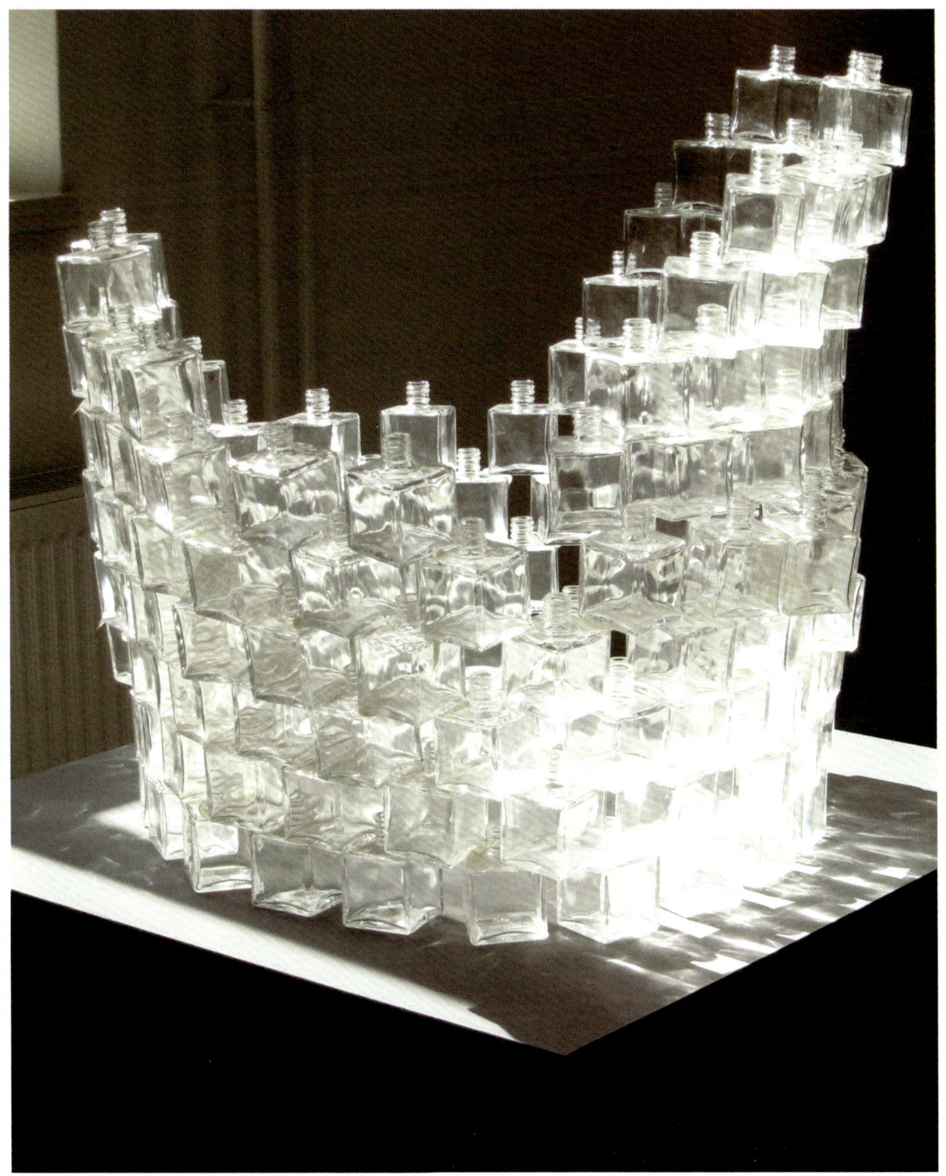

höhere Motive

2000, Plastic, lights, cables,
sockets, 100 × 260 × 240 cm

o.T.

2008, Glass, silicone, 46 cm

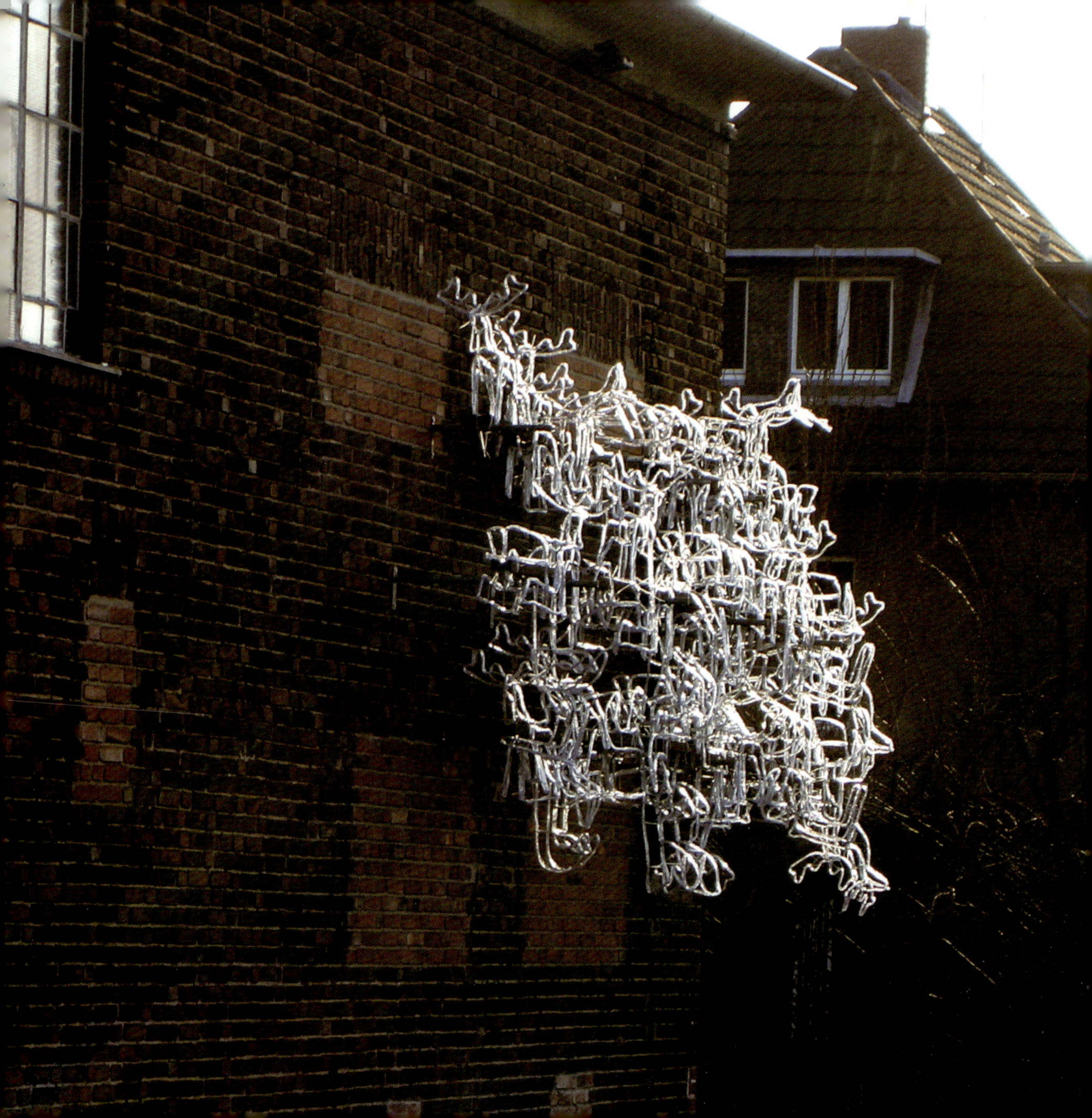

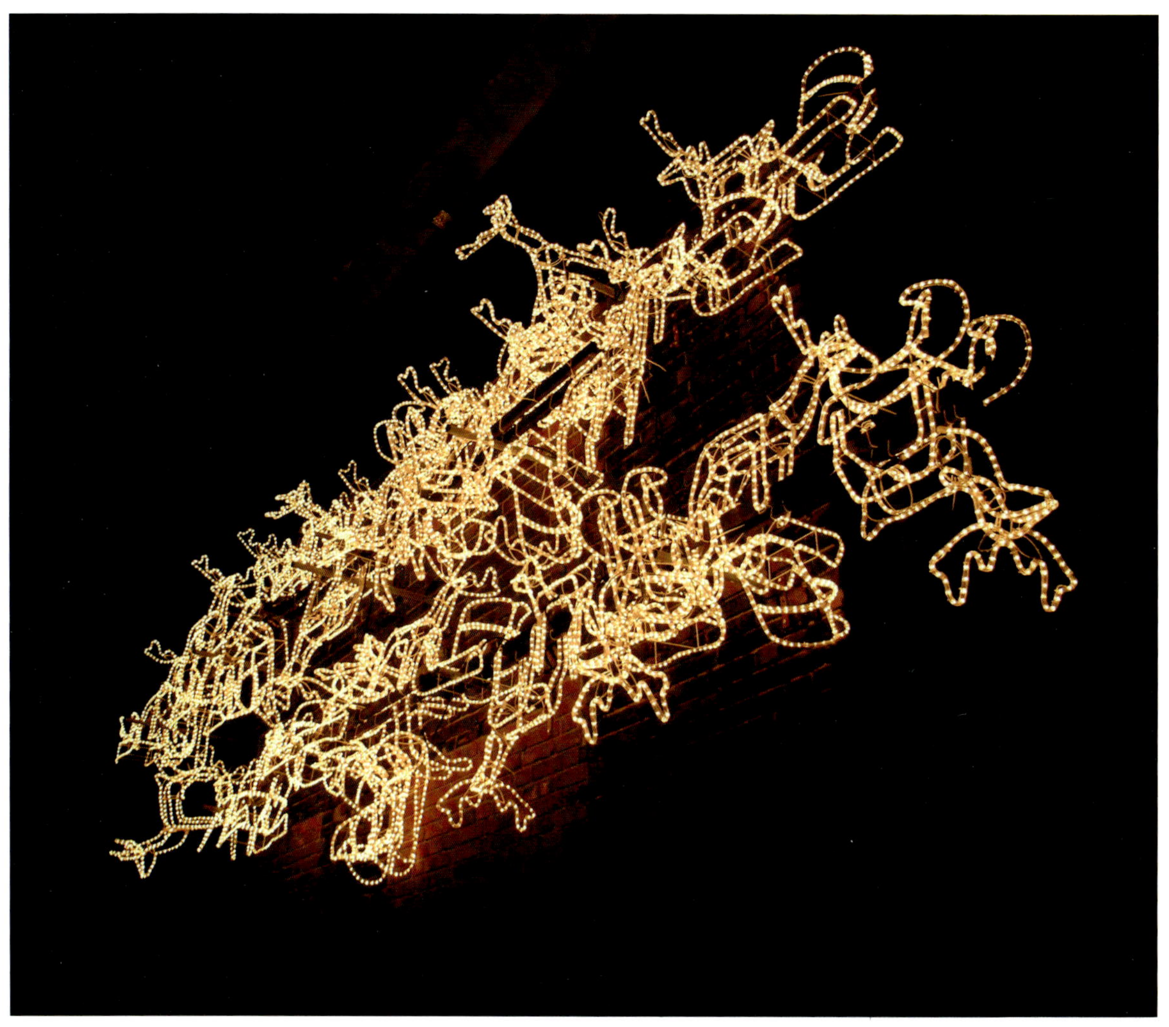

Mele Kalikimaka

2006, Iron, plastic, lamps, cables, 250 × 650 × 60 cm, Fuhrwerkswaage, Köln

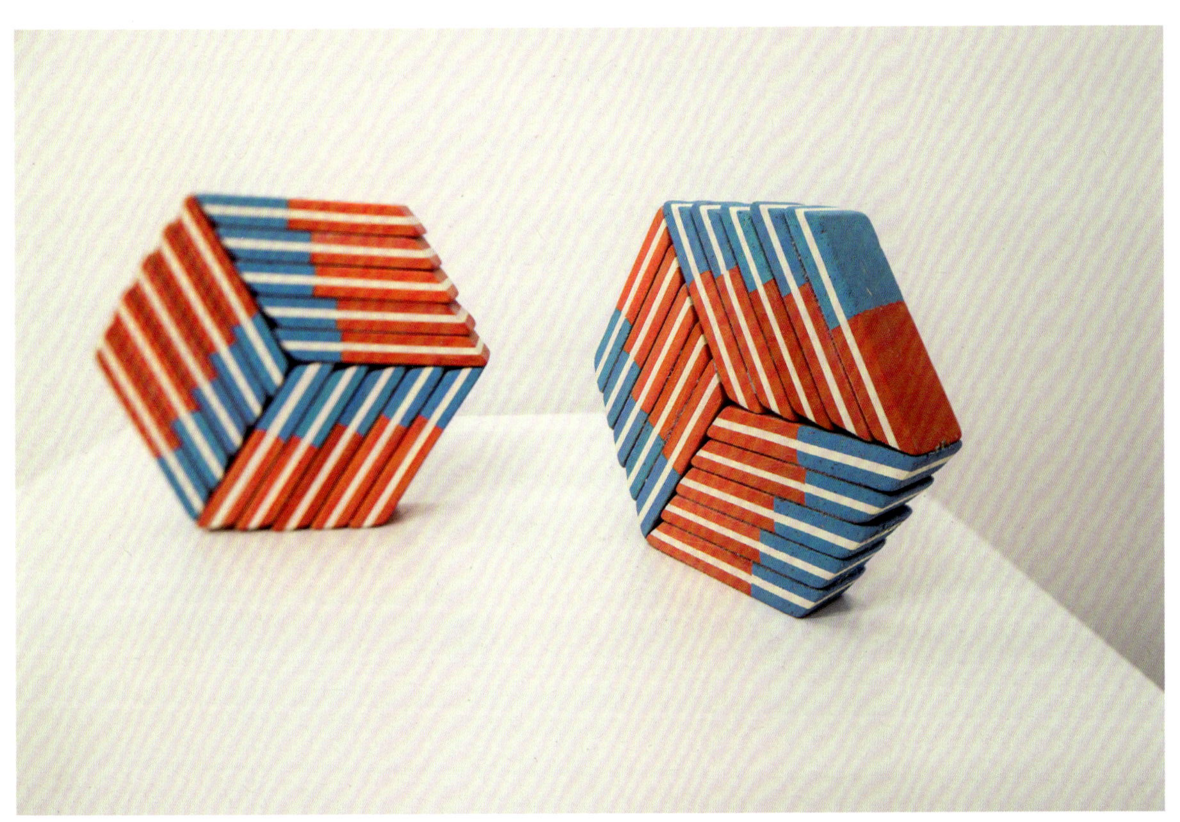

Radierarbeit, Edition

2009, Rubber, 12 × 12 × 2 cm

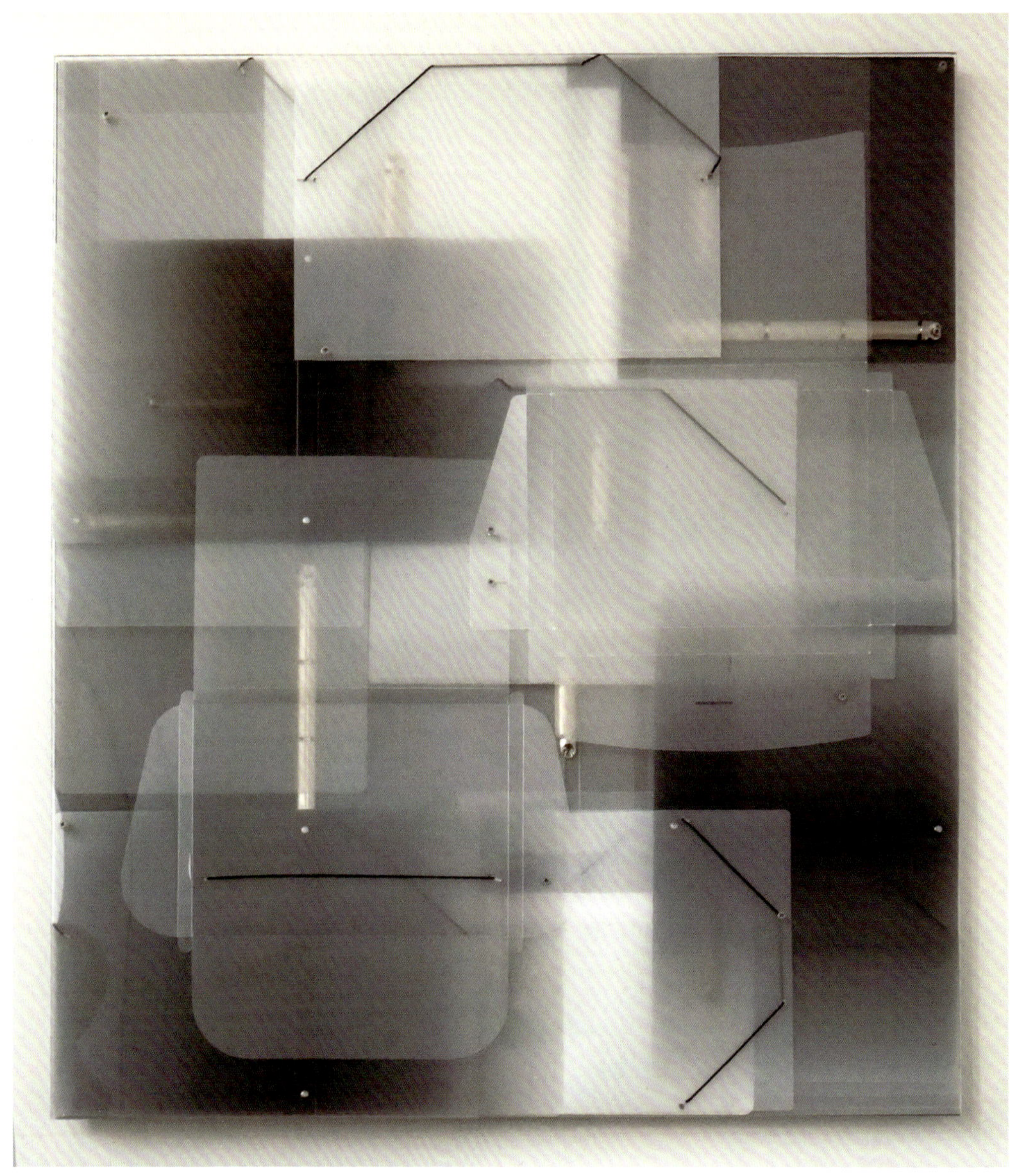

Bregenz

2011, Plastic,
109 × 93 × 3 cm

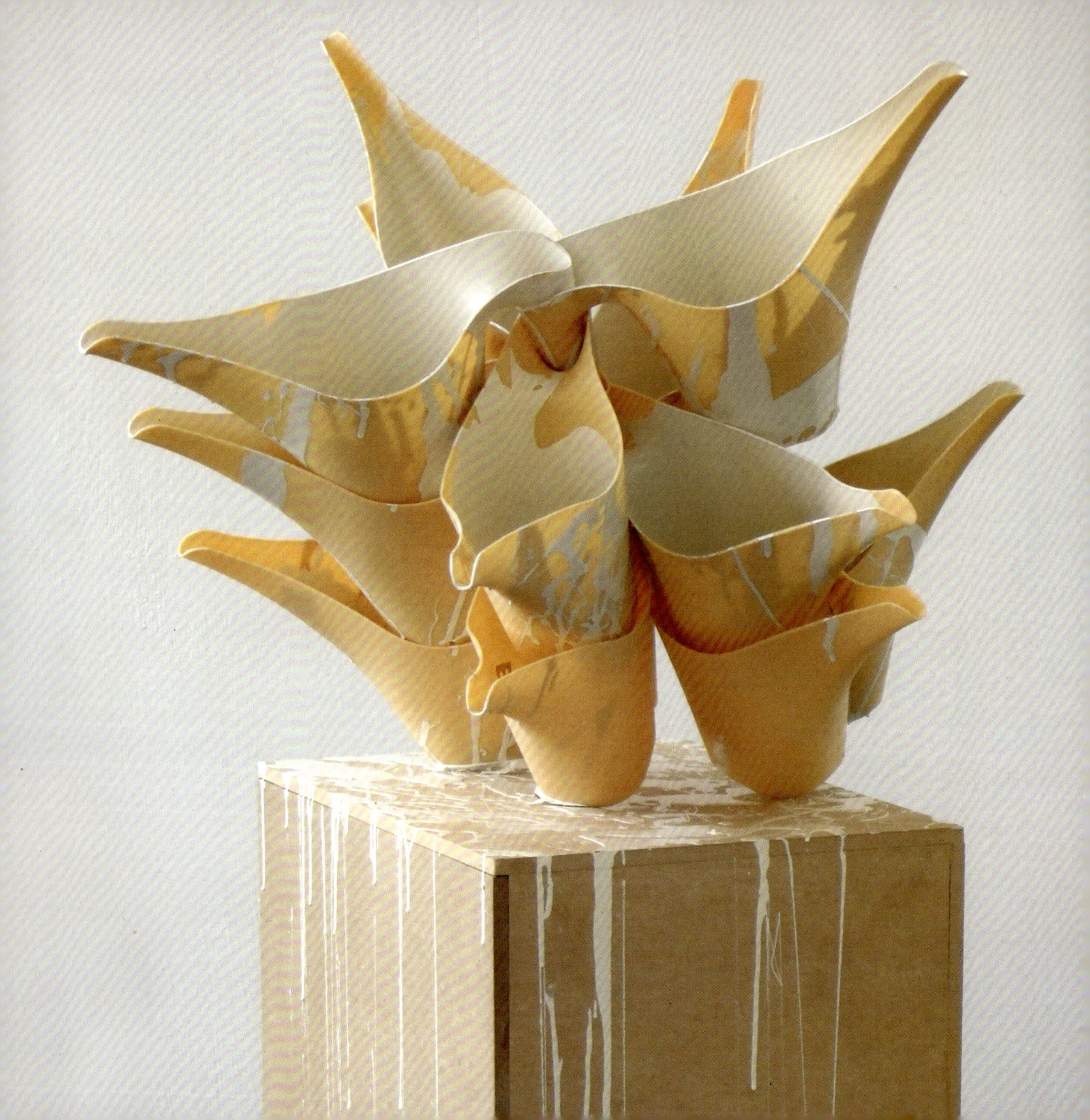

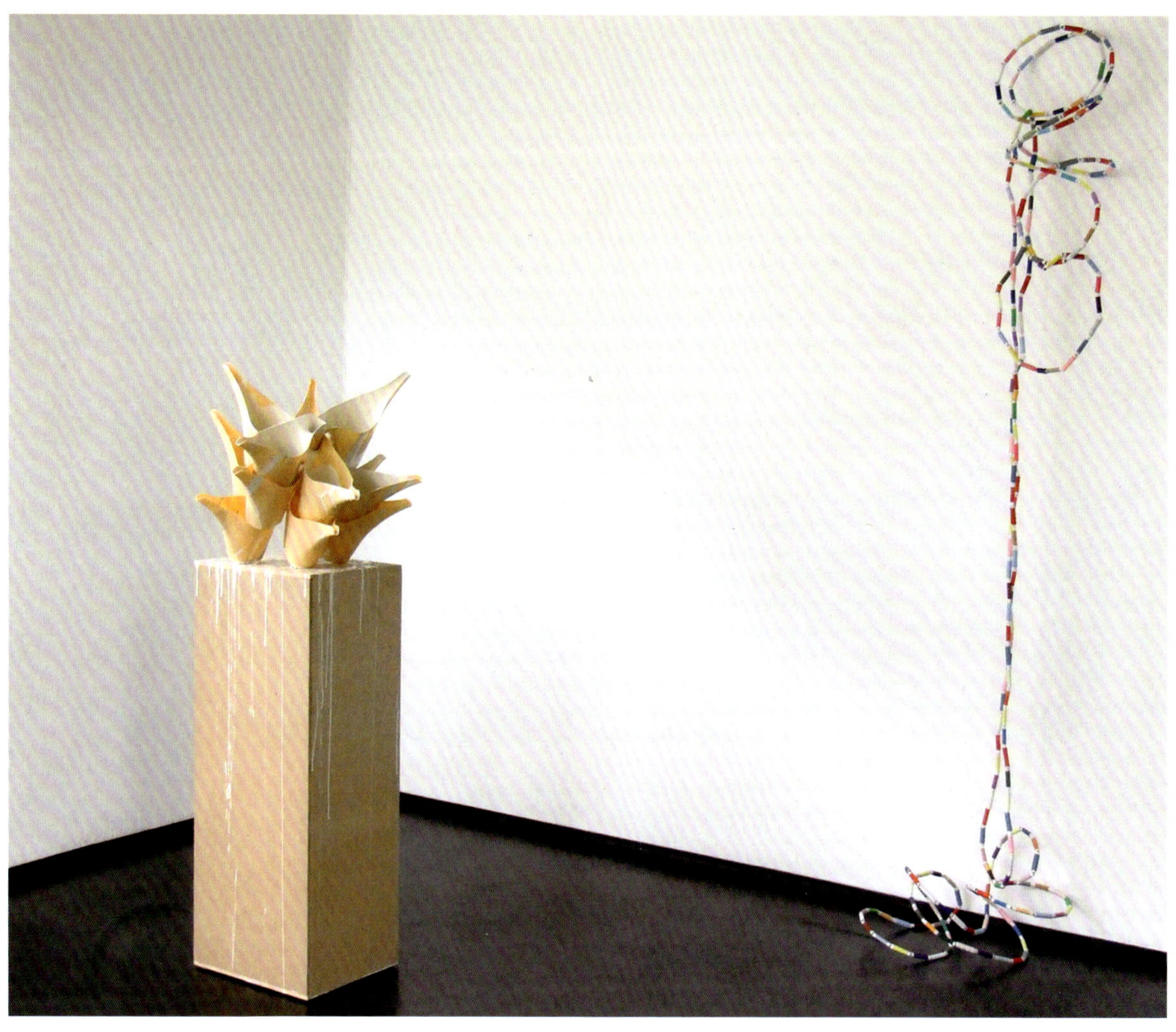

Auslaufmodell

2008, Plastic, MDF, acrylic paint, 152 × 60 × 50 cm

Liebeszeug

2008, Yarn, textile tape, iron wire

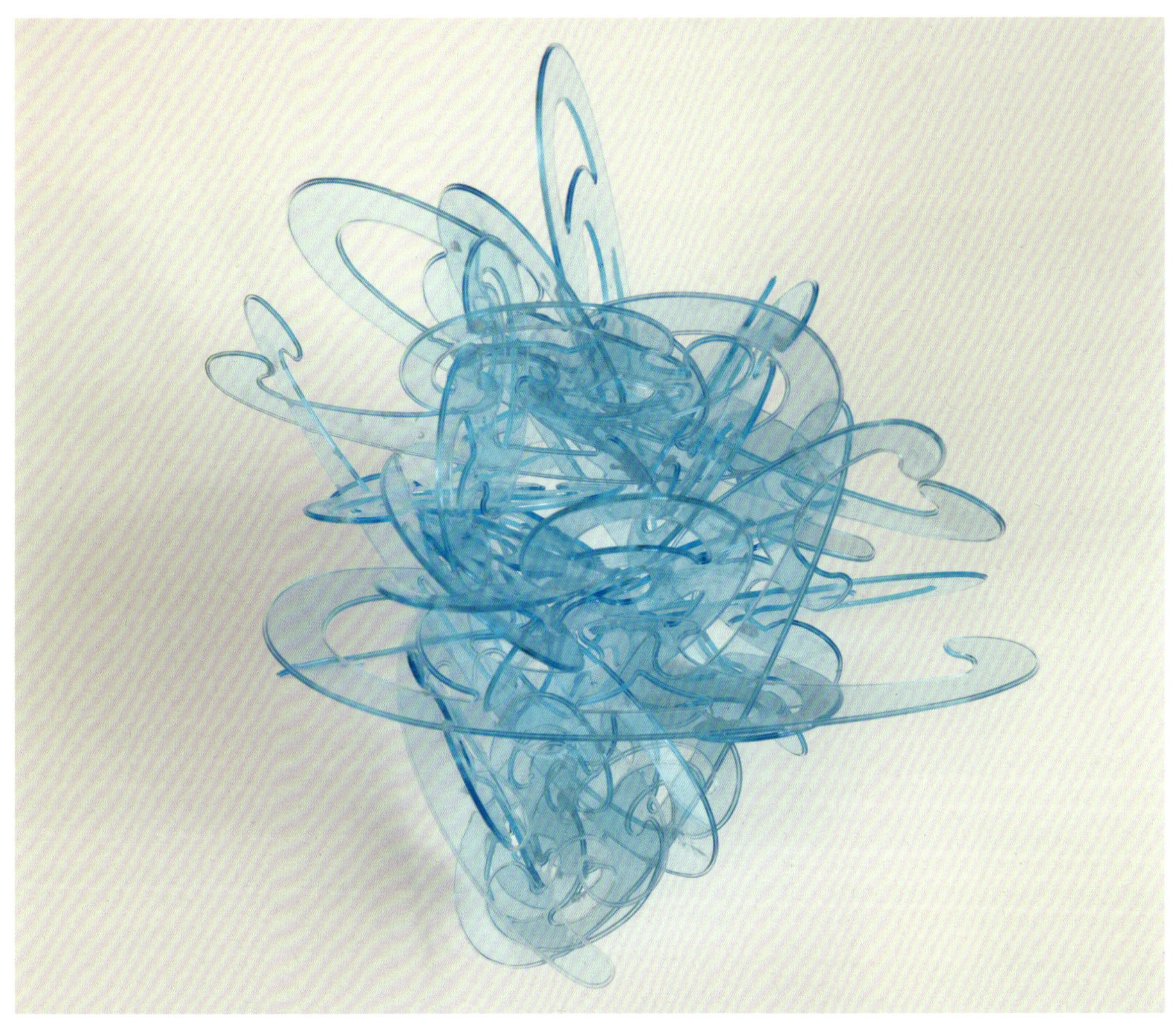

o.T.

2012, Plastic, Private collection

Brüssel

2013, Plastic, 95 × 95 × 3 cm

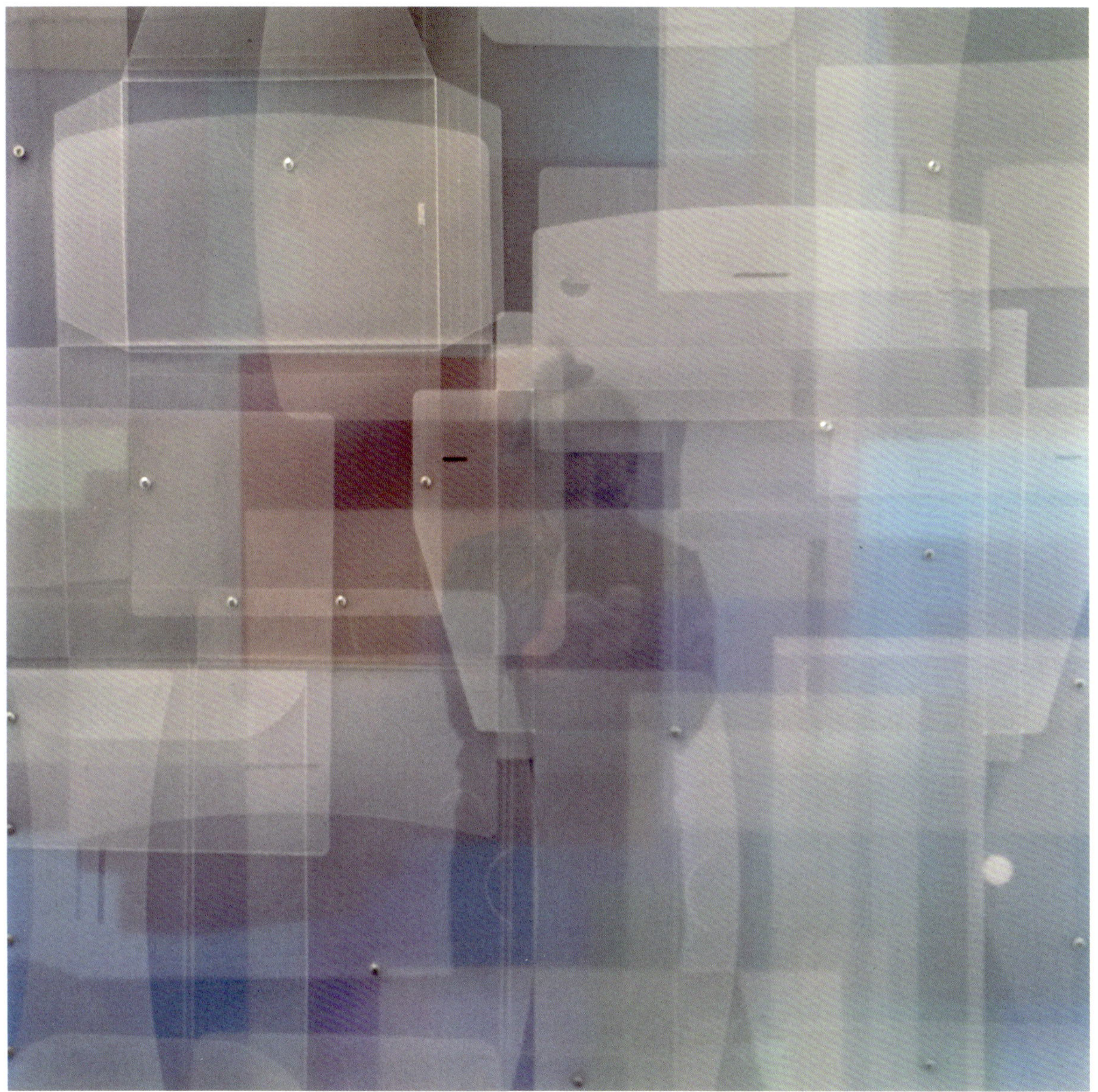

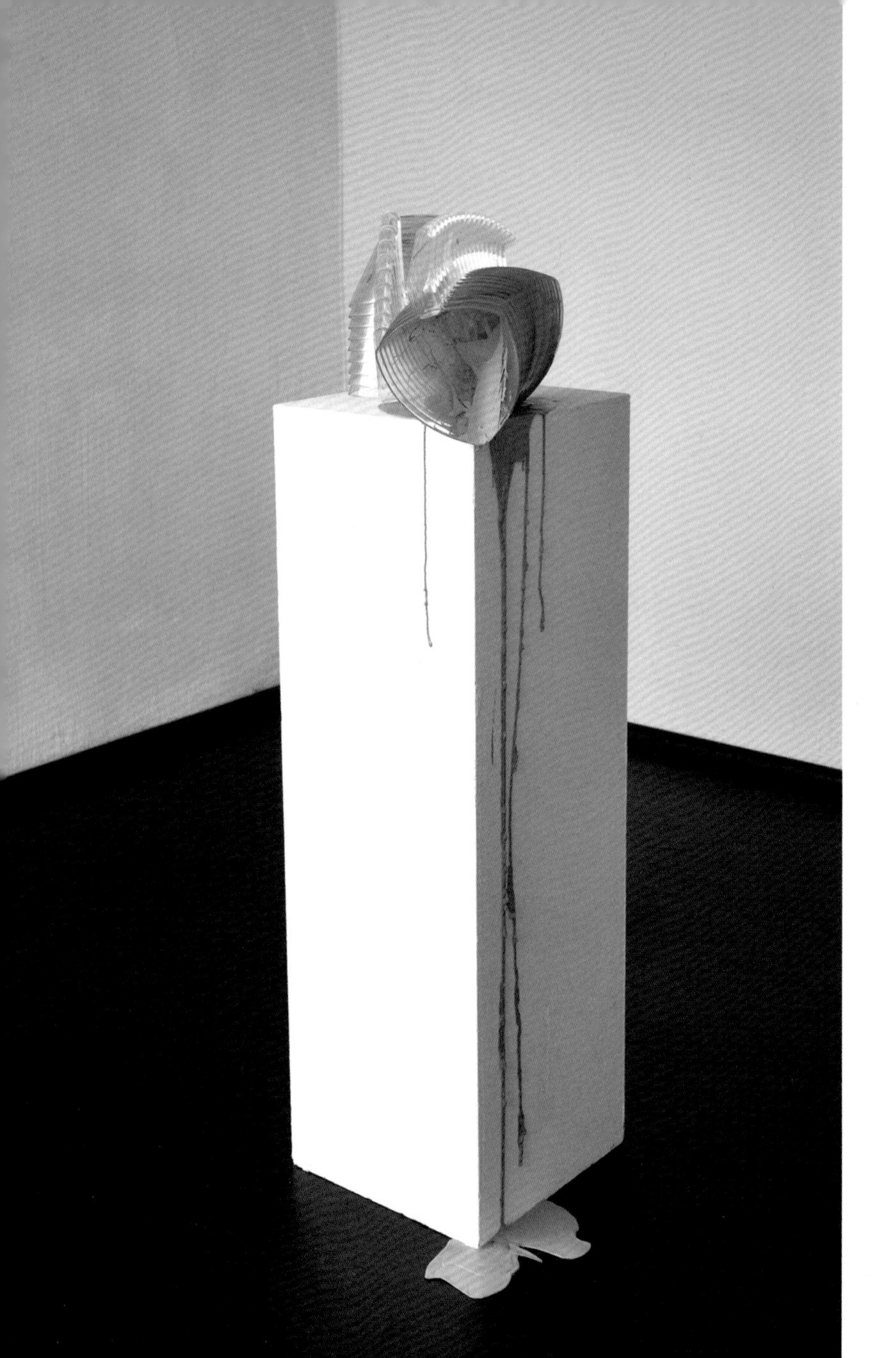

Modell Überfluss

2011, Polyethylene, acrylic varnish, wood,
130 × 40 × 40 cm

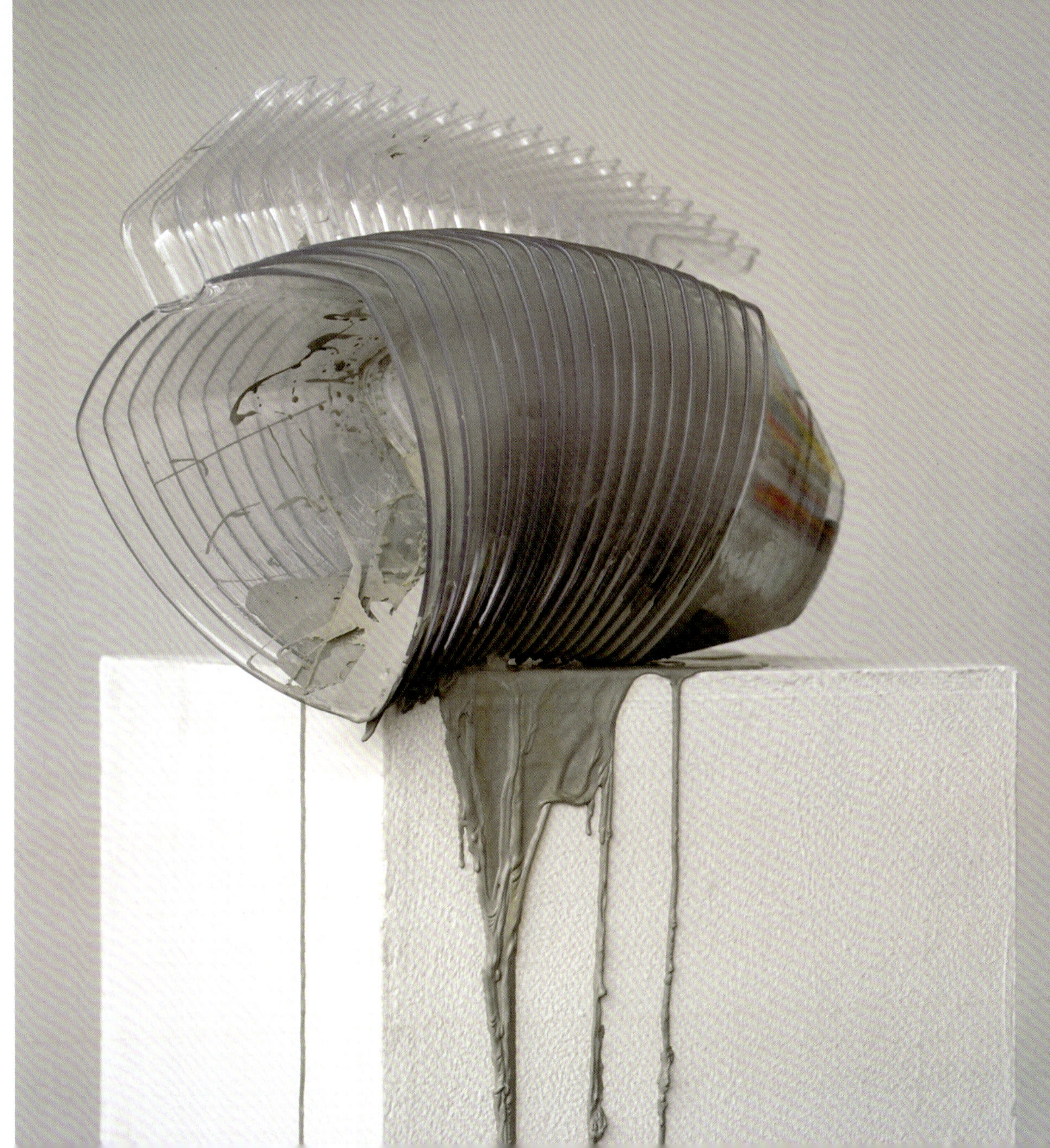

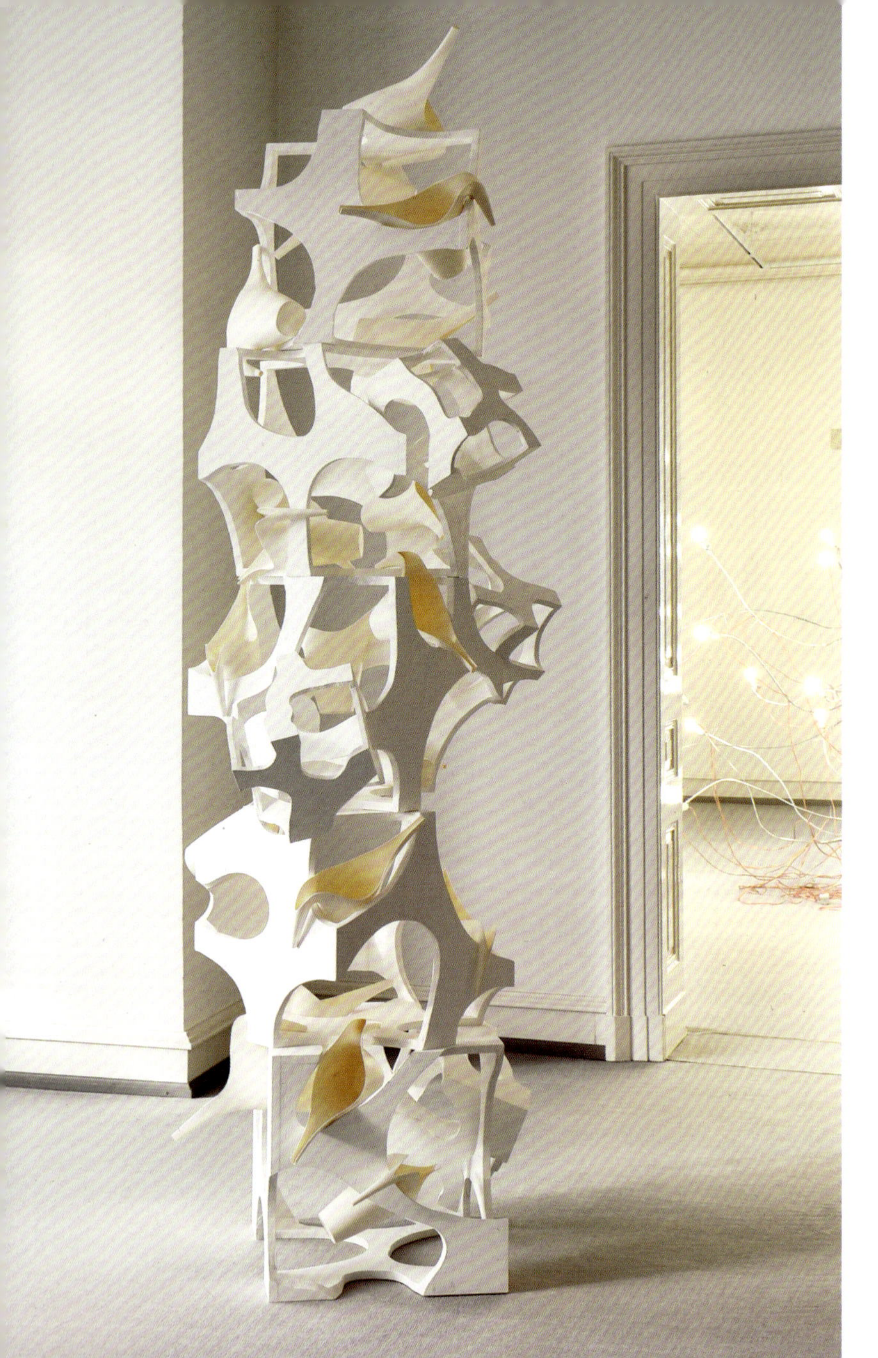

Sommerloch

*2012, MDF, plastic, 210 × 60 × 60 cm, Kunstmuseum
Villa Zanders, Bergisch Gladbach*

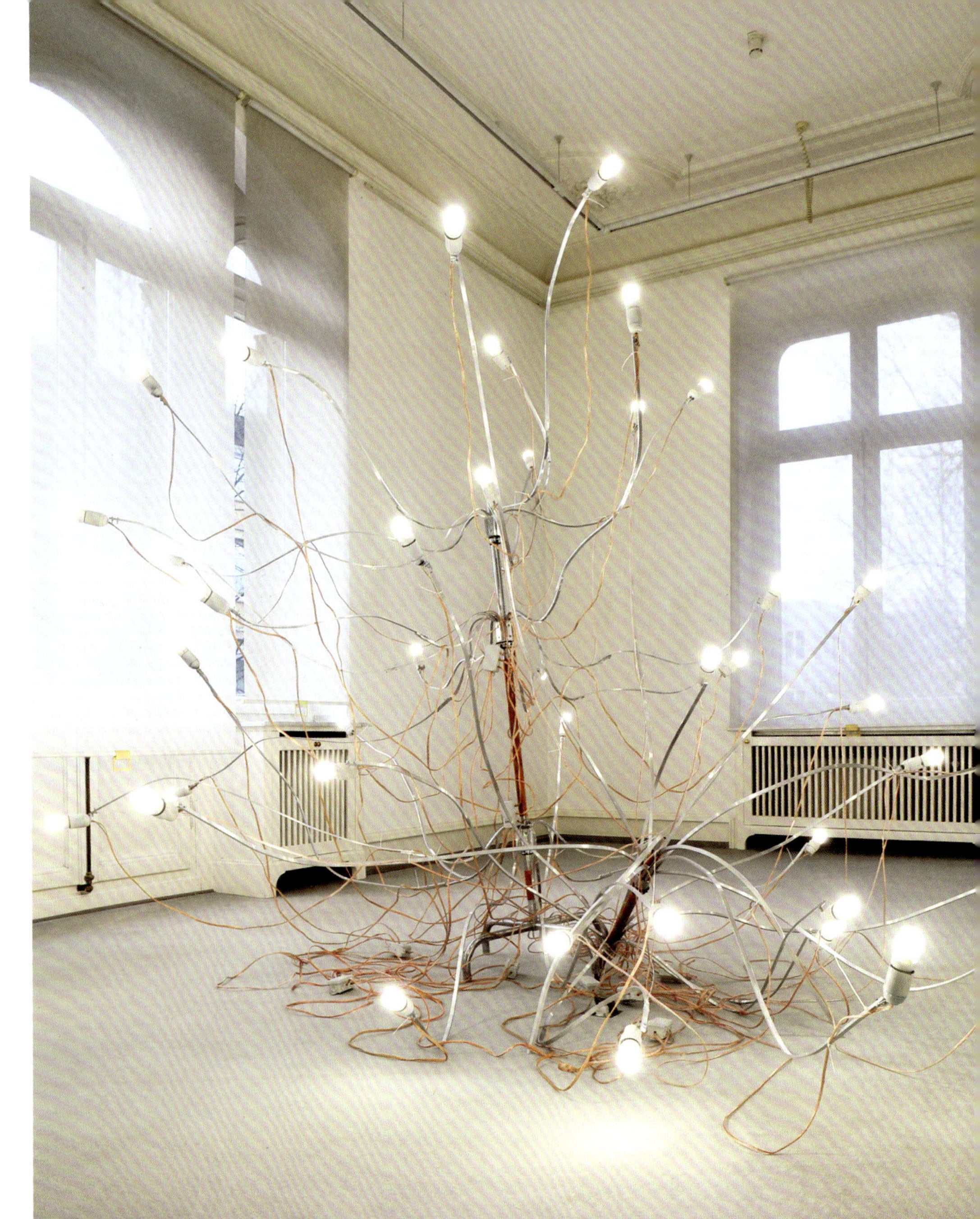

EU-Leuchter

2012, Aluminium, copper, energy saving lamps, 240 × 350 cm, Kunstmuseum Villa Zanders, Bergisch Gladbach

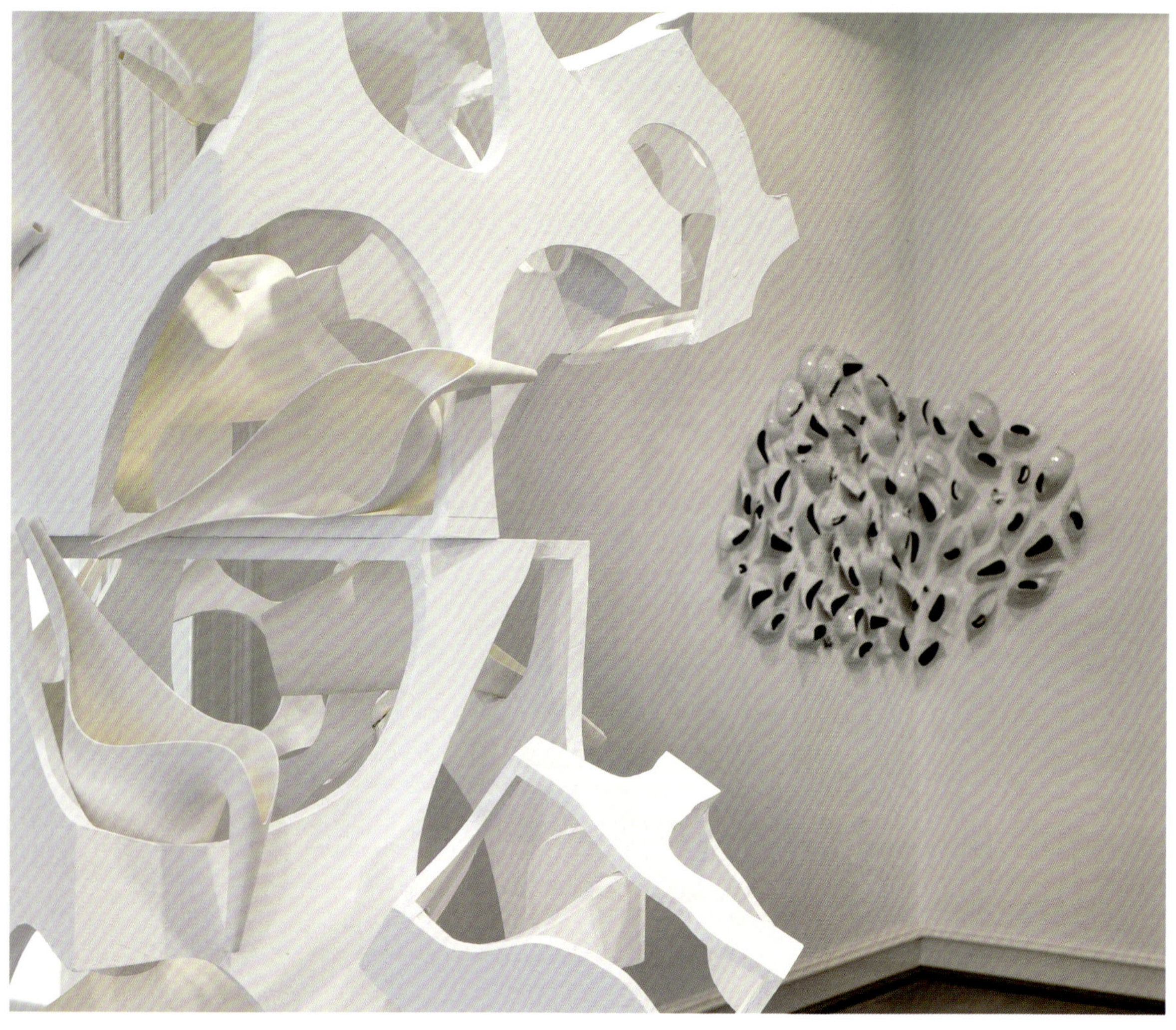

Sommerloch (Detail)

2012, MDF, plastic, 210 × 60 × 60 cm

Schwarze Löcher

2012, Plastic, tape, 85 × 80 × 60 cm, Kunstmuseum Villa Zanders, Bergisch Gladbach

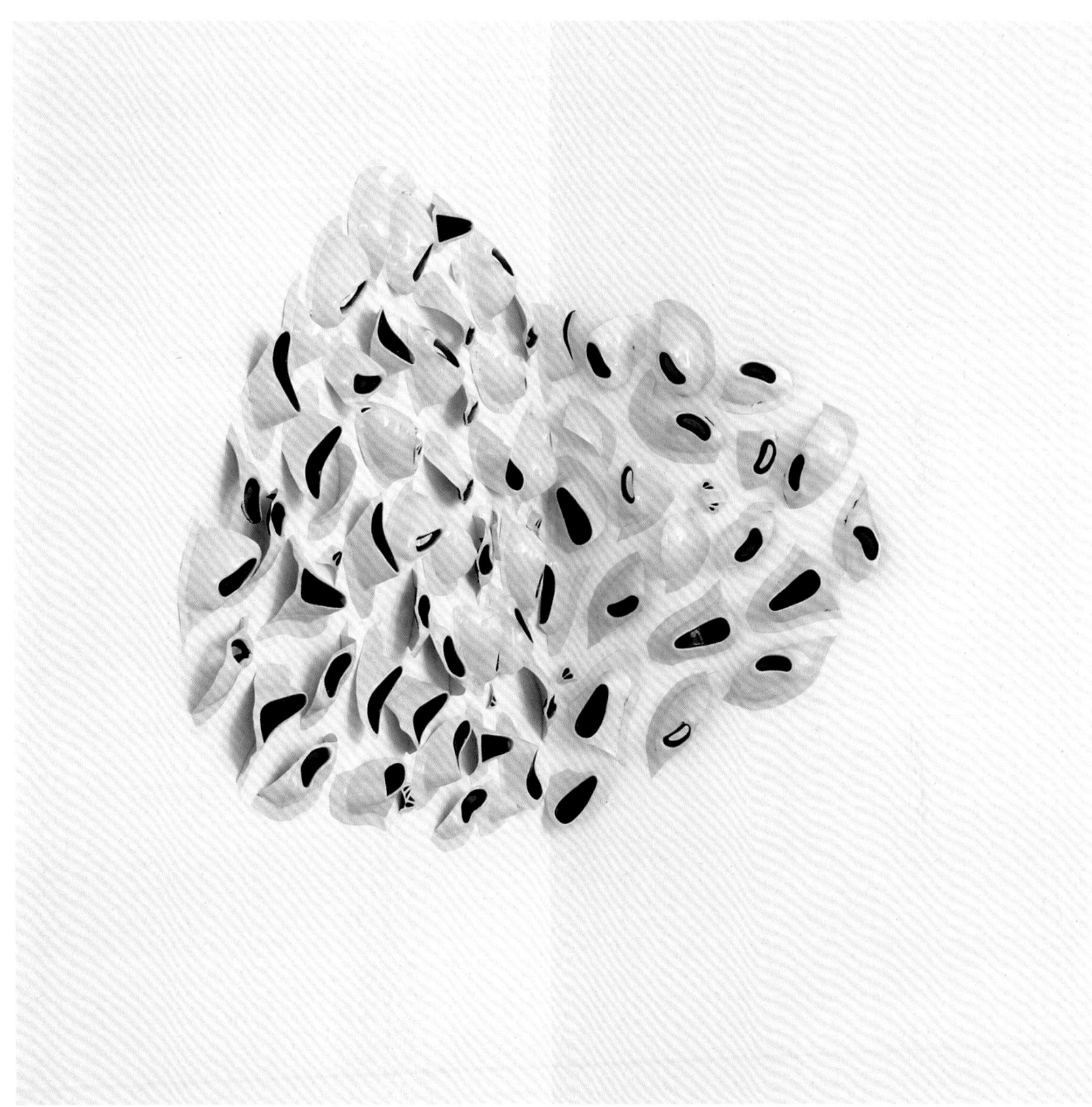

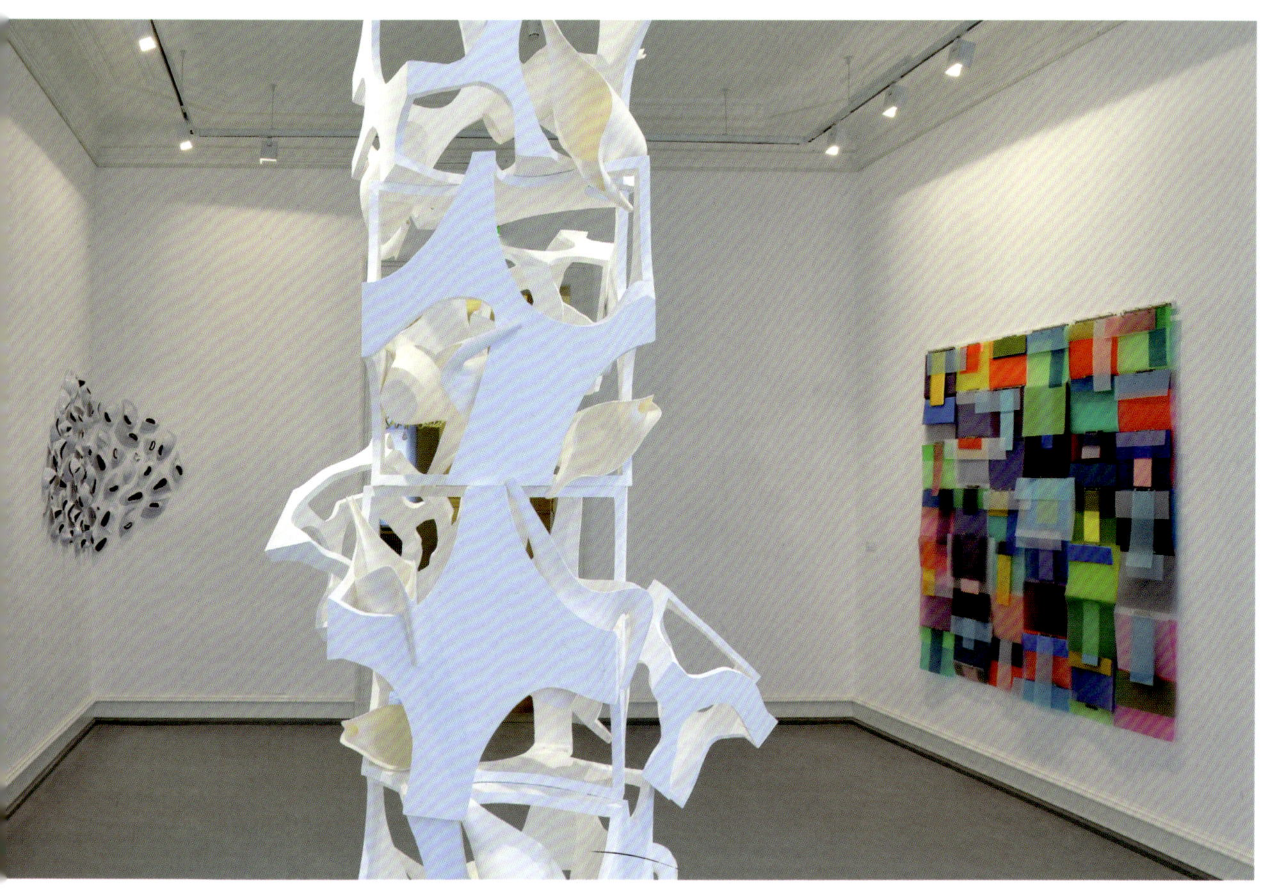

Ausstellungsansicht, Kunstmuseum Villa Zanders, Bergisch Gladbach

Abordner

2011, Plastic, wood, metal, 195 × 200 × 3 cm

146

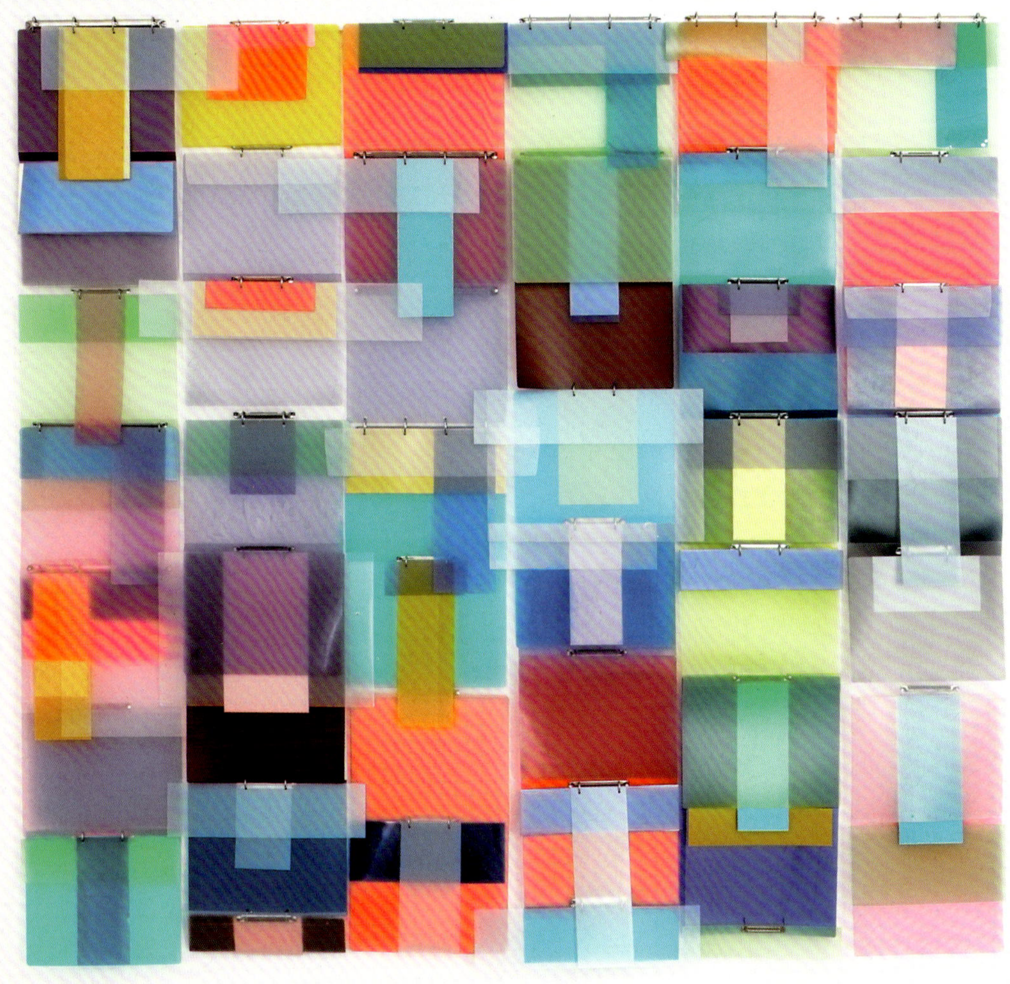

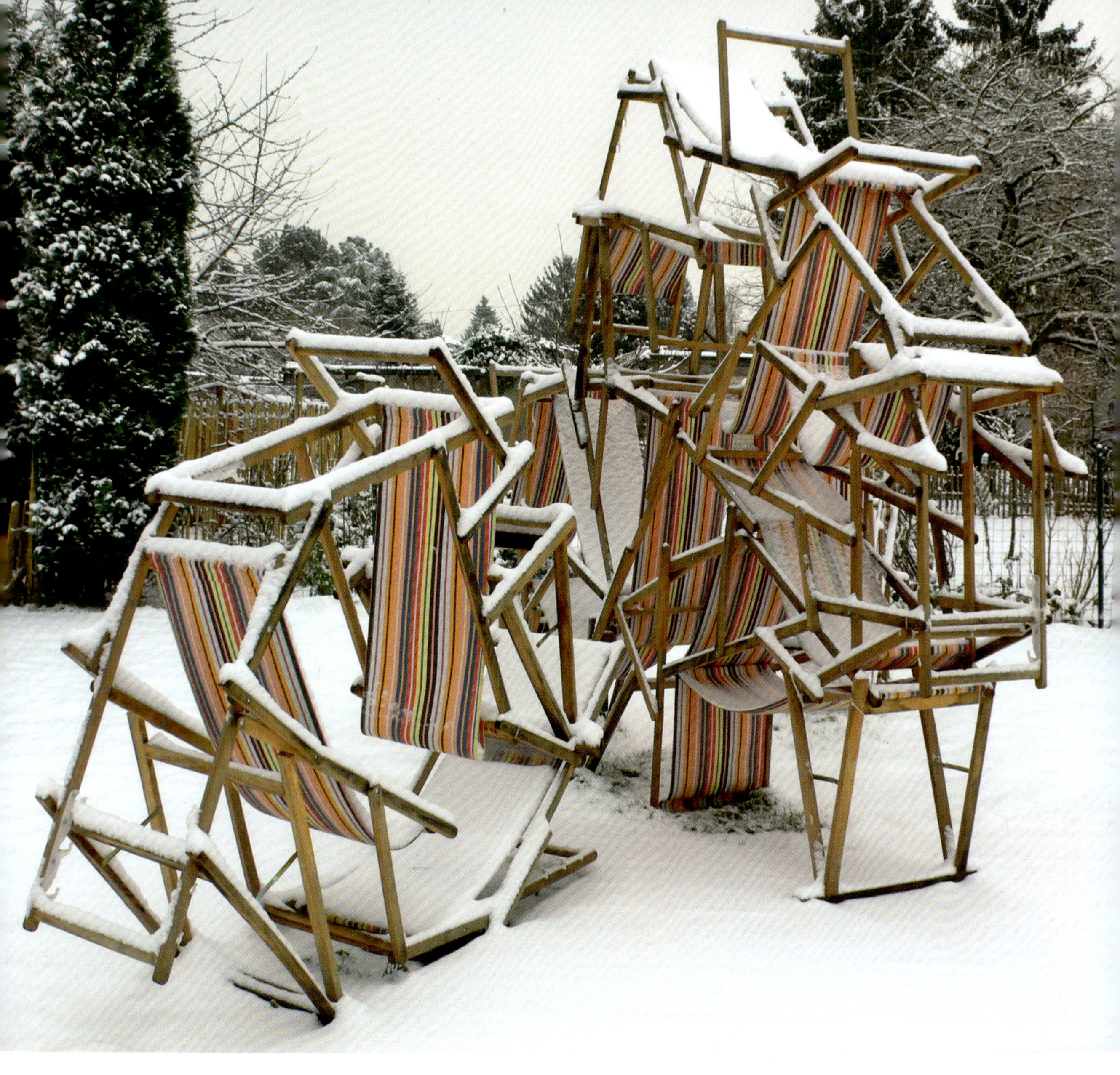

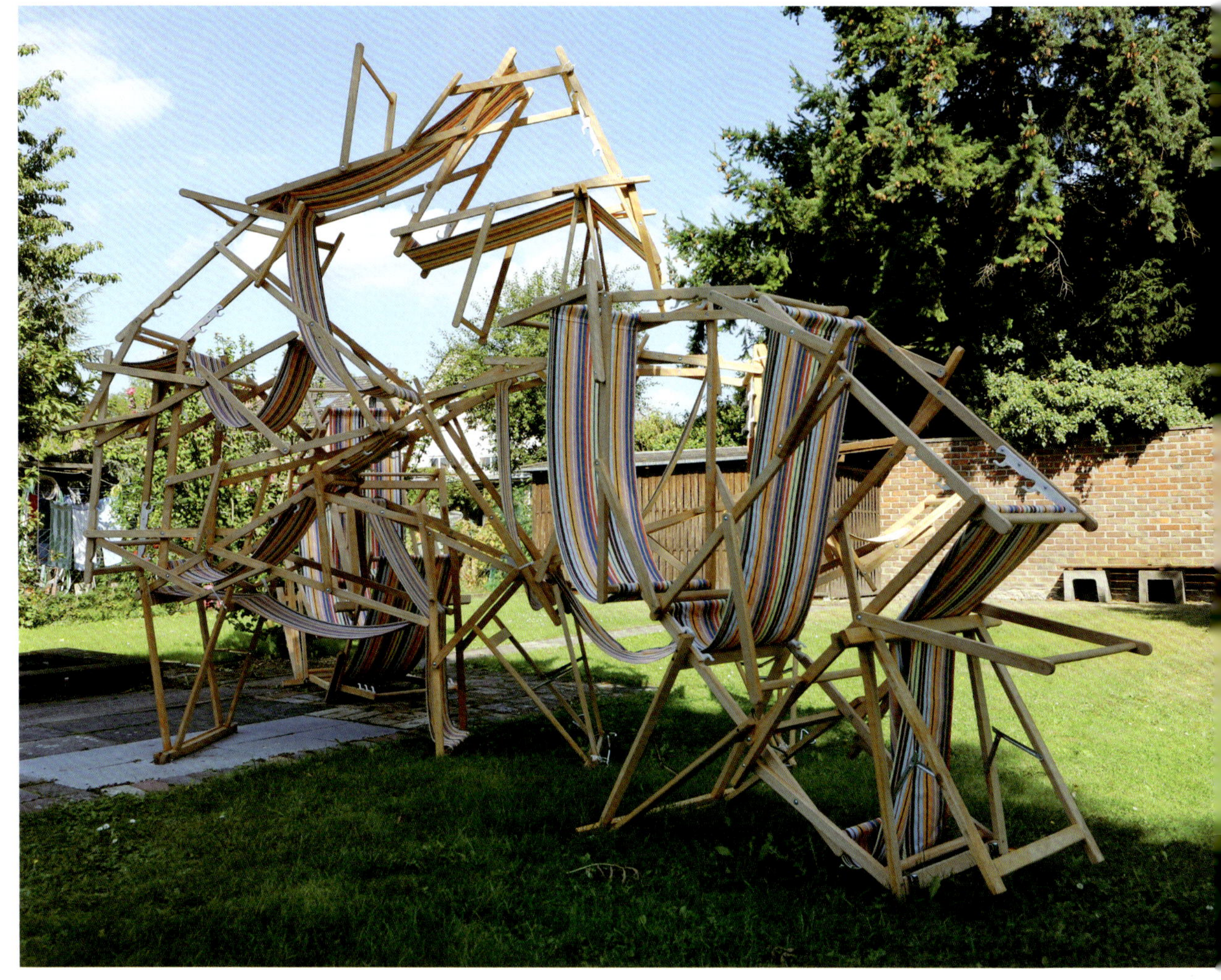

Fliegestühle

2012, Wood, textiles, metal, 240 × 350 × 200 cm

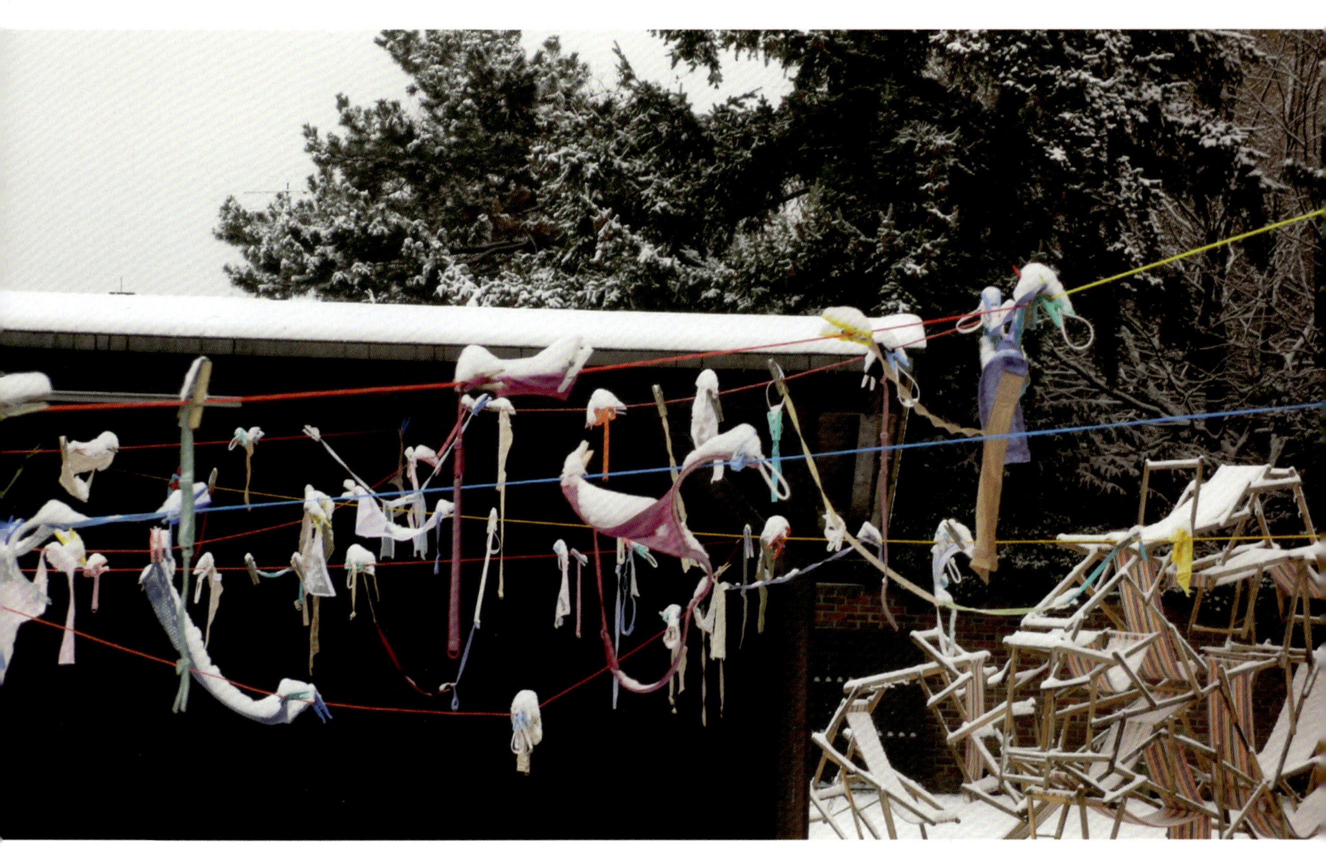

Installation für die Ausstellung **Luftveränderung, Köln-Weiß**

2012, Textiles, clotheslines

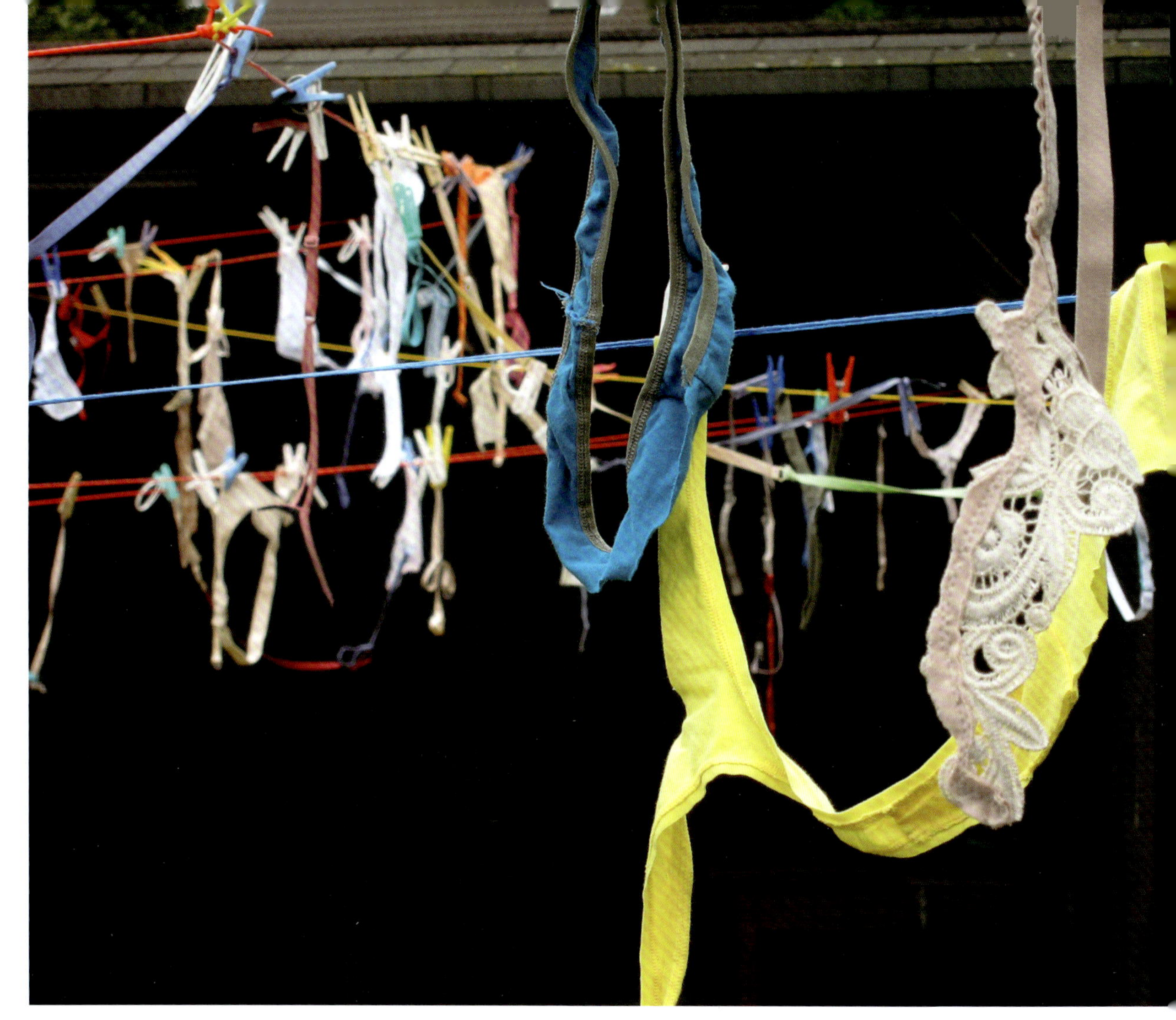

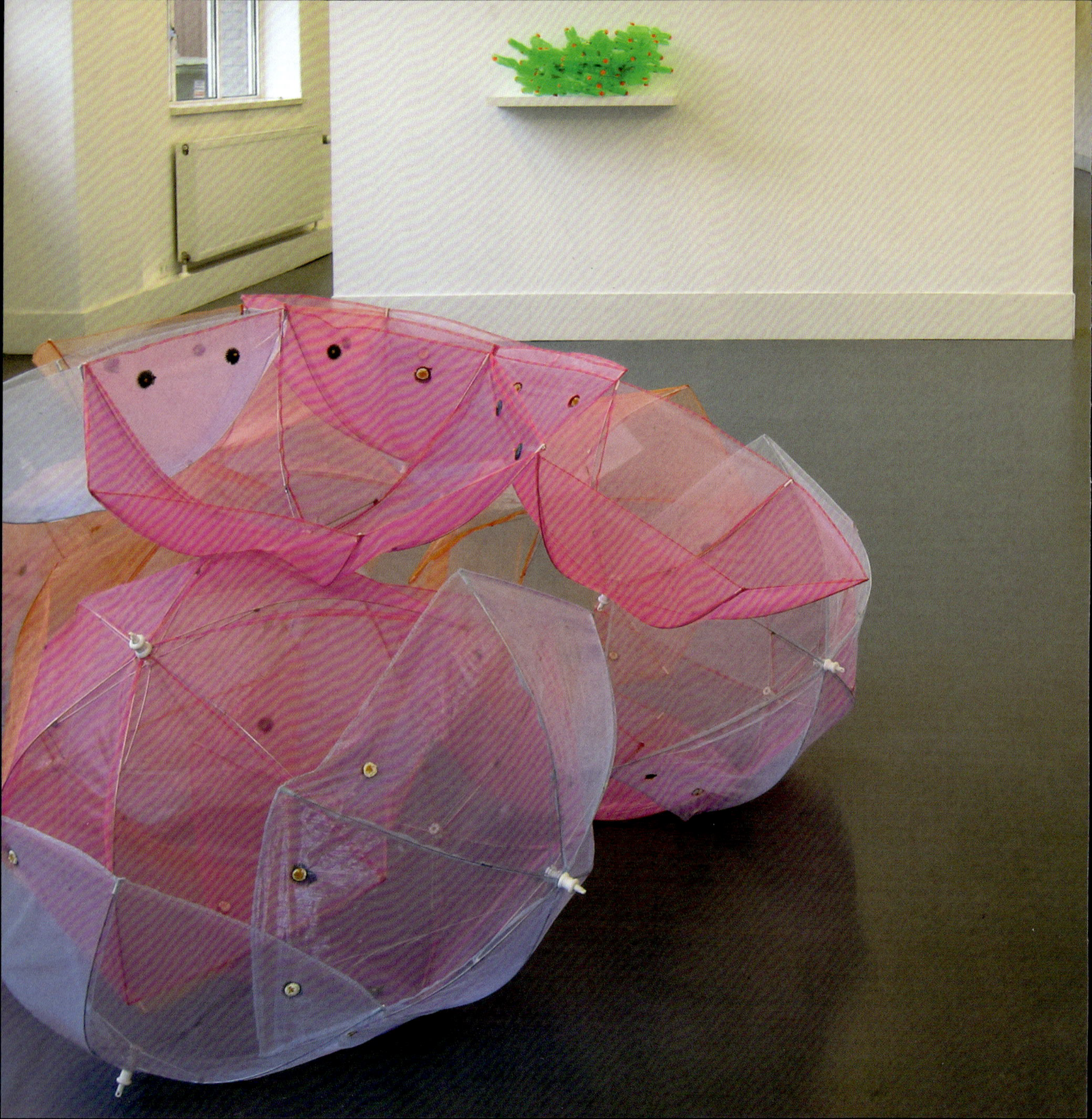

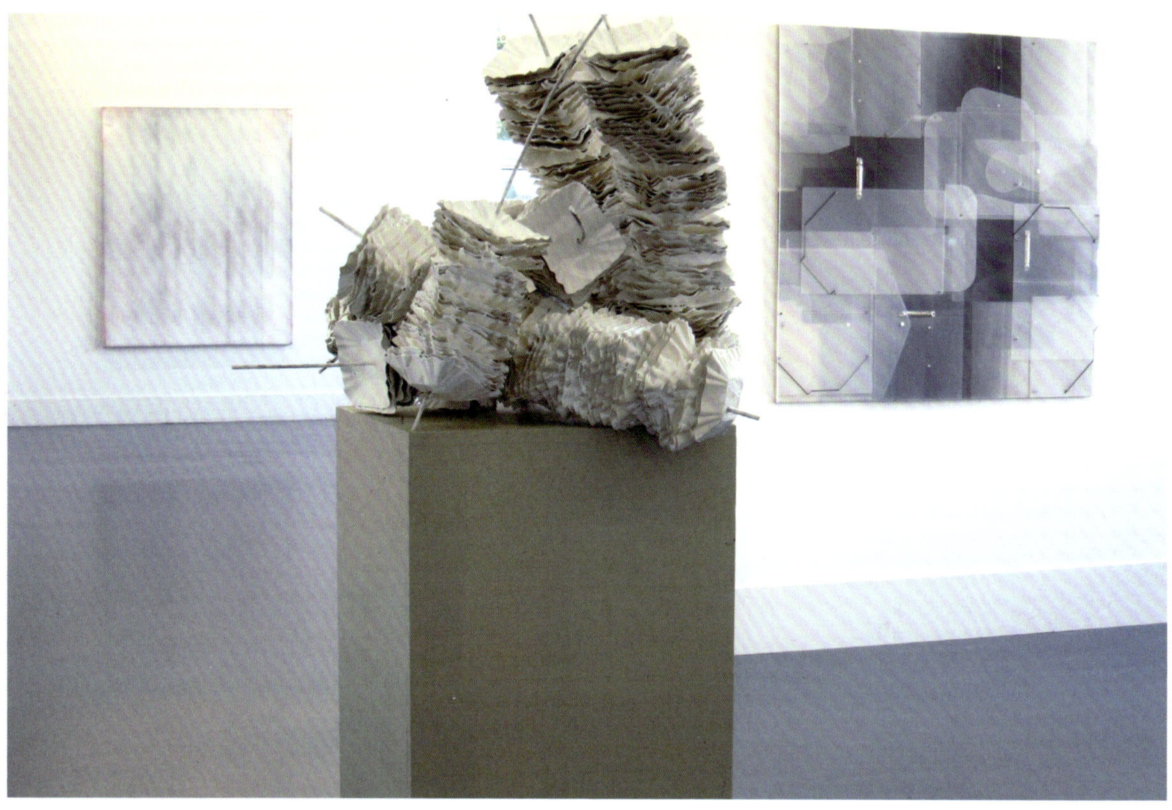

Jus Juchtmans

sans saucisse

2012, Cardboard, paint, metal, 60 × 50 × 60 cm

Bregenz II

2011, Plastic, 110 × 110 × 2 cm

Sommertag

2006, Textiles, metal, plastic, c. 70 × c. 155 cm

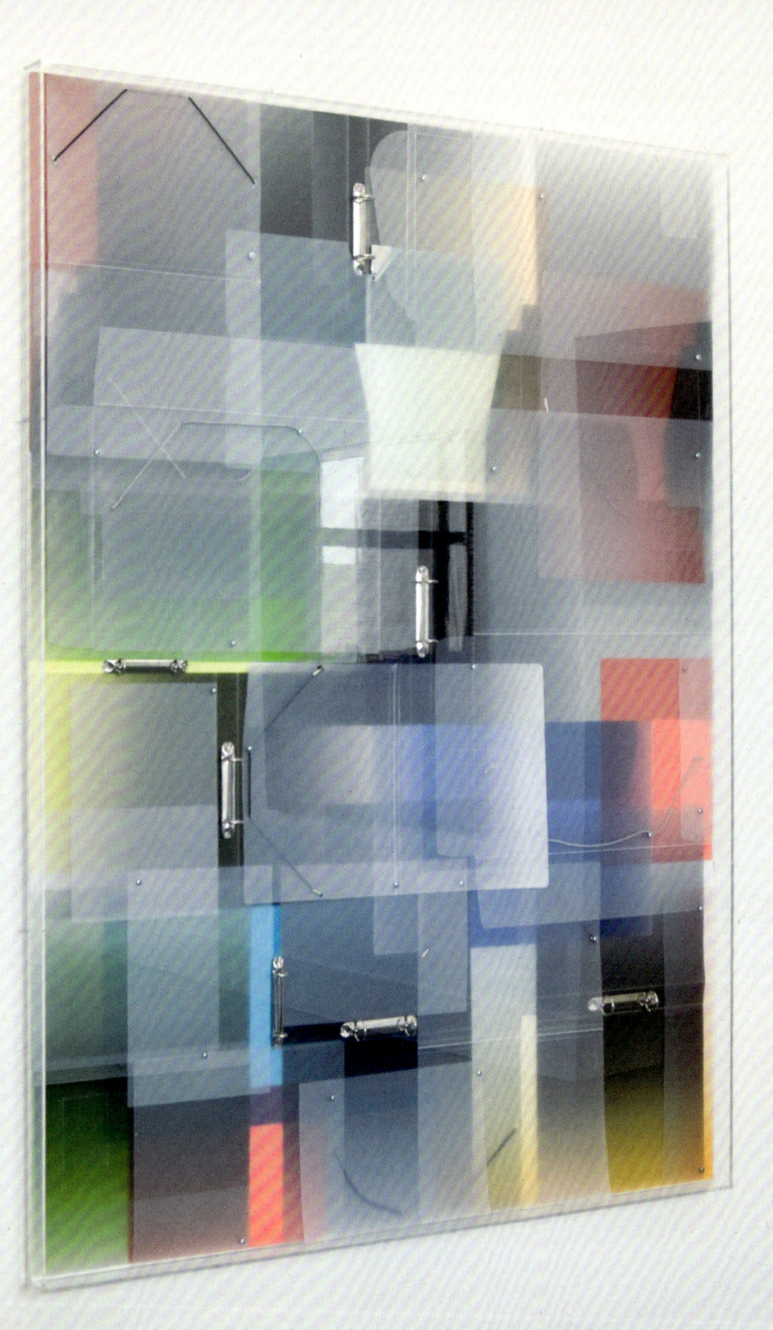

Budapest

2011, Plastic, MDF,
150 × 100 × 3 cm

Jus Juchtmans

Bel Air

2010, Glass, silicone,
55 × 60 cm

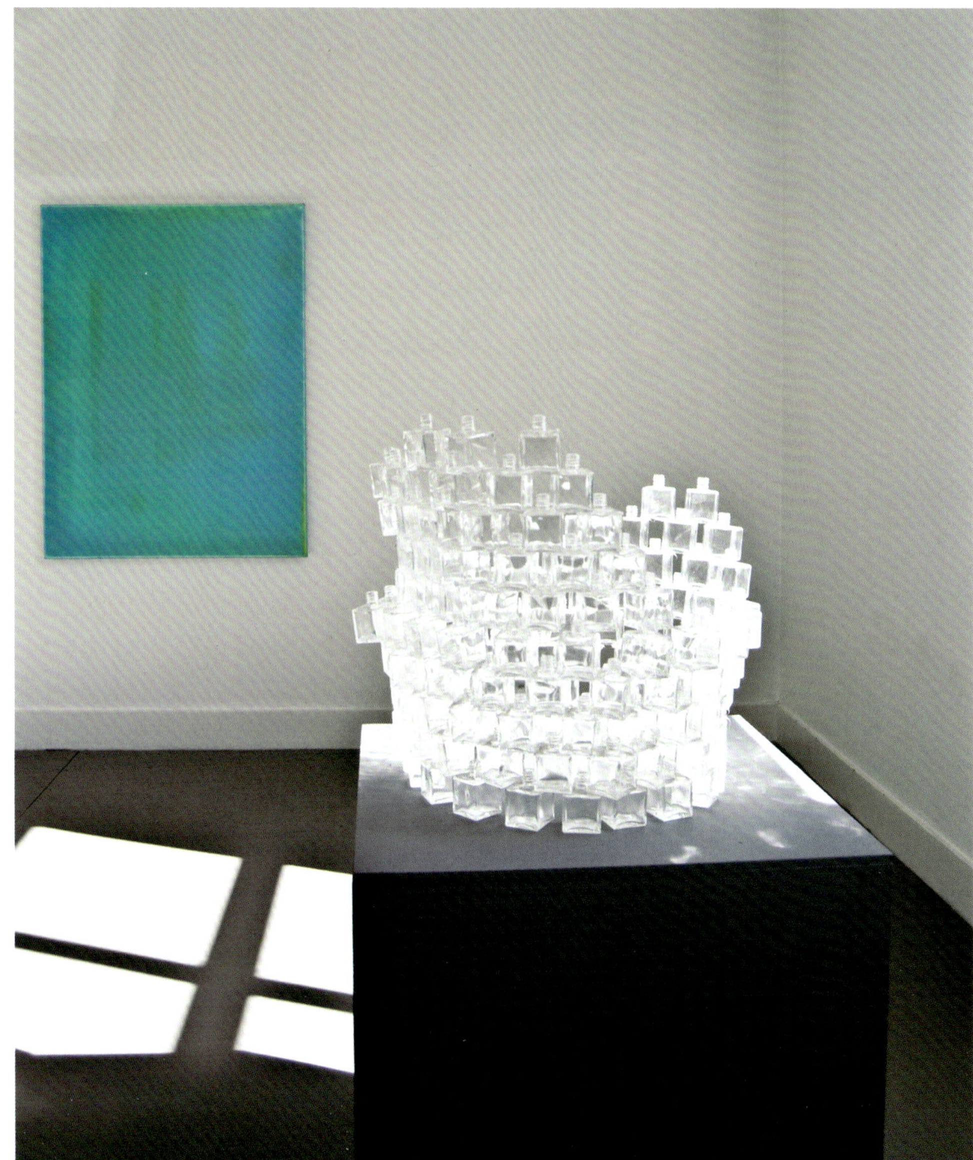

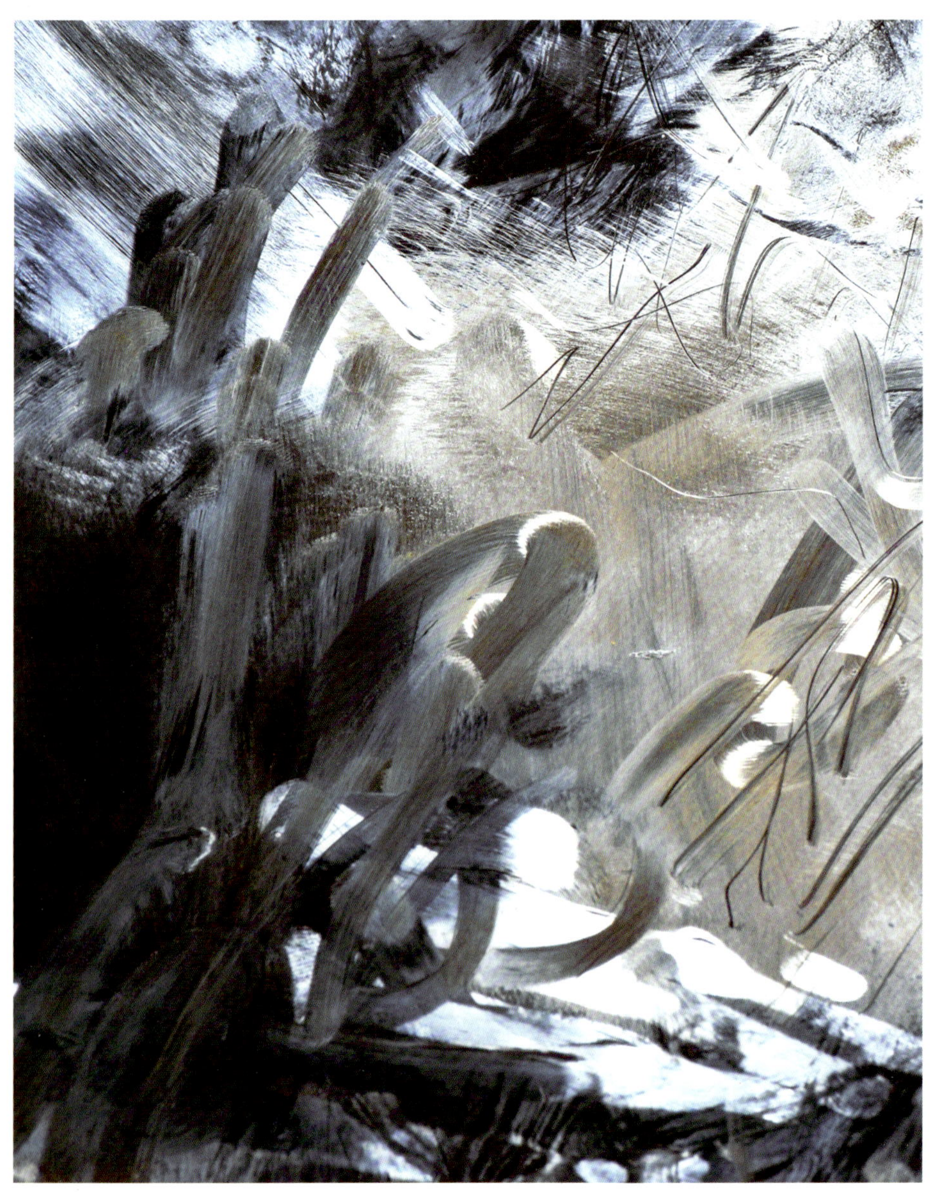

Sweatprint (ohne Schnee)

2013, Photo on aluminium composite panel, 53 × 42 cm

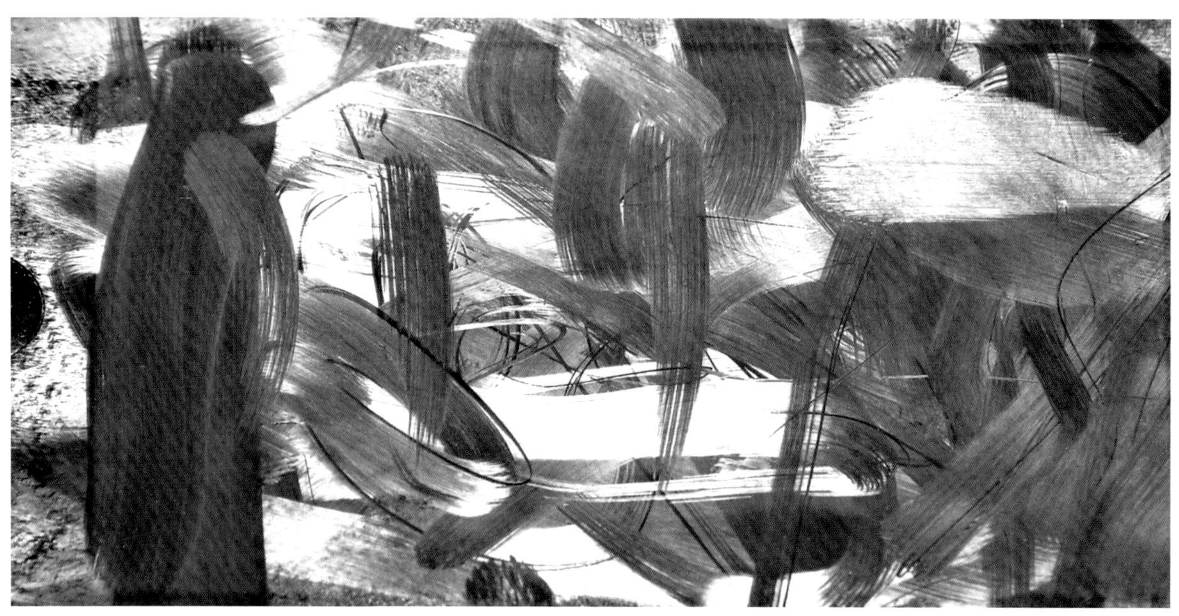

Sweatprint (chinesisches)

2013, Photo on aluminium composite panel, 31 × 62 cm

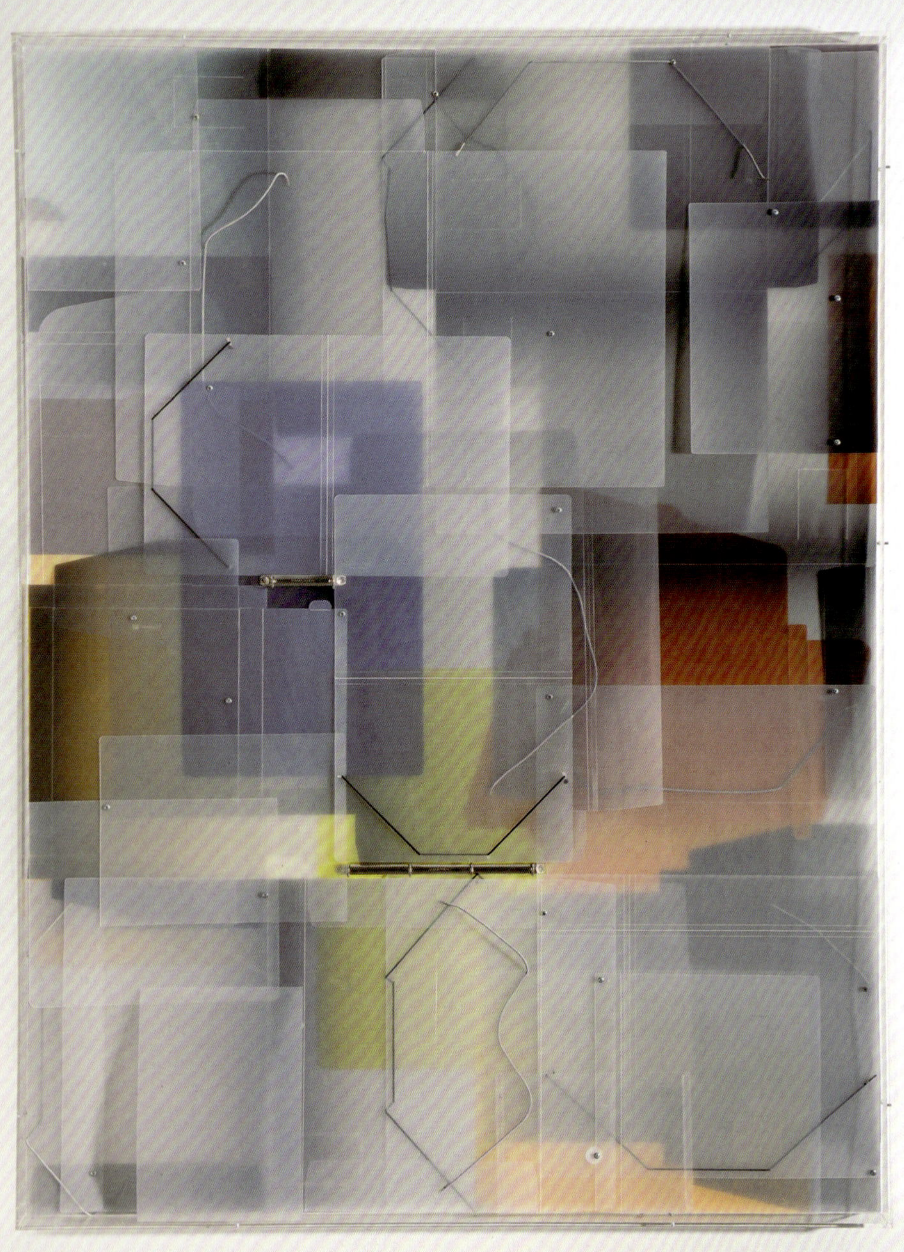

London

2012, Plastic, MDF,
150 × 100 × 3 cm, Museum für
Konkrete Kunst, Ingolstadt

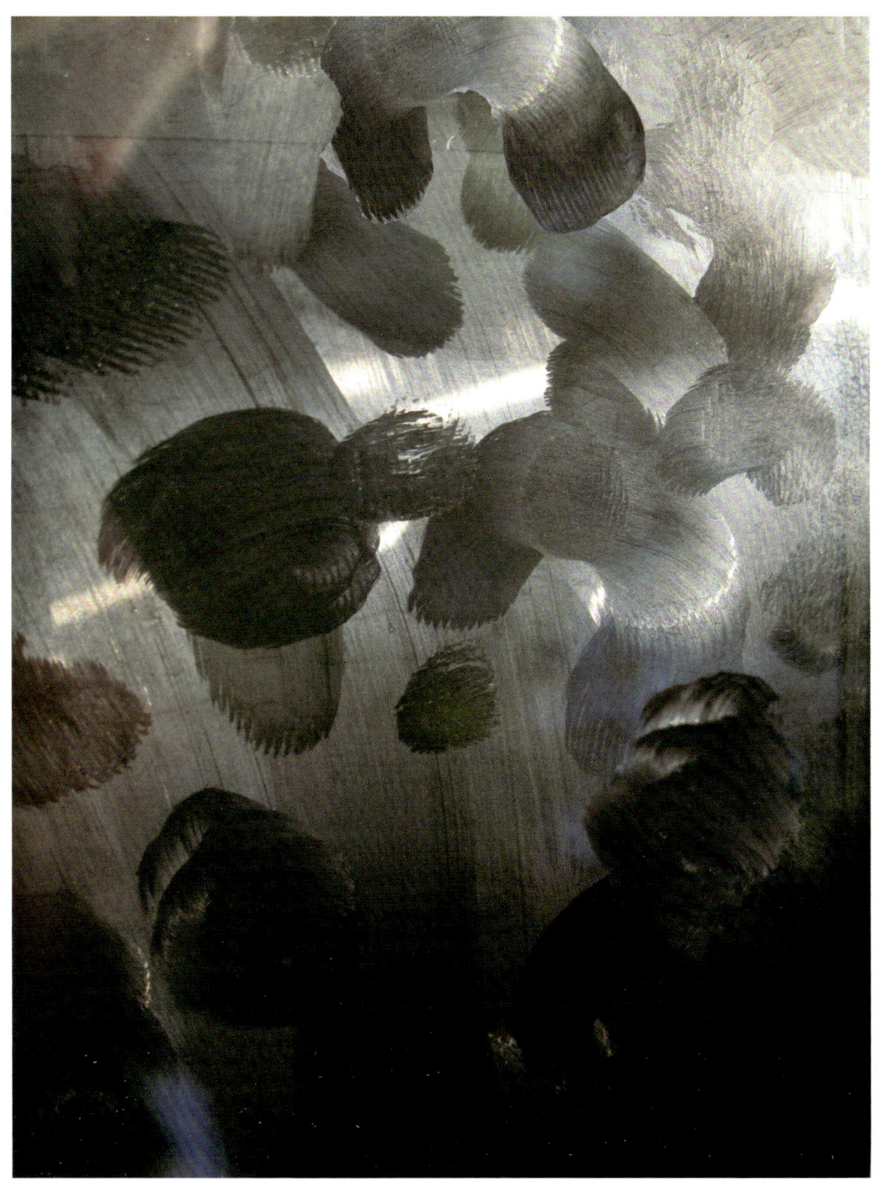

Sweatprint (heiter bis wolkig)

2012, Photo on aluminium composite panel, 42 × 32 cm, Private collection

Sweatprints are photos of the fingerprints on touchscreens.

Sweatprints sont des photos d'empreintes digitales sur des écrans tactiles.

Sweatprints sind Fotos von den Fingerabdrücken auf touchscreens.

Sweatprints son fotos de las huellas dactilares en las pantallas táctiles.

Le sweatprints sono foto delle impronte lasciate sui touchscreen.

Sweatprints zijn foto's van de vingerafdrukken op touchscreens.

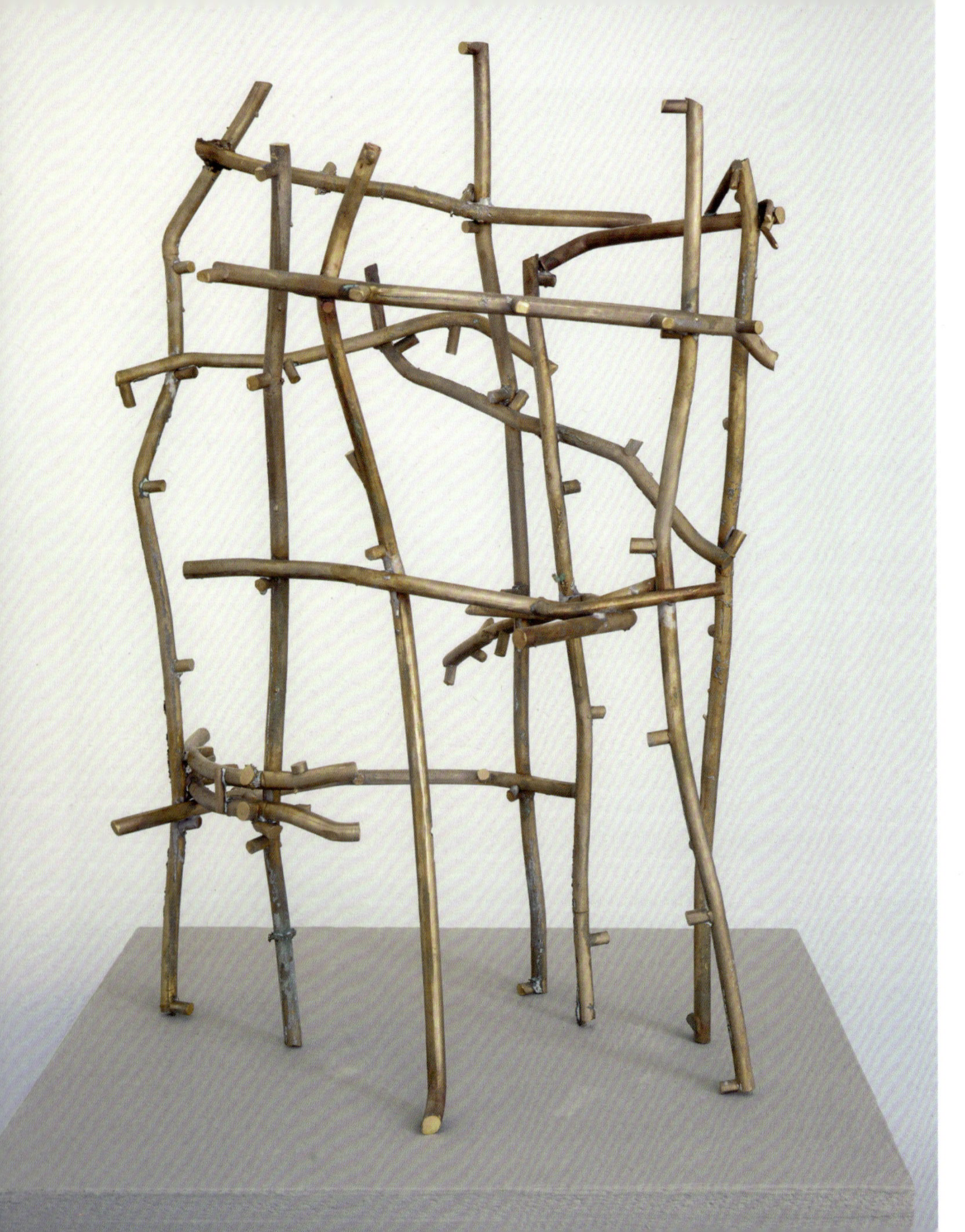

Gusspfeiffen 1

2014, Bronze cast pipes (remnants), 70 × 55 cm, Private collection

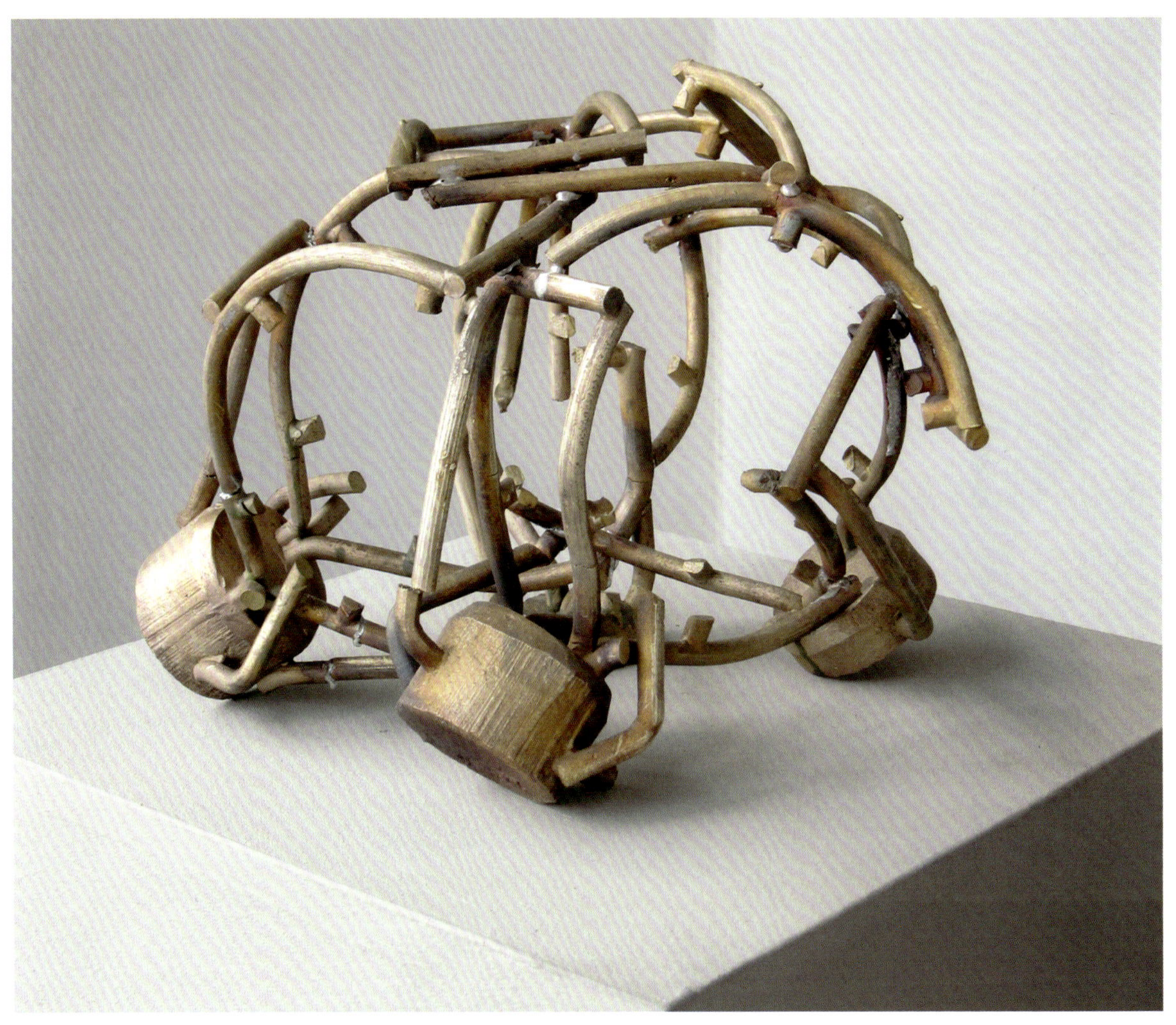

Gusspfeiffen 2

2014, Bronze cast pipes (remnants), Ø 35 cm, Private collection

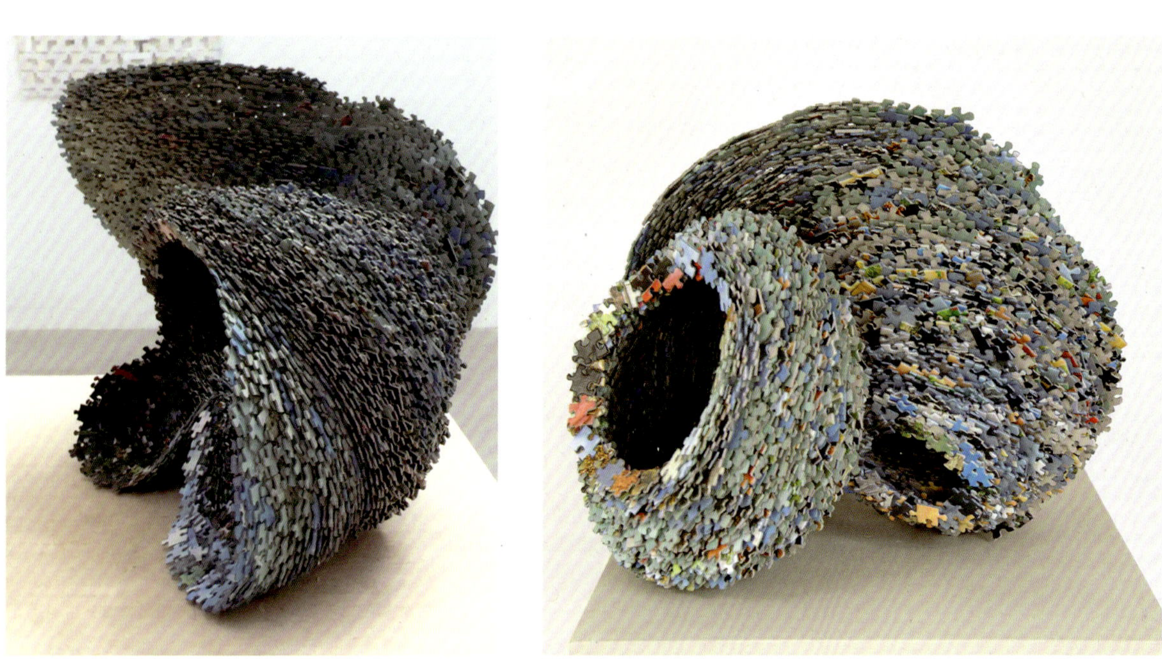

Stratigrafie 1, 2

2009–2017, Cardboard, adhesives, Kunstmuseum Villa Zanders, Bergisch Gladbach

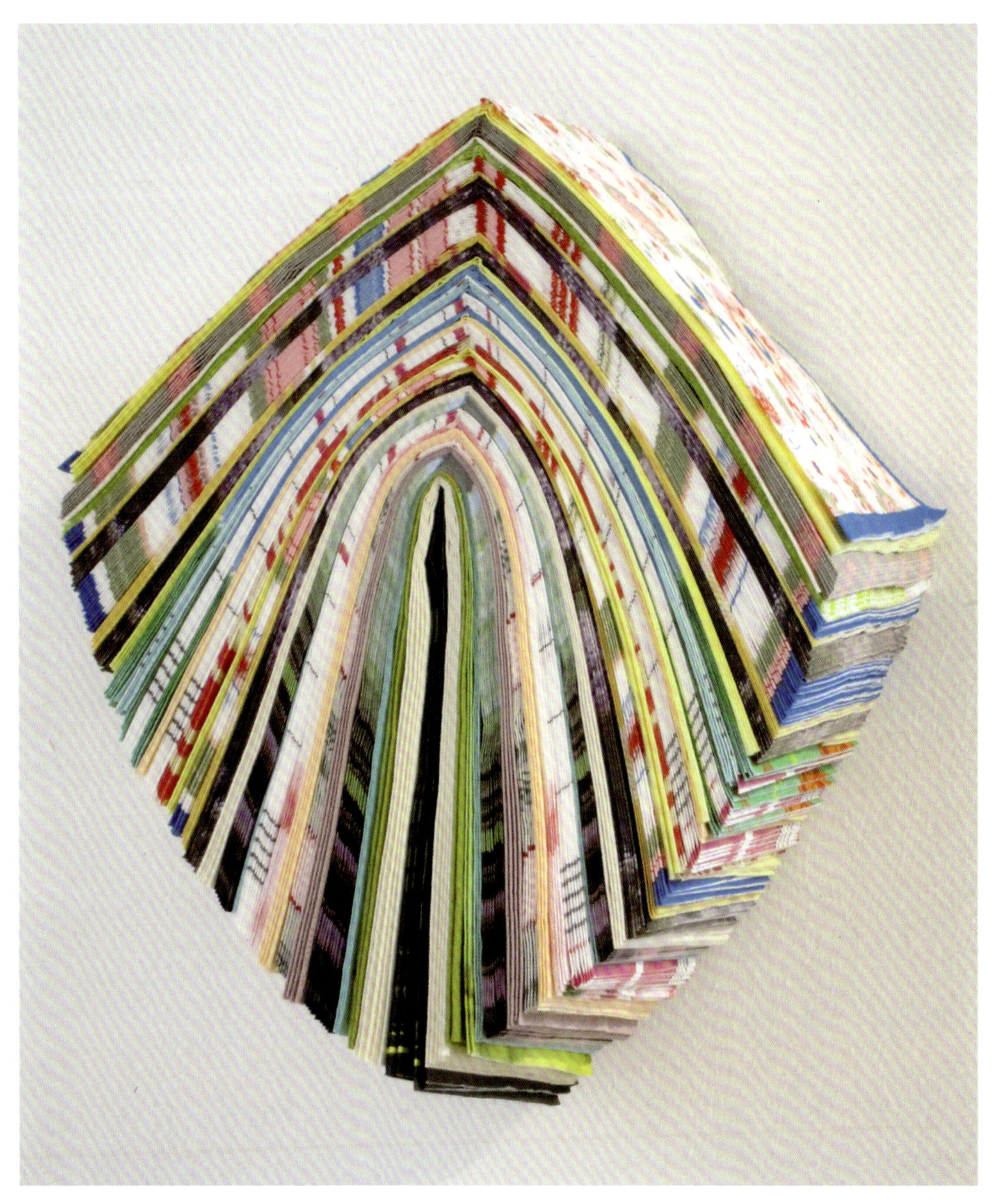

o.T.

2016, Napkins, metal,
30 × 23 × 18 cm

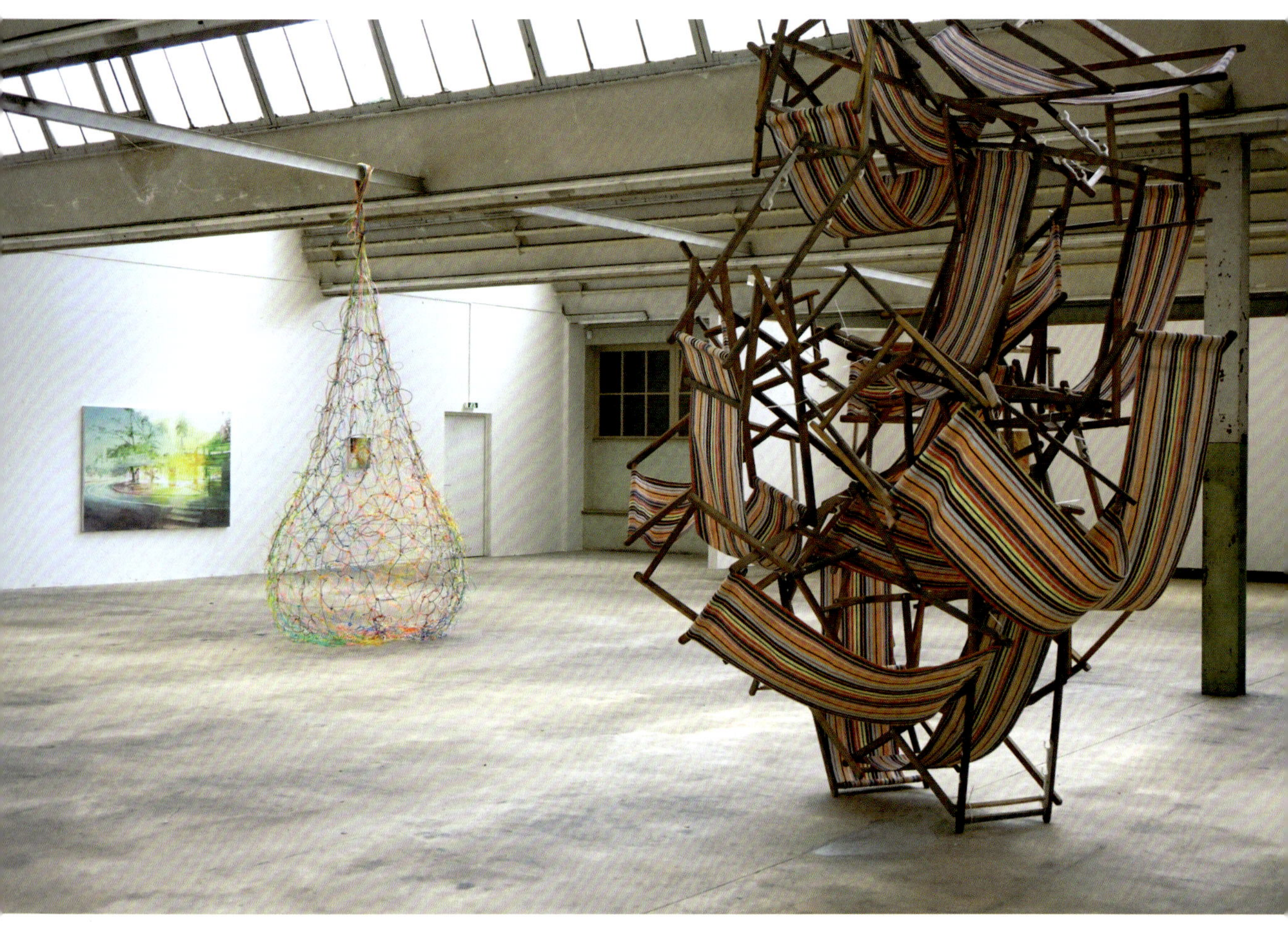

Anja Ganster

2014

Netzwerk

2015, Clotheslines, wire, spring steel, 350 × Ø 200 cm

Fliegestühle

2012, Wood, textiles, metal, 240 × 350 × 200 cm

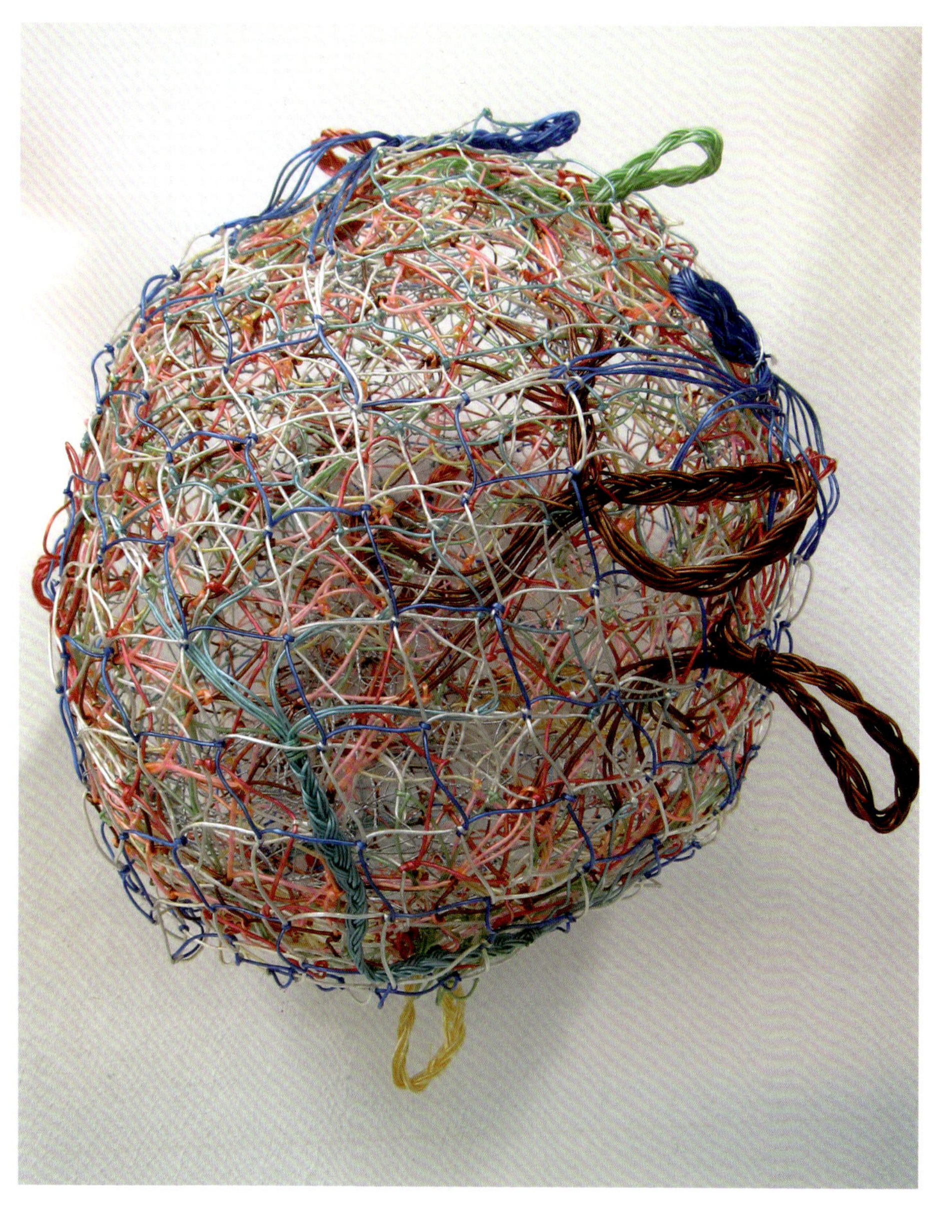

Nachverdichtet

2014, Wire, plastic

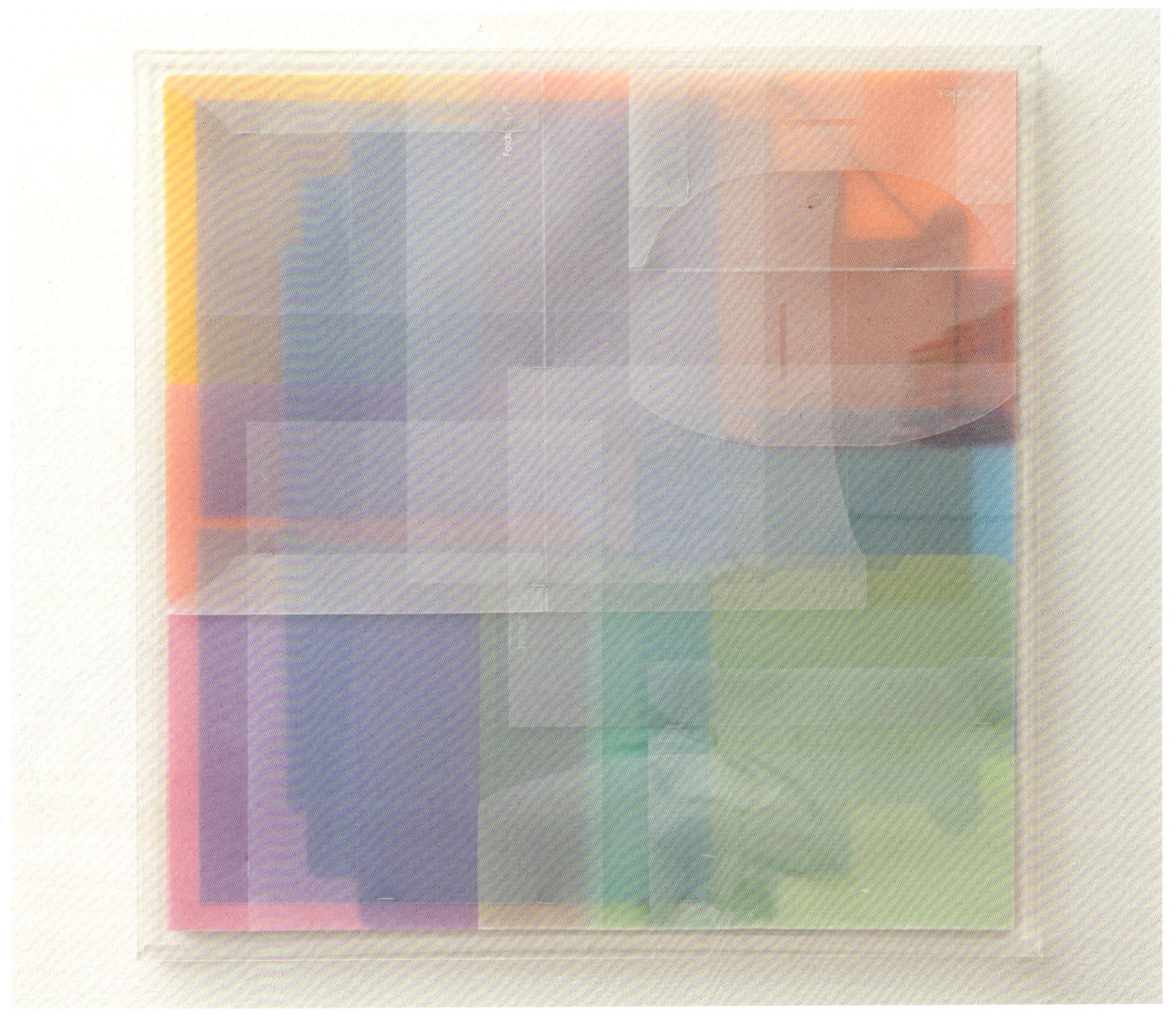

Rotenburg

2017, Plastics, MDF, 50 × 50 × 3 cm

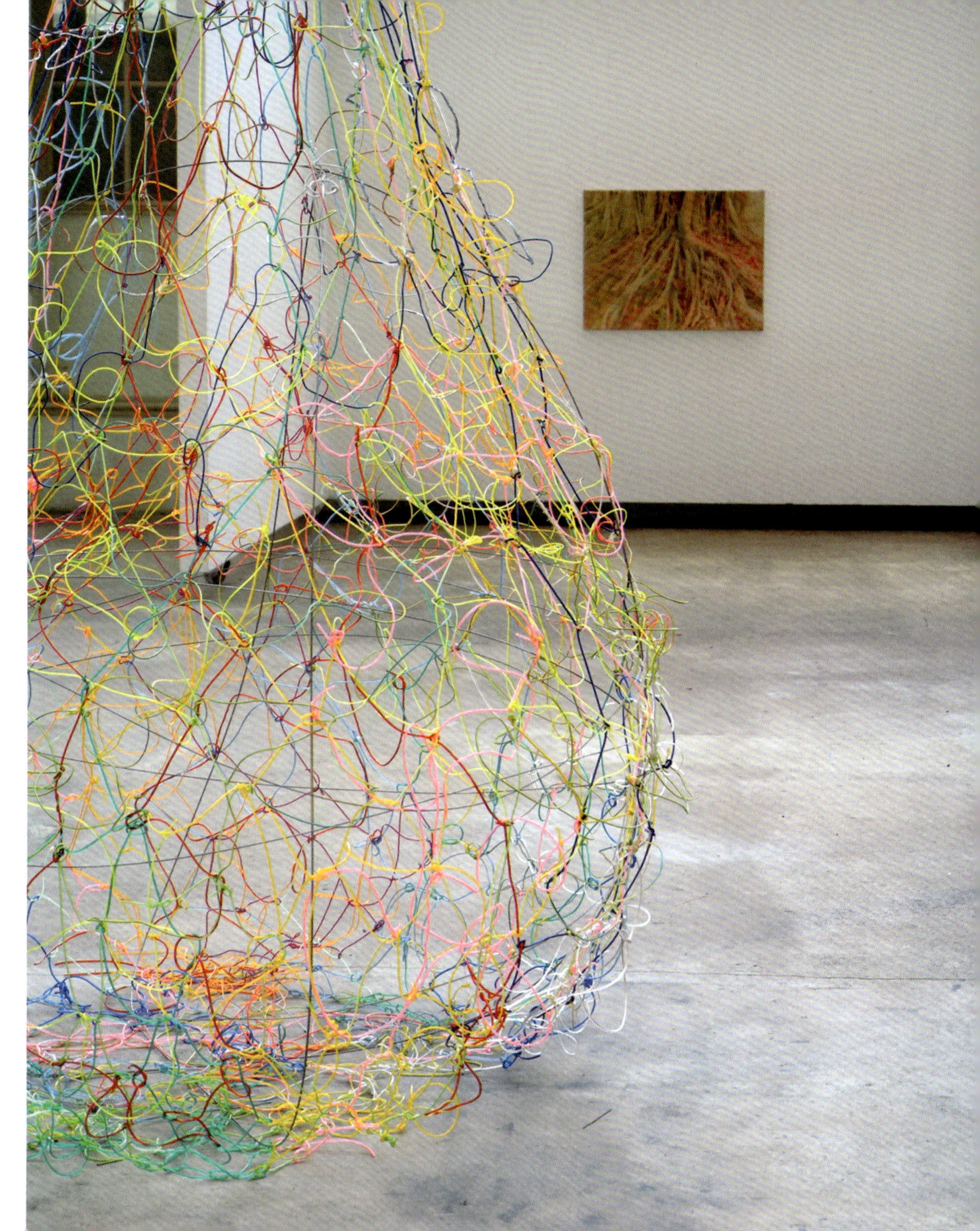

Anja Ganster

Netzwerk (Detail)

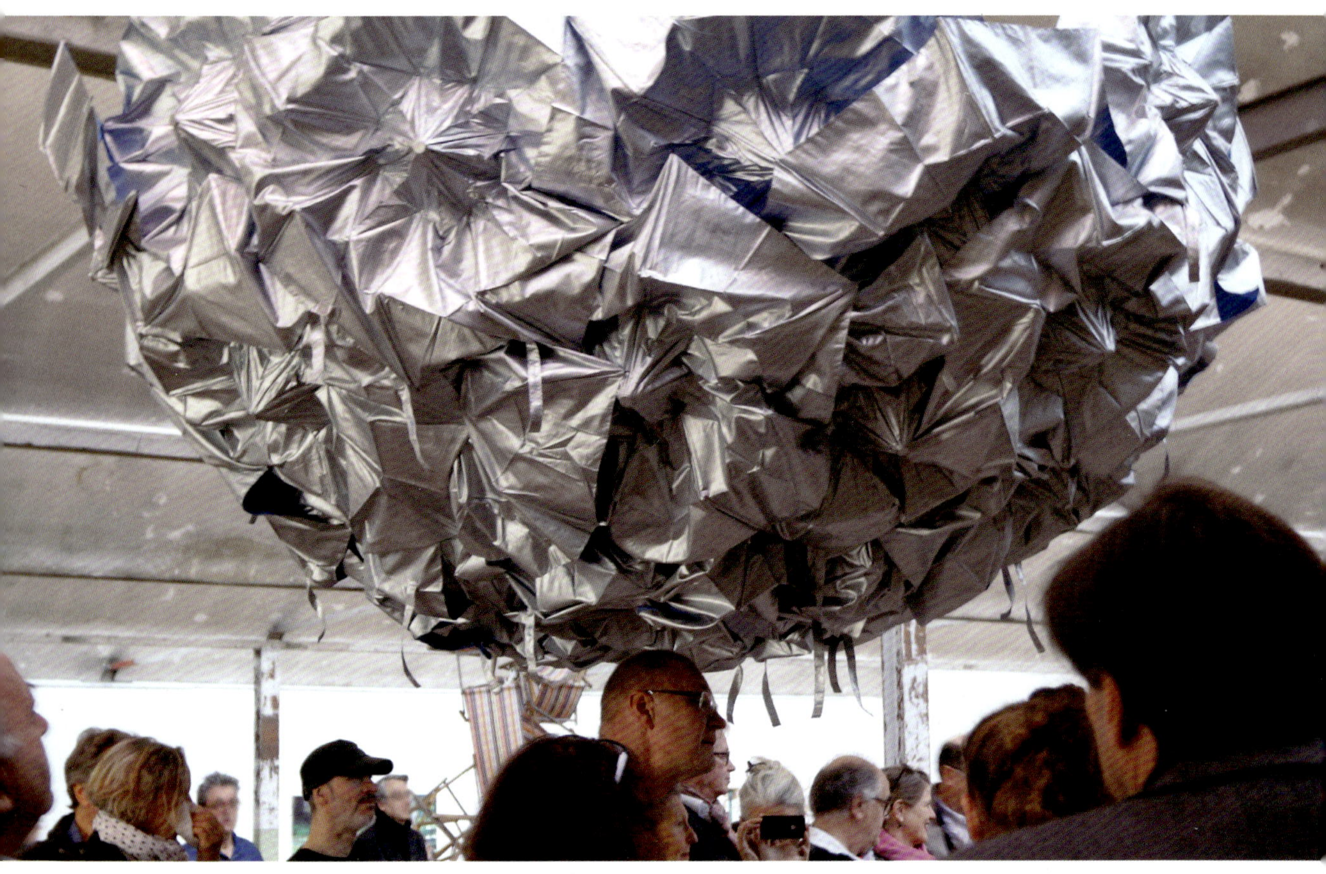

Flederschirm

2016, Metal, fabric, 160 × 250 cm

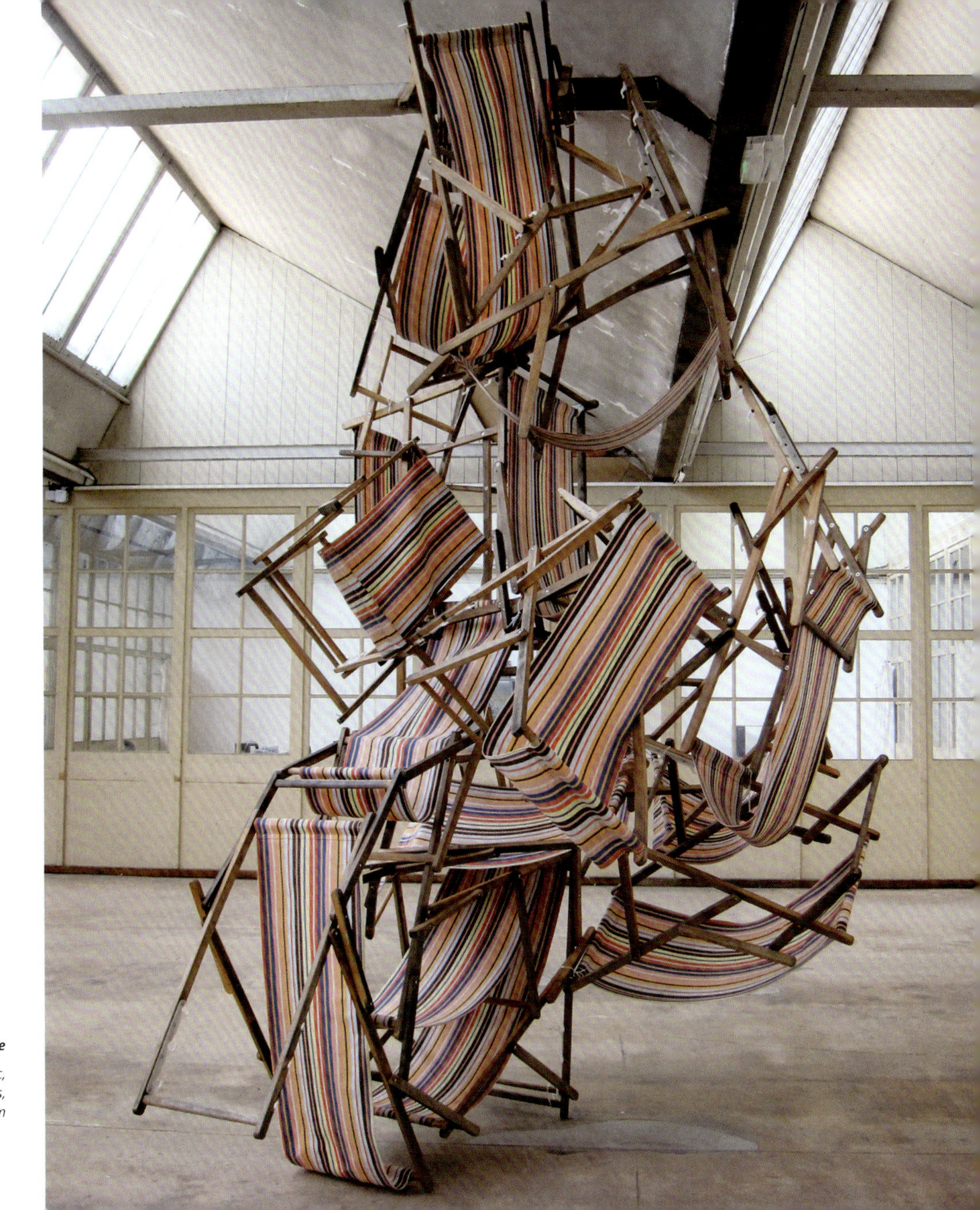

Fliegestühle

*2012/17, Wood, fabric,
metal, cable ties,
370 × 260 × 290 cm*

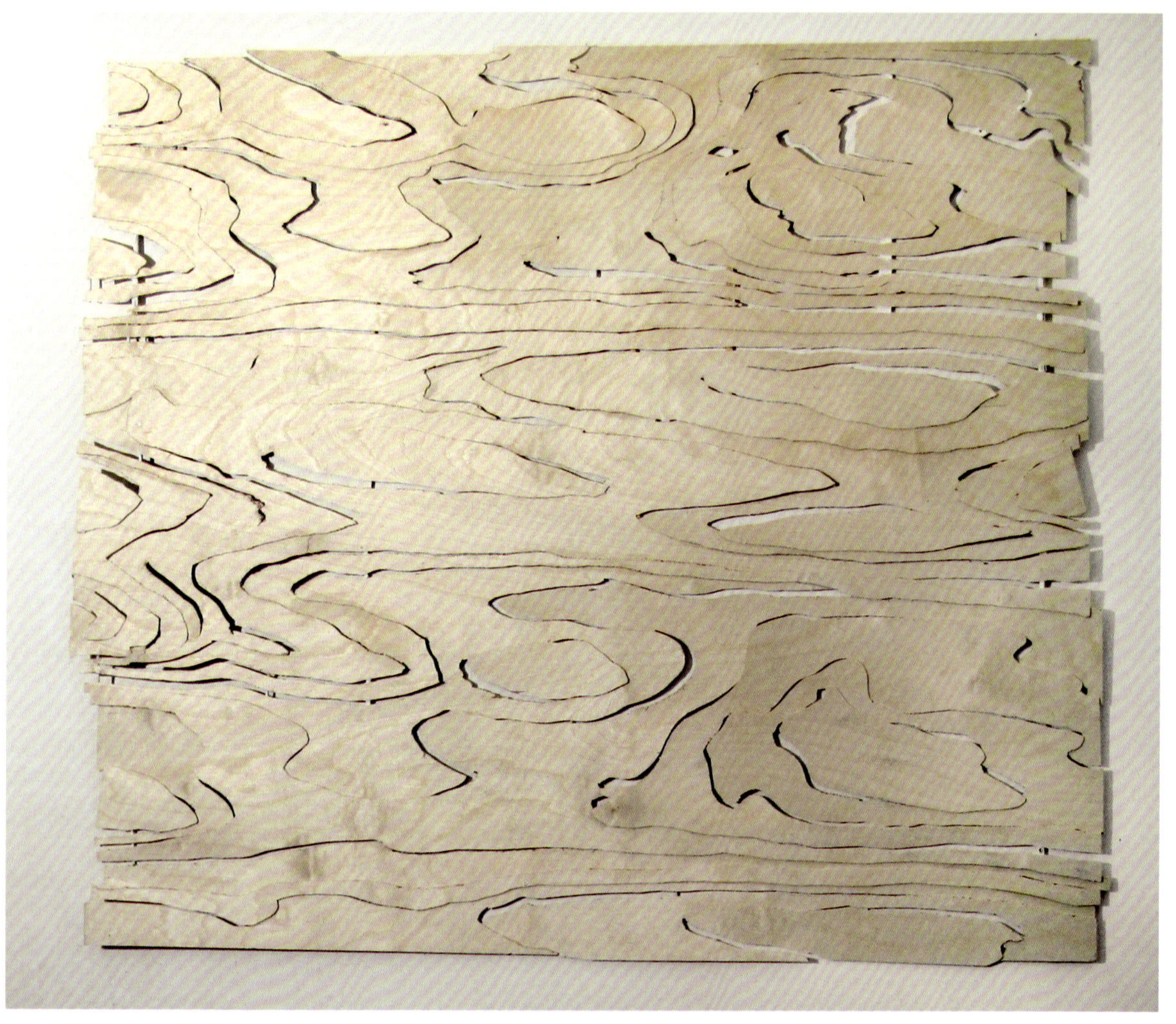

Große Welle

2013, Laminated wood, 89 × 114 cm

Aquaplaning I

2013, Mixed media, 180 × 250 × 70 cm

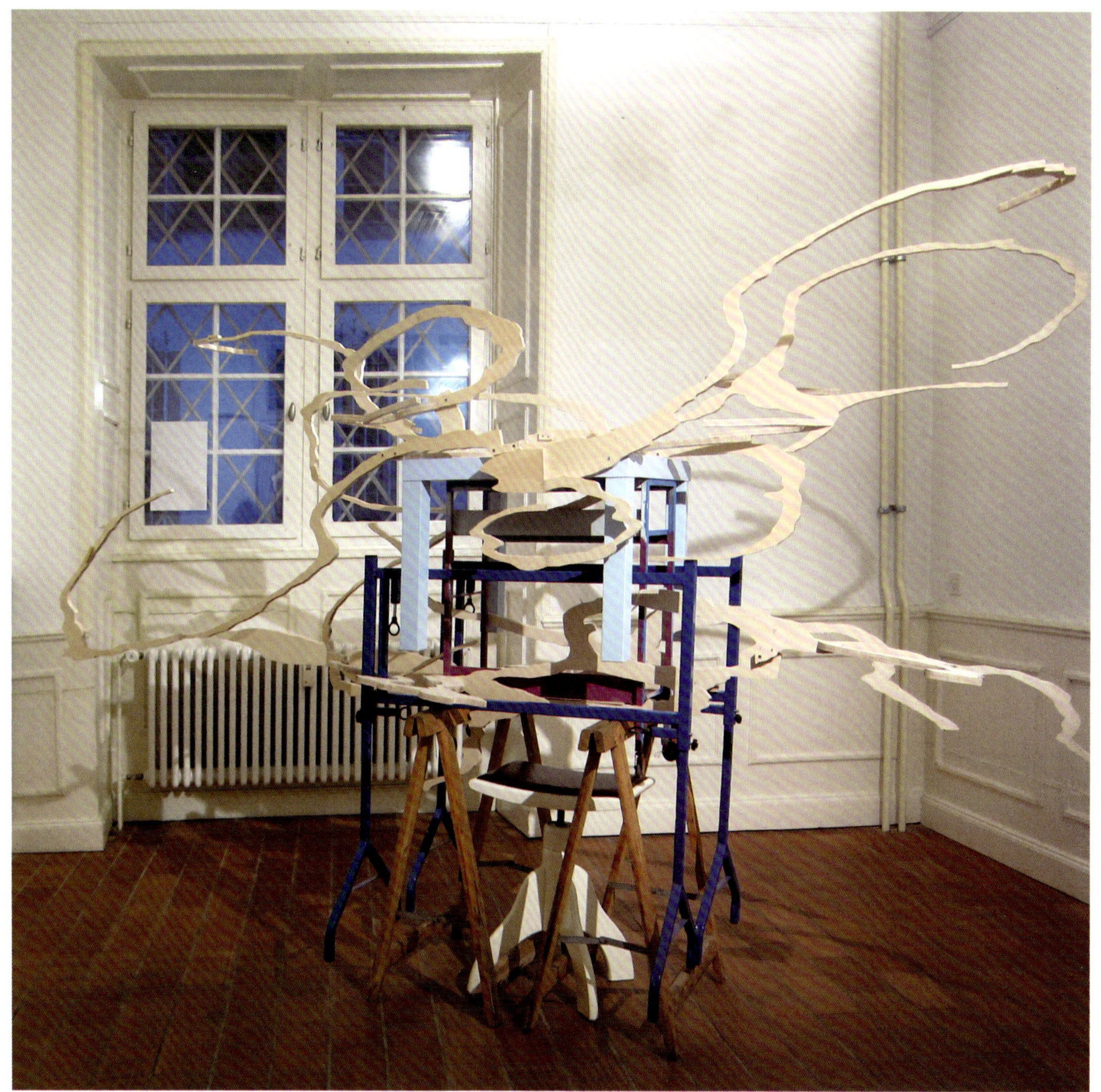

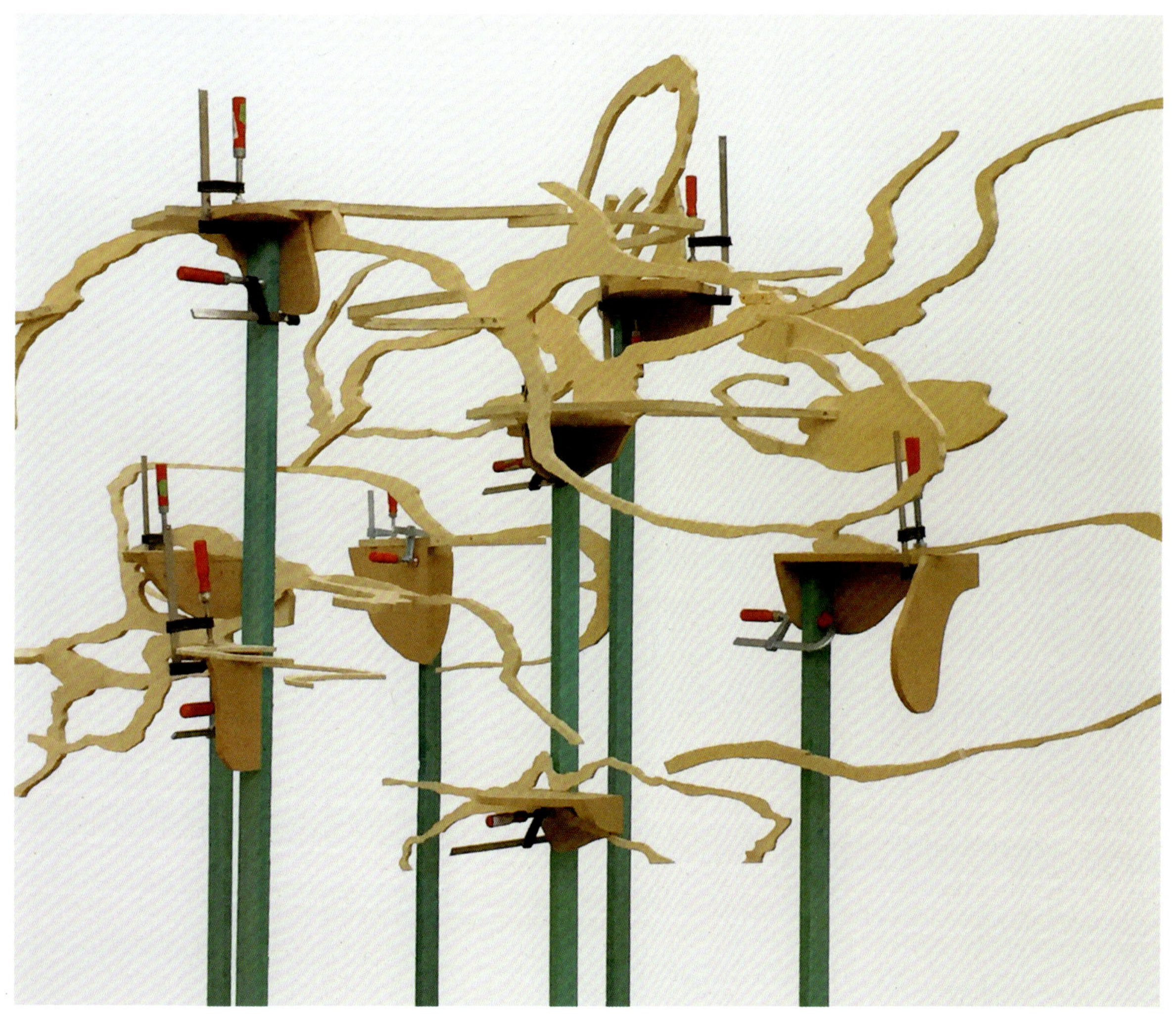

Aquaplaning II

2015, Wood, metal, 245 × 330 × 170 cm

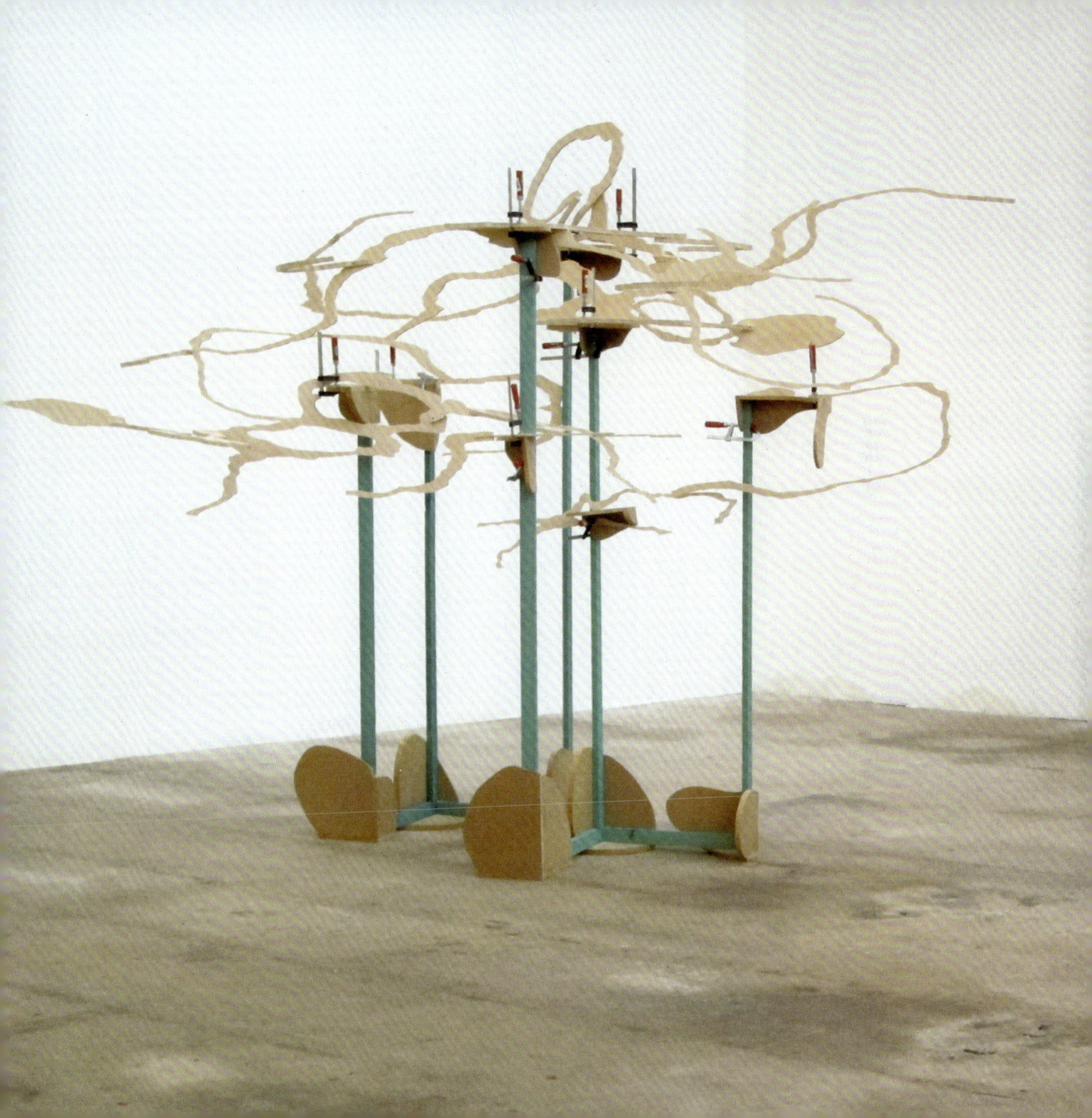

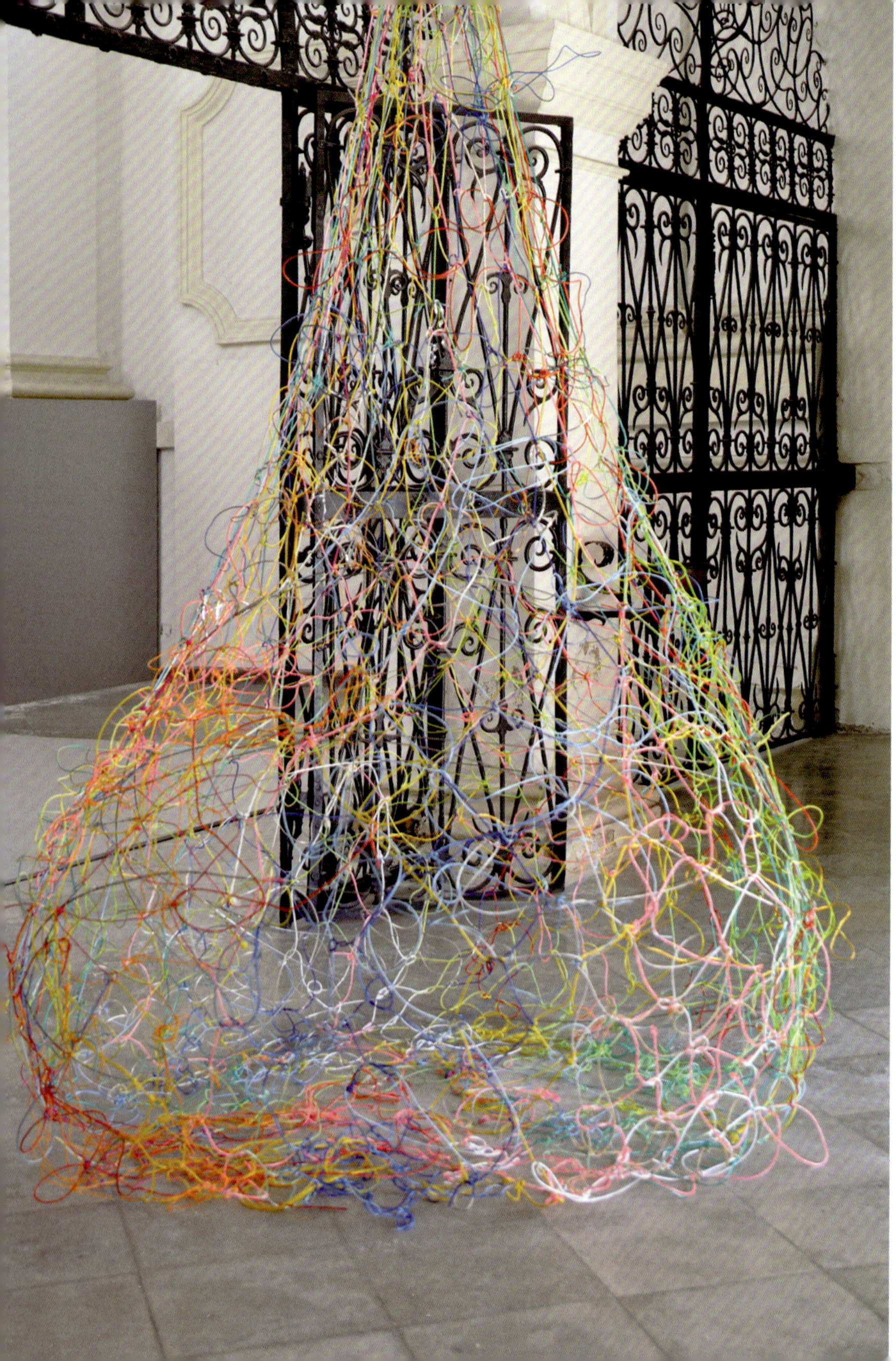

Netzwerk

2015, Clotheslines, wire, spring steel,
280 × 180 cm

o.T.

2016, Wood, table trestles,
600 × 185 × 320 cm, Studienkirche St. Josef,
Burghausen

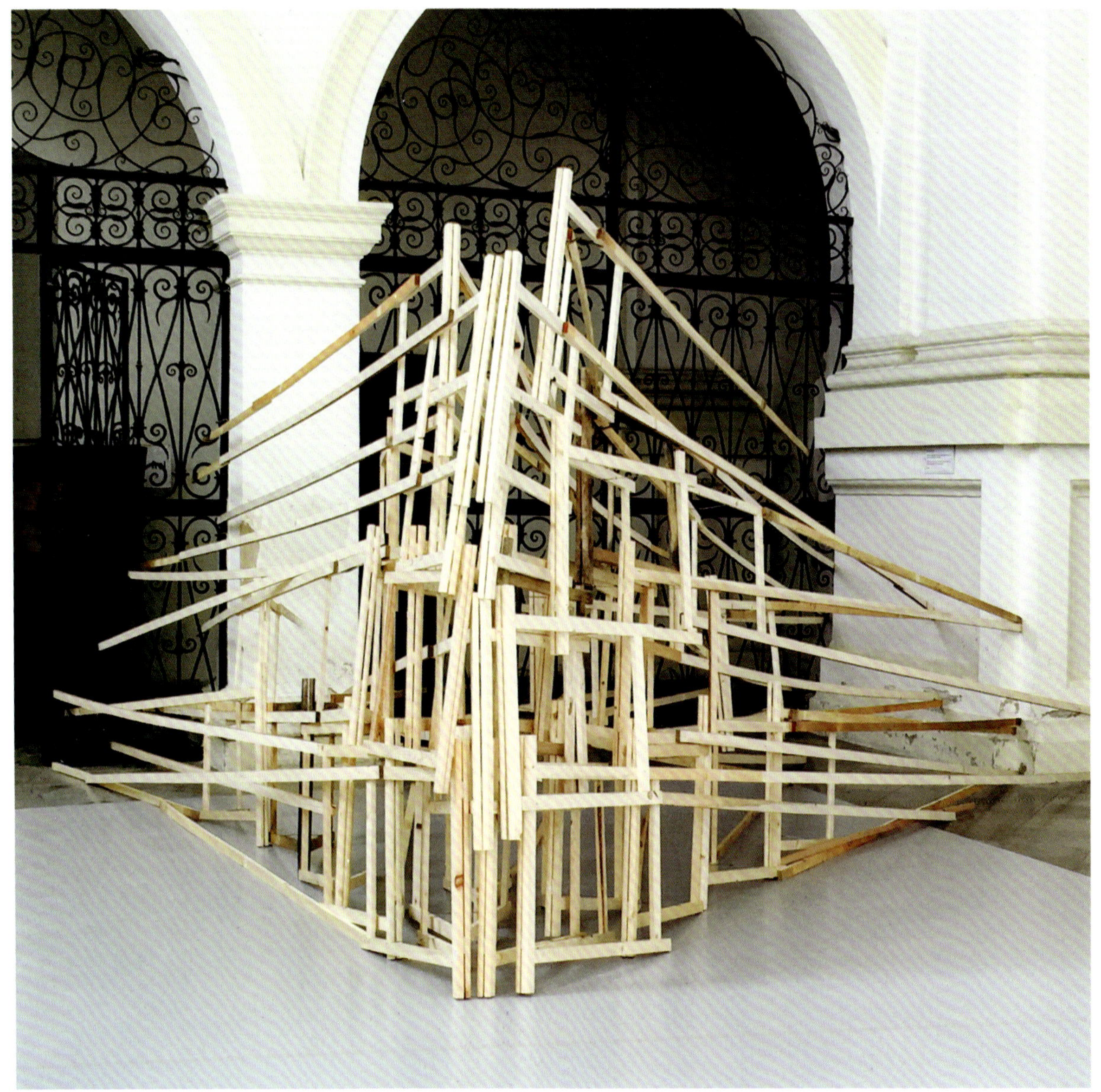

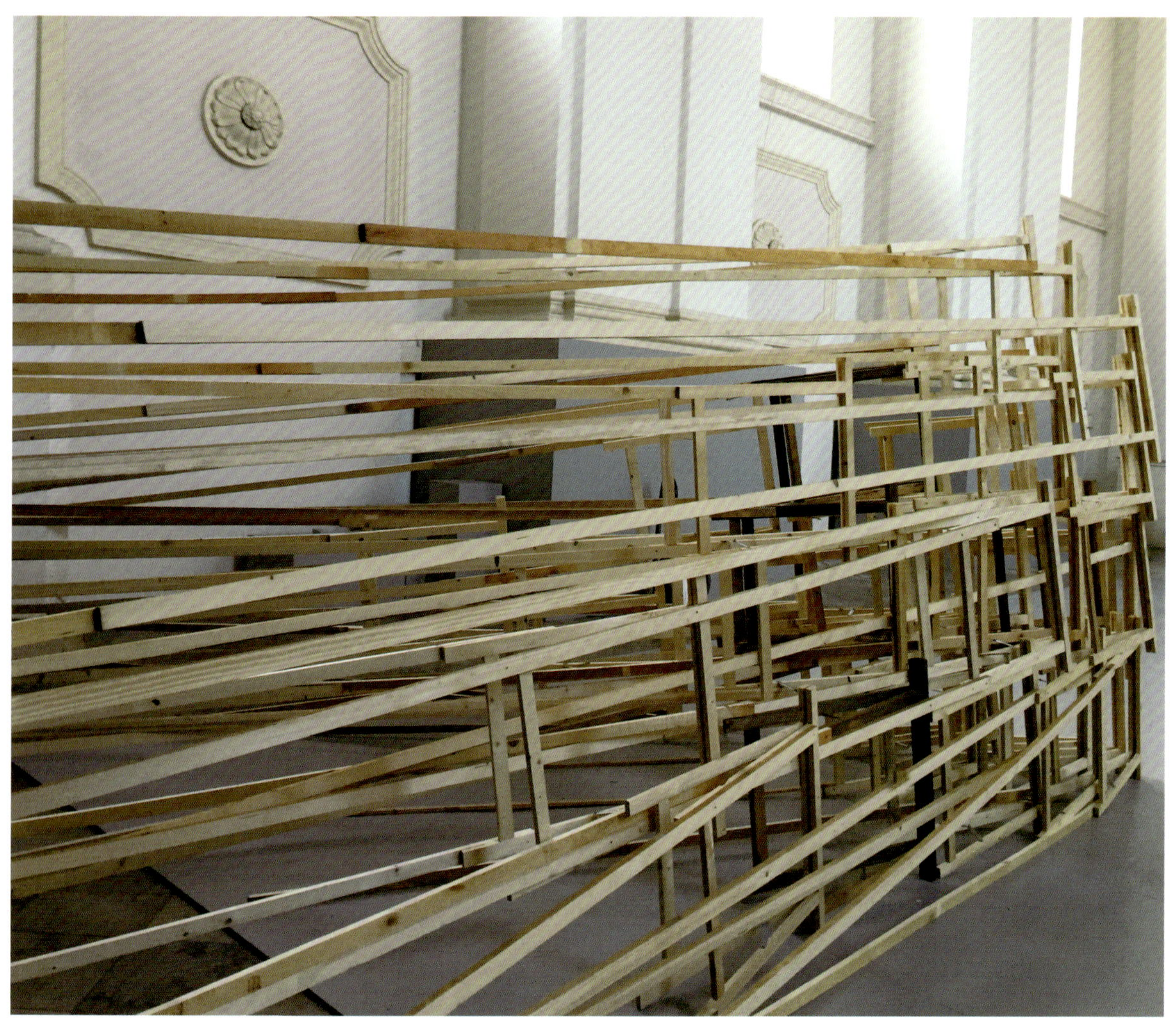

o.T.

2016, Wood, table trestles, 600 × 185 × 320 cm, Studienkirche St. Josef, Burghausen

Hangers

2017, Plastic, wood, Ø 54 × 10 cm

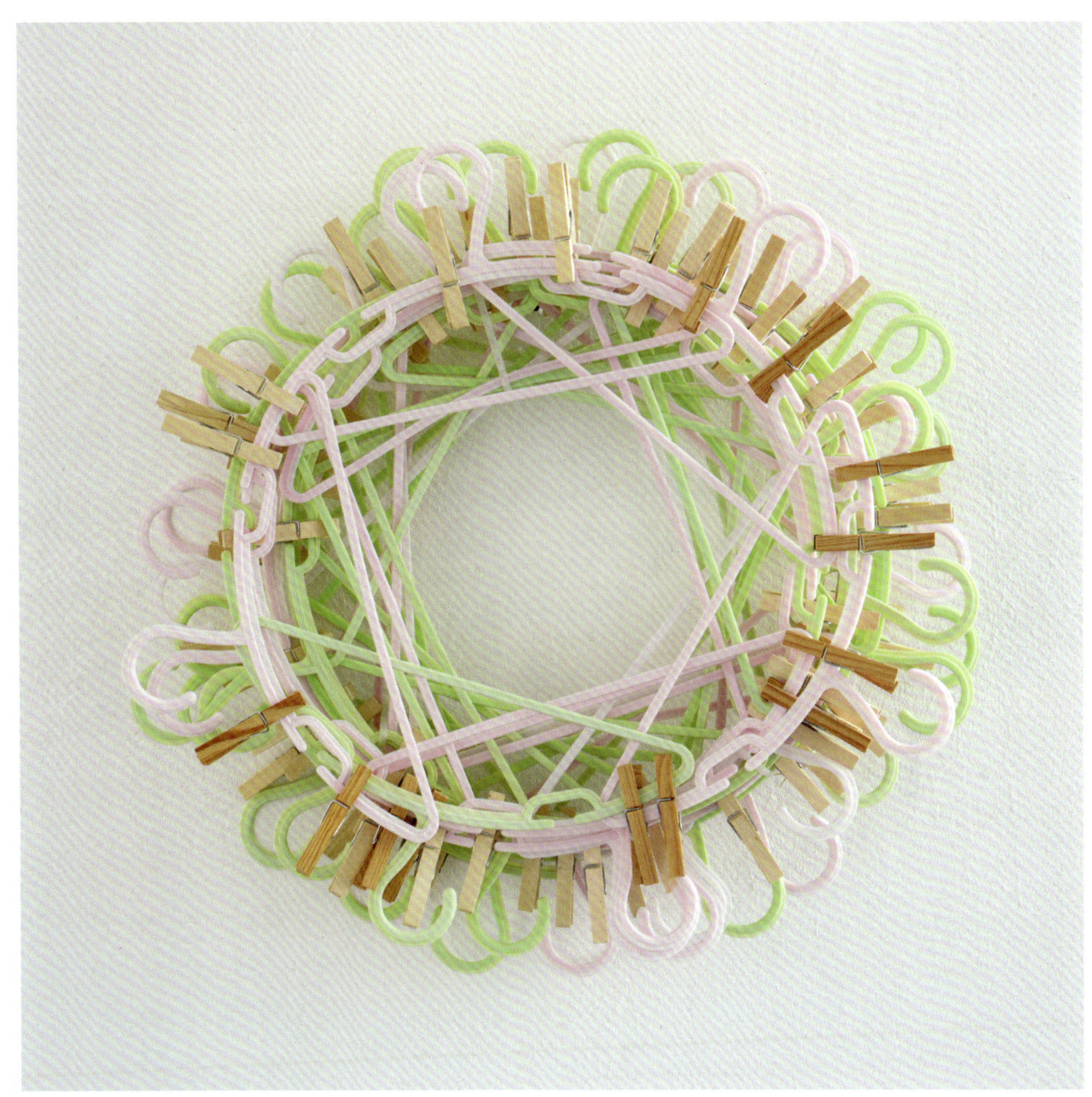

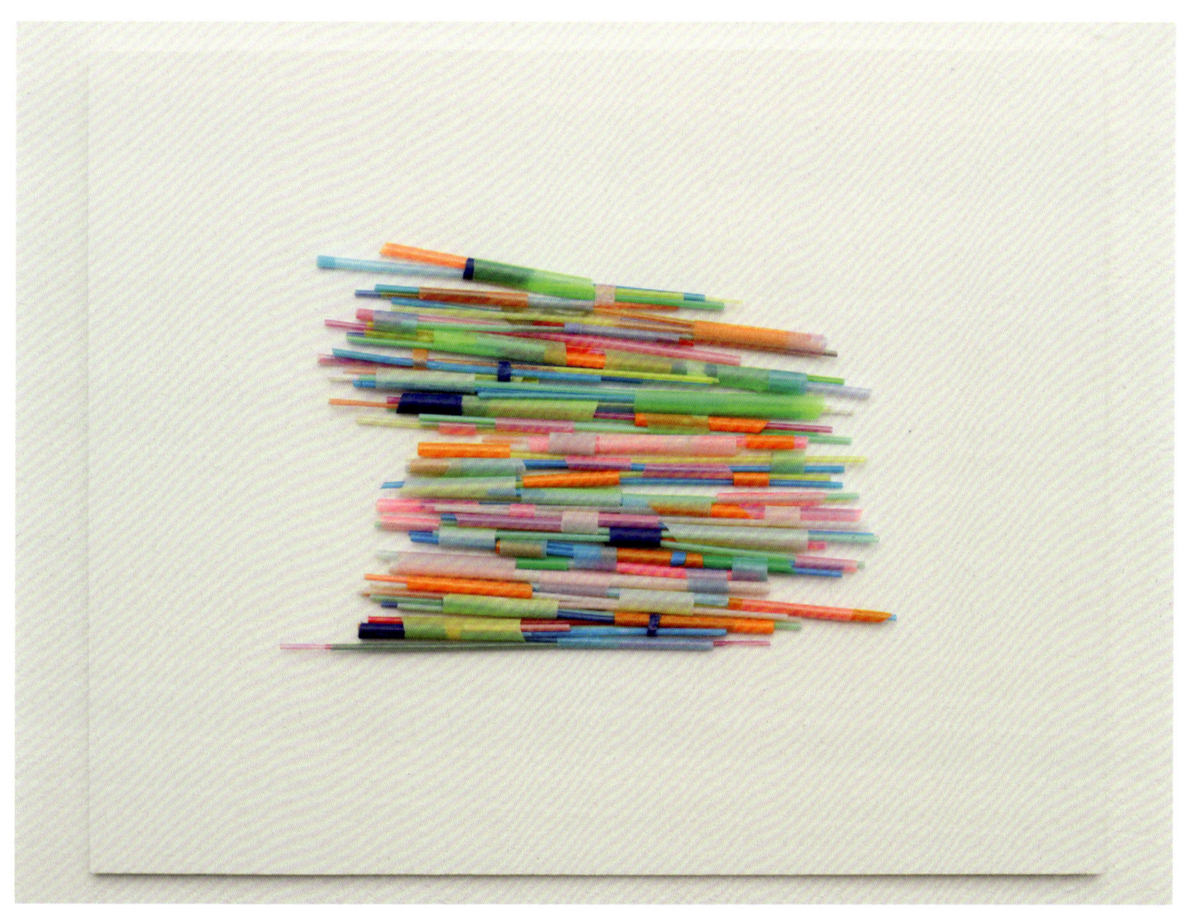

Sale

2017, Plastic, 40 × 50 × 2 cm

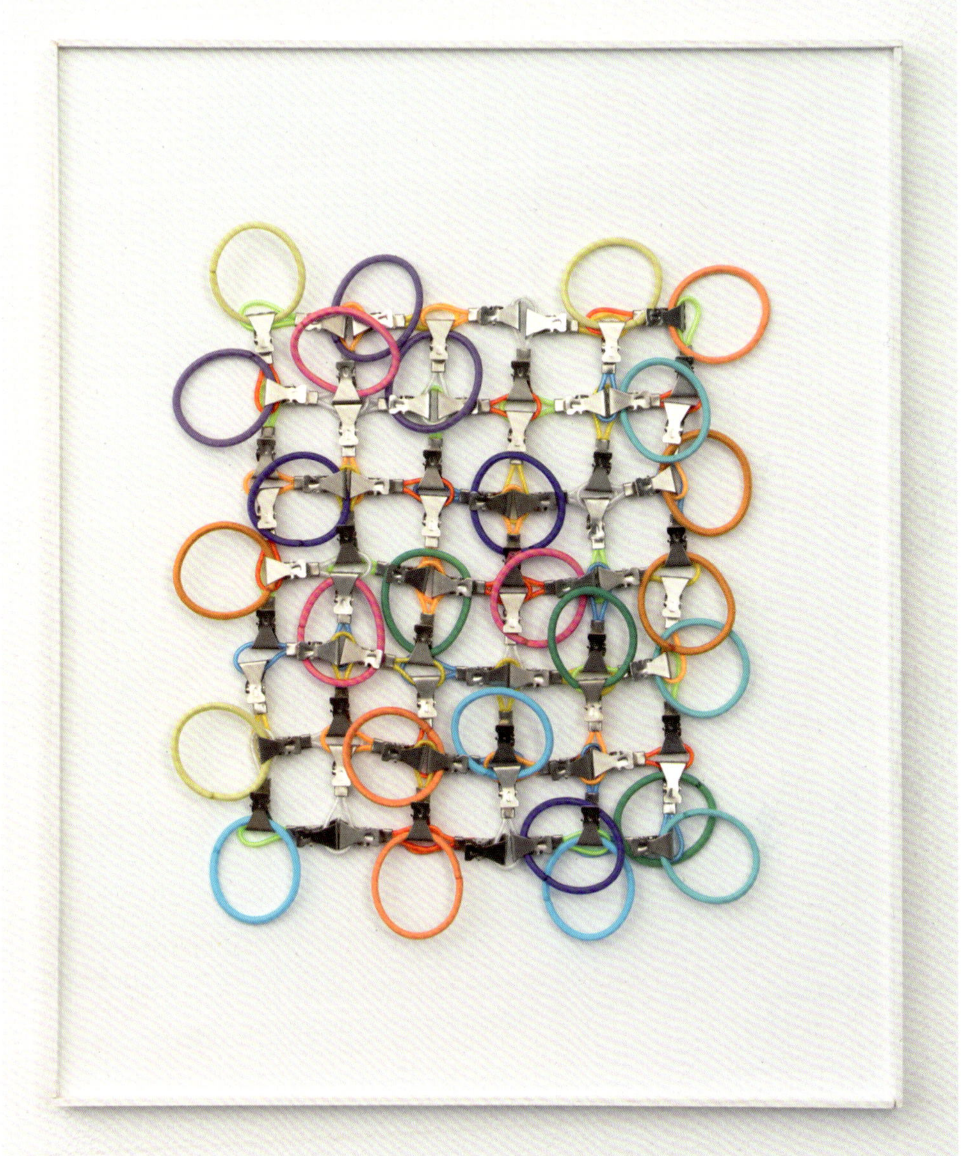

Halter

2016, Textile rubbers,
metal, 50 × 40 cm

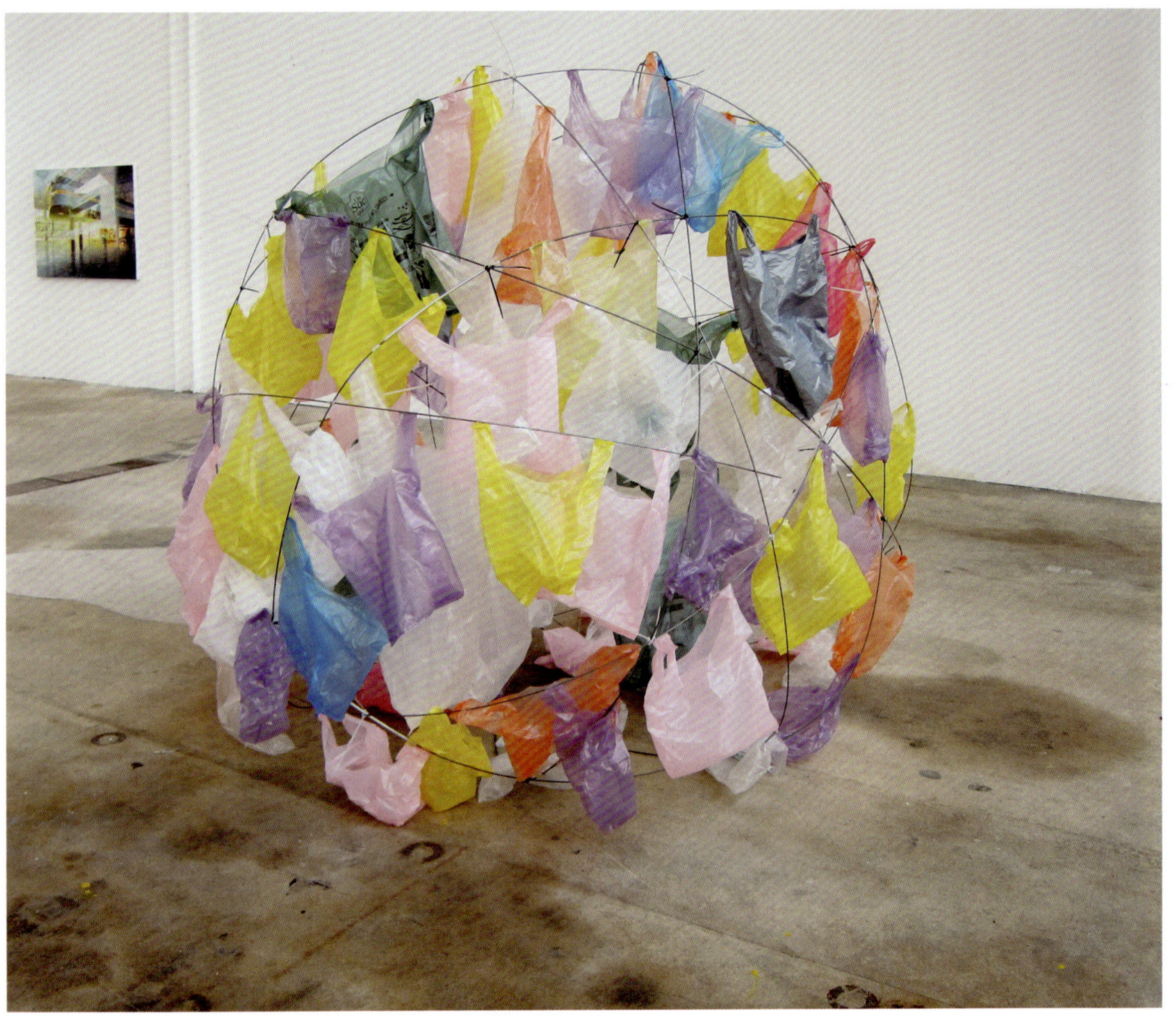

Anja Ganster

Tütenplastik

2015, Steel, plastic, 190 × 200 cm

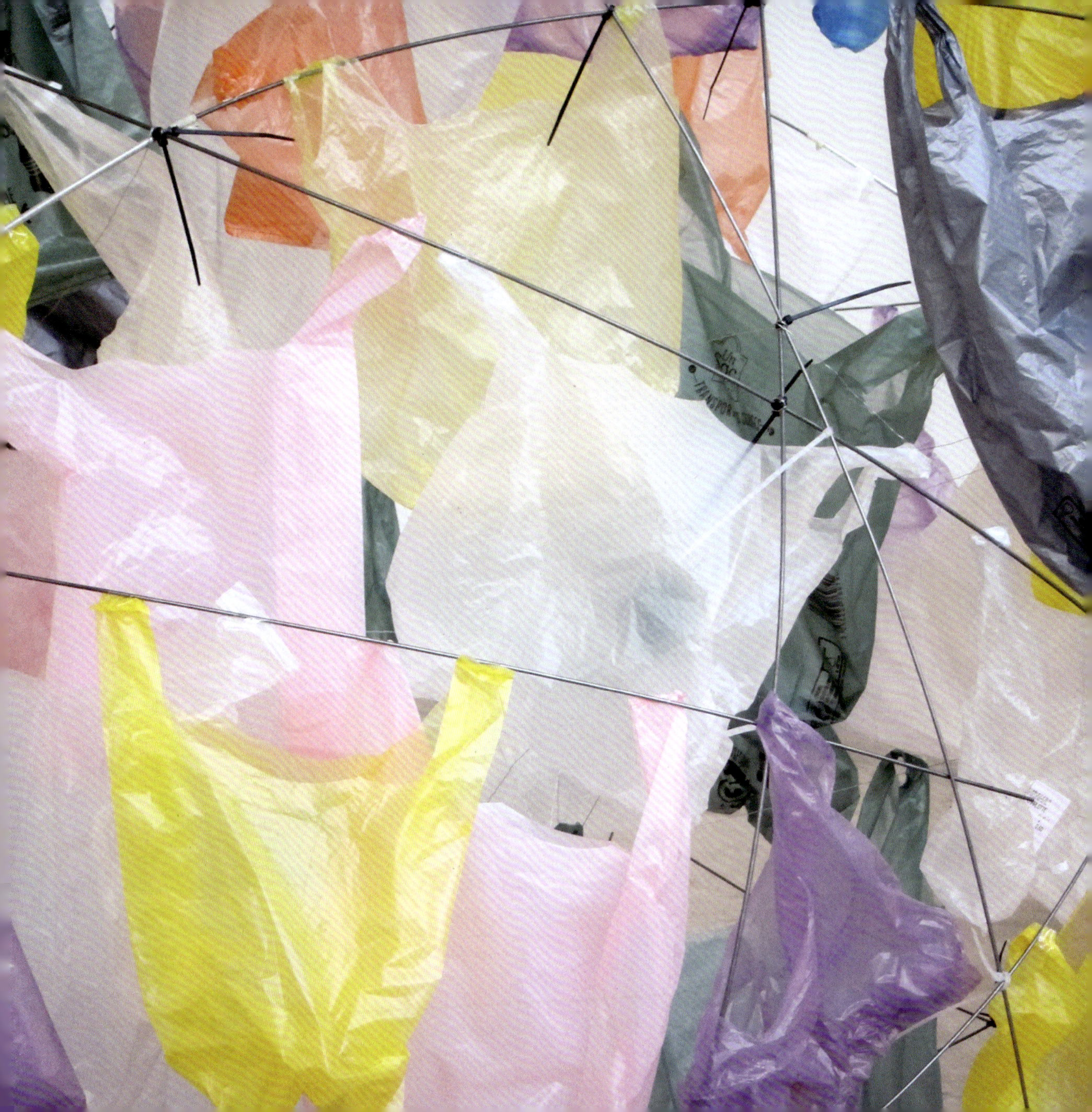

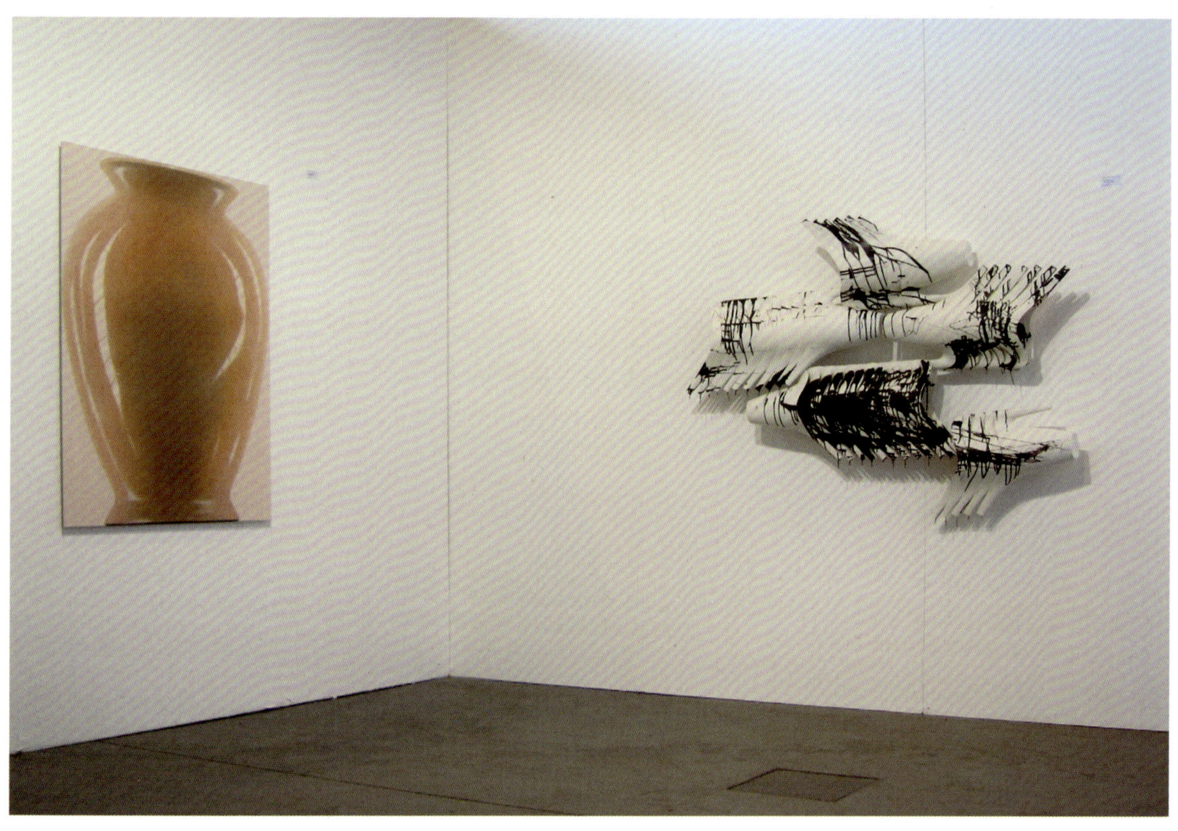

Thomas Kitzinger

Stracciatella

2016, Plastic, acrylic varnish, 115 × 125 × 15 cm

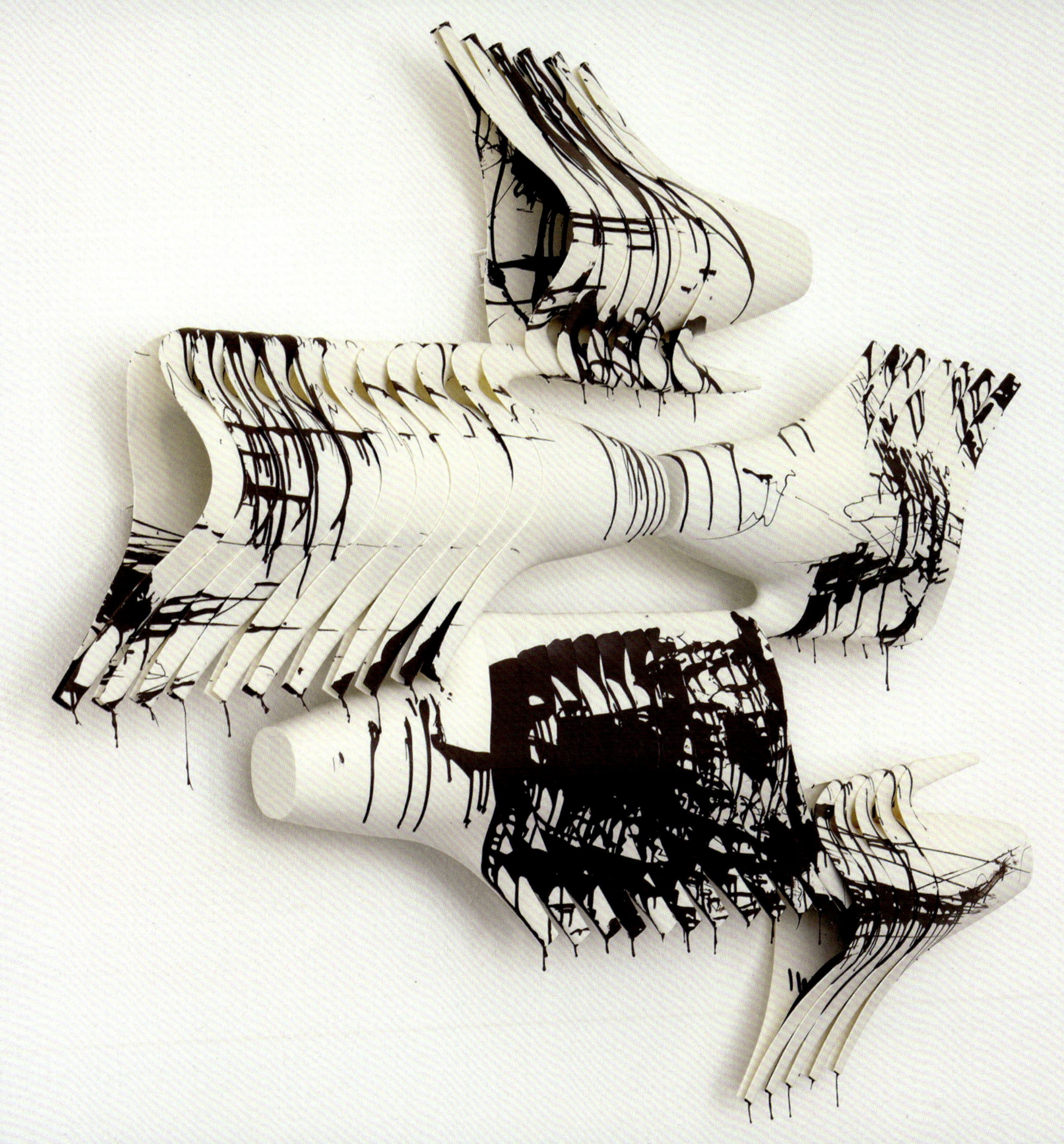

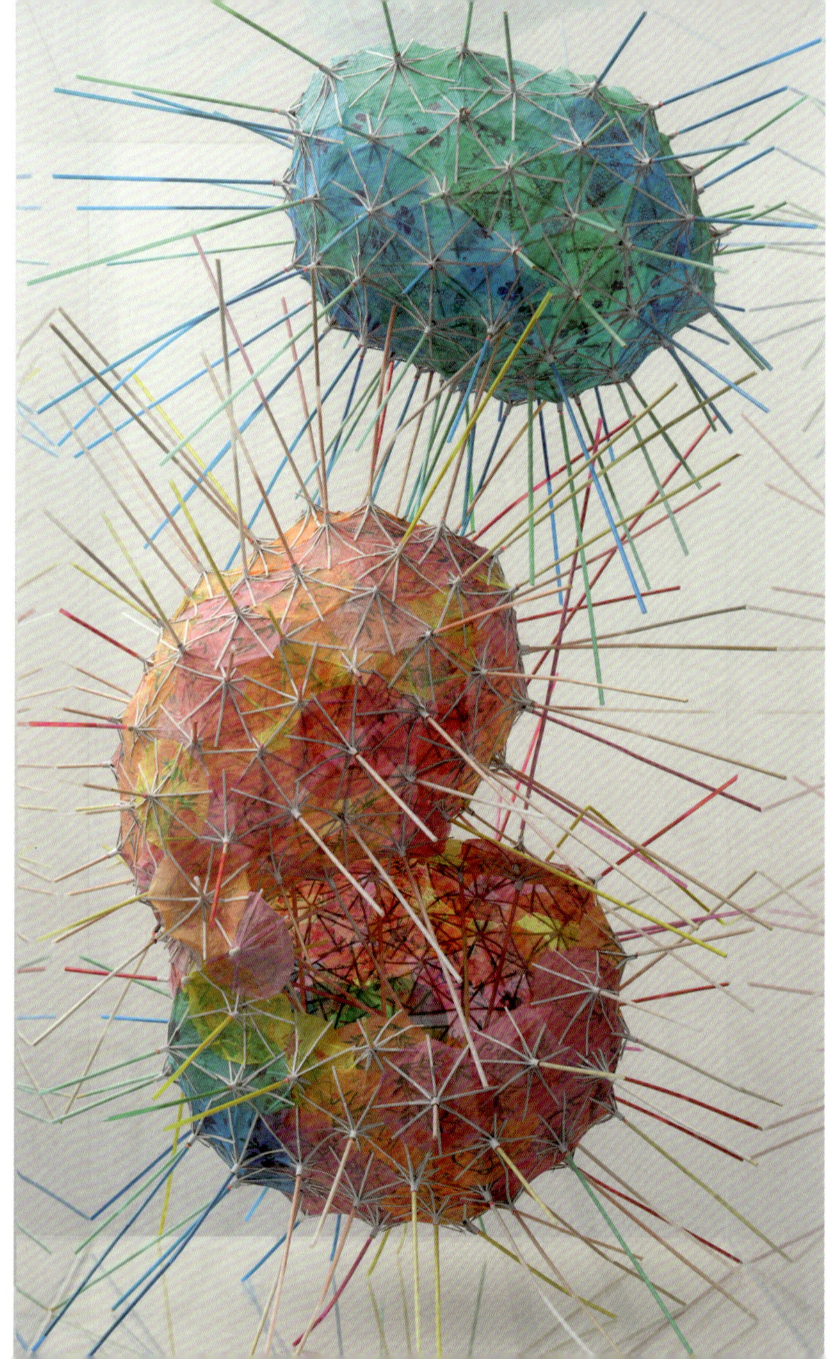

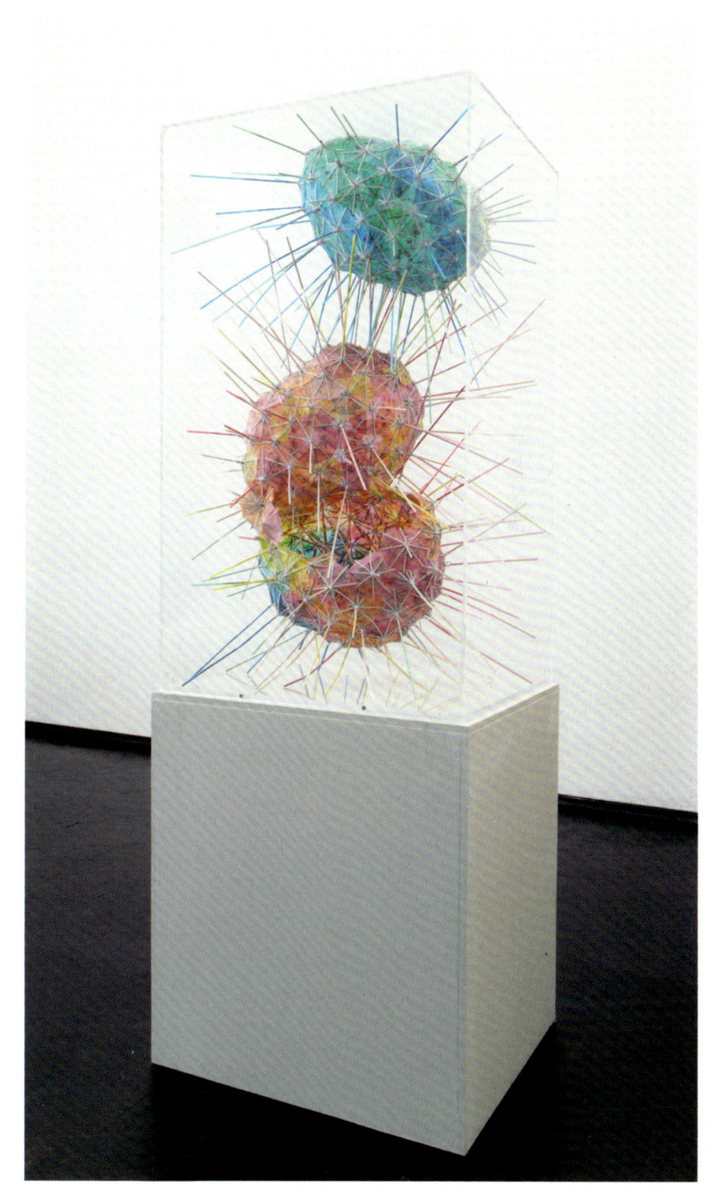

Sold

2017, Paper, wood, acrylic glass, 80 × 40 × 30 cm, Private
collection

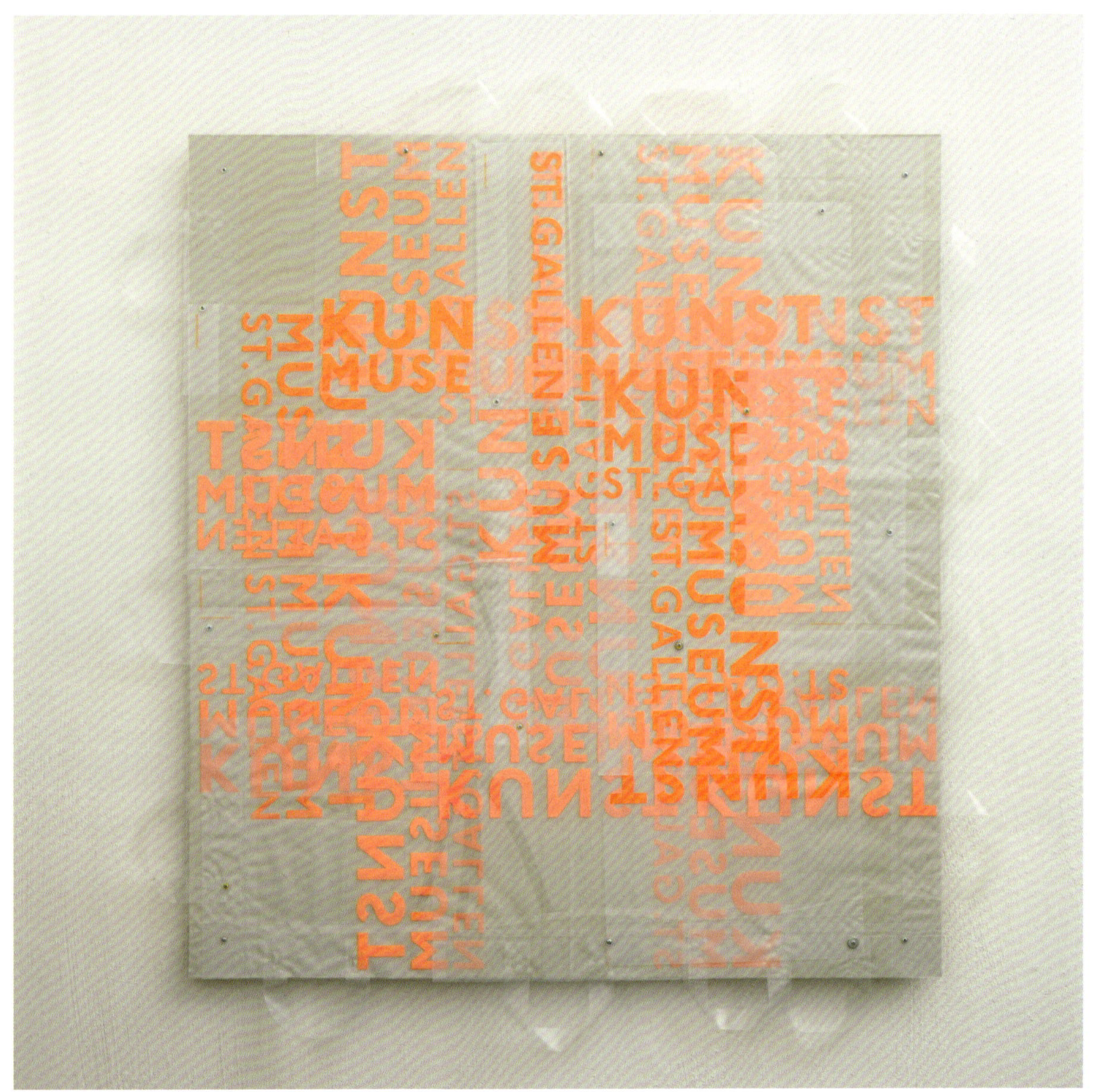

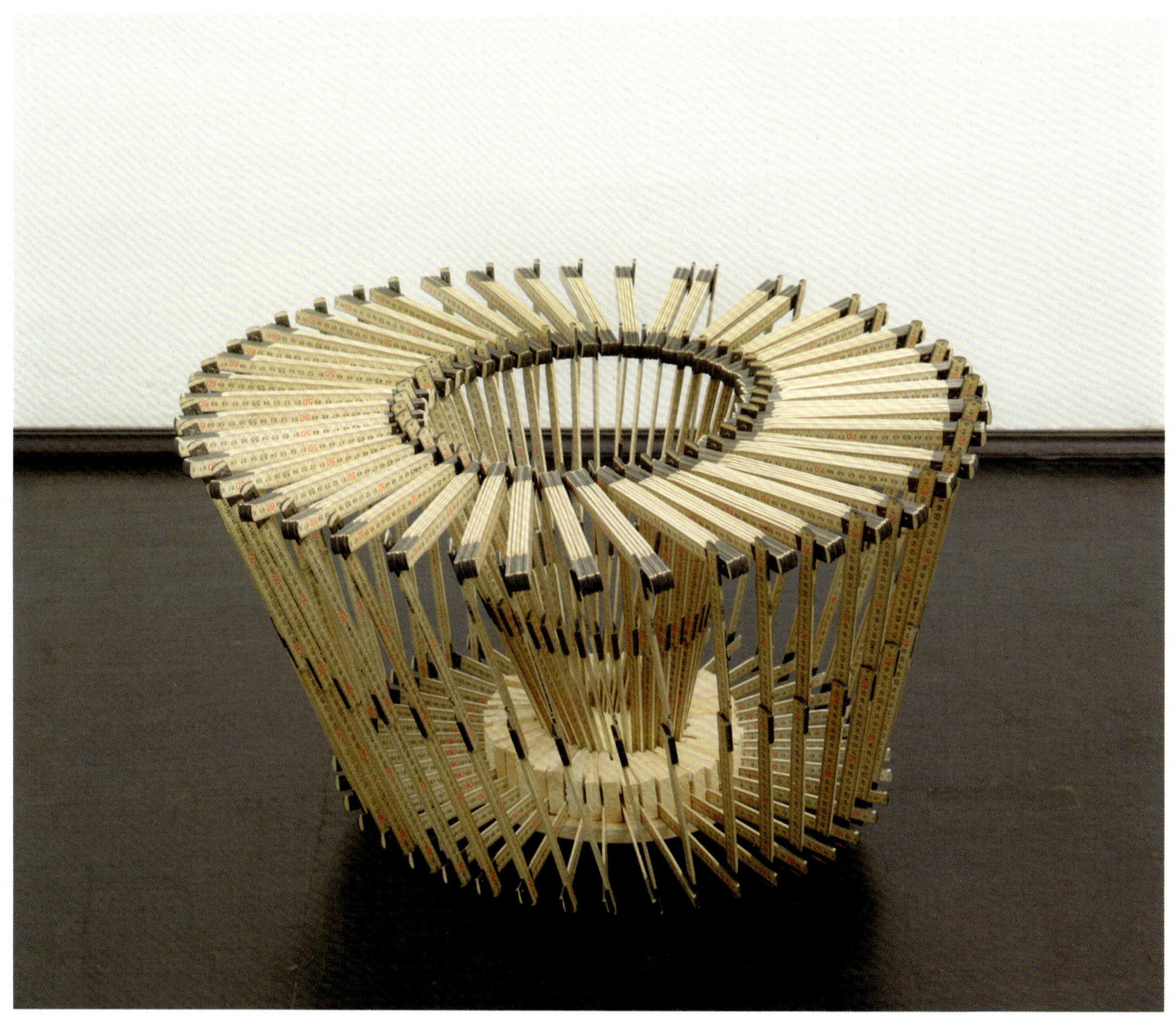

Sculpturefinder

2017, Wood, metal, plastic, 80 × 50 cm, Private collection

St. Gallen

2017, Plastic, MDF, 110 × 110 × 2 cm, Private collection

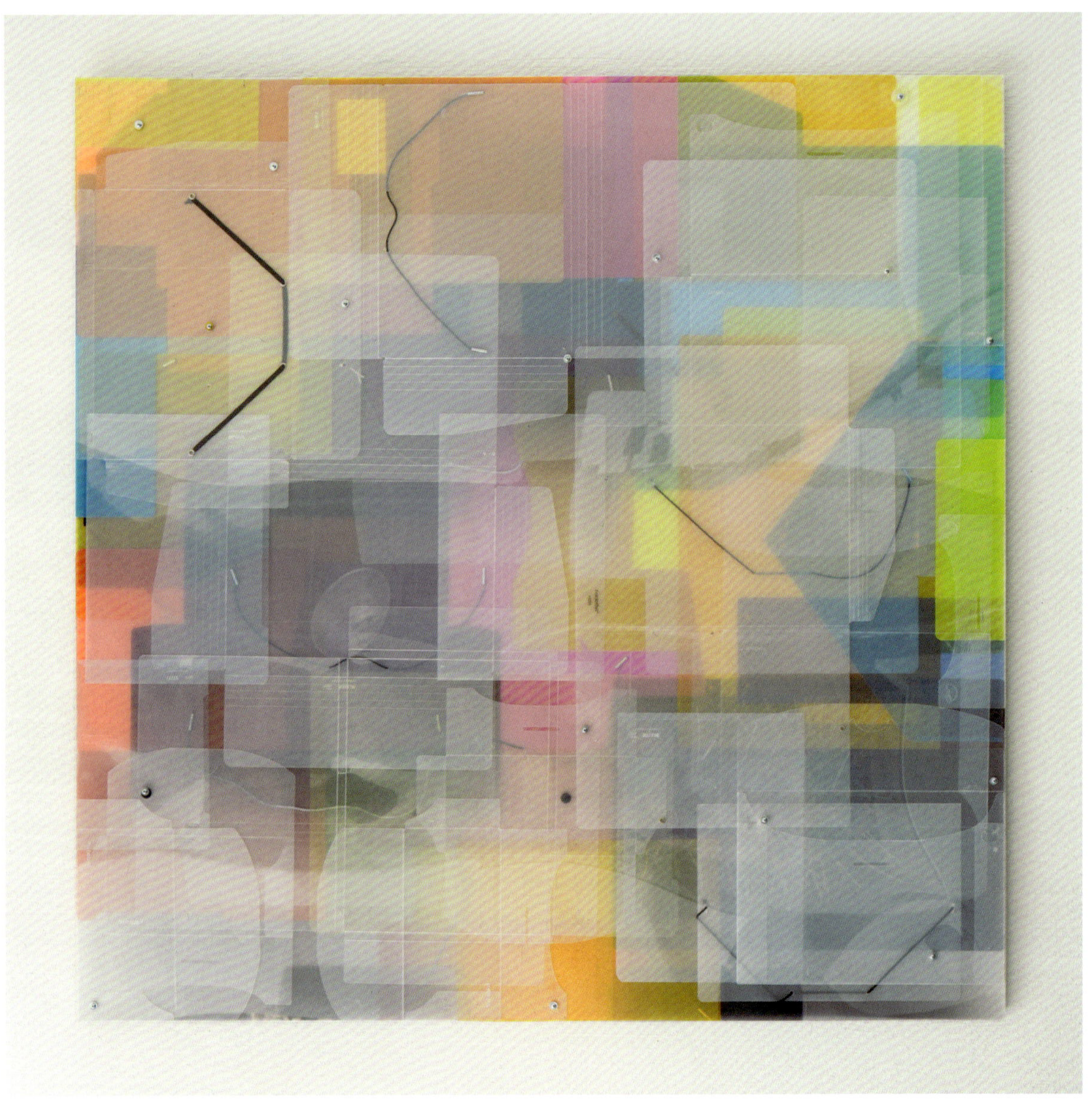

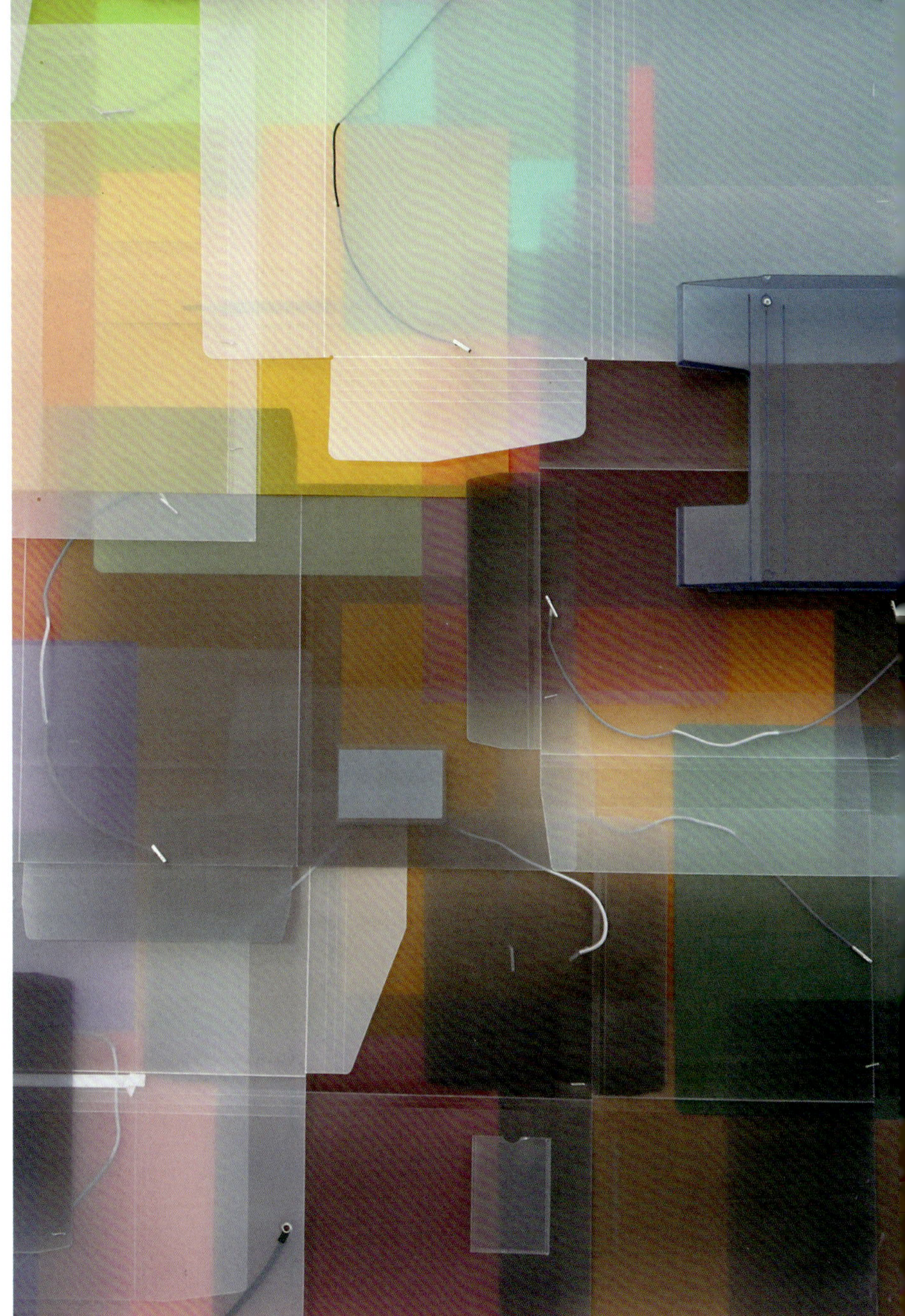

Dortmund

2017, MDF, plastic, 110 × 110 × 2 cm

**Wieviel Farbe kannst Du
noch ertragen? (Detail)**

*2017, Plastic, 350 × 570 × 50 cm, Museum für
Konkrete Kunst, Ingolstadt*

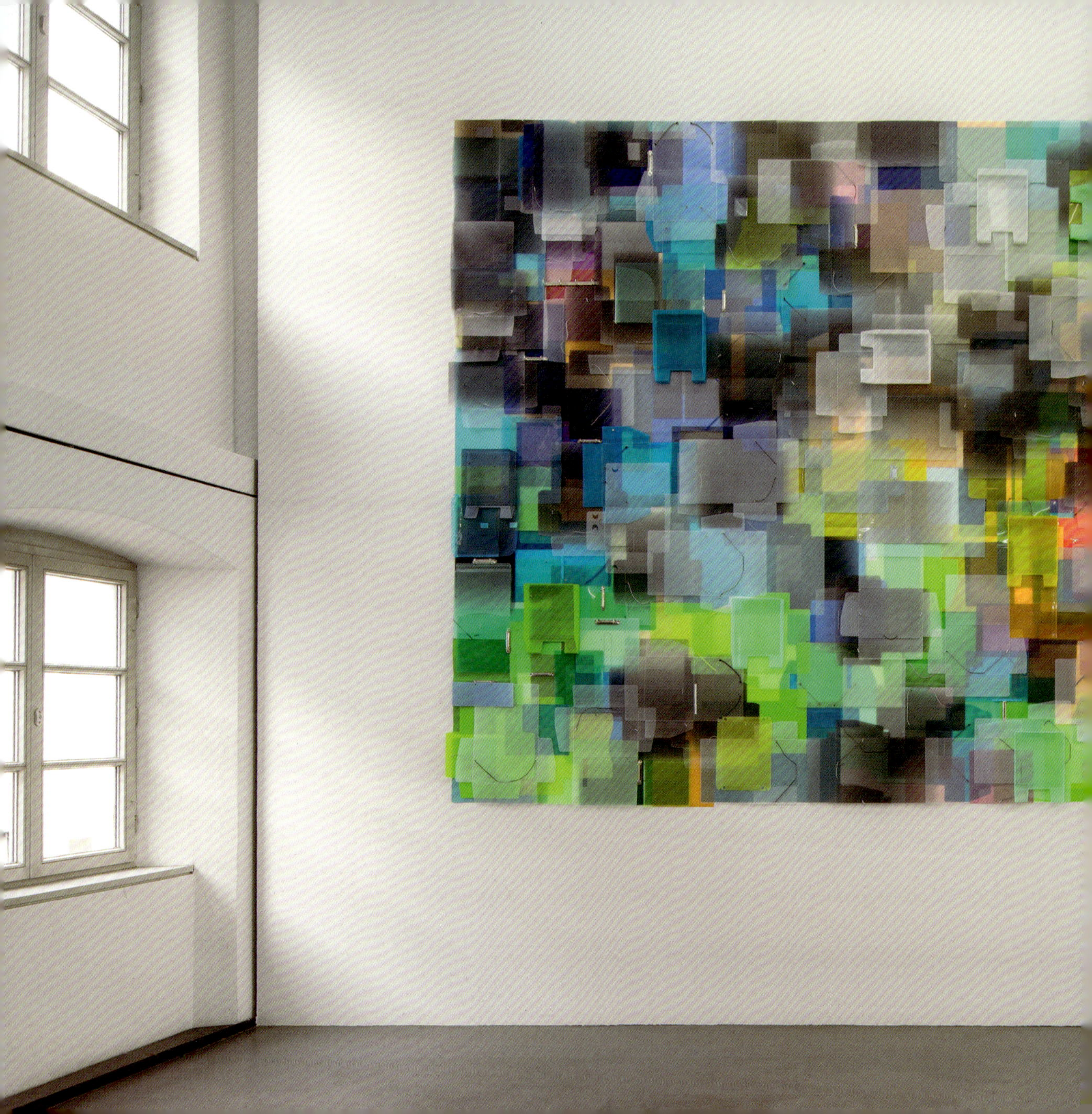

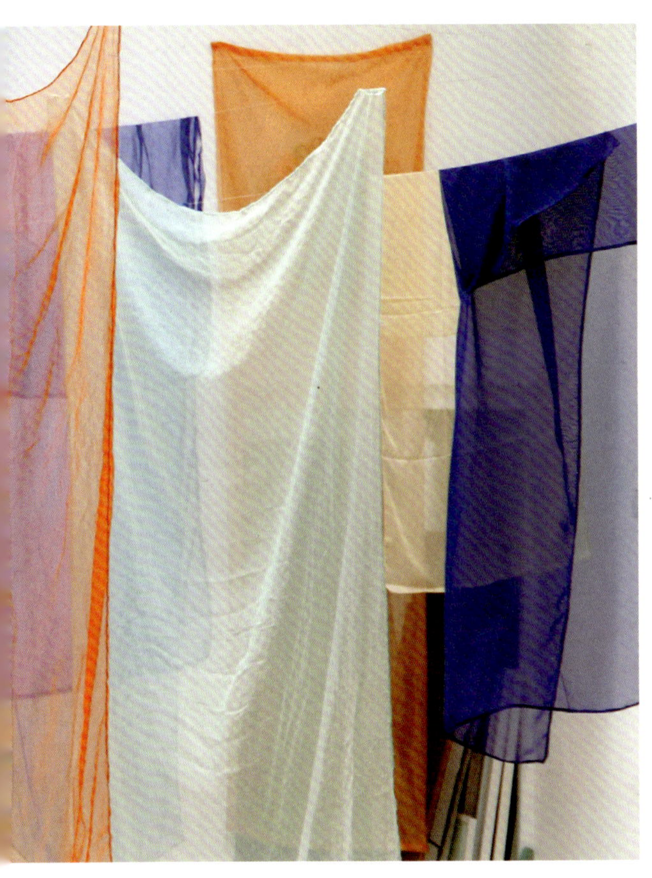

Wieviel Farbe kannst Du noch ertragen? (Detail)

2017, Plastic, 350 × 570 × 50 cm, Museum für Konkrete Kunst, Ingolstadt

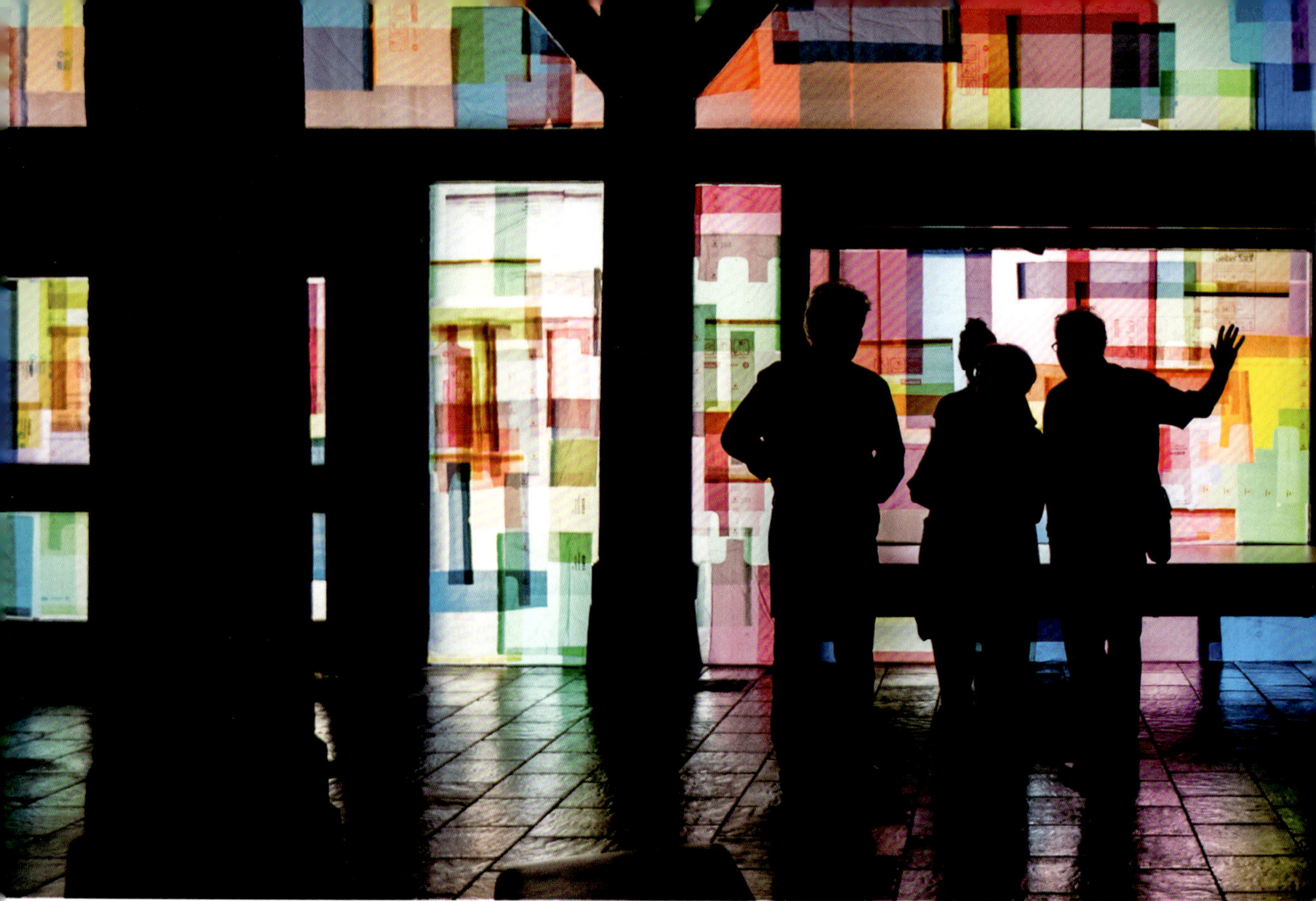

About the hustle and bustle of file covers after office hours

Back on the road you will rub your eyes and look again at windows covered with plastic film. Redecorating was your first thought, you remember. It only took one step to change sides. A transition from urban space to an exhibition, as if a switch were flipped. Like day and night.

The installation by Tina Haase in the Städtische Galerie im Kornhaus in Kirchheim unter Teck has two faces.

Au sujet des agissements des chemises de dossiers à la fermeture des bureaux

De retour dans la rue, tu te frotteras les yeux et, à nouveau, tu ne regarderas plus que les fenêtres recouvertes de films de plastique. La peinture, ça a été ta première pensée, tu t'en souviens. Il n'a fallu qu'un pas pour changer de côté. Une transition du milieu urbain à une exposition, comme si un interrupteur avait été enclenché. Comme le jour et la nuit.

Vom Treiben der Aktendeckel nach Büroschluss

Zurück auf der Straße wirst du dir die Augen reiben und wieder nur auf mit Plastikfolien verhängte Fenster blicken. Malerarbeiten, das war dein erster Gedanke, du erinnerst dich. Es brauchte nur einen Schritt, um die Seiten zu wechseln. Ein Übergang vom Stadtraum in eine Ausstellung, als ob ein Schalter umgelegt würde. Wie Tag und Nacht.

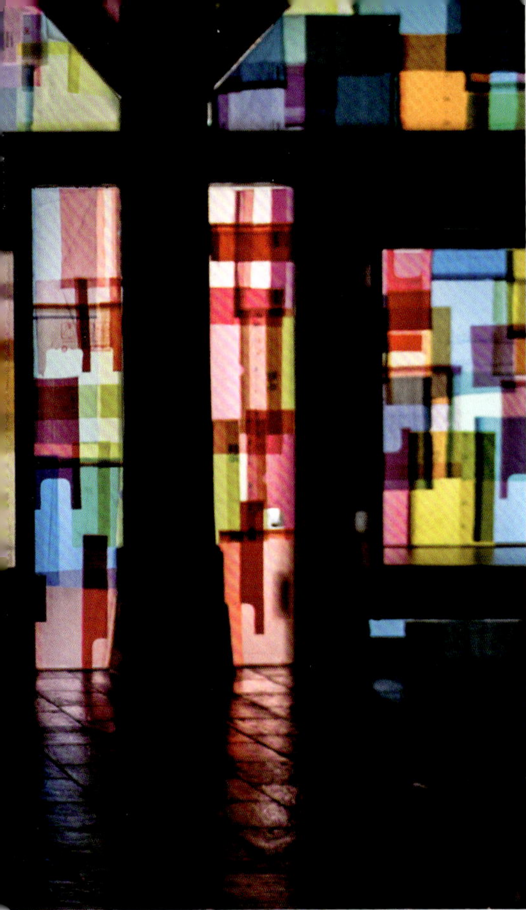

Situation bunt

2017, Plastic foils, 3500 × 25000 cm, Städtische Galerie im Kornhaus, Kirchheim unter Teck

Del ajetreo de las carpetas al momento del cierre en la oficina

De vuelta en la calle se frotará los ojos y mirará de nuevo a las ventanas cubiertas con papel de plástico. La pintura fue tu primer pensamiento, ¿recuerdas? Solo fue necesario un paso para cambiar de bando. Una transición del espacio urbano a una exposición, como si se accionara un interruptor. Como el día y la noche.

La instalación de Tina Haase en la galería municipal en el Kornhaus de

Del trambusto delle cartelle dopo l'orario d'ufficio

Di nuovo in strada ti strofinerai gli occhi e guarderai ancora una volta alle finestre ricoperte di pellicola di plastica. Imbianchini al lavoro, è stato il tuo primo pensiero, ti ricordi. È bastato un solo passo per cambiare atteggiamento. Un passaggio dallo spazio urbano a una mostra, come se un interruttore fosse stato schiacciato. Come il giorno e la notte.

Van de drukte van dossiermappen na kantoortijd

Op de terugweg wrijft u in uw ogen en kijkt u opnieuw naar de met plasticfolie bedekte ramen. Schilderwerk was uw eerste gedachte, u weet het nog. U hoefde maar één stap te zetten om van kant te wisselen. Een overgang van stedelijke ruimte naar een tentoonstelling, alsof er een schakelaar wordt omgedraaid. Als dag en nacht.

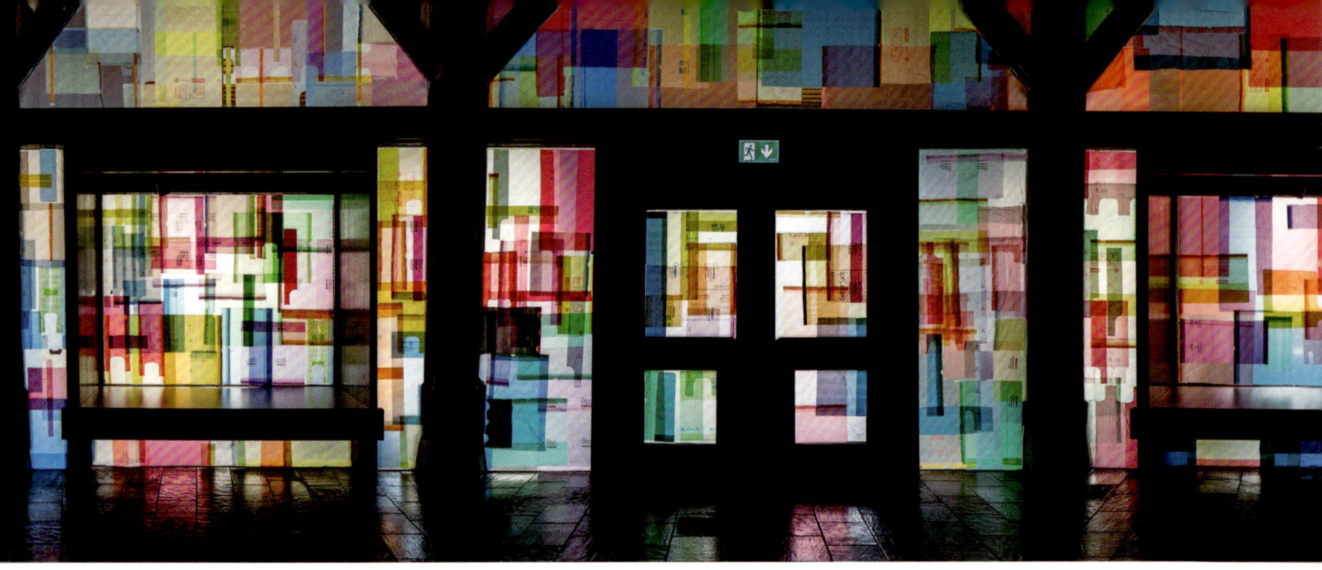

An external view, which is probably not even noticed by most passers-by. And if it is—an eyesore. Windows covered with plastic bags repel the eye rather than attract it. And the interior? A revelation! A room immersed in coloured light, which involuntarily reminds us of the sacred atmosphere of a church interior decorated with coloured glass windows, whereby the intensity of this colour effect is increased by a gentle progression from light to ever darker tones towards the depth of the room.

To have arrived here means to be lifted out of the flow of urban life. Another mode starts. The immobile inner attitude is released and lets the emotions flow. Spellbound amazement, excitement, but also amusement about the modest means of this transformation. It's all transparent. Garbage bags, whose astonishingly rich palette of colours, from pastel to brightly coloured, are

L'installation de Tina Haase dans la Städtische Galerie im Kornhaus à Kirchheim unter Teck a deux apparences. Une vue extérieure, que probablement seuls certains passants isolés remarqueront. Et dans ce cas, percevront comme une horreur. Les fenêtres recouvertes de sacs en plastique collés ont plus tendance à faire détourner le regard, plutôt que de l'attirer. Et l'intérieur ? Une révélation ! La salle immergée dans une lumière colorée, qui nous rappelle inconsciemment l'atmosphère sacrée d'un intérieur d'église aux vitraux multicolores, effet de couleurs accru par un changement progressif des tons du clair au foncé, au fur et à mesure que la luminosité diminue vers la profondeur de la pièce.

En être arrivé là signifie être attiré hors du flux de la vie urbaine. Un autre mode de perception se met e branle. L'état d'esprit se libère de son carcan et se laisse

Die Installation von Tina Haase in der Städtischen Galerie im Kornhaus in Kirchheim unter Teck hat zwei Gesichter. Eine Außenansicht, die vermutlich von den wenigsten Passanten überhaupt bemerkt wird. Und falls doch – ein Schandfleck. Mit Plastiktüten verklebte Fenster stoßen den Blick eher ab, als ihn anzuziehen. Und die Innenansicht? Eine Offenbarung! Ein in farbiges Licht getauchter Raum, der unwillkürlich an die sakrale Atmosphäre eines mit farbigen Glasfenstern ausgestatteten Kirchenraums erinnert, wobei die Intensität dieser Farbwirkung gesteigert wird durch einen sanften Verlauf von hellen zu immer dunkleren Tönen hin zur Tiefe des Raumes.

Hier angekommen zu sein bedeutet, herausgehoben zu werden aus dem Fluss des städtischen Lebens. Ein anderer Modus setzt ein. Die festgezurrte innere Haltung löst sich und lässt die Emotionen

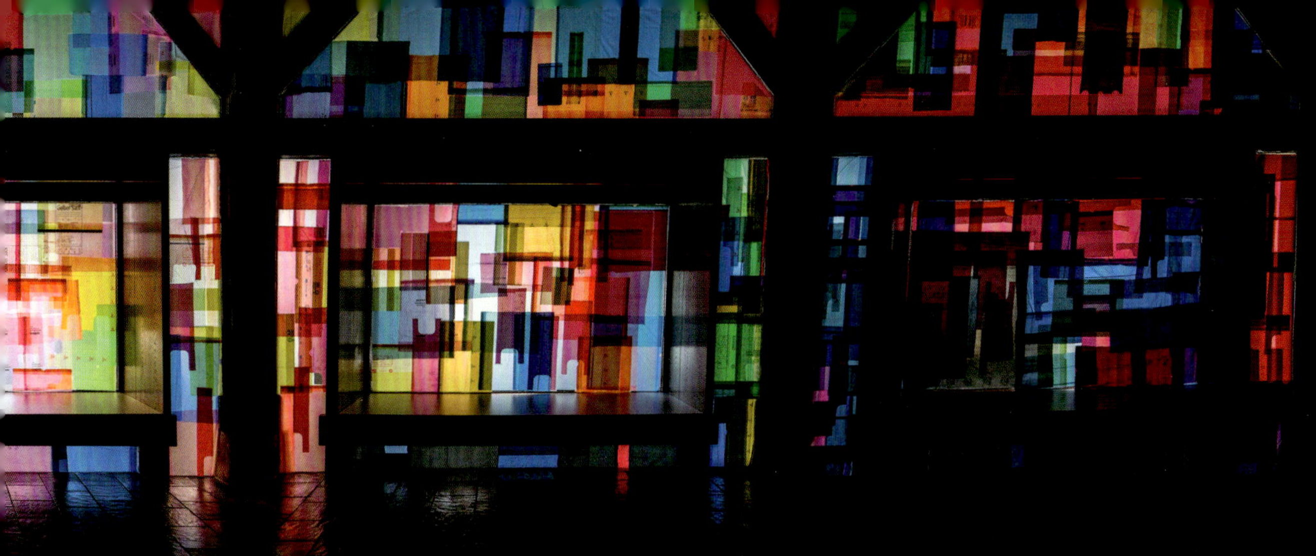

Kirchheim unter Teck tiene dos caras. Una externa, que probablemente ni apenas percibe una minoría de transeúntes. Y si se percatan, distinguen una mancha. Las ventanas pegadas con bolsas de plástico repelen la mirada en lugar de atraerla. ¿Y la interior? ¡Una revelación! Una habitación sumergida en luz de colores, que recuerda sin querer a la atmósfera sagrada del interior de una iglesia equipada con vidrieras de color, donde la intensidad de este efecto colorido se ve incrementada por una suave progresión de la luz a tonos cada vez más oscuros hacia la profundidad de la habitación.

Haber llegado aquí significa levitar sobre la vida urbana. Se inicia otro modo. La postura interior fija se libera y deja fluir las emociones. Asombro ensimismado, emoción, pero también alegría ante los modestos medios de esta transformación. Todo es transparente.

L'installazione di Tina Haase nella Städtische Galerie im Kornhaus a Kirchheim unter Teck ha due volti. Uno esterno, che probabilmente non viene nemmeno notato dalla maggior parte dei passanti – e, se lo è, solo come un elemento dissonante. Finestre ricoperte con sacchetti di plastica sono una vista più che altro repellente, non attirano lo sguardo. E l'interno? Una rivelazione! Una stanza immersa nella luce colorata, che ricorda involontariamente l'atmosfera sacra di un interno di chiesa con vetrate colorate, dove l'intensità di questo effetto cromatico è aumentata dalla leggera progressione dei toni dal chiaro allo scuro man mano che si procede verso il fondo della stanza.

Arrivare qui significa uscire dal flusso della vita urbana. Qui prende avvio un'altra modalità. Il rigido atteggiamento interiore si dissolve e lascia fluire le emozioni. Devoto stupore, eccitazione,

De installatie van Tina Haase in de Städtische Galerie im Kornhaus in Kirchheim unter Teck heeft twee gezichten. Een buitenaanzicht dat door de meeste voorbijgangers waarschijnlijk niet eens wordt opgemerkt. En indien wel – een schandvlek. Ramen beplakt met plastic zakken stoten het oog eerder af dan dat ze het aantrekken. En de binnenkant? Een openbaring! Een ruimte ondergedompeld in gekleurd licht, die onwillekeurig doet denken aan de heilige sfeer van een kerkinterieur met glas-in-loodramen, waarbij de intensiteit van de kleurenwerking wordt verhoogd door een zachte overgang van lichte naar steeds donkerder tonen dieper de ruimte in.

Hier aangekomen zijn betekent uit de stroom van het stadsleven te worden getild. Hier begint een andere modus. De vastgeroeste innerlijke houding wordt losgelaten en laat de emoties stromen. Aandachtige verbazing, opwinding,

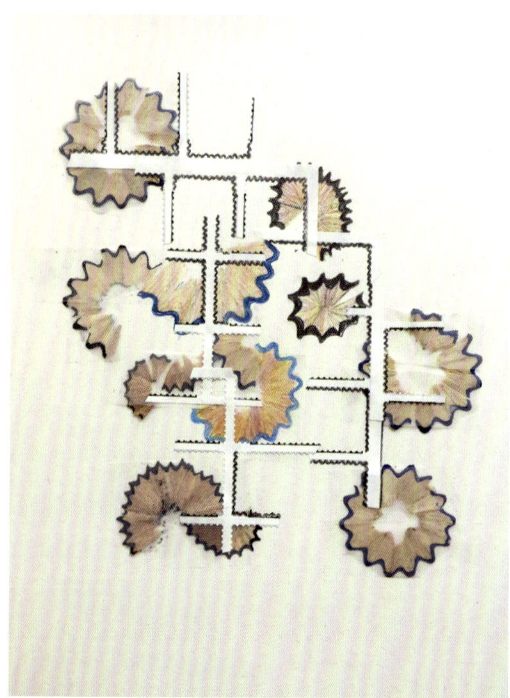

supposed to conceal their actual unappetizing purpose, provide valuable material for glass painting, thanks to their transparency. At least for the duration of this temporary installation. A moment between frivolity and magic, created from that which was produced for no other purpose than throwing it away.

Great art, from the cheapest thing the market has to offer. Tina Haase likes to use the term "forms of self-evidence" for her work: art draws on the possibilities that the object already offers. Plastic trays and folders are used to hold loose sheets together. But what if they are denied this? When the tray becomes aware of itself? "Trays

submerger par les émotions. Étonnement admiratif, excitation, mais aussi hilarité face aux moyens modestes utilisés pour cette métamorphose. Les sacs poubelles, dont la palette de couleurs étonnamment riche, allant du pastel aux couleurs vives, est censée faire oublier la fonction réelle et peu appétissante l'objet, deviennent, grâce à leur transparence, un matériau de qualité pour le vitrail. Un moment allant de la frivolité à la magie, né à partir d'un produit fabriqué dans le seul but d'être jeté.

Du grand art, produit à partir de ce que le marché nous offre de moins cher. Tina Haase aime utiliser pour son travail l'appellation « formes d'évidence » : l'art

fließen. Andächtiges Staunen, Erregung, aber auch Heiterkeit angesichts der bescheidenen Mittel dieser Verwandlung. Es ist ja alles durchschaubar. Mülltüten, deren erstaunlich reiche Farbpalette von pastellig bis quietschbunt über ihre eigentliche unappetitliche Bestimmung hinwegtäuschen soll, geben dank ihrer Transparenz einen vollwertigen Werkstoff für Glasmalerei. Wenigstens für die Dauer dieser temporären Installation. Ein Moment zwischen Frivolität und Magie, geschaffen aus dem, was zu keinem anderen Zweck als zum Wegwerfen produziert wurde.

Große Kunst, aus dem billigsten, was der Markt so hergibt. Tina Haase benutzt

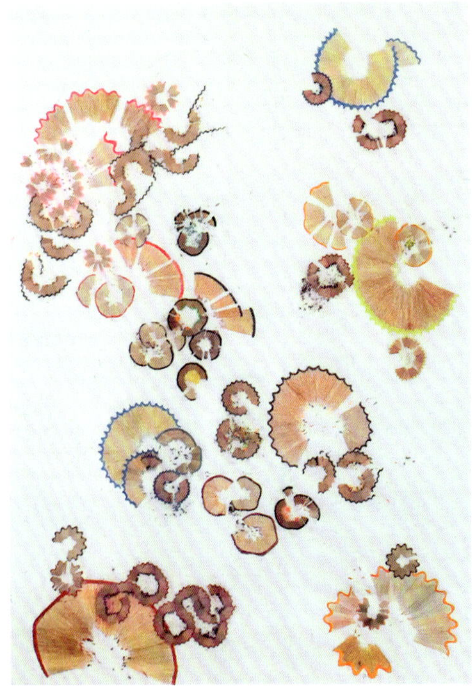

Las bolsas de basura, cuya paleta de colores va desde el pastel hasta los colores chillones, parece que ocultan su propósito poco apetecible. Gracias a su transparencia ofrecen un material de trabajo íntegro para la pintura de vidrio, al menos durante la duración de esta instalación temporal. Un momento entre la frivolidad y la magia, creado a partir de lo que se produjo con el único propósito de tirarlo.

Arte en mayúsculas partiendo de lo más barato que el mercado tiene para ofrecer. A Tina Haase le gusta utilizar el término "formas de lo sobreentendido" para su obra: el arte se basa en las posibilidades que el objeto ya ofrece.

ma anche un senso di allegria di fronte ai modesti mezzi di questa trasformazione. Tutto è trasparente. Grazie alla loro trasparenza, i sacchi della spazzatura, la cui tavolozza di colori sorprendentemente varia dai toni pastello a colori più vivaci e dovrebbe servire a nascondere l'effettivo utilizzo poco appetitoso, diventano materiale a tutti gli effetti per la pittura su vetro. Se non altro, per la durata di questa installazione temporanea. Un momento tra frivolezza e magia, creato con ciò che è stato prodotto solo per venir buttato via.

Arte di grande impatto, a partire dalla cosa più economica che il mercato abbia

maar ook vermaak over de bescheiden middelen van deze transformatie. Het is allemaal transparant. Afvalzakken, waarvan het verbazingwekkend rijke kleurenpalet, van pastel tot felgekleurd, hun eigenlijk onappetijtelijke doel moet verbergen, zijn door hun hun transparantie een volwaardig materiaal voor glasschildering. In elk geval voor de duur van deze tijdelijke installatie. Een moment tussen frivoliteit en magie, gemaakt van iets wat werd geproduceerd voor geen ander doel dan het weggooien.

Geweldige kunst, van het goedkoopste wat de markt te bieden heeft. Tina Haase gebruikt graag de frase 'vormen van vanzelfsprekendheid' voor haar werk:

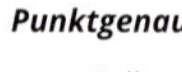

Punktgenau

2017, Collage, paper, plastic, 24 × 31 cm

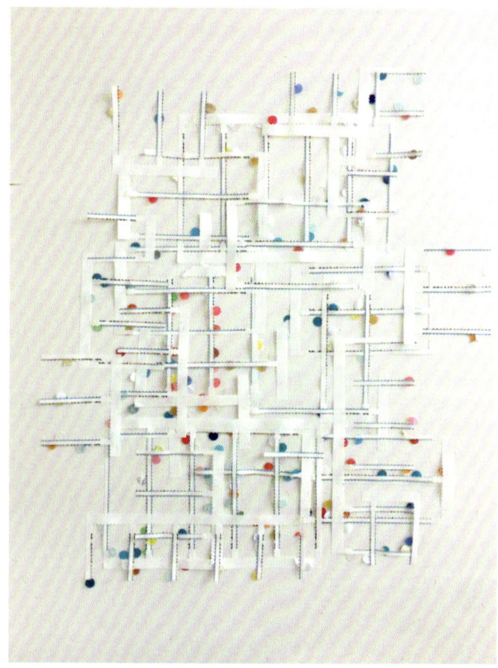

United" can apparently also join forces into a huge mural of 28 square metres, as could be seen in the exhibition "Out of Office" at the Museum für Konkrete Kunst in Ingolstadt. The standardised office material is transformed into superimposed color areas reminiscent of the pixels of a hugely enlarged digital photograph. What image would be created if the whole thing were reduced back to an imaginary original? The "self-evident form" is not self-evident. On the contrary, Tina Haase's works are as meticulously planned and prepared as art can be. Every single element has to find its place. The different colour values, but also the different degrees of transparency of the plastic, are cunningly

puise son inspiration dans le potentiel que l'objet lui apporte. Des casiers pour le rangement du courrier et des chemises en plastique sont normalement utilisés pour stocker ou ranger les feuilles volantes. Mais que se passe-t-il, si on les soustrait à cette fonction ? « Les casiers entre eux » peuvent probablement se métamorphoser en une horde formant un immense relief mural de 28 m², comme dans l'exposition « Out of Office » qui a eu lieu au Musée d'Art concret d'Ingolstadt. Le matériel de bureau standardisé n'est plus qu'une superposition de rectangles de couleurs évoquant les pixels d'une photographie numérique trop agrandie.

La « forme évidente » ne va pas de soi. Bien au contraire, les œuvres

für ihre Arbeit gerne den Begriff der „Selbstverständlichkeitsformen": Die Kunst schöpft aus den Möglichkeiten, die der Gegenstand schon mitbringt. Ablagen und Mappen aus Kunststoff dienen dazu, lose Blätter zusammenzuhalten. Was aber, wenn ihnen das verwehrt wird? Wenn die Ablage ganz zu sich selbst kommt? „Ablagen unter sich" können sich offenbar auch zu einem riesigen Wandbild von 28 m² Fläche zusammenrotten, wie in der Ausstellung „Out of Office" im Museum für Konkrete Kunst in Ingolstadt zu sehen war. Aus dem normierten Büromaterial werden übereinander verschobene Farbflächen, die an die Pixel einer ungeheuer vergrößerten digitalen Fotografie

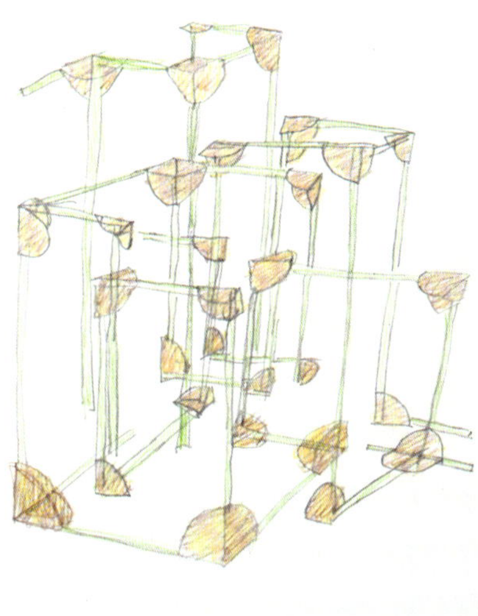

Los archivadores y carpetas de plástico se utilizan para mantener unidas las hojas sueltas. ¿Pero qué pasa si esto se les niega? ¿Cuando el archivador llega a sí mismo? "Entre archivadores" también se pueden agrupar juntas en un enorme mural de 28 metros cuadrados, como se puede ver en la exposición "Out of Office" en el Museo de Concretismo de Ingolstadt. El material de oficina estandarizado se transforma en áreas de color superpuestas que recuerdan a los píxeles de una fotografía digital de gran tamaño. ¿Qué imagen se crearía si todo se redujera a un original imaginado?

La "forma sobreentendida" no lo es tanto. Por el contrario, las obras de Tina Haase están trabajadas con tanto da offrire. A Tina Haase piace usare il termine "forme dell'ovvio" per il suo lavoro: l'arte attinge alle possibilità che l'oggetto già di per sé offre. Le vaschette portacorrispondenza e le cartelline di plastica vengono utilizzate per tenere insieme singoli fogli. Ma cosa succede se ciò gli viene negato? Quando la vaschetta portacorrispondenza ritrova se stessa? "Vaschette tra di loro" possono apparentemente trasformarsi in un enorme murale di 28 metri quadrati, come si può vedere nella mostra "Out of Office" al Museo di Concretismo di Ingolstadt. Il materiale standardizzato da ufficio si trasforma in aree di colore sovrapposte, che ricordano i pixel di una fotografia digitale estremamente kunst put uit de mogelijkheden die het object al biedt. Plastic dossiermappen dienen ertoe losse vellen bij elkaar te houden. Maar wat als ze dit wordt ontzegd? Als de map op zichzelf komt te staan? 'Dossiermappen onderling' kunnen blijkbaar samenscholen tot een enorme wanddecoratie van 28 m², zoals te zien was op de tentoonstelling 'Out of Office' in het Museum für Konkrete Kunst in Ingolstadt. Gestandaardiseerd kantoormateriaal werd getransformeerd tot over elkaar geschoven kleurvlakken die doen denken aan de pixels van een sterk vergrote digitale foto. Welk beeld zou er ontstaan als het geheel teruggebracht zou worden tot een denkbeeldig origineel?

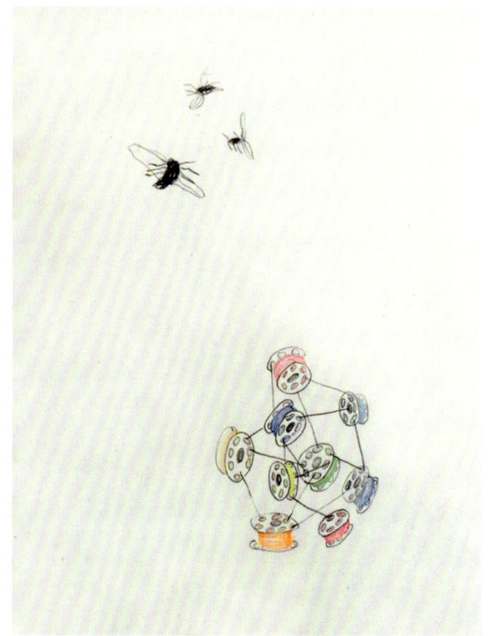

exhausted: file covers made of opaque, cloudy material, placed over the brighter colleagues, create blurriness. Only the subtle refraction of the seductive attractiveness of the colours conjures up this stupendous painterly effect from the plastic material. The ingenious layering ensures that the hard lines and right angles from the toolbox of Concrete Art come to life until a pulsating body of colour is created that is inspired by light. Arising out of the preference for plastic and its qualities as a colour and light medium, a growing interest in painting has developed in recent years. But how does a sculptor paint? Tina Haase simply paints her colour splashes, beautiful curls and arabesques freely in the room. This can be marvelled at in *Wush,* a short film

de Tina Haase sont réalisées aussi méticuleusement qu'une œuvre d'art puisse l'être. Chaque élément doit minutieusement trouver sa place. Les plus petites variations chromatiques, mais aussi les différentes transparences du plastique, sont accordées, quitte à atteindre un maximum de possibilités : les chemises en plastique à la transparence laiteuse, superposées avec leurs collègues aux couleurs crues laissent apparaître des effets flous. Mais c'est le jeu subtil et séduisant de la réfraction des couleurs qui fait naître du plastique cet effet pictural stupéfiant. L'ingénieuse superposition des surfaces permet, en puisant dans la boîte à outils de l'Art concret, de vivifier les contours saillants et les angles droits, afin de

erinnern. Welches Bild entstünde, wenn man das Ganze in ein imaginiertes Original zurückverkleinern würde?

Die „Selbstverständlichkeitsform" geht nicht von selbst. Im Gegenteil, die Werke von Tina Haase sind so akribisch durchgearbeitet wie es Kunst nur sein kann. Jedes einzelne Element muss umständlich seinen Platz finden. Die verschiedenen Farbwerte, aber auch die unterschiedlichen Transparenzgrade des Kunststoffs werden listig ausgereizt: Aktendeckel aus milchig eingetrübtem Material, den grelleren Kollegen übergeschoben, lassen Unschärfen entstehen. Erst die subtile Brechung der verführerischen Attraktivität der Farben zaubert aus dem Plastikmaterial diese stupende malerische Wirkung hervor. Die

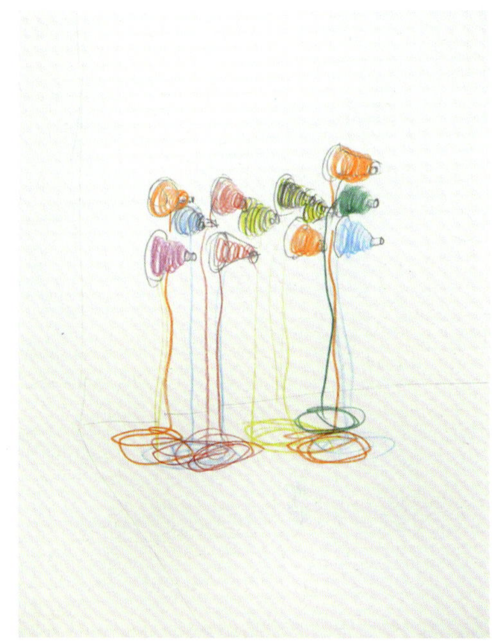

detalle que solo pueden ser arte. Cada elemento tiene que encontrar su lugar. Los diferentes grados de color, pero también de transparencia del plástico, se apuran con astucia: las carpetas hechas de material lechoso y turbio, empujadas por otras más brillantes, crean un efecto desenfocado. Solo la sutil refracción de la seductora atracción de los colores evoca este estupendo efecto pictórico del material plástico. La ingeniosa estratificación garantiza que las líneas duras y los ángulos rectos de la caja de herramientas del Concretismo cobren vida hasta crear un cuerpo de color animado que se inspira en la luz.

A partir de su preferencia por el plástico y sus cualidades como portador de color y luz, se ha desarrollado en

ingrandita. Quale immagine si creerebbe se il tutto venisse rimpicciolito a un originale immaginario?

La "forma dell'ovvio" non è ovvia. Al contrario, le opere di Tina Haase sono elaborate con la massima acribia. Ogni singolo elemento deve trovare il proprio posto. Lo spettro dei valori cromatici come pure i diversi gradi di trasparenza della plastica vengono abilmente portati all'estremo delle loro possibilità: le cartelline in materiale opaco e velato, posizionate su esemplari più brillanti, creano contorni sfocati. Solo la sottile rifrazione dei colori con la loro attrattiva seducente dà vita a questo impressionante effetto pittorico della materia plastica. L'ingegnosa stratificazione fa sì che le linee nette e

De 'vanzelfsprekende vorm' is niet vanzelfsprekend. Integendeel, aan de werken van Tina Haase is zo zorgvuldig gewerkt als maar kan aan kunst. Elk afzonderlijk element moet omstandig zijn plaats vinden. De verschillende kleurwaarden, maar ook de verschillende mate van transparantie van het plastic zijn slim uitgebuit: dossiermappen van melkachtig troebel materiaal die over de fellere collega's zijn geschoven, zorgen voor wazigheid. Slechts de subtiele lichtbreking van de verleidelijke aantrekkelijkheid van de kleuren tovert dit ontzagwekkend schilderkunstige tevoorschijn uit het plastic materiaal. De ingenieuze gelaagdheid zorgt ervoor dat de harde lijnen en rechte hoeken uit de gereedschapskist van concrete kunst

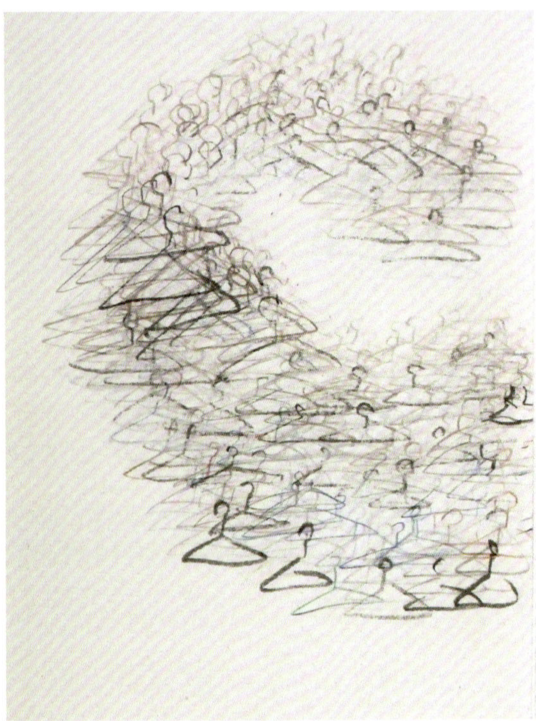

from 2016, with the usual simple setting: a group of people come together in a park and let colourful cloths fly through the air, in ever new constellations, individually, in circles or in wild confusion. And again it is the way in which these film images are put together through the editing and alienation techniques such as alternating the forward and backward running of the images, solarisation, fading etc., which turns the carefree and often very funny hustle and bustle into a dense structure of colours, forms and movements. The images are accompanied and repeatedly thwarted by the soundtrack in the background,

donner vie à ensemble coloré, d'où émane une luminosité subtile.

C'est de sa préférence pour le plastique et ses propriétés à transmettre la couleur et la lumière qu'est naît, ces dernières années cet intérêt croissant pour la peinture. Tina Haase peint tout simplement ses taches de peinture, ses gribouillages et ses arabesques sans support dans l'espace. On peut s'en émerveiller dans *Wush,* un court métrage réalisé en 2016, comme d'habitude dans un décor tout simple : dans un parc, un groupe de personnes se forme et laisse des tissus multicolores s'envoler, les constellations changent sans arrêt,

raffinierten Schichtungen sorgen dafür, dass sich die harten Linien und rechten Winkel aus dem Werkzeugkasten der Konkreten Kunst mit Leben füllen, bis ein pulsierender Farbkörper entsteht.

Aus der Vorliebe für Kunststoff als Farb- und Lichtträger hat sich in den letzten Jahren ein wachsendes Interesse an der Malerei entwickelt. Aber wie malen als Bildhauerin? Tina Haase malt ihre Farbkleckse, Kringel und Arabesken frei in den Raum. Zu bestaunen in *Wush,* einem Kurzfilm von 2016, mit gewohnt einfachem Setting: Eine Gruppe von Menschen kommt in einem Park zusammen und lässt bunte Tücher

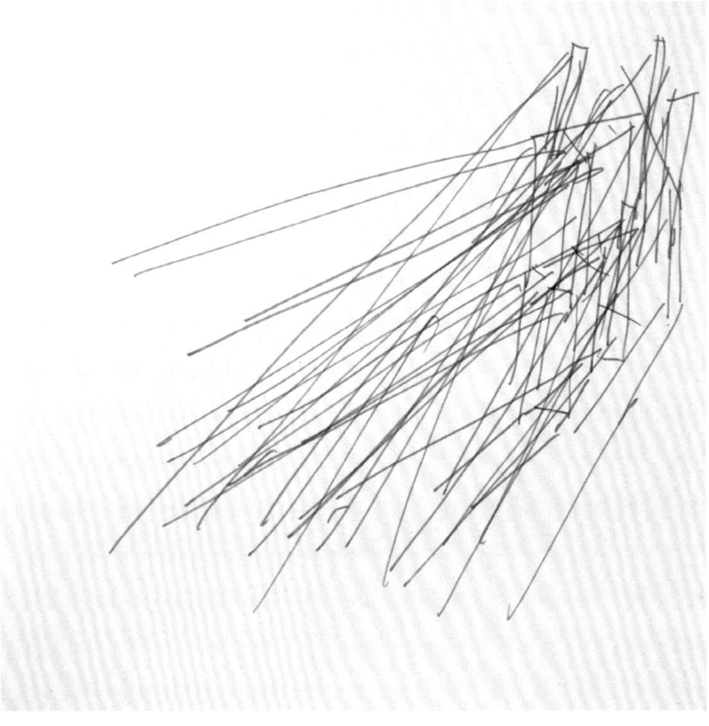

los últimos años un interés creciente por la pintura. ¿Pero cómo pintar como escultora? Tina Haase pinta sin tapujos manchas de color, rizos hermosos y arabescos en la habitación. *Wush* es un cortometraje de 2016 para deleitarse, con el escenario sencillo de siempre: un grupo de personas se reúnen en un parque y dejan que las telas de colores vuelen por el aire, en constelaciones siempre novedosas, individualmente, en círculos o en una salvaje confusión. Y de nuevo, es la manera en que estas imágenes de película se combinan a través de las técnicas de edición y alienación, como

gli angoli retti che l'arte concreta mette a disposizione prendano vita fino a creare un corpo cromatico animato dalla luce.

A partire dalla predilezione per la plastica e le sue qualità cromatiche e luminose, negli ultimi anni è cresciuto l'interesse per la pittura. Ma come può dipingere una scultrice? Tina Haase si limita a dipingere le sue macchie di colore, le belle volute e gli arabeschi liberamente nella stanza, come si può prendere atto in *Wush,* un cortometraggio del 2016 che ha la consueta semplicità di ambientazione: un gruppo di persone si riunisce in un parco e fa volare nell'aria panni coloratissimi, in costellazioni

tot leven komen, totdat een pulserende, door licht geïnspireerde kleur ontstaat.

Vanuit haar voorkeur voor kunststof en de kwaliteiten daarvan als kleur- en lichtdrager is de laatste jaren een groeiende interesse in schilderen ontstaan. Maar hoe moet je schilderen als beeldhouwer? Tina Haase schildert haar kleurvlakken, mooie krullen en arabesken gewoon vrij in de ruimte. Dit kan worden bewonderd in *Wush,* een korte film uit 2016, met de gebruikelijke eenvoudige setting: een groep mensen komt samen in een park en laat kleurige doeken door de lucht vliegen, in steeds nieuwe constellaties, afzonderlijk, in

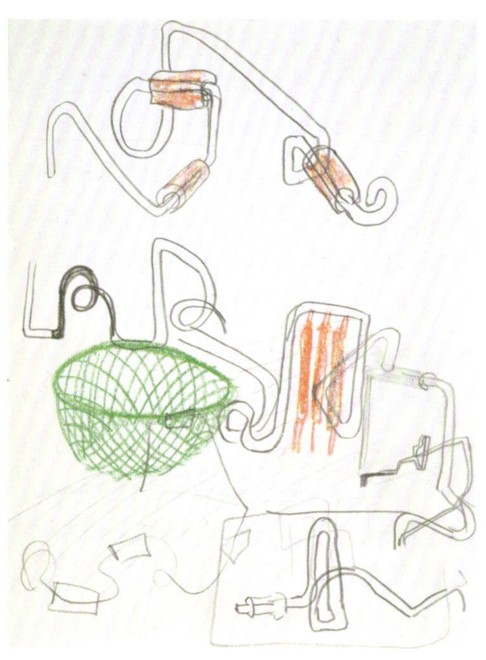

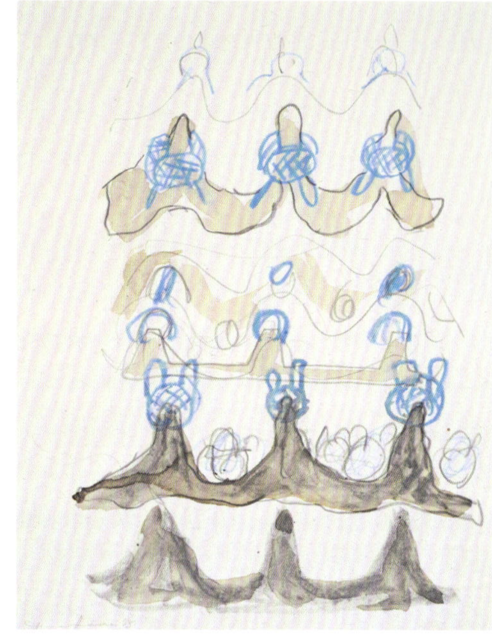

o.T.

2001, Crayons,
34 × 26 cm

o.T.

1998, Crayons,
34 × 26 cm

with sometimes gentle, sometimes off-key or quirky sounds. Painting and its protagonists are equally released from functionality. And obviously both of them enjoy it.

parfois chacun de son côté, d'autres fois en cercles ou même sans système apparent. Ensuite, le montage des images, mais aussi les techniques, avec lesquelles l'image est transfigurée, comme la projection en avant et en arrière des séquences, la solarisation, la surexposition etc., laissent apparaître dans toute cette agitation insouciante et souvent même amusante un monde de couleur, de formes et de vie. En fond sonore, les images sont accompagnées parfois en harmonie, souvent en dissonance, par des sons parfois légers, d'autres fois excentriques ou totalement bizarres. La peinture et ses acteurs sont les uns comme les autres entièrement libérés de toute fonctionnalité. Et évidemment, chacun y éprouve beaucoup de plaisir.

durch die Luft fliegen, in immer neuen Konstellationen, einzeln, im Kreis oder in wildem Durcheinander. Und wieder ist es die Art der Zusammenstellung dieser Filmbilder durch den Schnitt und durch Verfremdungstechniken wie wechselndes Vor- und Rückwärtslaufenlassen der Bilder, Solarisation, Überblendungen etc., die aus dem unbeschwerten und oft sehr lustigen Treiben ein dichtes Gefüge aus Farben, Formen und Bewegungen macht. Getragen und immer wieder konterkariert werden die Bilder durch die untergelegte Tonspur aus mal sanft, mal schräg bis schrullig versponnenen Klängen. Die Malerei und ihre Akteure sind gleichermaßen aus der Funktionalität entbunden. Und ganz offensichtlich zu beiderlei Vergnügen.

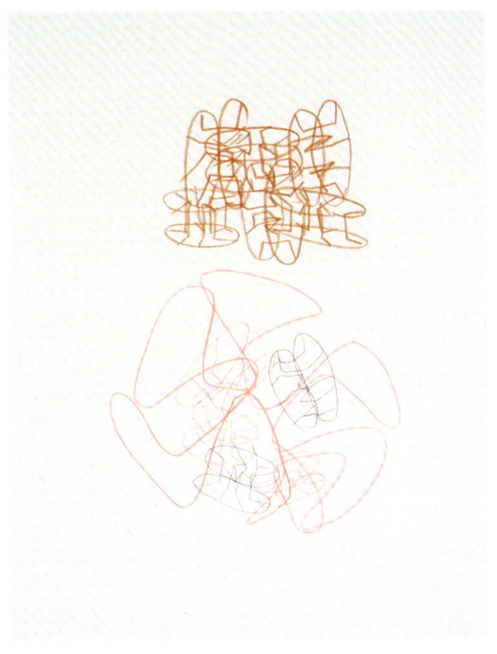

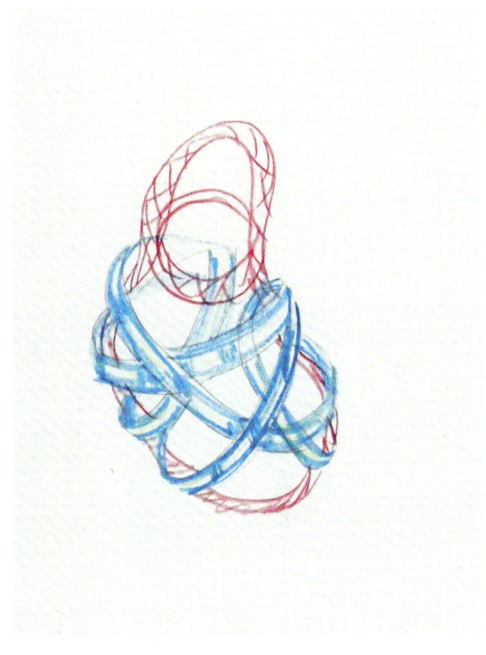

o.T.

1995, Crayons,
34 × 26 cm

o.T.

1995, Crayons,
34 × 26 cm

la alternancia del avance y rebobinado de imágenes, la solarización, el desvanecimiento, etc., lo que convierte el ajetreo despreocupado y a menudo muy divertido en una densa estructura de colores, formas y movimientos. Las imágenes son transportadas y de nuevo, contrarrestadas por la banda sonora subyacente, a veces se manera sutil, otras de soslayo e inclusocon melodías estrafalarias. La pintura y sus protagonistas también están liberados de la funcionalidad, evidentementepara entregarse a ambos placeres.

sempre nuove, singolarmente, in tondo o nella confusione più selvaggia. Ed è ancora il modo in cui queste immagini cinematografiche vengono assemblate attraverso varie tecniche di montaggio ed effetti speciali, come l'alternanza di scorrimento avanti e indietro, la solarizzazione, la dissolvenza ecc., che trasforma il trambusto spensierato e spesso molto divertente in una densa struttura di colori, forme e movimenti. La colonna sonora di sottofondo coadiuva o contrasta l'andamento delle immagini, a volte dolcemente, a volte con suoni dissonanti e addirittura stravaganti. La pittura e i suoi protagonisti sono tutti svincolati dalla loro funzionalità. E, come appare ovvio dalle immagini, con grande piacere di entrambi.

cirkels of in een wilde warboel. En ook hier is het de manier waarop deze filmbeelden tot stand komen door montage- en vervreemdingstechnieken zoals het afwisselend voor- en achterwaarts afspelen van de beelden, solarisatie, faden etc., die de onbezorgde en vaak erg grappige drukte omvormt tot een dichte structuur van kleuren, vormen en bewegingen. De beelden worden gedragen en herhaaldelijk tegengewerkt door de soundtrack op de achtergrond, met soms zachte, soms valse of vreemde klanken. De schilderkunst en haar protagonisten worden in dezelfde mate losgekoppeld van de functionaliteit. En vaak duidelijk tot beider genoegen.

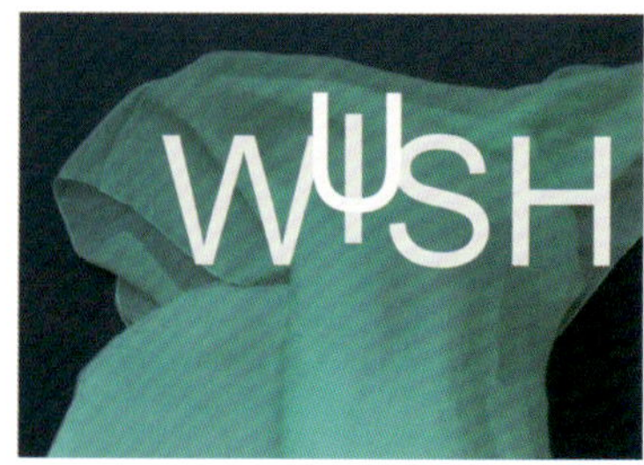
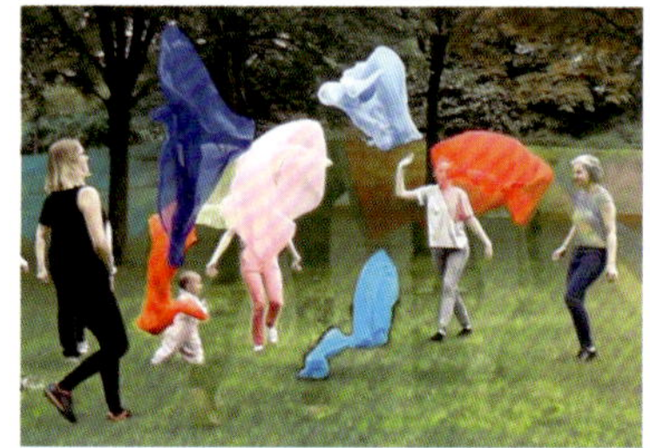
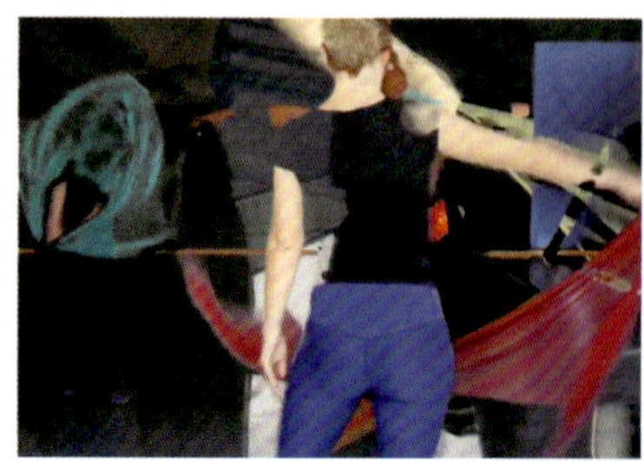
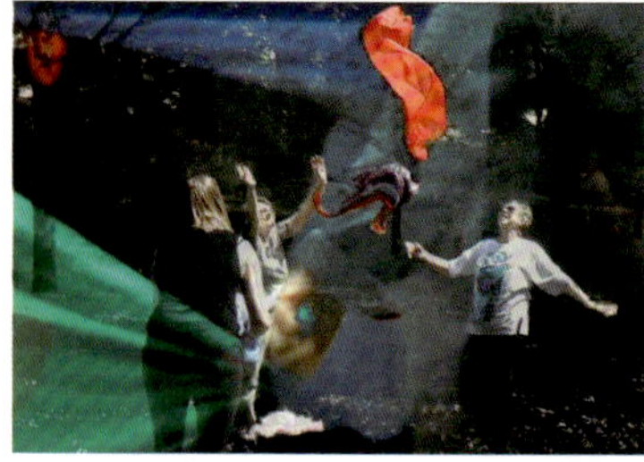
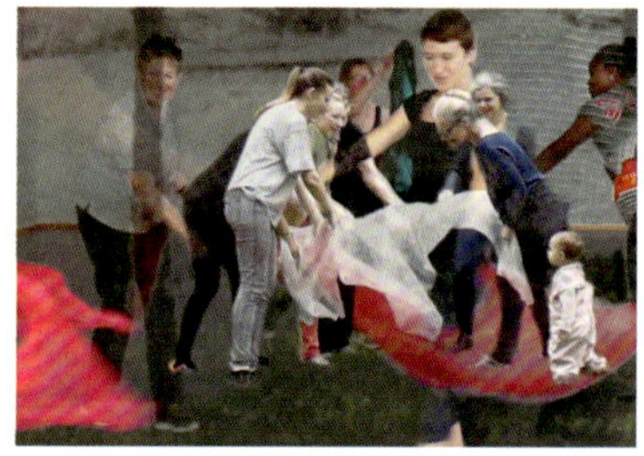
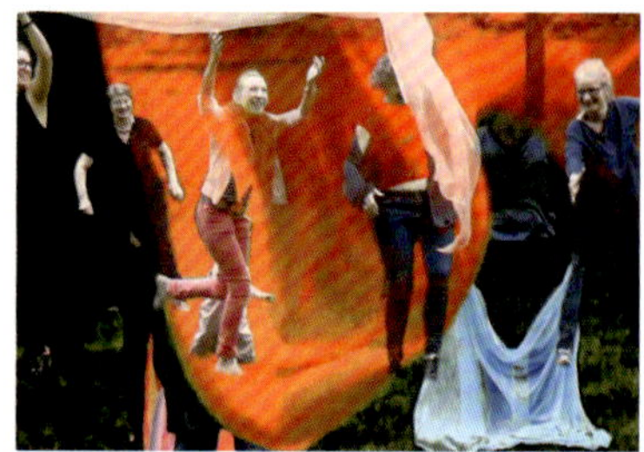
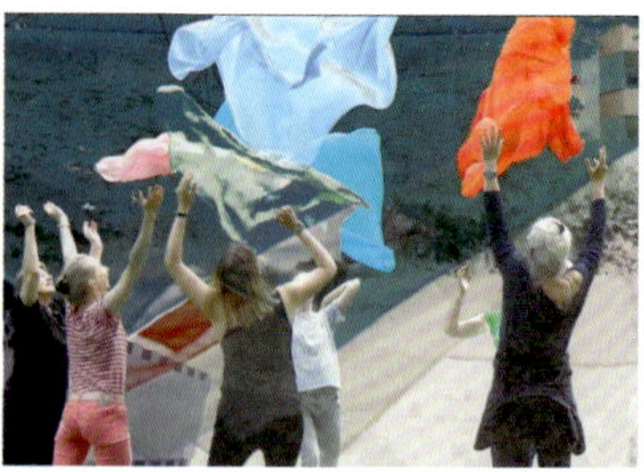
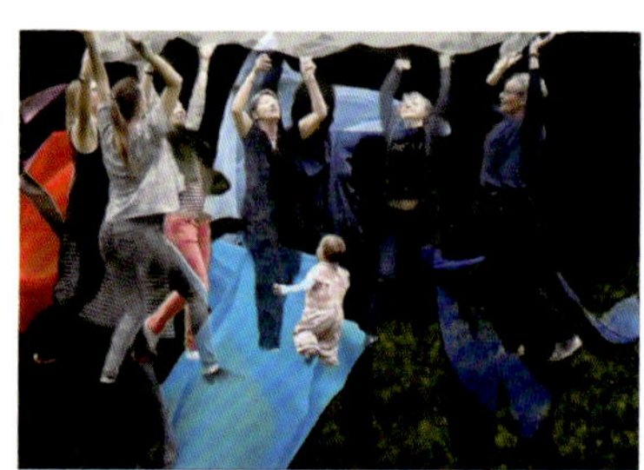
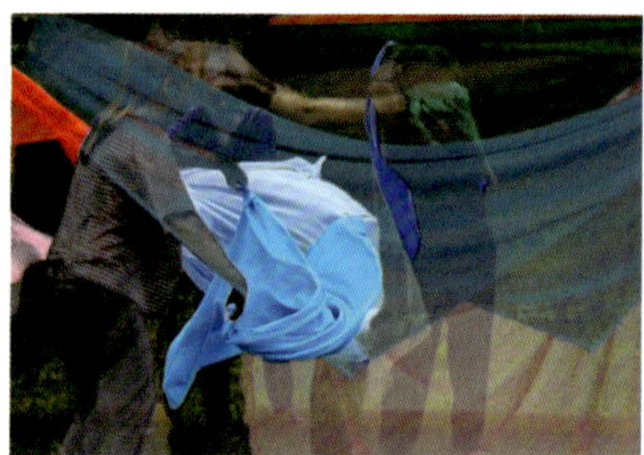

Wush

2017, 3:30 min, Editing Karin Hochstatter

People throw coloured cloths through the air. Overlays and delays create colourful depths of space with happy people.

Des gens lancent en l'air des tissus colorés. Des superpositions et des décalages naissent des effets de profondeurs composés d'éléments colorés et de gens heureux.

Menschen werfen farbige Tücher durch die Luft. Durch Überlagerungen und Verzögerungen entstehen farbige Raumtiefen mit glücklichen Menschen.

La gente lanza telas de colores por el aire. Las superposiciones y los retrasosos crean coloridas profundidades de espacio con gente feliz.

Alcune persone gettano in aria panni colorati. Sovrapposizioni e ritardi creano profondità colorate nello spazio in cui si muovono persone felici.

Mensen gooien gekleurde doeken door de lucht. Overlappingen en vertragingen creëren kleurrijke ruimtelijke diepten met gelukkige mensen.

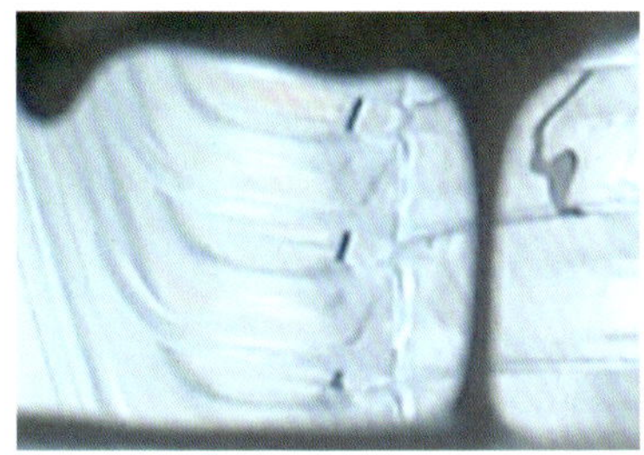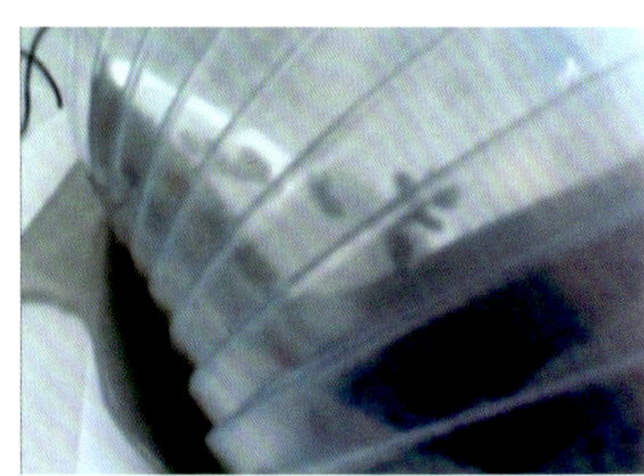

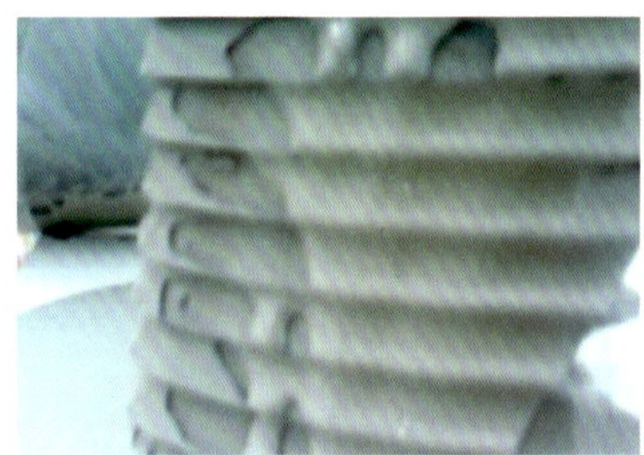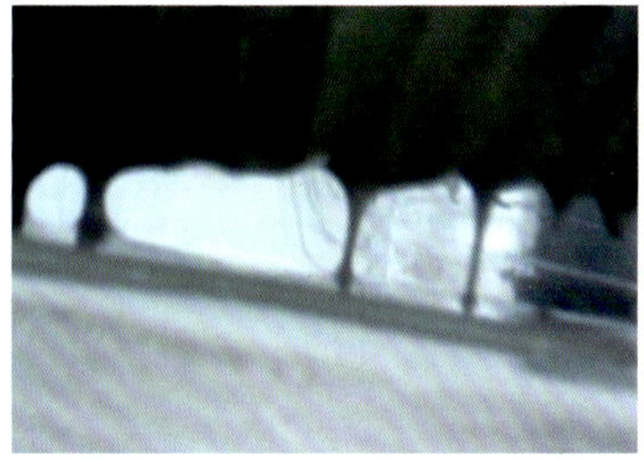

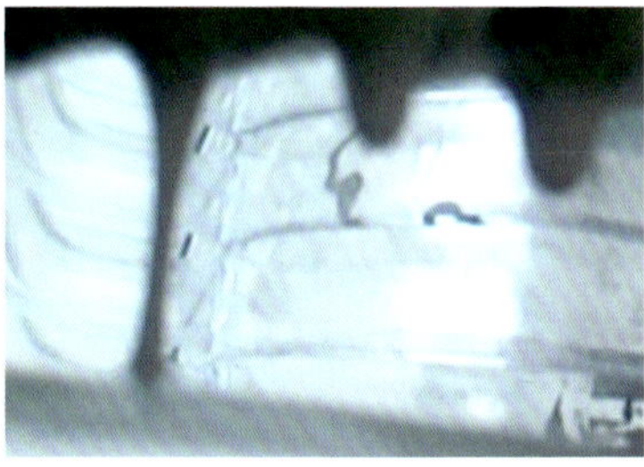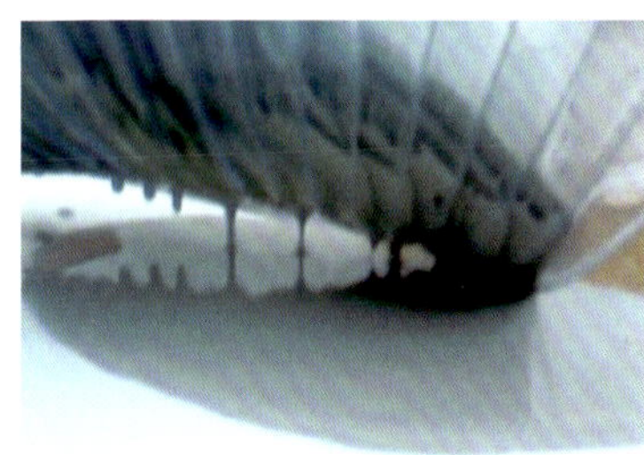

Peter Out

2015, 4:42 min

To heart-rending tones, the film *Peter Out* shows the pouring out of paint from 39 plastic watering cans.

Sur un fond sonore aux tonalités déchirantes, le film *Peter Out* (en anglais se vider lentement, ici dans le sens de déverser) montre 39 arrosoirs en plastique d'où coule de la peinture.

Zu herzzerreißenden Tönen zeigt der Film *Peter Out* (engl. Ausgießen) das Herausfließen von Lackfarbe aus 39 Kunststoffgießkannen.

A tonos desgarradores, la película *Peter Out* muestra el vertido de pintura de 39 regaderas de plástico.

Sullo sfondo di toni struggenti, il film *Peter Out* mostra 39 annaffiatoi in plastica nell'atto di versare vernice.

Op hartverscheurende tonen toont de film *Peter Out* het uitgieten van verf uit 39 plastic gieters.

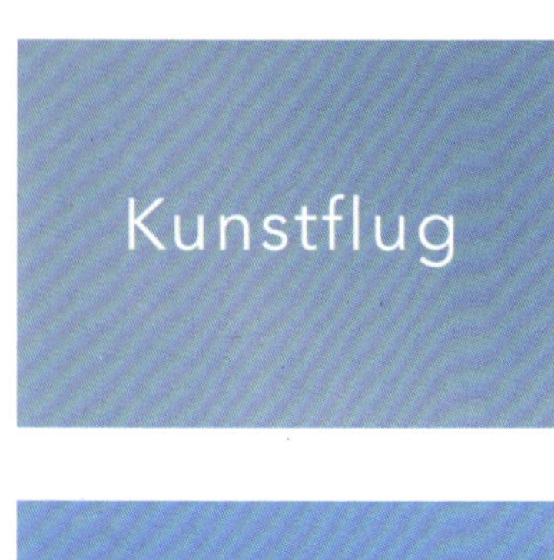

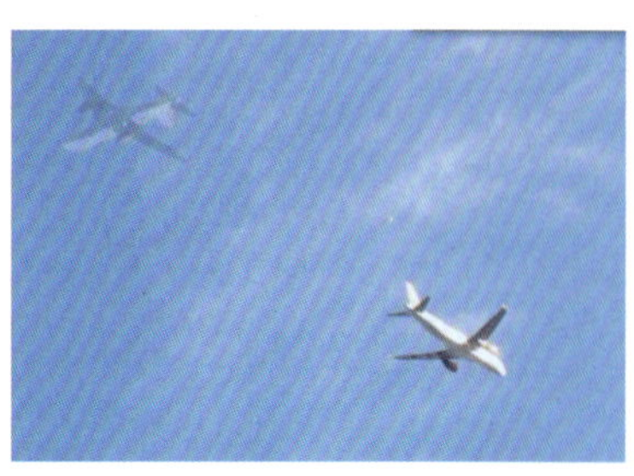

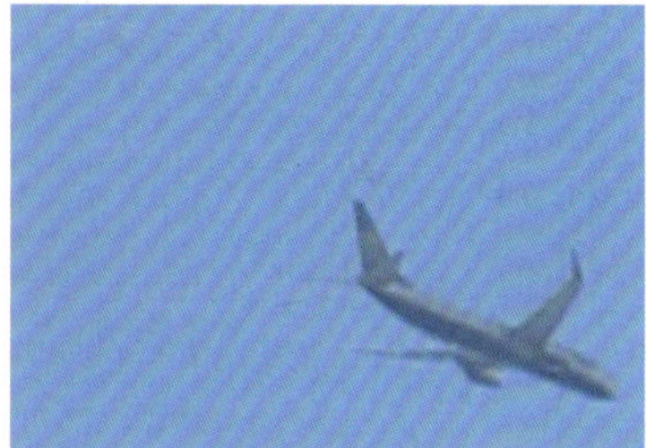

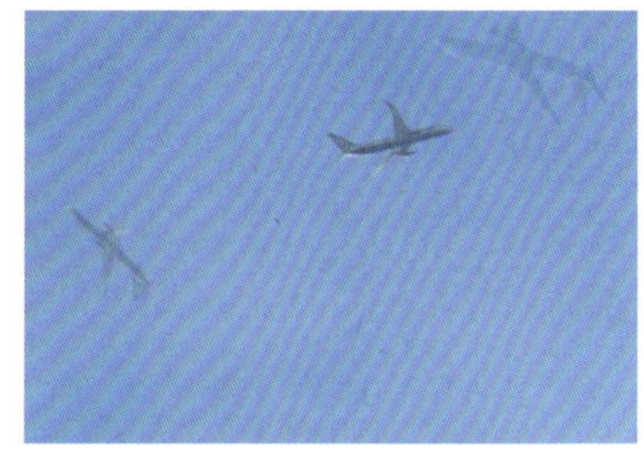

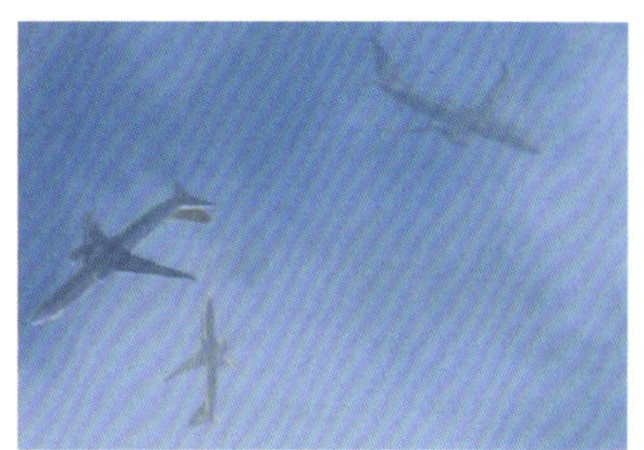

Kunstflug

2015, 3:47 min

The film *Aerobatics* creates crazy trajectories through changes of perspective and cross-fades, in which the heavy machines acquire certain similarities to insects.

Dans le film *Kunstflug* (en allemand voltige) les trajectoires des avions deviennent, à partir de changements de perspectives dans les prises de vue et grâce à la surexposition, complètement invraisemblables et font ressembler ces machines imposantes à des insectes.

Der Film lässt durch Perspektivwechsel und Überblendungen irrsinnige Flugbahnen entstehen, in denen die schweren Maschinen gewisse Ähnlichkeiten mit Insekten erhalten.

La película *Aerobatics* crea trayectorias insanas a través de cambios de perspectiva y fundidos cruzados, en los que las máquinas pesadas mantienen ciertas similitudes con los insectos.

Il cortometraggio ricrea traiettorie folli tramite cambi di prospettiva e dissolvenze incrociate. Le pesanti macchine mostrano vaghe somiglianze con insetti.

De film creëert krankzinnige trajecten door perspectiefwisselingen en cross-fades, waarbij de zware machines bepaalde overeenkomsten met insecten behouden.

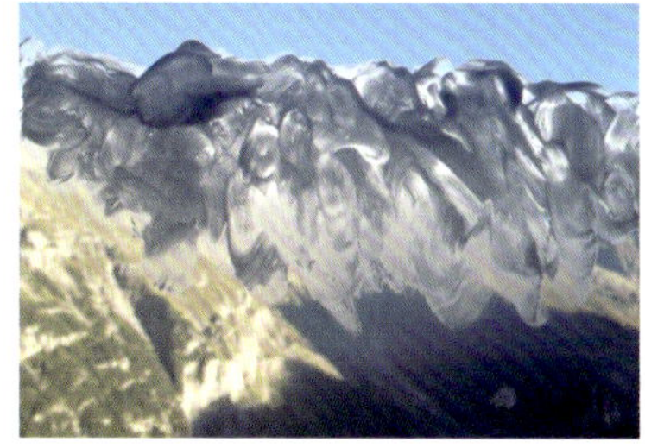 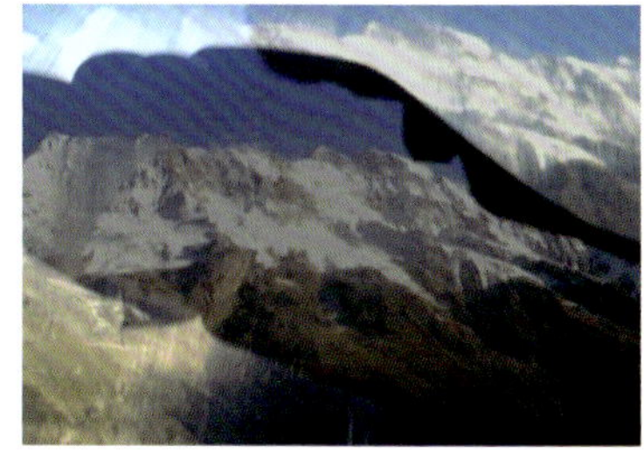

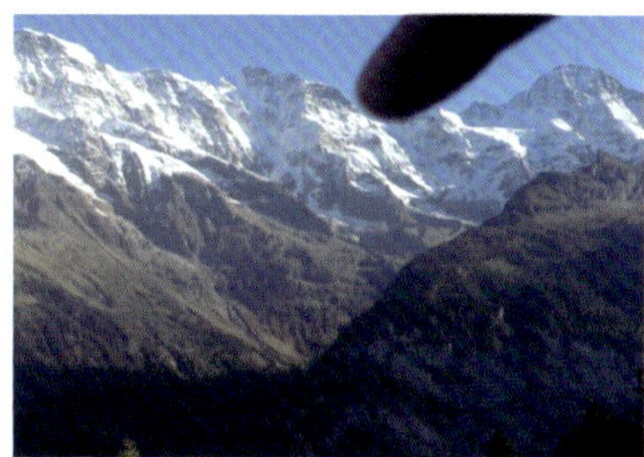 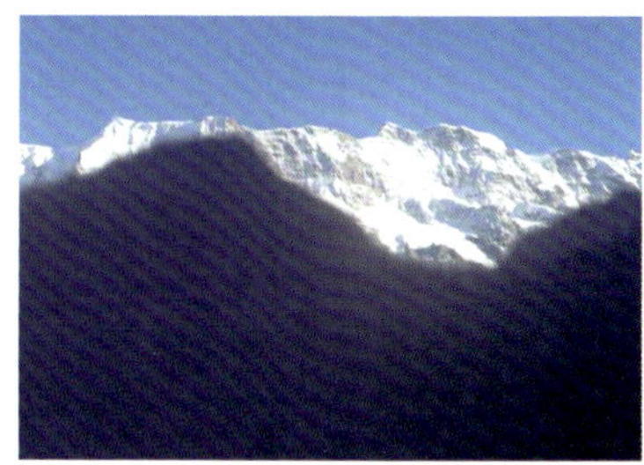

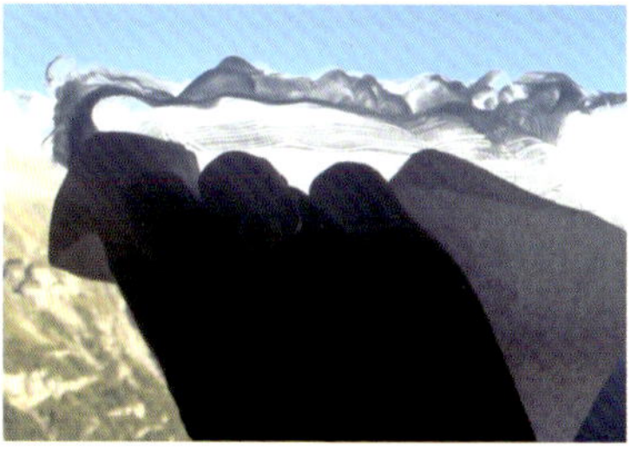 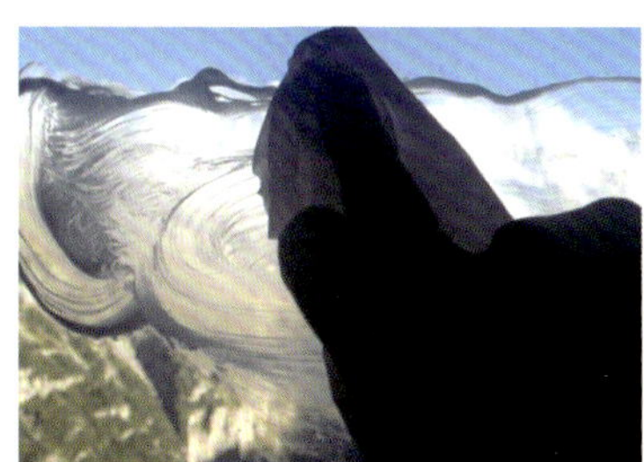

Almabrieb

2013, 3:12 min, joint production with Karin Hochstatter

Almabrieb shows the attempt to brighten up the mountains, which were once whiter.

Almabrieb montre la tentative de rendre aux montagnes leur blancheur d'autrefois.

Almabrieb zeigt den Versuch, die Berge, die früher einmal weißer waren, wieder aufzuhellen.

Almabrieb muestra el intento de iluminar las montañas, que alguna vez fueron más blancas.

Almabrieb mostra il tentativo di rendere più chiare le montagne, un tempo più bianche.

Almabrieb toont de poging om de bergen, die vroeger ooit witter waren, op te fleuren.

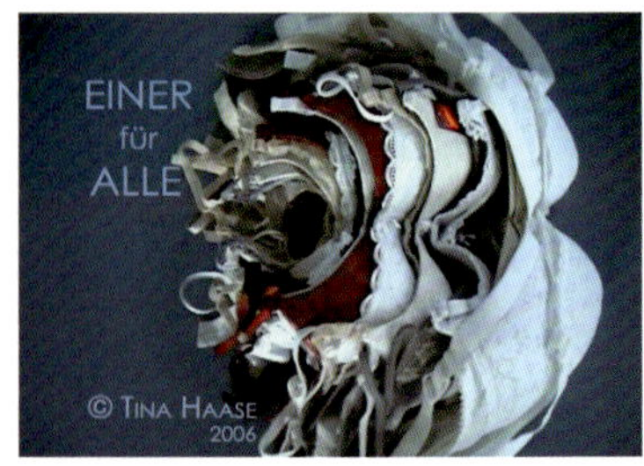

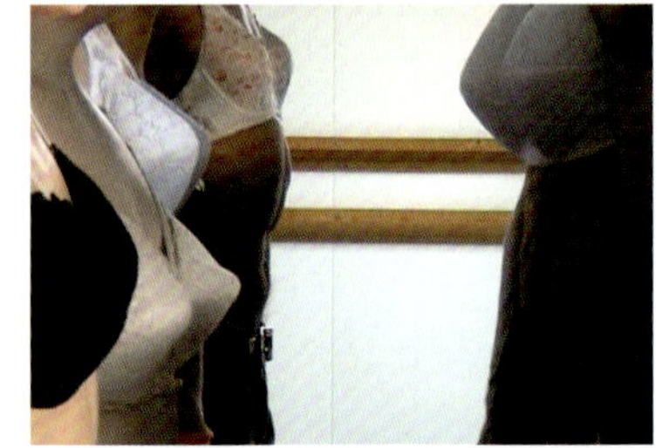
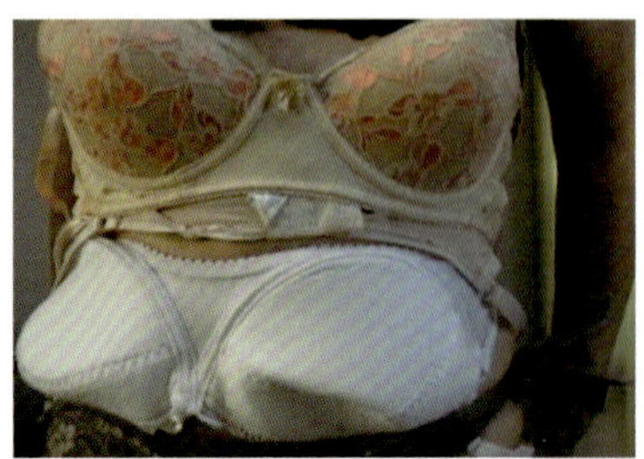
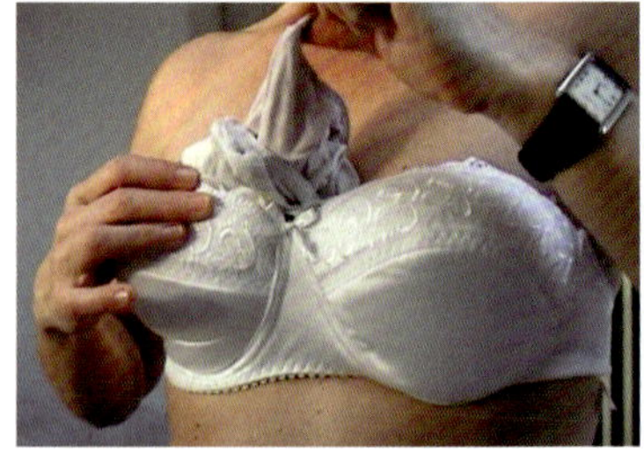
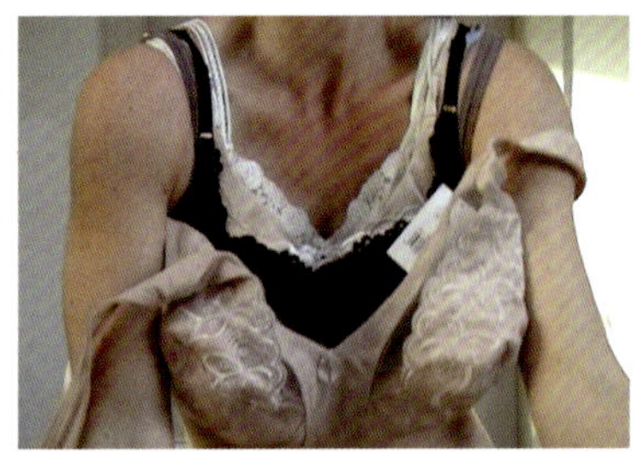
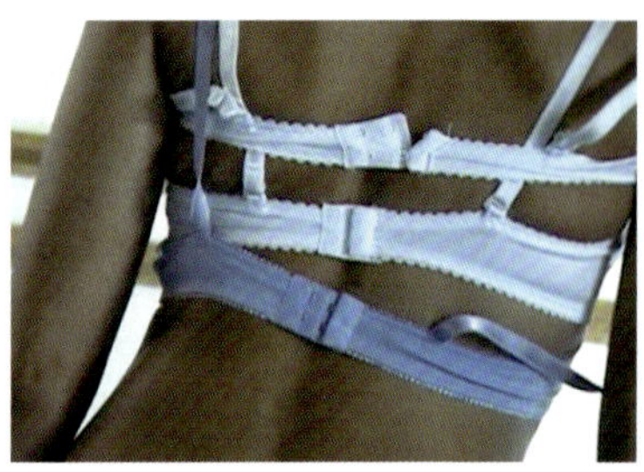
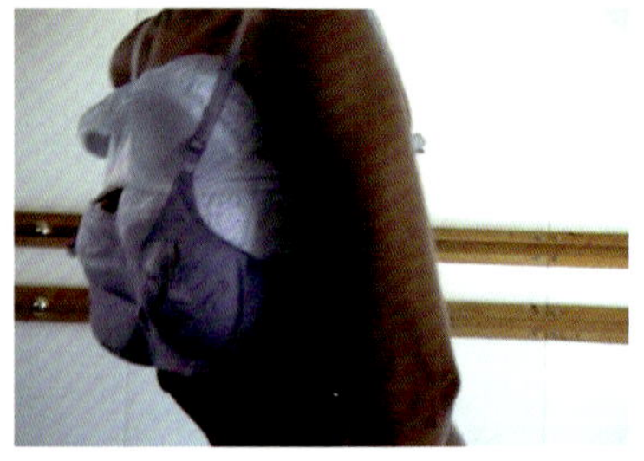
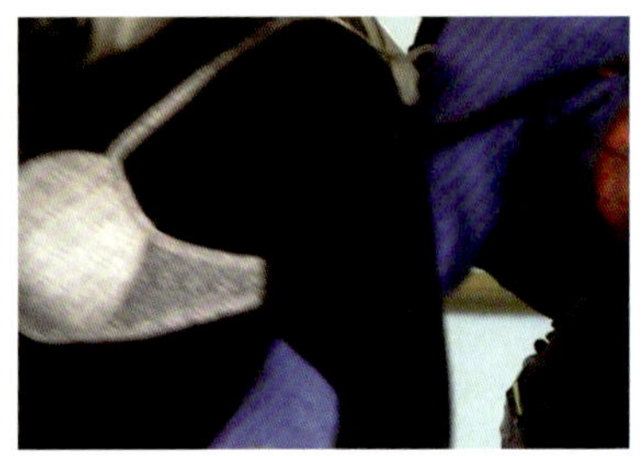
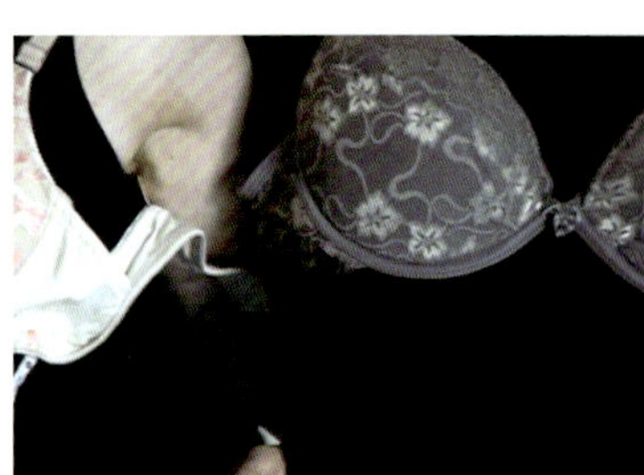

Einer für Alle

2009, 2:45 min, Editing Sandra Rausch

Using various bras as an example, the film shows what it's like when everyone should fit into one scheme.

À partir de l'exemple des soutiens-gorge, le film montre la difficulté à laquelle on doit faire face, quand on essaie de faire rentrer tout le monde dans le même moule.

Am Beispiel verschiedener BHs zeigt der Film wie es ist, wenn alle in ein Schema passen sollen.

Usando varios sostenes como ejemplo, la película muestra qué ocurre cuando todo el mundo debería encajar en un esquema.

Utilizzando vari reggiseni il film mostra cosa succede quando tutti si trovano a dover coincidere in un unico schema.

Aan de hand van verschillende bh's laat de film zien hoe het is als iedereen in één schema moet passen.

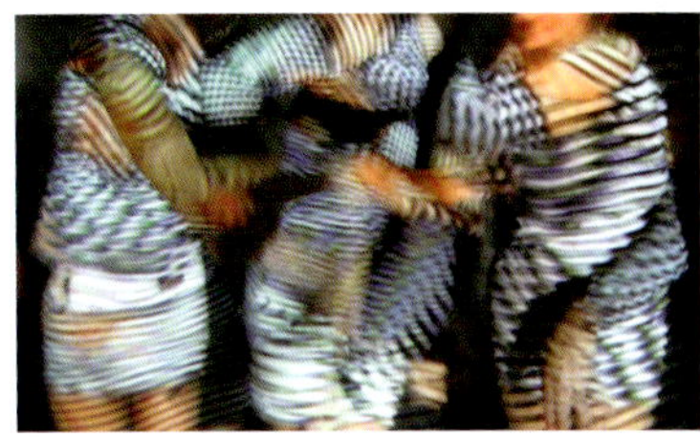 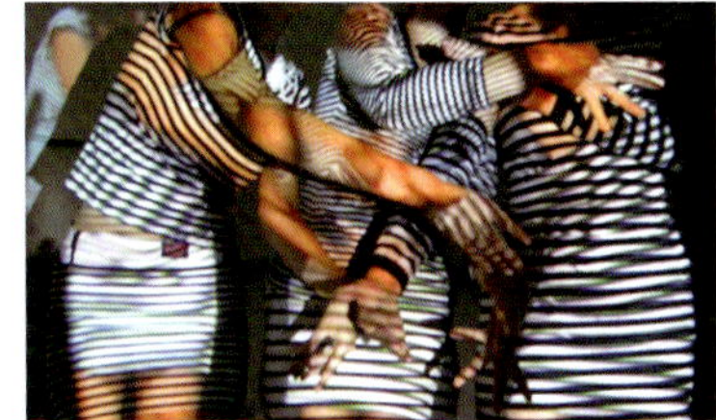 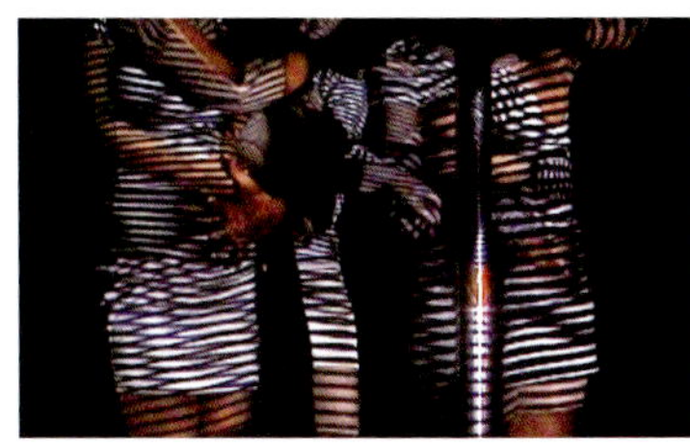

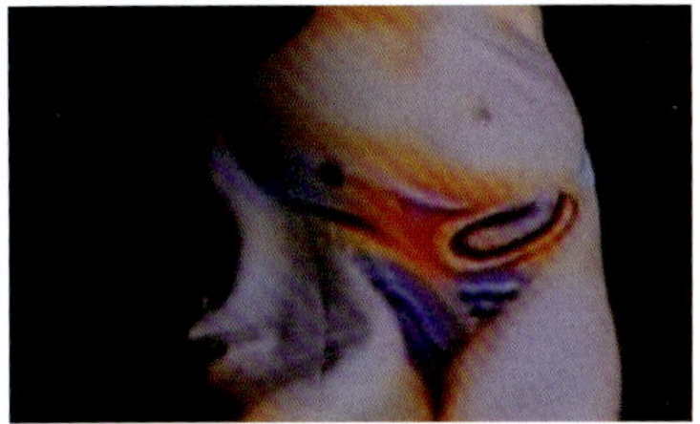 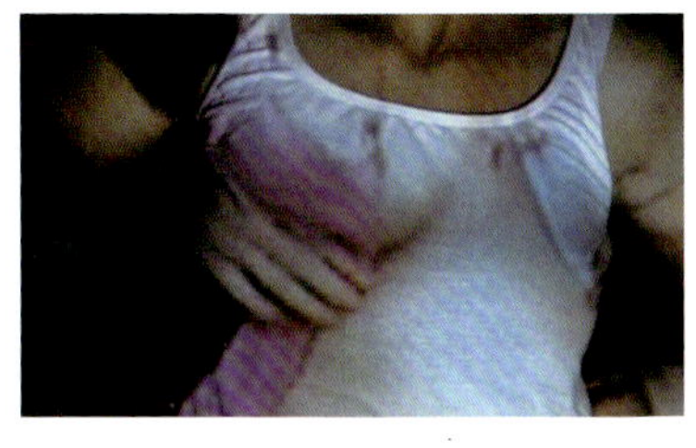 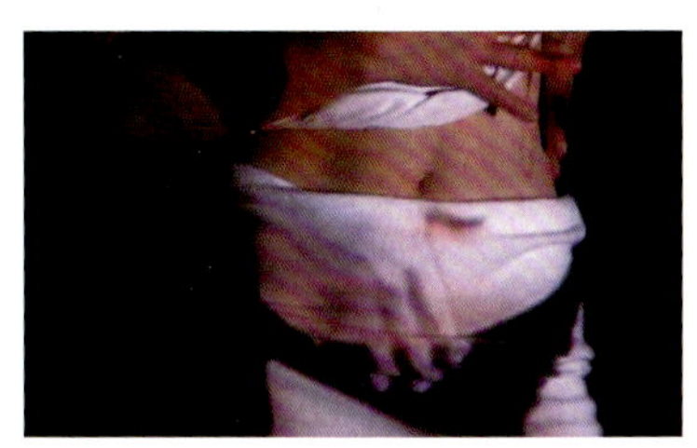

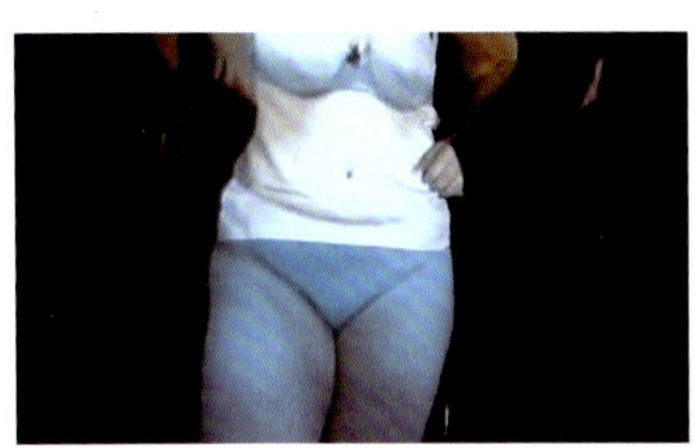 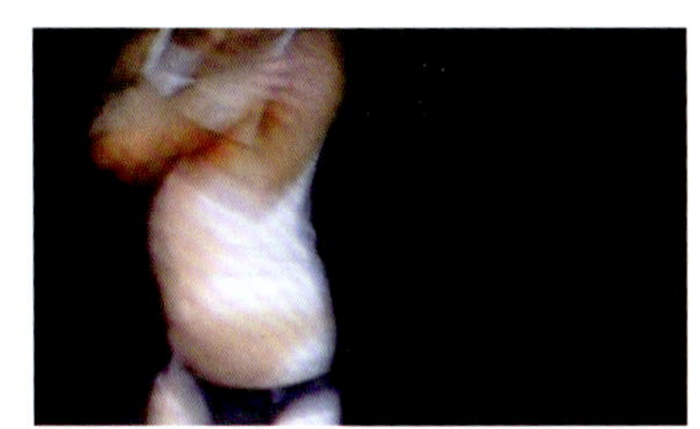 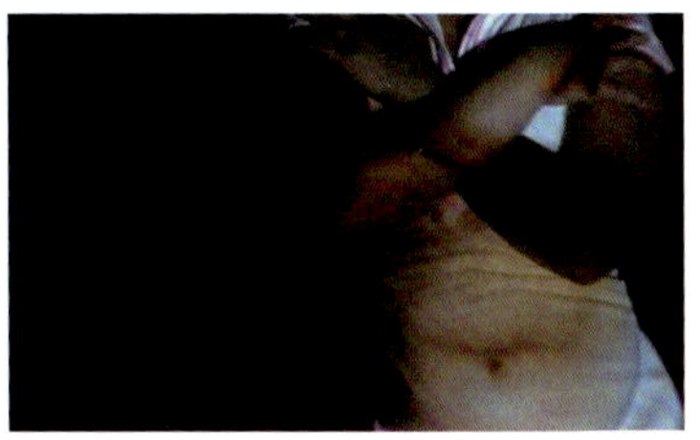

Nachtschattengewächse

2007, 45 min, Badehaus, Heidenheim

The performance was choreographed for a brothel in Heidenheim. Body projections on dancing performers show shifts of desire and reality, man and woman,fat and slim. Dream and resistance result in a picture noise in which nobody knows exactly what is real anymore.

La performance a été chorégraphié pour une maison close de Heidenheim. Les images projetées sur le corps des danseuses en mouvement représentent le décalage entre désir et réalité, entre l'homme et la femme, entre être gros et être mince. Le rêve et la résistance se traduisent par un bruissement des images dans lequel plus personne ne sait exactement ce qui est réel.

Die Performance wurde für ein Bordell in Heidenheim choreographiert. Körperprojektionen auf tanzenden Performerinnen zeigen Verschiebungen von Wunsch und Wirklichkeit, Mann und Frau, dick und dünn. Traum und Widerstand ergeben ein Bildrauschen, in dem niemand mehr genau weiß was real ist.

La actuación fue coreografiada para un burdel en Heidenheim. Las proyecciones corporales de los bailarines muestran cambios en el deseo y la realidad, en el hombre y la mujer, en lo bueno y en lo malo. El sueño y la resistencia dan como resultado un ruido de imagen en el que ya nadie sabe exactamente lo que es real.

La performance è stata coreografata per una casa di tolleranza di Heidenheim. I corpi proiettati sulle performer che danzano mostrano traslazioni tra desiderio e realtà, uomo e donna, grasso e magro. Sogno e resistenza producono un turbinio di immagini in cui nessuno sa più esattamente cosa sia reale.

De voorstelling werd gechoreografeerd voor een bordeel in Heidenheim. Lichaamsprojecties op dansende performers tonen verschuivingen van wens en werkelijkheid, man en vrouw, dik en dun. Droom en weerstand leiden tot een beeldruis waarbij niemand meer precies weet wat echt is.

Vita

1980 Studies at the Düsseldorf Art Academy
1986 Master student with Fritz Schwegler
1989 One-year Scholarship from the Minister of Culture NRW
1992 Chargesheimer Prize of the City of Cologne
1993 Förderkoje/Sponsored Booth Art Cologne
1994 Project scholarship MA Birmingham, Alabama, USA
2002 Art on Building Competition of the State of Brandenburg
2004 Professor of Design Theory at the University of Applied Sciences Niederrhein, Faculty of Design
2004/2007 Barkenhoff Scholarship
since 2007 Professor of Visual Arts, Technical University of Munich, Faculty of Architecture
2013/2015 Artist-Residences in Switzerland and France

Curriculum vitae

1980 Etudes à l'Académie des Beaux-Arts de Düsseldorf
1986 Élève du Conservatoire de Fritz Schwegler
1989 Bourse d'un an du ministre de la Culture de la Rhénanie-du-Nord-Westphalie
1992 Prix Chargesheimer de la ville de Cologne.
1993 Stand de soutien aux jeunes artistes à la Art Cologne
1994 Bourse de projet MA Birmingham, Alabama, USA
2002 Concours de l'Art dans un milieu architectural du Land de Brandebourg.
2004 Professeur de théorie de la mise en forme à l'université de sciences appliquées de la Basse-Rhénanie, faculté d'arts appliqués.
2004/2007 Bourse d'études Barkenhoff
depuis 2007 Professeur des Beaux-Arts, université technique de Munich, faculté d'architecture.
2013/2015 Résidences-artistiques en Suisse et en France

Vita

1980 Studium an der Kunstakademie Düsseldorf
1986 Meisterschüler bei Fritz Schwegler
1989 Jahresstipendium des Kultusministers NRW
1992 Chargesheimer Preis der Stadt Köln
1993 Förderkoje Art Cologne
1994 Projektstipendium MA Birmingham, Alabama, USA
2002 Kunst am Bau Wettbewerb des Landes Brandenburg
2004 Prof. Gestaltungslehre an der Fachhochschule Niederrhein, Fachbereich Design
2004/2007 Barkenhoff Stipendium
seit 2007 Univ.-Prof. Lehrstuhl für Bildende Kunst, TU München, Fakultät für Architektur
2013/2015 Artist-Residences in der Schweiz und in Frankreich

Exhibitions

Solo Exhibitions (Selection)

1990 and 92 | 94 | 96, 1999 Schneiderei Gallery, Cologne

1991 and 2000, 03, 08, 10, 14, 17 Galerie Ulrich Mueller, Cologne (K)

1994 Birmingham Museum of Art (with B. Werres and E. Haehnle) | USA

1994 Künstlerhaus Bregenz, Austria (K)

1994 and 1998, 01 Gallery InSitu, Aalst, Belgium

1995 Municipal Gallery Villa Zanders, Bergisch Gladbach (K)

1999 and 2007 Vanguardia Galeria de Arte, Bilbao

2012 Tina Haase, Jus Juchtmans, Gallery van den Berge, Goes, NL

Group exhibitions (selection)

1993 Recall Byblos, Ludwig Forum, Aachen (K)

1998 Plastic – The last years, Galerie Ulrich Mueller, Cologne

2005 Gekleurde Vormgeving, Stedelijk museum Aalst, Belgium (K)

2007 08 | 09 All colours permitted as long as they interfere with the commerce, 07 Muzeum Atelier 341, Brussels, Belgium, 08 Gallery of Contemporary Art BWA, Katowice, 09 Museum of Contemporary Art, Szczecin, Poland

2012 Salonstücke Reloaded, Municipal Gallery Villa Zanders, Bergisch Gladbach

2016 new ends II, Gerson Höger Galerie, Hamburg

2017 Out of Office, Museum of Concrete Art, Ingolstadt (K)

Expositions

Expositions monographiques (sélection)

1990 et 92 | 94 | 96 | 96, 1999 Galerie Schneiderei, Cologne

1991 et 2000, 03, 08, 10, 14, 17 Galerie Ulrich Mueller, Cologne (K)

1994 Musée d'Art de Birmingham (avec B. Werres et E. Haehnle) | États-Unis

1994 Künstlerhaus Bregenz, Autriche (K)

1994 &1998, 01 Galerie InSitu, Alost, Belgique

1995 Städtische Galerie Villa Zanders, Bergisch Gladbach (K)

1999 et 2007 Vanguardia Galeria de Arte, Bilbao

2012 Tina Haase, Jus Juchtmans, Galerie van den Berge, Goes, NL

Expositions collectives (sélection)

1993 Recall Byblos, Ludwig Forum, Aix-la-Chapelle (K)

1998 Plastique – Les dernières années, Galerie Ulrich Mueller, Cologne

2005 Gekleurde Vormgeving, Musée communal d'Alost, Belgique (K)

2007 08 | 09 All colours permitted as long as they interfere with the commerce (Toutes les couleurs sont autorisées tant qu'elles interfèrent avec le commerce), 07 Muzeum Atelier 341, Bruxelles, Belgique, 08 Galerie d'Art Contemporain BWA, Katowice, 09 Musée d'Art Contemporain, Szczecin, Pologne.

2012 Salonstücke Reloaded, Galerie municipale Villa Zanders, Bergisch Gladbach

2016 nouvelles fins II, Gerson Höger Galerie, Hambourg.

2017 Out of Office, Musée d'Art Concret, Ingolstadt (K)

Ausstellungen

Einzelausstellungen (Auswahl)

1990 und 92 | 94 | 96, 1999 Galerie Schneiderei, Köln

1991 und 2000, 03, 08, 10, 14, 17 Galerie Ulrich Mueller, Köln (K)

1994 Birmingham Museum of Art (mit B. Werres und E. Haehnle) | USA

1994 Künstlerhaus Bregenz, Österreich (K)

1994 & 1998, 01 Galerie InSitu, Aalst, Belgien

1995 Städt. Galerie Villa Zanders, Bergisch Gladbach (K)

1999 und 2007 Vanguardia Galeria de Arte, Bilbao

2012 Tina Haase, Jus Juchtmans, Galerie van den Berge, Goes, NL

Gruppenausstellungen (Auswahl)

1993 Recall Byblos, Ludwig Forum, Aachen (K)

1998 Plastik – Die letzten Jahre, Galerie Ulrich Mueller, Köln

2005 Gekleurde Vormgeving, Stedelijk museum Aalst, Belgien (K)

2007 08 | 09 All colours permitted as long as they interfere with the commerce, 07 Muzeum Atelier 341, Brüssel, Belgien, 08 Galerie für zeitgenössische Kunst BWA, Kattowitz, 09 Museum für Zeitgenössische Kunst, Stettin, Polen

2012 Salonstücke Reloaded, Städtische Galerie Villa Zanders, Bergisch Gladbach

2016 neue enden II, Gerson Höger Galerie, Hamburg

2017 Out of Office, Museum für Konkrete Kunst, Ingolstadt (K)

(K) Catalogue / Katalog

Recommended Literature · *Littérature recommandée* · Literaturempfehlungen

Beatrice Stammer, *Außerhalb von Mittendrin,* Hrsg. NGBK, Berlin 1991

Jens Peter Koerver, Gebrauchsinformation, in: *Tina Haase,* Hrsg. Mannheimer Kunstverein 1995

Thomas von Taschitzki, in: *Tina Haase,* Karin Hochstatter, Birgit Werres, Hrsg.: Kunstverein Köln rechtsrheinisch e.V., Köln 1998

René Hirner, Die Leichtigkeit der Dinge und der plastischen Formen, in: *Streifenweise,* Hrsg. Kunstmuseum Heidenheim 2000

Reinhard Ermen: Stapelware oder Die Geburt der Skulptur aus dem Geiste der Vervielfältigung, in: *Der geringste Widerstand,* Hrsg.: Galerie Ulrich Mueller, Köln 2002

Ingo Springenschmid, ACHSEN ZU SCHWE BE NDEN, in: *Tina Haase, zunächst sachlich.* Hrsg.Galerie Ulrich Mueller, Köln 2010

Petra Oelschlägel, Salonstücke 3, in: *Salonstücke reloaded,* Kunstmuseum Villa Zanders, Bergisch Gladbach 2013

Theres Rohde, Richtlinien, in: *Out of Office, Büro-Kunst oder das Büro im Museum,* Hrsg. Dr. Simone Schimpf und Dr. Theres Rohde, Museum für Konkrete Kunst, Ingolstadt 2017

The artist's work titles consist predominantly of puns that cannot be translated into other languages. Therefore only the German titles are mentioned in this volume.

Les titres des œuvres de l'artiste se composent principalement de calembours qui ne peuvent être traduits dans d'autres langues. Par conséquent, seuls les titres allemands sont mentionnés dans ce volume.

Die Werktitel der Künstlerin bestehen überwiegend aus Wortspielen, die sich nicht in andere Sprachen übersetzen lassen. Daher werden in diesem Band nur die deutschen Titel genannt, sofern vorhanden.

Los títulos de las obras del artista consisten predominantemente en juegos de palabras que no pueden ser traducidos a otros idiomas. Por lo tanto, en este volumen sólo se mencionan los títulos alemanes.

I titoli dei lavori dell'artista consistono prevalentemente di giochi di parole che non possono essere tradotti in altre lingue. Pertanto in questo volume sono citati solo i titoli tedeschi.

De titels van het werk van de kunstenaar bestaan voornamelijk uit woordspelingen die niet in andere talen vertaald kunnen worden. Daarom worden in dit boek alleen de Duitse titels genoemd.